MUSIC, SENSE AND NONSENSE

MUSIC, SENSE AND NONSENSE

COLLECTED ESSAYS AND LECTURES

ALFRED BRENDEL

The Robson Press

This updated edition published in Great Britain in 2015 by
The Robson Press (an imprint of Biteback Publishing Ltd)
Westminster Tower
3 Albert Embankment
London SE1 7SP
Copyright © Alfred Brendel 2015

Alfred Brendel has asserted his right under the Copyright, Designs and Patents
Act 1988 to be identified as the author of this work.

Essays from *Wunderglaube und Misstonleiter* (*Hymns of Harmony and Discord*)
© Carl Hanser Verlag 2014 München – reprinted by kind permission of the original
publisher.

Every reasonable effort has been made to trace copyright holders of material
reproduced in this book, but if any have been inadvertently overlooked the
publishers would be glad to hear from them.

ISBN 978-1-84954-905-9

10 9 8 7 6 5 4 3 2 1

A CIP catalogue record for this book is available from the British Library.

Set in Adobe Garamond Pro

Printed and bound in Great Britain by
CPI Group (UK) Ltd, Croydon CR0 4YY

MIX
Paper from
responsible sources
FSC® C020471
www.fsc.org

CONTENTS

CONVERSATIONS

PREFACE

SINCE THE LAST collection of my writings, *Alfred Brendel on Music*, appeared in 2007 a number of things have happened. I decided to stop my concert career while still in command of rhythm and nuances; sixty years of playing in public seemed sufficient. But I had already set my mind on what I wanted to do with the rest of my life: writing some more, lecturing, coaching, performing my poems with Pierre-Laurent Aimard or my son Adrian, collecting honorary degrees, looking at exhibitions, going to the theatre, watching films, re-reading my favourite books, and listening to all those works by Handel and Haydn that I hadn't encountered before. I feel lucky that most of it went as I imagined it would.

Next to my musical existence, I have always liked to operate with words. In some of my essays and lectures I've tried to clear my own mind, explain things to myself, give myself advice, and provide answers to questions to which I couldn't find satisfying ones in the literature available to me at the time of writing. Simultaneously, I entertained the hope that what I taught myself may be of some interest to others.

It gives me great pleasure to see this final compilation of my musical essays and lectures in print. My special thanks go to Jeremy Robson who started my life as a published author, and now ends it with this volume. To the edition of 2007, several pieces have been added, mostly written after I discontinued playing concerts in 2008. Repetitions of certain statements are not avoided if their inclusion seemed indispensable for the completeness of a piece. Older essays have been corrected but, on the whole, not updated. Within a sixty-year span of writing, there were bound to be changes of fact and opinion. I did not shy away from contradicting myself, or modifying some of my views. Each of my pieces has been supplied with the year of origin.

Two lectures on chamber music testify to my predilection for coaching string quartets. It has been particularly delightful to remain in touch with some of the finest ensembles of this kind and to witness the remarkable level of achievement of a number of young ones.

To mention all the musicians, friends and personalities whom I owe gratitude would fill another book. Let me single out Maria Majno for her never-ending care and perception, and Olivia Beattie and Victoria Godden for their tireless editorial work.

London, 2015
Alfred Brendel

MOZART

∾୰∾

A Mozart Player Gives Himself Advice

Unmistakably, Mozart takes singing as his starting-point, and from this issues the unin-
terrupted melodiousness which shimmers through his compositions like the lovely forms
of a woman through the folds of a thin dress.

FERRUCCIO BUSONI

L ET THIS BE the first warning to the Mozart performer: piano playing, be
it ever so faultless, must not be considered sufficient. Mozart's piano works
should be for the player a receptacle full of latent musical possibilities which
often go far beyond the purely pianistic. It is not the limitations of Mozart's pianoforte (which I refuse to accept) that point the way, but rather Mozart's dynamism,
colourfulness and expressiveness in operatic singing, in the orchestra, in ensembles
of all kinds. For example, the first movement of Mozart's Sonata in A minor K.310
is to me a piece for symphony orchestra; the second movement resembles a vocal
scene with a dramatic middle section, and the finale could be transcribed into a
wind divertimento with no trouble at all.

In Mozart's piano concertos, the sound of the piano is set off more sharply against
that of the orchestra. Here the human voice and the orchestral solo instrument will
be the main setters of standards for the pianist. From the Mozart singer he will learn
not only to sing but also to 'speak' clearly and with meaning, to characterise, to act
and react; from the string player to think in terms of up-bow and down-bow; and
from the flautist or oboist to shape fast passages in a variety of articulations, instead
of delivering them up to an automatic non-legato or, worse still, to an undeviating
legato such as the old complete edition prescribed time and again without a shred
of authenticity.

A singing line and sensuous beauty, important as they may be in Mozart, are not,
however, the sole sources of bliss. To tie Mozart to a few traits is to diminish him.
That great composers have manifold things to say and can use contradictions to their
advantage should be evident in performances of his music. There has been altogether

too much readiness to reduce Mozart to Schumann's 'floating Greek gracefulness' or Wagner's 'genius of light and love'. Finding a balance between freshness and urbanity ('He did not remain simple and did not grow over-refined', said Busoni), force and transparency, unaffectedness and irony, aloofness and intimacy, between freedom and set patterns, passion and grace, abandonment and style among the labours of the Mozart player: this is only rewarded by a stroke of good luck.

What is it that marks out Mozart's music? An attempt to draw a dividing line between Haydn and Mozart could perhaps help to answer the question. Mozart some-times comes astonishingly close to Haydn, and Haydn to Mozart, and they shared their musical accomplishments in brotherly fashion; but they were fundamentally different in nature. I see in Haydn and Mozart the antithesis between the instru-mental and vocal, motif and melody, C. P. E. and J. C. Bach, adagio and andante, caesuras (amusing and startling) and connections (seamless), daring and balance, the surprise of the unexpected and the surprise of the expected. From tranquillity, Haydn plunges deep into agitation, while Mozart does the reverse, aiming at tran-quillity from nervousness.

Mozart's nervous energy – his fingers were constantly drumming on the near-est chair-back – can be recognised in the fidgety or spirited agitation of many final movements, as one heard them in performances by Edwin Fischer, Bruno Walter or Artur Schnabel. When Busoni denies Mozart any nervousness, I have to disagree. Like melodiousness shimmering through the folds of a dress, 'chaos' now and then, even in Mozart, can be 'shimmering through the veil of order' (Novalis).

The perfection of that order, the security of Mozart's sense of form, is, as Busoni puts it, 'almost inhuman'. Let us therefore never lose sight of the humanity of this music, even when it gives itself an official and general air. The unimpeachability of his form is always balanced by the palpability of his sound, the miracle of his sound mixtures, the resoluteness of his energy, the living spirit, the heartbeat, the unsen-timental warmth of his feeling.

Between Haydn the explorer and adventurer, and Schubert the sleepwalker, I see both Mozart and Beethoven as architects. But how differently they built! From the beginning of a piece, Beethoven places stone upon stone, constructing and justify-ing his edifice as it were in accordance with the laws of statics. Mozart, on the other hand, prefers to join together the most wonderful melodic ideas as prefabricated components; observe how in the first movement of K.271 he varies the succession of his building-blocks, to the extent of shaking them up as though in a kaleidoscope. Whereas Beethoven draws one element from another, in what might be called a procedural manner, Mozart arranges one element after another as though it could not be otherwise.

Mozart, more than most other composers, expresses himself differently in minor and in major keys. That he could also compose in a procedural manner is demonstrated by his two concertos in minor keys, K.466 and 491, which so greatly impressed Beethoven. Original cadenzas for these two works unfortunately do not exist. Neither the dynamic spaciousness of the D minor concerto nor the contrapuntal density of the C minor concerto is compatible with the usual type of improvisational cadenza in Mozart's concertos in major keys. Rather more conceivable are cadenzas in the manner of Bach's Fifth Brandenburg Concerto, which carry on the intensity of the movement, transporting it in a broad arc to the next entrance of the orchestra.

Mozart is made neither of porcelain, nor of marble, nor of sugar. The cute Mozart, the perfumed Mozart, the permanently ecstatic Mozart, the 'touch-me-not' Mozart, the sentimentally bloated Mozart must all be avoided. There should be some slight doubt, too, about a Mozart who is incessantly 'poetic'. 'Poetic' players may find themselves sitting in a hothouse in which no fresh air can enter; you want to come and open the windows. Let poetry be the spice, not the main course. It is significant that there are only 'poets of the keyboard'; a relatively prosaic instrument needs to be transformed, bewitched. Violinists, conductors, even Lieder singers – so usage would suggest – seem to survive without 'poetry'.

One look at the solo parts of Mozart's piano concertos should be enough to show the Mozart player that his warrant leaves that of a museum curator far behind. Mozart's notation is not complete. Not only do the solo parts lack dynamic markings almost entirely; the very notes to be played – at any rate in the later works that were not made ready for the engraver – require piecing out at times: by filling (when Mozart's manuscript is limited to sketchy indications); by variants (when relatively simple themes return several times without Mozart varying them himself); by embellishments (when the player is entrusted with a melodic outline to decorate); by re-entry fermatas (which are on the dominant and must be connected to the subsequent tonic); and by cadenzas (which lead from the six-four chord in quasi-improvisational fashion to the concluding *tutti*).

Luckily, there are a good number of Mozart's own variants, embellishments, re-entries and cadenzas, and they give the player a clear idea of his freedom of movement. In re-entries and cadenzas the main key is never deviated from; in embellishments and variants the prevailing character is never disturbed. Mozart's variants sometimes show a subtle economy which, I assume, was not in keeping with contemporary convention.[1] The view that empty spots must stay empty because the performer cannot possibly claim to possess Mozart's genius has been overcome today; it was an attitude produced by misguided reverence, which did not expect or trust the player to have the necessary empathy with Mozart's style. The case of the Rondo in A major K.386 is instructive; thanks to the recent discovery of the last pages of Mozart's manuscript, we now realise that the final twenty-eight bars of the Rondo, as we used to know it, are not by Mozart but by Cipriani Potter, which no one would otherwise have noticed.

It is precisely in those passages where Mozart's text is sketchy that the player must know exactly what Mozart wrote and how he wrote it, and not put his faith in editors. Anyone who takes on Mozart's piano concertos will have to devote some time to studying the sources. A particular case in point is the so-called 'Coronation' Concerto K.537. Most of the left hand is not worked out at all. In the middle movement, which is plagued by a complete lack of emotional contrast, the same four-bar phrase appears no fewer than ten times in virtually identical guise. Here the richest ornamentation will be needed if the effect is not to resemble the pallid charm of certain Raphael Madonnas, which the nineteenth century adored, just as it did this movement, unembellished. It is not at all easy to understand why a version of this lovely work fabricated after Mozart's death is still generally played today, as though nothing about it could stand to be improved.

Additions to Mozart's text are in some instances obviously required, in others at least possible. An appendix to the Bärenreiter complete edition prints a lavishly embellished version of the F sharp minor Adagio from the Concerto in A major K.488; it is probably the work of a pupil, and apparently was part of Mozart's musical estate. What is elaborated in this manuscript is in no way satisfactory, but it does provide a clue that embellishment is permitted. As to how one is to go about it, Mozart's own models, and no others, are the ones to be guided by. The embellishments by

---

1   In his C minor Concerto K.491 the extremely delicate shifts of harmony, part-writing and rhythm at the returns of the initial theme should be savoured without further additions.

Hummel or Philipp Karl Hoffmann do not even try to follow Mozart's example; they are foreign to his style and frequently overcrowded with notes to such a degree that, to get all of them in, the relatively flowing tempi of Mozart's middle movements must be pulled back to largo. The additions by Hummel and Hoffmann do make us aware that the 'gusto' of performance style could change quite quickly and drastically; this should give pause to those who try to get at Mozart by concentrating too single-mindedly on Baroque practice.

The player's delight at filling in the white spots on Mozart's musical map in such a way that even the educated listener does not prick up his ears must stay within bounds. The player must not be seduced into overdoing it or into living too much for the moment. When improvising embellishments becomes a parlour game gleefully played to flummox the orchestra, when the player sets out in every performance to prove to himself and all present that he is indeed spontaneous, he is in danger of losing control over quality. I think he will be more deserving if he makes a rigorous selection from a supply of versions he has improvised at home, rather than risking everything on the platform by trying to play Mozart as though he *were* Mozart.

One of the additions that is possible but rarely necessary, since in most cases it merely doubles the orchestra, is continuo playing. Once I relished accompanying the bass line of the orchestra, but today I usually limit myself to taking a hand occasionally in energetic passages and to giving almost imperceptible harmonic support to some piano cantilenas. At a time when there were neither conductors, nor full scores, the basso continuo, apart from giving the soloist his harmonic bearings, served mainly to co-ordinate the players' rhythm. Nowadays one can reasonably expect the soloist to be familiar with the score (lately even Lieder singers are expected to have taken a glance at the piano accompaniment); and naturally we expect the conductor to keep the orchestra together. Basso continuo playing therefore seems to have a point only in special cases, such as when the four Mozart chamber concertos (K.413–15 and 449) were performed without winds. But the difference between *solo* and *tutti* must not be lost.

Even a composer like Mozart could make a mistake. Artur Schnabel's precept that the performer must accept the whims of great composers though he may be quite unable to fathom them must not be allowed to go so far that errors remain unrectified. Schnabel himself provided some examples of reverential blindness, as when, for example, in the middle movement of the Concerto in C minor K.491, he played a bar, with wind accompaniment, precisely as Mozart inadvertently let it stand. Here, as in one bar of the finale of K.503, Mozart apparently wrote the piano part first and then, when writing in the orchestral parts, changed his mind about the harmony. In doing so he forgot to adjust the piano part to the new harmonic situation. The result is cacophony and a divergence in the leading of the bass line that is unthinkable in Mozart. If the player, in rare instances, puts Mozart's text right, it does not mean that he presumes himself to be equal, or indeed superior, to Mozart.

With the *alla breve* of the middle movement of K.491, Mozart seems to set us a riddle, but for once without giving us 'the solution with the riddle' (to quote another of Busoni's Mozart aphorisms). Paul and Eva Badura-Skoda have gone to some lengths to explain why Mozart must have made a mistake with this marking. In its note values, the movement is twice as slow as the *alla breve* movements in Concertos K.466, 537 and 595. As confirmed by the textbooks of the period, and by Beethoven's metronome figures, the *alla breve* marking stands not only for counting half-bars but also for a considerable increase in tempo. Yet there are exceptions, as Erich Leinsdorf was kind enough to point out to me, and the second movement of K.491 is one. Leinsdorf mentioned, among others, some examples from *The Magic Flute* (Overture: Adagio; No. 8: Finale I-Larghetto; Act II: March of the Priests; No. 18: Chorus of the Priests; No. 21: Finale II-Andante) where the *alla breve* 'should be translated to a contemporary conductor meaning: in four, my boy, not in eight'. But there is also the Aria with gamba 'Es ist vollbracht' ('It is accomplished') from Bach's *St John Passion* where Bach indicated, above the 3/4 of the middle section, the words *alla breve*, suggesting the 'next faster unit': in three, not in six. The old complete edition, which altered several of Mozart's tempo markings arbitrarily, transformed the *alla breve* in the first movement of the Concerto in F major K.459 into 4/4 time, thereby doing precisely what this piece cannot tolerate: it is meant to move along not *alla marcia*, as we are constantly told in commentaries and hear in performances, but dancingly and in whole bars.

Mozart was not a flower child. His rhythm is neither weak nor vague. Even the tiniest, softest tone has backbone. Mozart may dream now and then, but his rhythm stays awake. Let the tempo modifications in Mozart be signs of a rhythmic strength that counterbalances emotional strength; above all in variation movements, it will surely be permissible to graduate the tempo at times, to set off the variations from one another. Mozart may lament – and that lamentation can reach a pitch of solitary grief – but he does not moan and groan. Two-note patterns should be 'sighed' only when the music really demands sighing. Not only singers should be aware of the difference between a suspension, which has a purely musical role, and an appoggiatura, whose role is emotional and declamatory, stressing the pathos of two-syllable words.

Is Mozart's music simple? For his contemporaries it was frequently too complicated. The idea of simplicity has become downright embarrassing in this century. There is a 'kitsch' of plainness, especially noticeable in the literary glorification of the 'simple life' and in a longing for the 'popular vein'. What was all right for the Romantics is thought to be reasonable enough for their descendants. Simplicity in playing Mozart must not mean subjecting diversity to a levelling process or running away from problems. Simplicity is welcome as long as the point is to avoid superfluity. But to 'concentrate only on what counts' in Mozart is questionable. Everything in his music counts, if we leave out a few weaker works or movements, of which there are some even among Mozart's piano concertos, for example the early pieces preceding that wonder of the world, the 'Jeunehomme' Concerto K.271.

The identity of Mlle Jeunehomme has recently been disclosed thanks to the efforts of the Austrian scholar Michael Lorenz: her name was Victoire Jenamy, born in Strasbourg 1749 as the oldest child of the famous dancer Jean-George Noverre. What remains mysterious, however, is the sudden supreme mastery that unfolds in the work composed for her. Here it is revealed for the first time that Mozart is both 'as young as a youth, and as wise as an old man' (Busoni). And from this point on, the Mozart player must shoulder a burden of perfection that goes beyond his powers.

(1985)

Minor Mozart: In Defence of His Solo Works

THE UNDERESTIMATION OF Mozart's sonatas and other solo piano works begs for reflection. We readily extol composers for their 'greatest' and 'most personal' or exemplary achievements. Bach is granted primacy in organ music, sacred choral music and in fugue; Mozart primacy in opera, the piano concerto and the string quintet; Beethoven highest rank with the symphony and sonata, and – according to our preferences and perspective – either Haydn or Beethoven supremacy with the string quartet. In this vein not only have the piano sonatas of Haydn and Schubert been long neglected; Mozart's sonatas, unlike his concertos, have received less than their due. A widespread prejudice regards them as teaching matter for children, as secondary pieces for domestic use imbued with the taste of their age, as works in which Mozart made it easy for himself and the player. Ernst Bloch refers to the 'still uncharacteristic, not yet fully realised sonatas', and finds that in Mozart, everything remains 'of course somehow like porcelain'. It seems inevitable at this point to break some porcelain.

Mozart's fame as a pianist reaches back to his early years. His first six sonatas K.279–84 already served him as 'difficult sonatas', which he performed by heart. Mozart designated only the so-called 'Sonata facile' K.545 as 'a little piano sonata for beginners'. Paradoxically, it belongs to the most treacherous pieces of the repertory, as every self-critical pianist of age and experience will know. The reduction to the most essential, which we so admire and dread in Mozart's pianistic writing, is carried here to a masterly extreme. Two great pianists comment on this state of affairs. Artur Schnabel quips that Mozart's sonatas are 'too simple for children, too difficult for artists'. Anton Rubinstein put it differently: 'Strange, that one usually gives Mozart to children to play! One should give his music to the big, fully grown children.'

Woe, if these children are not truly mature! The pianist who has just surmounted the chords and double octaves of Brahms's B♭ Concerto will be keenly aware how much every note counts in Mozart's solo works. The performer is left alone here with every nuance, every small decision – a great deal more so than in Mozart's piano concertos. The responsibility to these few proffered notes is immense, yet needs to be carried off lightly. It is as if huge searchlights illuminated everything, while the player must act as if they did not blind him.

In the concertos the orchestra is not only a framework and partner to the pianist

but also a guide to questions pertaining to the musical text. Although dynamic indications are largely missing in the piano part, the specifications in the full score can
supplement much that relates to character and articulation. How much more precarious is the pianist's situation with those sonatas that bear few, or as in the 'Sonata
facile', no dynamic indications at all! One sits here alone in front of bare notes to be
infused with dynamic life, whereas in other piano works, especially those in minor
keys – the Sonatas in A minor and C minor, the A minor Rondo, the B minor Adagio – a great deal is specified: these works are marked with a care and even obsession
for detail that drives many Mozart players to the brink of despair. This circumstance
creates an entirely different kind of embarrassment, namely one in which an Apollonian equilibrium is upset, with climaxes not underplayed but emphasised, and (already
in early works like K.282) contrasts startlingly juxtaposed, blunt crassness seemingly
yielding to the utmost nervous refinement. This performance style specified by Mozart
does not at all fulfil the expectations of many of today's musicians and listeners, shaped
as these are on the one hand by the notion of a sweet, tender, pampered Mozart, who
would correspond to the *galant* scenes not of Watteau, but of Lancret or Pater, and on
the other by a 'pure', simple, demurely virginal wax-figure image that reflects above all
the taste of the Biedermeier, the 'Nazarenes' and the purism of the 1950s. The rococo
notion was expressed in 1889 by Anton Rubinstein as follows: 'The character of the
time in which Mozart lived was moulded by mannerism, refinement and artificial-
ity of manners and costumes'. Rubinstein speaks of polite and gentle bowing and of
dances, which only slowly burst into leaps and jumps. 'As strange as it may seem, we
thus find the entire character of the age and its manners mirrored in the music.'[2] The
Biedermeier-Nazarene idea surfaces in a letter of the 25-year-old Paul Klee to his second wife, the pianist Lili Stumpf, though with an invitation to contradiction. To Klee,
who as is well known also played violin, Mozart seemed 'psychologically not too rich in
contrast, especially in moods of darkness and beyond melancholy'. In his view, lament
was rare here; rupture or conflict did not appear, and in the realm of chamber music,
the player could not venture much more than to avoid wrong notes. From such an
impression of passivity, it is not a long way to Ernst Bloch's astonishing claim 'that on
the whole Mozart reveals a dead, unbearably arithmetic dimension'.

---

2   Anton Rubinstein, *Die Meister des Klaviers* (Berlin: Harmonie, Verlagsgesellschaft für Literatur und
     Kunst, 1889).

While the appreciation of his other music has progressed enormously, this picture of Mozart's solo piano music still hangs on. The cause may have to do with an antiquated idea of the 'spinet' (for which these works are allegedly written) as promoting a prettified image of the music. The idea widely entertained about the possibilities of Mozart's keyboard instruments is of course just as inappropriate as the concept of a prim, lavishly seasoned, artificially intricate rococo aesthetic. Mozart's piano music – like that of most great composers – is but rarely derived from the sound of the keyboard itself: its expressive potential, colours and power transcend by far the limits of the most advanced pianos of the age. Thus there were in the first decades of the nineteenth century at least three orchestral versions of the C minor Fantasy K.475, including one by Mozart's student Ignaz von Seyfried, who also orchestrated the C minor Sonata K.475.[3] This is hardly remarkable, since purely pianistic passages are exceptional in these works. On the other hand, I find next to many orchestral features in the Fantasy some pronounced operatic elements: the sublimity and passion of *opera seria*. (That Seyfried also concocted an opera *Ahasverus* with the help of piano works by Mozart goes definitely too far.)

In the opera, song and language are inseparably connected. Instrumentalists should perhaps always honour the maxim that a good Mozart interpreter must at each moment sing and speak – which can even take the form of rests infused with a telling quality, a device conspicuous in the C minor Fantasy. Sándor Végh told me that he appeared as a young violinist in concerts of the great Schaljapin. The intervals between the arias, which the singer spent with a steak and bottle of wine in the dressing room, were given over to Végh and his solos. One evening Végh noticed that instead of devoting himself to this steak as usual, Schaljapin sat in a loge and listened to his playing. After the concert he said: 'You sing beautifully, but you speak too little.' (Schaljapin had already said the same to another striving artist, Gregor Piatigorsky.) Végh, as he explained, later took Casals as a model for musical speech. More recently, the balance in many historically oriented performances has been tipped so strongly in the direction of declamation that one is tempted to beg for more song.

We are indebted to the sound of historic orchestral instruments for confirming that the flattened-out Mozart of yesteryear – who permitted no strong *forte*, and no disturbing accents – was but a fiction. Already earlier, interpreters such as Gustav

---

3   The other two arrangements are by Josef Triebensee and Carl David Stegmann.

Mahler, Bruno Walter or Edwin Fischer had offered counter-examples. And Richard Strauss had perceived how the whole range of human sensitivity was distilled in Mozart's purely instrumental creations. To him, the effort to erect a unified style of Mozart interpretation in the face of these infinitely subtle and richly shaped images of the human soul seemed foolish and superficial. Mozart's solo works contain the same diversity. After a year of preoccupation with this repertory I was myself surprised, by how effortlessly and naturally the performer of this music can fill large halls. At the same time, even the limits of the modern instrument seem so often transcended that one leaves the podium with a sense of having conducted or sung rather than played the piano. On the one hand, the player needs to display an 'extrahuman sense of form' (Busoni), and humanise the structures of works like the little C major Sonata or the B♭ major Sonata K.333 (315c) (which is dated in the Koechel catalogue more than five years too early). On the other end of the scale, he must hold together the music, where Mozart 'carries the language capacity of his epoch to the breaking point and nearly to its end' (Hans Werner Henze), as in the Andante of the Sonata K.533.

Whether Mozart should be regarded as a revolutionary (Tschitscherin), as an innovator (Stendhal: 'He resembles no one'), as neither (Harnoncourt) or as a conservative revolutionary (Alfred Einstein) has remained a point of disagreement. Even if Mozart was no revolutionary, it doesn't follow that he offered nothing new. Mozart's early biographer Franz Xavier Niemetschek saw Mozart's novelty as a synthesis of what already existed, whereas Henze finds it in his alienation and exaltation. But don't works like the early E♭ major Concerto K.271 and *Die Entführung*, in which the freshness of the new is joined by absolute mastery, go still further? Composers like Reichardt and Zelter responded to Mozart's surprises with exasperation. Time and again, Mozart's instrumental music appeared to his contemporaries as unnatural, teeming with unnecessary difficulties and uncalled-for contrasts. The admiring Ernst Ludwig Gerber wrote in 1790 that even erudite ears would need to listen to Mozart's works repeatedly. The Apollonian roller had not yet smoothed him out. A later Mozart enthusiast, George Bernard Shaw, recalled the reproaches of Mozart's day – 'too many notes,' the 'noise' of his instrumentation, the lack of 'true' melody, the 'attacks' against the human ear – and asked himself where such irritation could still be lurking.

I would like to venture an answer from my own experience: it is still there. In any event this depends upon what we as listeners and players think Mozart was like. The majority of listeners stretch out their legs before them and expect from Mozart joy, crispness, grace and satisfaction, as if there were no *Requiem*, no *Idomeneo* and *Don Giovanni*, no C minor Mass and C minor Serenade, no G minor Symphony and G minor chamber works. It seems as if many wish to suppress the dark and deadly Mozart, as Nietzsche did:

> Do present practitioners of musical performance really believe that the highest duty of their art is to give every piece as much *high relief* as is possible, and convey at any price a *dramatic* language? Is this, when for instance applied to Mozart, not actually a sin against his spirit, that bright, sunny, tender, reckless spirit of Mozart's, whose seriousness is kindly, not frightful, whose pictures do not jump out of the wall to plunge the audience into fear and flight. Or do you mean that Mozartian music would be identical with the 'music of the stone guest'? And not only Mozart's, but all music?[4]

We do not want to exaggerate and subordinate the whole of Mozart to the stone guest's perspective. Nor should we take Stendhal literally when he says that compared to Rossini and Cimarosa, Mozart offers neither lightness nor comedy. Nonetheless, I believe that the weight of those relatively few works in the minor that Mozart wrote in fact balances his works in the major, whether these be serene, comic, inward or tinged with melancholy. The pieces in the minor do more than just present a dark backdrop to Mozart's brilliance. Furthermore, is Mozart's seriousness charitable? Is it not the sublimity of tragedy? The composer who, already as an eight-year-old, seems to have been able to improvise arias of love and fury with a mischievous face, the master who housed in himself as 'performer and portraitist' (Busoni) any character you name, must have felt compelled at times to leave the cherished play-acting behind. When he writes in C minor or D minor we may perceive in his music neither the human being contemplating death and despair or longing for oblivion, nor the creature that gives expression to its encounter with the uncanny, the monstrous or, as Goethe would have said, the demonic. In parts of the C minor Mass, in the choruses of *Idomeneo*, in the maestoso of the Commendatore or in the C minor

---

4   'Der Wanderer und sein Schatten' (*Menschliches, Allzumenschliches*, No. 152), p. 165.

Adagio with Fugue (K.546) the music as it were no longer participates. Like fate itself it appears immovable before us: not as consoling best friend, not as the agent of longed-for release through death, but as the sublime, implacable Other before which we are mute and powerless. The 'extrahuman' dimension is manifested here not only in the perfection of form but also in a transcending power of emotion.

I know of no other composer as fundamentally transformed while writing in minor keys, and none except Gesualdo and Wagner, who made such unforgettable use of chromaticism. (For Wagner himself, Mozart was 'the great *Chromatiker*'.) The pianist stands especially close to Mozart's minor mode works, since the largest number of his instrumental compositions in the minor are devoted to the piano – Mozart's instrument – as solo pieces, concertos or chamber music. Here again, we must disregard one of those oversimplifications, which would withhold from one artist what is readily granted to another. Beethoven was declared the supreme master of C minor, while Mozart became identified with the sphere of G minor. Yet the largest number of Mozartian works in the minor – one third – are in C minor. An understanding of Mozart's handling of the minor mode must begin here. Mozart leaves us without recourse or resolution in this key. (Only the Wind Serenade K.388 ends in major, and it remains open whether its close in major really manages to console.) The great, never surpassed slow movement of the *Jeunehomme* Concerto K.271 forges the way: Gluck, elevated to Mozartian heights.

The last of the pianistic works in minor is the B minor Adagio K.540: passion music as interior monologue. The engagement with Bach and Handel had enriched Mozart's music especially since 1782. Much in the later works would be unthinkable without, such as the bravura of double counterpoint displayed for connoisseurs in the Allegro of the exquisite F major Sonata K.533 – a piece in which the player must determine virtually all of the dynamics himself. Mozart shows how challenging he can be, as he brings together counterpoint and operatic elements, learnedness and wit, new and old. The goal of being 'neither too easy nor too difficult', as Mozart once put it to his father – that balance of 'making effects' while also writing for the initiated – does not adequately describe this work. To this day the Sonata has remained a piece for the initiated. The contrapuntal development of its Andante collapses into a dissonant inner turbulence, very nearly dislocating the formal equilibrium. In this movement, communicative utterance is virtually stifled. Whoever is irritated by Mozart's serene loveliness – as evidently was Busoni – should realise

from this Andante, from the beginning of the 'Dissonance' Quartet, the trio of
the B♭ major Quartet K.589 or the F minor works for mechanical organ K.594 and
616, how boldly Mozart could darken beauty. The two movements of K.533 display
a musician who shows not only what he can do, but what he dares to do. Regret
has been expressed over Mozart's use of the Rondo, K.494, composed one and a
half years earlier, as the third movement of the sonata. True, the vigorous inserted
cadenza-like passage of twenty-seven measures, which relates structurally to the other
movements, does not attempt to put into question the basically graceful character of
the whole. Yet nothing could resolve the preceding tensions more thoroughly than
the lightness which remains gently suspended even in the subterranean bass register
of the closing measures. Mozart bids us farewell with a delicately ironic antithesis
to those disturbing pages in D minor and G minor, in which the Andante had so
nearly met its destruction.

(1991)

BEETHOVEN

~~~

Notes on a Complete Recording of
Beethoven's Piano Works

I MUST BEGIN WITH a qualification: this first recording of Beethoven's piano works, which I made for Vox-Turnabout between 1958 and 1964, is not entirely complete. There seemed to me little virtue in rescuing from oblivion works that are totally devoid of any touch of Beethoven's mastery and originality. It was without regret, therefore, that I omitted pieces like the deplorable Haibel Variations, which could have been written by any of Beethoven's contemporaries, as well as certain student exercises, *Albumblätter*, studies, sketches and curiosities, most of which were never intended for publication – pieces, that is, which are merely of interest to the historian. These include the total output of the Bonn period (among which are the Variations on a March of Dressler by the twelve-year-old Beethoven and the two preludes through all the major keys, curiously published later on as Op. 39), the Easy Sonata in C major, Woo 51, the Variations on the 'Menuet à la Viganò' by Haibel which I have already mentioned, the pieces Woo 52, 53, 55 (the Prelude in the style of Bach), 56, 61 and 61a, as well as the little dance movements Woo 81–6, of which I retained only the Six Écossaises, Woo 83, although in all likelihood these are transcriptions of an orchestral score, and the single extant copy, passed down by Gustav Nottebohm, may well be dubious in some of its detail. It is not for nothing that virtuosi have been stimulated again and again to make arrangements of these spirited pieces.

If I mention the fact that I concluded the series at the age of thirty-four, this is not to plead for mitigation, but to acquaint the reader with a circumstance that may explain certain features of these interpretations. Nothing was further from my mind than to suppose that I could present in my recordings anything like a definitive solution of the Beethoven problem. Nor was it my intention to supply the musical illustrations to any fashionable theory of Beethoven interpretation. I just plunged into an adventure, the consequences of which I could no more foresee than could the record company that had put its trust in me.

My work on the Beethoven series took five and a half years. One of the crosses the artist has to bear is that the date of a recording is so rarely indicated on the record sleeve. He is all too easily blamed or, almost worse, praised for interpretations that have lost some of their validity, at least as far as he himself is concerned. People expect an artist to develop, and yet they are only too ready to impale him, like an insect, on one of his renderings. The artist should have the right to identify his work with a certain phase of his development. It is only the continuous renewal of his vision – either in the form of evolution or of rediscovery – that can keep his music-making young.[5]

The recordings of Beethoven's variation works, with the exception of the *Diabelli Variations*, were made in three stages between December 1958 and July 1960. There followed, at the turn of 1960–61, the last five sonatas, together with the Fantasy, Op. 77. In March 1962 I played the Sonatas Op. 31, Nos. 1 and 2, Op. 57 and Op. 90; in June and July of that year all the remaining sonatas between Op. 22 and Op. 81a. The early sonatas from Op. 2 to Op. 14 were recorded in December 1962 and January 1963. (By coincidence, I concluded my work on the thirty-two sonatas on my thirty-second birthday.) Finally, in July 1964, I played the miscellaneous pieces and the greatest of all piano works: the *Diabelli Variations*.

I recall a cold winter morning in a rather dilapidated Baroque mansion in Vienna; the logs in the fireplace of the hall where we recorded crackled so loudly that we had to throw them out of the window onto the snow. Several changes in recording technique, and in the room and instrument, proved unavoidable. In the event, there were five groups of recordings: 1) the variation works, 2) the late sonatas, 3) the middle-period sonatas from Op. 22 on, 4) the early sonatas, 5) the miscellaneous pieces and the *Diabelli Variations*. The initiated will know that even the same concert grand does not stay the same over several months; that exactly the same microphone position – as if there were a jinx on it – does not always give the same results; that even technically satisfactory tapes may be distorted beyond recognition in the disc-pressing process. On some of the pressings of the late sonatas the dynamic range was reduced almost to uniformity; moreover, empty grooves of standard length were inserted between the movements, whether or not this suited

---

5   In recent years, serious record companies have provided the date and place of the recording on the sleeve or in the accompanying booklet. Less serious ones mislead the purchaser in updating older recordings by giving dubious copyright dates instead.

the context or the composer's instructions, the reason given being that the customers liked it that way.

Beethoven's piano works pointed far into the future of piano building. Decades had to pass after his death before there were pianos – and pianists – equal to the demands of his 'Hammerklavier' Sonata, Op. 106.

If one tries to play on Beethoven's Érard grand of 1803, which is kept in the instrument collection at the Vienna Kunsthistorisches Museum, one thing becomes evident at once: its sound, dynamics and action have surprisingly little in common with the pianos of today. The tone of each single note has a distinct 'onset'; within its intimate confines, it is livelier and more flexible, and also more subject to change while it lasts. The difference in sound between bass, middle and top register is considerable (polyphonic playing!). The treble notes are short-lived and thin, and resist dynamic changes; the treble range is not conducive to cantilenas that want to rise above a gentle *piano*. Even in the clear and transparent, somewhat twangy bass register, the dynamic span is much narrower than on our instrument. One begins to see the reason for the permanent accompanying *piano* in the orchestral textures of Beethoven's piano concertos – even though, admittedly, the orchestral sound of his period cannot have been much like ours. If I had to compare the demands the Érard and the modern Steinway make on the physical power of the player, I would tend to think in terms of those made on a watchmaker and on a removal man!

A few years later, with the pianos of Streicher and Graf, a new, more rounded, more even and neutral sound came into being which, while dynamic scope continued to increase, became the norm throughout the nineteenth century. This sound is more closely related to the piano sound of today than to that of the older Hammerklavier, whose timbre was still derived from that of the harpsichord and clavichord. But by the time this new sound had become established, Beethoven had already composed a large portion of his piano works, and was afflicted by deafness.

We have to resign ourselves to the fact that whenever we hear Beethoven on a present-day instrument, we are listening to a sort of transcription. Anyone still having illusions about that will be disabused by a visit to a collection of old instruments. The modern concert grand, which I naturally used for my recordings, not only has the volume of tone demanded by modern orchestras, concert halls and ears; it also – and of this I am deeply convinced – does better justice to most of Beethoven's piano works than the Hammerklavier: its tone is far more colourful, orchestral and rich in contrast, and these qualities do matter in Beethoven, as can be seen from his orchestral and chamber music. Some of the peculiarities of a Hammerklavier can only be approximated on a modern grand – for instance the sound of the *una corda* and even more the whisper of the *piano* stop. (In the studio, however, finesses of this kind did not always turn out as I wished, either because damping noises obliged me to change my style of playing, or because the technical specifications of the microphone did not permit me to go below a certain dynamic level.)

One must translate other characteristics of the Hammerklavier as best one can. The octave glissandi in the Prestissimo of the 'Waldstein' Sonata, for example, were easier to execute on the older instrument: on the deep, heavy keys of a Steinway they can be brought off only by the use of brute force, which causes them to lose their scurrying *pianissimo* character. Very conscientious pianists, who cannot bear an untidy note, curb the tempo here and play wrist octaves. The only safe method of preserving the *pianissimo* character of this section without the help of a *piano* stop lies in imitating the sliding progress of the glissandi by distributing the passages between the hands, while reducing the bass octaves to their lower part.

The variation works do not conform to the concept of Beethoven, the Olympian. Most of them are unknown even to pianists. Beside the sonatas, many of the variation works appear to be outpourings rather than structures. This is in the nature of the form, which derives from the improvisatory treatment of given material. The attraction (as well as the unevenness) of many variation works stems from the fact that something of the casualness and spontaneity of an improvisation survives in them. The charm of the moment, the lightness, mobility, sharp characterisation, the humorous turn are here more important than organic growth. (Admittedly, this does not apply to the masterpieces of the genre: the *Diabelli Variations*, the Op. 34 and Op. 35 sets and possibly the problematic C minor Variations.) In the witty, roguish finales we get a glimpse of Beethoven's art of improvisation, which otherwise only manifests itself – in a different, more passionate vein – in Op. 77, the Fantasy without basic tonality. Beethoven's at times rather peculiar sense of humour disports itself quite freely here – as for instance in the delightful 'Kind, willst du ruhig schlafen', my favourite piece in the lighter style, or in 'Venni amore'. In the 7th, 16th, 21st and 22nd variations of 'Venni amore', incidentally, there are distinct anticipations of Brahms, which make it quite obvious that the bearded successor of Beethoven must have known this work, and also 'Das Waldmädchen'. 'Quant'è più bello l'amor contadino' and 'Nel cor più non mi sento' (both after Paisiello) will give unalloyed pleasure to the innocent mind as also the Six Easy Variations on an original theme in G major. The Variations on 'Rule, Britannia' are full of bizarre quirks; those on Salieri's 'La stessa, la stessissima' test the performer's sense of humour. It is surprising that some of these works made their first appearance in the LP catalogue on this occasion.

What the pianist can learn, and the listener enjoy, in the variation works will be of advantage to both of them when they approach the sonatas. The variation works teach promptness of reaction, exactness and delicacy of characterisation, and the ability to regard nearly every variation as having its own separate identity. When compared to the suite with its well-established formula of movements, the sonata too contained many new personal, private, characteristic elements which must have baffled the eighteenth-century listener. We also learn to be wary of over-dramatisation in the sonatas, and begin to see the concept of the heroic Beethoven as a one-sided view representative of the bourgeois nineteenth century.

The miscellaneous piano pieces show us that Beethoven was also a master of the small form, though he rarely turned his attention to it. They are either loosely gathered and small-scale collections, such as the Bagatelles Op. 33 and Op. 119 and the Écossaises; or they are held together by an inner unity, such as the sublime 'trifles' of Op. 126 with which Beethoven took his leave of the piano. By themselves stand the spirited, sparkling Polonaise, the hectic Fantasy, and the three Rondos: the two gracefully feminine ones of Op. 51, and the wild, masculine *alla zingara* work of his early Vienna days.

This last piece has an interesting history. It was published posthumously in 1828 under the title 'Die Wuth über den verlorenen Groschen ausgetobt in einer Kaprize' ('The Rage over the Lost Penny, Vented in a Caprice'); but only in 1832 was the so far unused opus number 129 affixed to it. In contrast to Czerny and Lenz, Hans von Bülow insisted with almost comical emphasis that this Rondo was a late-style work, repudiating any doubt on that point as 'worthy of the Kalmuck Oulibichev'.[6] The manuscript, discovered by Otto E. Albrecht in 1945, refutes Bülow's (and Hugo Riemann's) view: it also contains sketches for works dating from 1795–98. It can be deduced from the state

6 *Translator's note*: Alexander Oulibichev (1795–1858), an early Russian biographer of Beethoven.

of the manuscript that it served as the basis of the original edition, which was prepared by an unknown hand (Czerny? Schindler?), and certainly not by Beethoven himself. The title current today has been added to the manuscript in different handwriting. In Beethoven's own hand are the superscription 'Alla Ingharese quasi un Capriccio' and the designation 'Leichte Kaprize' on the flyleaf. The manuscript bears all the marks of a sketchy first draft: uncompleted passages, particularly in the left-hand accompaniment, mistakes in part-writing and a complete lack of dynamic markings and articulation signs. Unfortunately, it was only after my recording that I came across Erich Hertzmann's thorough investigation of the autograph in the *Musical Quarterly*, XXXII, 1946, as well as the manuscript itself, so that not all the mistakes of the original edition have been expunged from my performance. An exact text of the piece can be found in the edition I prepared for the *Wiener Urtext* series.

The beautiful 'Andante favori' and the C minor Allegretto are remnants of Beethoven's work on the Sonatas Op. 53 and Op. 10, No. 1, respectively. The wonderful, well-known 'Für Elise' (or Therese) and another, later *Albumblatt* in B flat major, a memento to Marie Szymanowska, can hold their own with the best of the Bagatelles, while the Op. 119 and Op. 126 sets look ahead to the Romantic cycles of Schumann, from *Papillons* to *Kreisleriana*.

The study of a composer's works appears to me a more profitable pursuit than any pilgrimage to tombs and shrines, or, for that matter, the perusal of a large quantity of critical writing about him. A great deal has been written about Beethoven's sonatas, most of it of negligible value. (On the other hand, despite Donald Francis Tovey's outstanding attempt, I do not yet know of any exhaustive analysis of the *Diabelli Variations*.)[7] Generally, all one can expect is a little amusement, albeit at the author's expense: thus, a Beethoven biographer from the beginning of this century tells us that the 'Waldstein' Sonata 'had at some time acquired the nickname "Horror", presumably because of the thrusting, agitated figuration and the surprising modulations of its opening which are apt to make one shudder.' The author's shudderings are based on a misunderstanding: the 'Waldstein' Sonata is known in France as 'L'Aurore'.

---

7   This has been splendidly remedied by William Kinderman's monograph (Clarendon Press/Oxford University Press, 1987).

Among the older Beethoven literature, the commentaries of Czerny, *Über den richtigen Vortrag der sämtlichen Beethoven'schen Klavierwerke* ('On the proper performance of all Beethoven's works for the piano'), newly edited by Paul Badura-Skoda, are well worth reading; of slightly lesser importance are the writings of Anton Felix Schindler, Ferdinand Ries and Wilhelm von Lenz. The interest of Prod'homme's book *The Piano Sonatas of Beethoven* lies in its inclusion of some of Beethoven's sketches.

Czerny, taking the Cello Sonata, Op. 69, as an example, describes the repeated striking of two notes connected by a tie, an effect later known as *Bebung*, which may also be intended in the Adagio of Op. 106 and in the recitative of Op. 110. The information he gives on the later works is scanty. Yet he does make this comment on the variations of Op. 109: 'The whole movement in the style of Handel and Seb. Bach' – a remark which startled me only for a moment. It is rather amusing to see how indignant the self-important and unreliable Schindler, Beethoven's first biographer, waxes about Czerny's at times clumsy, but generally sensible and honest, commentaries. Anyone nowadays venturing to play the first movement of Op. 10, No. 1 in the manner recommended by Schindler would cause some shaking of heads. His suggestion to add two crotchet rests between each phrase in bars 16–21 makes the passage sound rhetorically overblown, while his addition of two fermatas in bar 93 and a caesura before the *fp* in bar 94 I find downright silly.

Among the more recent books on the sonatas, that of my teacher Edwin Fischer is outstanding; while containing only a fraction of what Fischer had to say about these works, the loving care with which his often quite unobtrusive advice is given makes it more useful than many more exhaustive investigations. Bülow's and Artur Schnabel's editions of the sonatas may, on account of their copious footnotes, jokingly be counted among the Beethoven literature. Both deserve respect as manifestations of strong personalities, and are highly stimulating owing to the temperaments of their authors. Both frequently invite disagreement. Bülow is the first editor to be credited with the attempt to retrace mentally Beethoven's compositional processes; unfortunately, his intellectual method was not equal to his purpose, and he could not pay sufficient attention to the original material. Schnabel, whom I respect as one of the great pianists of his time, was in many ways anti-Bülow: he removed the latter's autocratic 'corrections', but accepted a number of obvious mistakes in the original texts with a kind of pedantic deference. In his choice of readings, I find Heinrich Schenker generally more convincing than Schnabel, who is said to have been not too happy about his edition in later years. Both Bülow and Schnabel invented highly original fingerings, as did Eugen d'Albert, who had a fondness for playing bass notes with the thumb; in his comments, however, he was more sparing of words than his colleagues. At the well-known disputed passage in the 'Hammerklavier' Sonata, before the entry of the first movement's recapitulation, he just says 'A sharp, of course'. As a matter of fact, I play A natural.

Of all the analyses, those by Tovey, Schenker and Erwin Ratz (Op. 106) proved more helpful to me than Riemann or Nagel.[8]

For a player to study autographs and first prints is more than a hobby; in spite of modern *Urtext* editions, it is frequently a necessity. When does an *Urtext* edition deserve to be so called? When, basing itself on all existing original sources, it reproduces the text as the composer might have wished to see it, while at the same time discussing mistakes, omissions and doubtful passages in detailed critical notes, quoting all divergent readings, and substantiating editorial decisions. Heinrich Schenker's exemplary edition of the sonatas and the widely esteemed Henle edition come closer to these requirements, without entirely fulfilling them; the edition by Craxton and Tovey regrettably ignores many of Beethoven's articulation markings, while giving phrasing indications of dubious value. The definitive editorial work is still to be done.

Using the early prints as the point of reference, I myself corrected a large part of the variation works, since at the time of recording no tolerably reliable edition of the second volume was yet in existence. In connection with the recording of the miscellaneous pieces (Bagatelles, Rondos, etc.) I began to prepare an *Urtext* edition of all those pieces I was including in my gramophone series. Certain important documents, however, did not come to my notice until after the recording sessions were over – as for instance the autograph of the 'Easy Caprice' and the London first editions of some works, the significance of which was not realised until Alan Tyson's book *The Authentic English Editions of Beethoven* (Faber & Faber) was published in 1963.

Let me give one or two examples:

The London first edition (The Royal Harmonic Institution) of the Sonata Op. 106 has in bar 116 of the Adagio as first semiquaver in the right hand an F sharp,

---

8   Since this article was written, several new books merit attention. To mention only three: Jürgen Uhde's
     Beethovens Klaviermusik (Reclam, 3 volumes), Rudolph Reti's *Thematic Patterns in Sonatas of Beethoven*
     (Faber & Faber), and Charles Rosen's *The Classical Style* (Faber & Faber).

in contrast to the usual D sharp of the Vienna first edition (Artaria) and all later editions known to me.

This F sharp not only strikes me as stronger and nobler, it also fits better into the melodic line of the second subject: the three note motive (rising third, falling second) determines its structure up to bar 120.

In other cases I mistakenly relied on the well-known *Urtext* editions, as the following will illustrate:

The six-times-repeated F, of the pedal point in bars 373–8 of the Fugue in Op. 106, was tacitly provided with ties by Schenker, but these belong only to the overlying trill on B flat. The logical argument in favour of re-striking these notes is furnished by bars 379–80: the sixfold F reappears here, this time in rhythmic diminution.

In the Polonaise, Op. 89, we find the following sequence (bars 19–21, also 64–6):

The Henle edition altered, without comment, the bass of the third crotchet of bars 19 and 64 into B flat,[9] thus depriving this *pianissimo* passage of its special harmonic piquancy. Both these examples are in contradiction to the sources.

I have since changed my mind about the execution of certain details, so that today, in the ninth variation of the 'Eroica' Variations, Op. 35, I would play the acciaccaturas in bars 13–17 not before, but together with the left hand. In some cases my reading was inaccurate, or my fancy permitted itself an indefensible variant, as in Op. 28, second movement, bars 72–3. I apologise!

---

9   In recent reprints the error has been corrected.

Every generation of musicians is unconsciously influenced by the editions with which it has grown up. My own generation, at least in Central Europe, became accustomed to using editions which respect the text of the composer. Yet necessary though it is to reject the accretions foisted upon the music by the older editors, the restored text is all too easily invested by its users with an autonomous significance which it does not merit. All of us are apt to forget at times that musical notes can only suggest, that expression marks can only supplement and confirm what we must, first and foremost, read from the face of the composition itself.

I should therefore like to propose that the words *Werktreue* and *Texttreue*[10] be banished from the vocabulary. They have become the feather bed of the academic Classicists. The 'fidelity' referred to here smacks overmuch of 'trust': blind trust, that is, in the self-sufficiency of the letter; trust in the notion that the work will speak for itself as long as the interpreter does not interpose his personality. Let there be no misunderstanding: it is far from my intention to set myself up as the advocate of self-indulgence. The virtuoso who unhesitatingly adapted the music of the past to his own style of playing and composing belongs to a bygone age.[11] Gone are the days when the 'edition', the revision made by a famous virtuoso or teacher, was more important than the original text. That state of affairs, commonly associated with the successors of Liszt, dates back, incidentally, to much earlier times. Carl Czerny – the teacher of Liszt and pupil of Beethoven – did not have any scruples about publishing with Diabelli under his own name a 'Grand Duo brillant à quatre mains', with the minutely engraved subtitle 'arrangé d'après la Sonate de L. van Beethoven, Oeuv. 47'. This is nothing other than a piano duet arrangement of the 'Kreutzer' Sonata! (see p. 25)

---

10   *Translator's note: Werktreue*, commonly used in German musicology, signifies the performer's fidelity to the intentions of the composer, *Texttreue* his fidelity to the text of a work. Since no simple English translation offers itself, I have decided to use the German terms in the context of this essay as well as in the title of its supplement, in the hope that – *pace* the author's distrust if not of the words, then of their implications! – they will be accepted by the English music lover with the kindness he has bestowed on the word *Urtext*.

11   Or maybe not, as the cult status of Glenn Gould suggests.

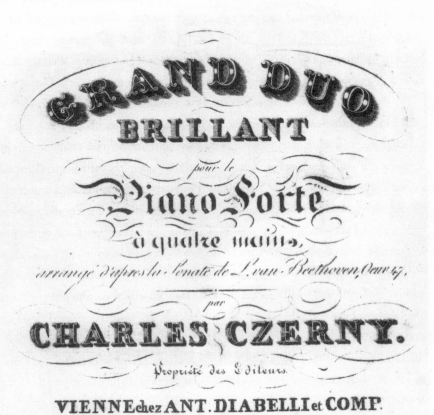

The title page of Czerny's piano duet arrangement of Beethoven's 'Kreutzer' Sonata.

(Collection Hermann Baron)

The Romantic era did not yet know a historically minded style of interpretation. People played everything 'the way they felt', their minds scarcely accessible to arguments of historical propriety. (Editors like Bischoff and Kullak, who aimed at meticulously cleaning the musical text of additions, remained outsiders.) This attitude appeared natural and legitimate until the time when tonality began to disintegrate. In other words, when one could no longer compose or improvise 'modern' cadenzas for Classical piano concertos, the practice of interpreting Classical works in a 'modern' manner also became obsolete. The innocent self-assurance of the virtuoso was gone – a revolutionary development indeed. In its wake there evolved the editing techniques of the *Urtext* publication. The investigation of the performing traditions of past ages produced, apart from some misconceptions, a number of genuine insights, which affected the style of Mozart interpretation in particular. The first era of 'historicism' in the short history of public concert-giving had dawned. Its repercussions on the late Romantic age itself both fascinated and inhibited more than one generation of performers. The loss of self-confidence was often followed by a rigid faith in the letter. People began to play every sort of appoggiatura on the beat, and string quartets would play all four parts equally loudly just because Beethoven had marked them all with the same *forte* or *piano*. The harshness thus created was considered Classical by many, and still is today in some circles. The dogma according to which every whim of the composer, however unreasonable, must be accepted with reverence, absolved performers from the effort of thinking for themselves. No engraver's error in a first print, no slip of the pen in an autograph was so absurd that it could not be hailed as a bold stroke of genius.

During the same period, the gramophone record established itself. At first a convenient means of preserving the fleeting, unrepeatable impression of a performance, the record, and with it the recording artist, soon laid claim to greater things: all elements of improvisation must stand back in favour of an ideal performance, a definitive rendering divested of any fortuitous aspects. The taking of risks – for which one needs self-confidence – lost its attraction and relevance. The image of the machine in its impassive efficiency gained power over many minds; it became an obsession to strive for perfection. In mistrusting their own nature, artists denied themselves access to the nature of music. The usual symptoms of this are that emotions become either completely dried up or wilfully superimposed. Often, both extremes are to be found in the same person; the vital area between them remains largely unfrequented.

We artists of today have to bear the burden of this paternal heritage, and we feel drawn towards the great ones among our grandfathers.

What, then, should the interpreter do? Two things, I believe. He should try to understand the intentions of the composer, and he should seek to give each work the strongest possible effect. Often, but not always, the one will result from the other.

To understand the composer's intentions means to translate them into one's own understanding. Music cannot 'speak for itself.' The notion that an interpreter can simply switch off his personal feelings and instead receive those of the composer 'from above', as it were, belongs to the realm of fable. What the composer actually meant when he put pen to paper can only be unravelled with the help of one's own engaged emotions, one's own senses, one's own intellect, one's own refined ears. Such an attitude is as far removed from sterile 'fidelity' as it is from transcription-mania. To force or to shun the 'personal approach' is equally questionable; where this does not come of itself, any effort is in vain.

The second requirement, that of giving the music the strongest possible effect, can be seen as an attack on the same problem ('What is appropriate to the music?') from a different angle. But let no one imagine that the greatest possible effect can be equated with the noisiest – or, for that matter, the least noisy – public acclaim. The crucial distinction is not between, on the one hand, that incessant, extrovert high tension so beloved of naïve listeners, and, on the other, the kind of music-making that fancies itself in the garb of a penitential hair shirt. Those performances that are historically 'most correct' are not always the ones that leave us with the most cherished memories. It would be wrong to modify such memories after the event on Christian Morgenstern's humorous principle that 'what may not be, cannot be'. It is our moral duty to make music in as visionary, moving, mysterious, thoughtful, amusing, graceful a manner as we are able to; but this raises the question, 'What is it that will move, shatter, edify or amuse our contemporaries?' There results the paradox that a consummate musical inter-pretation in which time and occasion seem to have been transcended, in which the shackles of historicism seem to have been broken and thrown off, can only be achieved in concord with our own age. The musical masterwork is a power-house of multiple energies. To release those that will strike the noblest, the most elemental resonance in modern man – it is this task that raises the *Urtext* inter-preter above the status of museum curator. A task, also, that should restore to him some of his lost self-confidence.

(1966)

Werktreue – An Afterthought

O N ACCOUNT OF my essay on Beethoven's piano works, I have been branded an opponent of *Werktreue*, while the actual arguments I brought against this by now rather antiquated word were conveniently forgotten. My strictures were directed against the formation of the word and the pedantic aura surrounding it, not against its real meaning, which, however, is rarely intended. In any case, the proper meaning of *Werktreue* is at best marginal and suggestive; *Texttreue*, by comparison, is rather more concrete. As my essay shows, my reasons for disliking this word do not lie in any supposed hatred of a father figure, in any attitude of protest against the authority of the composer, which would indeed ill befit a musical interpreter. But equally, I have never considered myself to be merely the passive recipient of the composer's commands, preferring to promote his cause of my own free will and in my own way.

I have been made immune to blind faith by the years I spent under the Nazi régime. In the slave mentality of that era, not only words like 'faith' and 'fatherland', but also the word 'fidelity' suffered shameful abuse. Even a fairly harmless word like 'work', when used in conjunction with 'fidelity', strikes a militant pose; for me, after all these years, the term *Werktreue* still smacks of credulous, parade-ground solemnity.

The Vienna of the post-war years – a further background to my aversion – presented a mixed picture, musically speaking. Furtwängler and Clemens Krauss, each in his own way, set their seal on the Philharmonic Concerts and on the wonderful sound of the orchestra. The Nicolai Concerts of Furtwängler, in which Beethoven's Ninth was regularly played, were high points in my musical calendar; but so were the New Year Concerts of Krauss with their inimitable, ironically detached performances of the waltzes and polkas of the Strauss family. In the Vienna State Opera company were a number of young female singers whose looks rivalled the splendour of their voices. Mozart's operas, though still lacking the appoggiaturas abolished in Gustav Mahler's time, were performed with a freshness and an enthusiasm hardly equalled since.

The teaching of music in Vienna, on the other hand, was dominated by a strict Classicism. Having recently come across Busoni's writings, I admired his aesthetics, which ran counter to the Viennese literal-mindedness, and was impressed by the aristocratic reserve of his reply to the polemical attack in Hans Pfitzner's pamphlet *Futuristengefahr* ('The Futurist Danger'). After recording Busoni's *Fantasia Contrappuntistica* for a small, now defunct gramophone company, I played it again in 1954 before a sparse Viennese audience. Busoni's concept of a 'Young Classicism' had no more to do with the academic Classicism prevalent in Vienna than with the sort of 'new music' which was performed there in those days. It was quite a time before twentieth-century music began to recover from the dislocation of 1938, and the gap was temporarily filled by works of a neo-Classical or neo-Baroque stamp. Piano students played Beethoven as if he had learned composition from Hindemith. Romanticism was disparaged as something vague, disorderly, dreamy, Utopian; something that might be right for the Philharmonic Concert audiences, but not for people with more progressive tastes. It was identified with pathos, sentimentality, luxuriance, frequent arpeggio chords and the neglect of strict time-keeping. Modernity was equated with anti-Romanticism. There seemed to be no place for illusions in the stark reality of those years. What went unnoticed was that Classicism itself was one of the illusions of the moment. Despite an occasional undercurrent of aggressiveness, and despite its apparent reluctance to take itself seriously, Classicism simulated an order which no longer existed.

Since then, the meagre frame of music has acquired more body. Schubert's sonatas and Mahler's symphonies have experienced a nostalgic revival or, rather, been truly discovered by performers and a wider audience. 'Austere' is no longer the highest epithet that can be bestowed upon a musical rendering. Radio stations no longer suppress resonance; the spatial nature of sound has re-established itself. Musicians show their colours once again. They are tired of excessive calculation, and give a chance to chance.

Parallel to this development, a change has overtaken the interpretation of the music of the past. There is no danger now that a new generation of pianists will 'invest the text with an autonomous significance which it does not merit'. Indeed, the prevailing ambition to do better than just reel off the notes piously and phlegmatically reminds one at times of those conductors of the old school who concealed their lack of textual learning behind the assertion that 'all music is at best an arrangement'. Perhaps in the age of aleatory music a reminder that the observance of the notated text is obligatory would not come amiss.

To read music correctly does not only mean to perceive what is written down (although this in itself is far more difficult than is commonly assumed), but also to *understand* the musical symbols. Though the correct perception of these symbols is only a starting point, the attention given to it is of decisive importance to the process that follows: a faulty foundation endangers the stability of the whole edifice. To go to the original sources rather than take the various editors on trust, to find out which are the proper sources to consult, then to look these up in libraries or obtain photocopies of them – all this is not a waste of time, nor does it distract from the essentials. Even Bülow would not have persisted in his arguments against the repeat in the finale of the 'Appassionata' if the autograph of this work had been known to him, for in it the words 'la seconda parte due volte' are written out by Beethoven for good measure.

Beethoven's autographs are often difficult to read, but it would be wrong to conclude from this that his notation, let alone his composition, was imprecise. The chaotic side of Beethoven's nature, so startlingly apparent form the scrawl of his handwriting, is brought to order in the finished compositions. The effort it cost him to achieve that order gives it its particular stability. However, Beethoven's untiring labour over details hardly ever interferes with his conception of the whole. On the contrary: in some of the early works the detail is not always worthy of the grand design; in some of the middle-period works the detail is at times lost in the wide expanse of the whole, receding into the background as if viewed through the wrong end of a telescope; and in some of the works between the 'Appassionata' and the late sonatas the notation is surprisingly careless on occasion, as in the left-hand line of the second movement of the Sonata in F sharp, Op. 78, or the rhythmic value of notes at the end of phrases. But these are only exceptions which prove the rule that Beethoven's self-discipline exerted its strict control even when he was taking the most adventurous risks.

The text of the 'Hammerklavier' Sonata, the autograph of which is lost, is a special case, and it poses a whole series of problems. On the one hand, the structure of this gigantic work appears to be a triumph of logic without equal; and yet, on the other, there is Beethoven's letter to his former pupil Ferdinand Ries, who was then living in London, in which he gives him permission to destroy this structure: he may transpose, if he wishes, the order of the two middle movements (the London first edition does in fact have the Adagio before the Scherzo), and he may, 'if necessary', omit the introduction to the Fugue. Beside such a proposition, Busoni's idea of putting the Adagio and Fugue into a programme without the first two movements appears positively innocuous. Beethoven's letter cannot be explained away as an act of negligence. Could it be that in this rare instance chaos predominated, turning the creator against his own creation?[12] The metronome marks have an equally detrimental effect: with one exception, they are all hurried, not to say maniacally overdriven. In the first movement particularly, the prescribed tempo cannot be attained, or even approached, on any instrument in the world, by any player at all, be he the devil incarnate, without a grievous loss of dynamics, colour and clarity.

My recommendation to young pianists is to put their reading ability to the test by means of Béla Bartók's Suite Op. 14 and Alban Berg's Sonata Op. 1. (The aid of a tape recorder is indispensable.) Compared with the subtly differentiated symbols which Bartók and Berg use to convey their intentions, Beethoven's notation is still sketchy: a new technique of notation was in the making. It is therefore all the more important to observe *every sign* written down by Beethoven. His ability to notate the essential without overloading the text with instructions has been equalled by very few later composers, and bettered by none. To a greater extent than in the piano works of Mozart, Beethoven's expression marks are founded in the logic of the composition.[13] Among the most important gifts a Beethoven player can have is the power to visualise, in an almost geographical sense, the entire panorama of varying dynamic levels embodied in a work – like looking at a landscape and taking in at a single glance its valleys and mountain tops.

Beethoven's notation is more modern than that of his contemporaries, with the possible exception of Carl Maria von Weber. One can take it more literally than Mozart's, in whose piano music every degree of marking is to be found, ranging from the excessive to the non-existent, and in which, moreover, symbols taken from the sphere of the string player (bowings) and the singer (accents, dynamics) have to be translated into their pianistic equivalents. In his notation Beethoven rejected a number of Baroque conventions. Schubert, and even Chopin and Schumann, occasionally notate divided

---

12   Beethoven's severing of his greatest fugue from the Quartet in B flat, Op. 130, is another case of apparent self-destruction. The 'Grosse Fuge' was composed as its finale and obviously belongs there. Beethoven substituted a comparatively lightweight rondo, which is now usually played, and agreed that the 'Grosse Fuge' would be published separately, in its string version as Op. 133, and in a piano four-hand version of its own as Op. 134. Beethoven's consent may have had commercial reasons: he needed money, and the publisher offered him separate fees for each version of the fugue.

13   This does not mean that there are no mistakes, misjudgements, vagaries or ambiguities in Beethoven. Misjudgements of balance are familiar to anyone who has had practical experience of his piano concertos. The *piano* entry of the soloist in the development of the first movement of the G major Concerto (bar 192) was, as Nottebohm has already observed, later changed by Beethoven into a *forte* much to the benefit of clarity. And in the London first edition of the Sonata Op. 31, No. 3, it is interesting to see that the main subject of the finale is marked *forte*, whereas the Vienna first edition, published at about the same time, has *piano*.

triplets as dotted rhythms, but there are not many instances in Beethoven's piano music, after the stormy second subject in the Rondo of the Sonata Op. 2, No. 2, where dotted rhythms have to be adapted to triplets. In his commentaries on Beethoven's piano works, Czerny points out that in the Adagio of the 'Moonlight' Sonata the semiquaver of the melody should always fall *after* the accompanying triplet note, a remark which shows how foreign such a procedure still was to contemporary practice. In Beethoven's use of the turn, the Baroque manner of execution has survived in one or two cases, whereby the rhythm of figure *a* is played as in figure *b*:

a) 𝄽   *b)* 𝄽

This applies in pieces of moderate tempo and graceful or coquettish character. (A slur over group *a* would be a counter-indication, for then the semiquaver would have to retain its full length.)

Among Beethoven's expression marks, there are some whose particular significance I should like to investigate.

1)   Beethoven's accentuation signs: *sforzando, fortepiano, rinforzando*

What is a musical accent? Is it a sudden dynamic impact, fading into a *diminuendo*, as visually suggested by the > sign? The pianist, whose instrument has acquired the reputation of a percussion instrument, should be particularly wary of automatically interpreting it this way. Yet it is above all the *sforzandi* of Beethoven that receive the most unthinking treatment: on all instruments, it has become habitual to 'stab' at them.

What, then, is an accent? A note (or chord) the intensity of which must be underlined. This can be done in various ways. A *sf* may swell out a note; it may plummet into it; it may have a *cantabile* character – on orchestral instruments, an increase in vibrato may be sufficient to lift out an *sf* note from its neighbours. With many of Beethoven's *sforzandi*, a note will retain its intensity over its whole duration, or over the greater part of it. Accompanying voices, moving in shorter note values, will often support the intensity of the longer note.[14]

---

14   Piano Concerto Op. 15, first movement, bar 97; third movement, bars 28–32. Piano Concerto Op. 19, second movement, bars 31–4.

Here we have a clear case for breaking the general rule that one *sf* applies only to one single note. (In Mozart, it is not unusual for the effect of a *sf* to extend over several notes, until the next *piano*.)[15]

What is the pianist to do, since in theory he cannot influence the sound of a note once it is struck? In the first place, he must rid himself completely of the prejudice that to do so is impossible. Singing, as an idea and a reality, must become second nature to him to the extent that even the recalcitrant piano will be at his service. The sound of sustained notes on the piano can be modified a) with the help of accompanying voices, if there are any; b) with the help of syncopated pedalling; c) with the help of certain movements which make the pianist's conception of *cantabile* actually visible to the audience. Such movements will strongly affect not only the onset of the note, but also its preparation and continuation. But there are some *crescendi* on a single note which only the suggestive power of the artist in the concert hall will convey.

Let me now discuss the individual accentuation signs.

There is no general rule determining the quality and quantity of a *sforzando*. It is governed by its musical significance, which has to be discovered by the player in each instance. In a lyrical context, it will rarely be violent. If it occurs in a *ff* passage, the player will have to husband his strength in order to make the accent stand out above the general level of tone. Not every *sf* is unprepared. It is possible for a *sf* to give added radiance to the climax of a rounded phrase, or to lend some of its weight to the preceding note or group of notes. When he means a *sf* to decrease gradually, Beethoven gives it a *diminuendo* pin.

The *fortepiano* must be taken at its face value: as a *forte* which is followed by a *piano* as quickly as possible. The same principle applies to the signs *mfp*, *ffp* and *fpp*. In the orchestra, *fp* means that the *piano* should occur within the note so marked, unless that is very short; it is, then, a vehement accent with its centre of gravity at the start of the note. On Beethoven's Hammerklaviers with their rapidly fading tone, a *fortepiano* chord like the one at the beginning of the 'Sonata Pathétique' still had an orchestral quality. The sound, as Schindler reminds us, should have died away almost completely before one plays on. (Edwin Fischer

---

15   K.595, first movement, bars 54, 57, etc. K.331, first movement, variation 1. K.456, second movement, variation 1.

and Eduard Erdmann attempted, with varying success, to produce orchestral *fp* effects on the modern grand by tricks of pedalling.) In general, however, *fp* in piano music will mean that it is the succeeding note that has to be played softly. By comparison, Schubert's *fp* direction is much less absolute: it often trails away in a spacious *decrescendo*. Beethoven's *fp*, besides denoting an abrupt accent, may stand for something else: it may mark out the last note of a longish *forte* passage which is to be succeeded by a sudden *piano*. In contrapuntal piano writing, the *fp* may also serve to underline and sustain the note of longest value while the other parts fall back at once to *piano*. This is the opposite of the sustained *sf* note which, as I have said, receives the support of the accompanying parts.

In the sign *sfp*, the *sf* has relative, the *p* absolute meaning.

The *rinforzando* is used by Beethoven in two ways:

i)   as a *cantabile* emphasis on one or several notes, usually in a lyrical context (it does not by any means always extend over several notes, as is shown by the *rinforzandi* in the slow movements of the Sonatas Op. 7, Op. 10, No. 2 and Op. 10, No. 3);

ii)   in his later works, as a signal that *all* the notes up to the next dynamic sign should be played with greater insistence, usually in preparation for the dynamic climax to be reached during a *crescendo*. Instead of the climactic moment, however, there may be a surprising *subito piano*, as in the second movement of Op. 109.

The word *sforzato* is used by Beethoven only in the first movement of the *Emperor* Concerto. There, it asks for the player's energetic attention to the outer notes of an extended section, the figuration of which he should not mistake for a neutral background. On the contrary, these passages should provide rhythmic orientation to the melodic line of the wind instruments. It goes without saying that in bar 136 ff. this resistance will have to be confined within narrow dynamic limits if the bassoon is to remain audible.

In Beethoven's notation, the accentuation mark in most common use since the nineteenth century > indicates slight accents that do not achieve the intensity of a *sf*.

2)   *pianissimo* and *dolce*

Whereas the dynamic degrees between *p* and *ff* can serve a wide range of expressive purposes, according to the character of the passage, Beethoven's *pianissimo* is mostly what Rudolf Kolisch called a '*pianissimo misterioso*'. We enter into a sphere distinctly removed from *piano*, a sphere of awe and wonder. His *dolce*, too, has its own emotional climate: my translation is 'tenderly committed'. *Dolce* tells the player: 'Identify yourself with this phrase; do not control it from outside.' It begs for loving attention and flinches from mechanical coldness.

3) *espressivo*

I should like to refer to three *espressivo* markings in Beethoven's late sonatas. In the first movement of Op. 101 we find *espressivo semplice*. In the last movement, there is a *dolce poco espressivo*, and in the second movement of Op. 109, a *poco espressivo* occurs twice, followed a few bars later by an *a tempo*. What do these directions tell us? In the first place, it is highly illuminating to discover that *espressivo* and *semplice* are not mutually exclusive, as the general manner of *espressivo* playing might lead one to believe. Secondly, we learn that *dolce* and *espressivo* emit different emotional signals. The heartfelt gentleness of *dolce* generally keeps away from minor keys. *Dolce* is soothing, or conveys tender rapture. However luminous it may be, it shines with an inner light, whereas *espressivo* distinctly addresses the outer world. Where the two appear together (as *dolce poco espressivo* in Op. 101, or as *cantabile dolce ed espressivo* in the first movement of Op. 106), the *dolce* is to be given additional weight. For that is what *espressivo* demands: a perceptible increase in emotional emphasis over the foregoing passage. The philological justification for drawing out the tempo a little under the pressure of this emphasis is provided by the tempo indications of Op. 109.

4) Pedal

Beethoven writes pedal marks:

  i)   perhaps most frequently when pedal points are to be suggested in the bass, as in the Rondo of the 'Waldstein' Sonata;

  ii)   in a delicately veiled atmosphere (Czerny speaks of an 'Aeolian harp'): for example in the Largo of the C minor Concerto, and in the recitative in the first movement of the Sonata Op. 31, No. 2;

  iii) when all the notes of a chord or arpeggio are to be sustained, but this cannot be done by the hands alone;

iv) when the pedal is to be used in a way unexpected by the player, as in the hammered chords in the Presto of Op. 27, No. 2, or the diminished seventh chords in the third movement of Op. 101;

v) when the duration of the pedal sound is to be precisely defined against surrounding rests: for example in the two arpeggio chords before the epilogue in the slow movement of the G major Concerto, where a subdivision into semiquaver rests occurs.

It can be seen that Beethoven notates the pedal only when he wishes to obviate misunderstandings, or when aiming at unusual effects.

5) *ritardando*

Czerny's *School of Piano-Playing*, Op. 500, (1842), enumerates the circumstances in which a slowing of the tempo may suggest itself, even though none is notated by the composer. According to Czerny, 'A *ritardando* may be made to advantage

i) in passages which form a return to the main subject;

ii) on notes which lead up to a single small part of a *cantabile* line [?];

iii) on sustained notes that are to be struck with particular emphasis, and which are followed by shorter notes;

iv) during the transition to a new tempo, or to a movement wholly different from the preceding one;

v) immediately before a fermata;

vi) when a very lively passage, or some brilliant figure-work, gives way to a *diminuendo* introducing a soft, delicate run;

vii) on ornaments consisting of a large number of quick notes which cannot be squeezed [!] into the correct tempo;

viii) occasionally in heavily marked passages, where a strong *crescendo* leads to a new movement or to the end of the piece;

ix) in very whimsical, capricious or fanciful movements, in order to highlight their character better;

x) finally, in almost every case where the composer has put *espressivo*; and

xi) at the end of every long trill forming a halt and a cadence in *diminuendo*, as well as on gentle cadences in general. (NB: It is understood that the word *ritardando* as used above includes all other terms which indicate a greater or lesser slowing of the tempo.)'

These observations of Czerny's, as well as the musical meaning of various passages marked *ritardando*, make it clear that up to the middle of the nineteenth century no distinction was made between *ritardando* and *ritenuto*. A *ritardando* (or *rallentando*) mark may therefore tell us either to *become* gradually slower, or to *be* slower at once. An awareness of this will make it much easier for us to perform convincingly the *rallentando* passages in the first movement of Op. 2, No. 2.

The same Czerny who regards tempo modifications as a prerequisite of beautiful playing tells us apropos of Beethoven's First Piano Concerto:

> In fast passages, the player must not forget that some orchestral instruments usually play along with him, either by way of furnishing an accompaniment or in the execution of a melody. In such passages, therefore, he must restrain his humour more fully than in the rendering of a solo piece, and at rehearsal everything that may be necessary in this respect must be diligently dealt with.

('Humour' in the language of the time means 'whim' or 'caprice'.)

Another remark of Czerny's illuminates the performing conventions at the beginning of the last century even more: 'In Beethoven's last concerto works it is expedient for the director of the orchestra to conduct from his own copy of the clavier part, since the correct rendering of these works cannot be divined [!] from the violin part.'

The scores of concertos were frequently published many years after the solo and orchestral parts, if they were published at all. The practice of conducting concertos from the first violin part had survived into our century, as I learned during my student days in the late 40s. The teacher of the conducting class at the Graz Conservatory set me the laborious task of reconstructing the score of the First Violin Concerto by Spohr from the orchestral parts. When the elderly librarian, himself a retired Kapellmeister, handed me the orchestral material, he just shook his head and said, 'What do you need a full score for? In my day we conducted this sort of thing from the violin part!' What would our hypersensitive ears make of a performance, mounted after a single rehearsal, of a work whose meaning had to be 'divined' by the musicians, none of whom knew the score? How anxiously everyone must have kept time to avoid utter confusion!

Like most great writers for the piano, Beethoven was in no lesser degree a composer for ensemble music. The soloist should therefore never completely lose contact with the performing style of the orchestra or string quartet, unless he happens to concentrate on those composers who wrote exclusively for the piano, as is the case with Chopin, the young Schumann and the young Liszt.

My relations with the metronome are on the cool side, and I resent it if the classics are subjected to the rhythmic discipline of a jazz musician. The great conductors, who allow an orchestra to breathe, should be our model; their tempo modifications will often differ from those of the average soloist. Liberties in tempo of a 'humorous' kind, which a good orchestra would not play nor a good conductor conduct, are usually out of place in the performing of Beethoven's sonatas as well. Despite his self-sufficiency, the pianist will be able to claim exemption from the rules of ensemble playing only where the symphonic framework of a sonata is broken up by recitatives or improvisatory passages, where particular eloquence is desired (as in the fifth Bagatelle of Op. 33, marked *con una certa espressione parlante*), and in those capricious finales which Beethoven, according to Czerny, 'played humorously'.

While I readily believe the reports of Beethoven's contemporaries that, at least in his early years, his piano playing 'mostly stayed strictly in time', surely that kind of timekeeping has nothing in common with the metronomic awareness one acquires through acquaintance with jazz and Stravinsky.

If someone intends to play something with the utmost simplicity, he will in the first place try to achieve this by an absolute evenness of tone and rhythm. It may be years before he realises that his vision of the desired effect has, paradoxically, closed his eyes to the best way of achieving it. The projection of simplicity can be a very complex business. An exceptional reservoir of nuances – even though they may remain unused – and a considerable degree of sensitivity and inner freedom are required if the result is not to be, instead of simplicity, emptiness and boredom. Similarly, on the subject of musical time, a 'psychological' tempo is to be distinguished from the metronomic one: an interpreter who follows the flow of the music as naturally as possible – and by 'natural' I refer of course here to the nature of the music, not to that of the player – will always give the 'psychological' listener the impression that he is 'staying in tempo'.

Those of my readers who are more at ease when they can use their own discretion will now feel relieved. I share their feelings. But the free elements – fire, water and air – will not carry us unless we have first practised our steps on firm ground. We follow rules in order to make the exceptions more impressive. From the letter we distil our vision, and on turning back observe the letter with new eyes. The growing precision of our understanding should enhance, and not diminish, our sense of wonder.

(1976)

Form and Psychology in Beethoven's Piano Sonatas

I SHOULD SAY AT the outset that the remarks that follow are those of a practical musician, and they apply first and foremost to practical performance. Further, although I find it necessary and refreshing to *think* about music, I am always conscious of the fact that *feeling* must remain the alpha and omega of a musician; therefore my remarks proceed from feeling and return to it.

Beethoven's piano sonatas are unique in three respects. First, they represent the whole development of a genius, from his beginnings to the threshold of the late quartets. There the *Diabelli Variations* and the last set of Bagatelles round out the picture. Secondly, there is hardly a work among them that is not worth playing – in contrast to many of the sets of variations, for example, which tend to be uneven. I find it impossible to share Busoni's low opinion of Beethoven's early works. If we must divide Beethoven's works into three periods in line with Liszt's pronouncement, 'L'adolescent, l'homme, le dieu', then the young Beethoven already stands there as a great composer. We must not take the term 'adolescent' too literally, however: after all, Beethoven was twenty-four when his Opus 1 was published. Thirdly, Beethoven does not repeat himself in his sonatas; each work, each movement is a new organism.

I like to think of every masterpiece as a phenomenon in its own right. In doing so, the usual way of looking for relationships and analogies within a certain style is of no great use to me. There are people who want to put everything into pigeonholes: Beethoven is allowed to be fierce and heroic, but not graceful; Mozart is allowed to be graceful and crisp, but not melancholy; Bach has to be majestic; the late eighteenth century is neatly divorced from the early nineteenth, and so on. As an interpreter that is, in my threefold function of curator, executor and obstetrician, I am not interested in clichés, but in what is special and unique.

I should like to illustrate my standpoint with two quotations. The first is from an essay by Werner Schmalenbach, the curator of one of Germany's larger art collections. He says:

> It is not the duty of an art museum to give a documentation of art history, nor is it its duty to teach the history of art. History and style can be taught from reproductions; masterpieces have something quite different to say … In a museum

only artistic incomparability counts; this has nothing to do with artistic style, for works of art are thoroughly comparable in style, independent of their quality.

Next I should like to quote Donald Francis Tovey, who wrote, in connection with Beethoven's Sonata Op. 54:

> It resembles all Beethoven's other works, great and small, late, middle and early, in this – that it can be properly understood only on its own terms. If Beethoven uses an old convention, we must find out how it fits the use he makes of it, instead of imagining that its origin elsewhere explains its presence here. If Beethoven writes in a form and style which cannot be found elsewhere, we must, as Hans Sachs says, find its own rules without worrying because it does not fit ours.

Having spoken of the variety in Beethoven's sonatas, we really ought to ask ourselves what the word 'sonata' means and what interpretations the term allows. We can distinguish between three meanings: the first and oldest stands for an 'instrumental piece' as opposed to the vocal 'cantata'; the second means a cyclic work that has two or more movements without being a suite; and the third refers to the so-called 'sonata form' which was defined not earlier than 1827 by Heinrich Birnbach and later, in 1838, by Adolf Bernhard Marx. We are all familiar with the usual description of sonata form today: exposition (principal theme followed by one or more subsidiary themes in the dominant or mediant), development, recapitulation (in which the subsidiary theme returns in the tonic) and coda. This description is an oversimplification: there are plenty of sonata forms it does not measure up to, for one reason or another. For example, we find sonata forms that make do with a single theme, among them two by Beethoven: the third movement of Op. 10, No. 2 and the second movement of Op. 54. Two others of his sonatas arc without sonata form entirely, namely Op. 26 and Op. 27, No. 1. On the other hand, there are two sonatas with no fewer than three sonata forms: Op. 10, No. 1[16] and Op. 31, No. 3; and a whole list of sonatas with two.

Again I should like to quote Tovey, as he draws attention to two interesting characteristics of the sonata:

---

16 The second movement of Op. 10, No. 1 is a sonata form without a development section, unless one accepts the broken chord in bar 45 as the shortest development section ever written.

> The sonata is an essentially dramatic art form, combining the emotional range and
> vivid presentation of a full-sized stage drama with the terseness of a short story;
> … As the sonata forms accomplish their designs more quickly than they can sat-
> isfy their emotional issues, they retain the division into separate pieces inherited
> from the earlier suite forms, which are their decorative prototype.

I quite agree with Tovey's bringing out the sonata's dramatic nature and emotional
engagement as emphatically as he does. The sonata frees itself from the ceremonial
attitude of the suite. It is, for fanciers of the eighteenth century, startlingly 'private'.
'Sonatas are like studies of the several mental attitudes and passions of Man,' said
Abbé Pluche in 1732.[17] If we attempt to define the drama of Beethoven's sonata
form more precisely, we are bound to notice that it is a drama in which the character of the principal theme predominates. Beethoven himself did speak about the
'battle between the two principles', but his remarks are rather vague, or else Schindler did not understand him quite correctly. However great the difference between
the themes, however violently they may clash in the development, the character
of the principal theme dominates. The principal theme reigns like a king surrounded
by his court. Not until Schubert's sonatas is this maxim called into question, and
the terms 'principal theme' and 'subsidiary theme' lose their meaning at times; then
the themes face each other like distant planets. This enlarged field of tension was
expanded still further by Liszt in his Sonata in B minor, the most powerful post-
Schubert sonata structure. Here the defiance of the principal theme does not have
the last word; the tranquillity of the fifth and last theme ends the piece.

However, the sonata (or quartet, or symphony) did make one concession to the
ceremonial at first: it took into its cycle of movements the minuet, one of the most
formal of all suite movements. But here, too, the form began to evolve in a more
spontaneous direction. The result was the scherzo.

Czerny is mistaken in assuming that Beethoven invented the scherzo. That honour apparently goes to Haydn, who used two kinds of scherzo or scherzando, both
jocose and brisk, but different as to form and rhythm. One is in 3/4, one beat to a
bar, and related to the minuet, with a contrasting trio before the literal repeat; the
other is in 2/4, usually appearing as a finale, with no firm bonds to a definite form.

---

17   *Le spectacle de la nature*, 2nd edition, Vol. 7, 1745, p. 116.

In Beethoven's sonatas we have a 2/4 scherzo in sonata form as the second movement of the Sonata Op. 31. No. 3, but also a 3/4 scherzo in rondo form as the finale of Op. 14, No. 2. The connecting link between all the divergent forms is, as I have said, the scherzando character.

Something similar happens with the minuet. We distinguish between the actual minuet in strict minuet form, and the *tempo di minuetto*, a movement tied to no particular form, whose principal theme has minuet character. Beethoven generally underlined the formality of his minuets and the dramatic quality of his scherzos. The minuet character in his piano works can be described in two words: *dolce* and *grazioso.* In this respect he was much more orthodox than Haydn and Mozart, whose minuets are open to practically any emotion compatible with three strict crotchet beats. We can call to mind majestic, energetic, passionate, even wild minuets (think of Mozart's Symphony in G minor, k.500); in such instances nothing more than the formal shell of the ceremonial remains.

Let me approach the subject of form and psychology from another angle. What do we do when we want to perceive the particular attributes of a personality as clearly as possible? We compare it to a personality of a different nature. Thus we may compare the sonata composer Beethoven with the sonata composer Schubert. In Beethoven's music we never lose our bearings, we always know where we are; Schubert, on the other hand, puts us into a dream. Beethoven composes like an architect, Schubert like a sleepwalker. This is not to say, of course, that Schubert's craftsmanship is shoddy, or that Beethoven's music remains prosaic: I mean that the attitudes of the two masters to the problems of composition were different by nature.

Before I present technical proof to support my analogies of architect and sleepwalker, I should like to talk about the difference between Classical and Romantic form, as seen by a performer. When a Classical or 'Classicistic' piece is played without any great emotional involvement but with a certain solid craftsmanship, the form of the piece can nevertheless prove to be a firm framework that will in many instances carry the performance.

Now Romantic music, performed in this way, would give a completely different result, as a rule. Only insight into the psychology of the piece can bring about the vision of form – form is disclosed by emotion.

In other words, if I compare Classical form to a drawing, anyone can see the lines and outlines of the drawing, even if he is unable to perceive what the drawing is all about. Romantic form, on the other hand, could be compared to a drawing that is invisible except to the understanding eye.

Now I should like to offer the proofs I promised. Looking at the first movements of Beethoven's sonatas (which are usually in sonata form), we notice that Beethoven generally constructs his principal themes by a technique I should like to call, for want of a better name, the technique of foreshortening. The principal theme of Op. 2, No. 1 is a simple example.

The succession of harmonies up to the fermata is foreshortened according to the following scheme: two two-bar units, two one-bar units, three half-bar units. Motivic and rhythmic foreshortenings add to the process. This technique dominates not only the thematic construction but, in a much more complex way, the organisation of the whole movement.

The technique of foreshortening, or at least the rudiments of it, can be traced back via Mozart and Haydn to Bach and the Baroque chaconne. So far as I know, it is not mentioned in contemporary textbooks on composition, but it must have been well known. Even the waltz theme by Diabelli that Beethoven used for his set of Variations is constructed in that technique.[18] But no one used foreshortening so consistently and with such a degree of complexity as Beethoven. I would venture to say that it is a driving force of his sonata forms and a basic principle of his musical thought. Later I shall say a few words about how this technique works. It gives Beethoven's music its inexorable forward drive, while Schubert's music at times almost conveys the impression of a passive state, a series of episodes communicating mysteriously with one another. Accordingly, it is not unusual for Schubert to invent his themes as a period or Lied.

---

18   Instead of relying on harmonic or melodic organisation of Diabelli's waltz, Beethoven chose its foreshortened structure as the common denominator for his Thirty-three Variations, and without it would hardly have been compelled to write them at all.

We learn more about the architect and the sleepwalker from their treatment of harmony. Schubert was fond of daring tensions between distant keys; his predilection for chromatic neighbouring keys is notorious. The polarity of C major and C sharp minor dominates the *Wanderer* Fantasy, for example; the polarity of F minor and F sharp minor dominates the F minor Fantasy for four hands. The macabre finale of the Sonata in C minor has subsidiary sections in D flat and C sharp minor on one side, and in B major on the other. And the first movement of the unfinished Sonata in C major takes a risk that puts them all in the shade, namely a subsidiary theme starting in B minor. It often happens that chromatic neighbours appear next to one another abruptly and glaringly. Schubert strides across harmonic abysses as though by compulsion, and we cannot help remembering that sleepwalkers never lose their step.

In Beethoven a new movement or theme in a chromatic neighbouring key is unthinkable. (Before him, however, that tireless adventurer Haydn had in his great Sonata in E flat major a slow movement in E major; and there is an earlier example in C. P. E. Bach.) When Beethoven does make his way to a distant key – which happens only rarely, and then with logical preparation – there are far-reaching consequences for the whole work. Recall the first movement of the 'Hammerklavier' Sonata in B flat major, Op. 106: the appearance of B major in the development, and even more so the modulation to B minor in the recapitulation, give rise, as Erwin Ratz has shown, to formal and psychological problems that it takes all of the remaining movements to solve.[19] One is tempted to say that the harmonic problems of the first movement constitute the rest of the movements and make them necessary. Incidentally, Beethoven follows a definite key symbolism in the 'Hammerklavier' Sonata. An entry in one of his sketchbooks reads 'B minor, black key'. Set against it, the tonic B flat major is perceived as the key of luminous energy. Accordingly, the fugue subject is in the positive B flat major, but its retrograde form is in the negative B minor. Now, the scales of B flat major and B minor have two notes in common, G and D. The mediant keys of G major and D major negotiate between the two poles; they move in a sphere of lyrical deliverance and consolation, a sphere that becomes out-and-out religious in the second fugue subject.

As I said earlier, Classical form can be compared to a drawing whose lines are

---

19 Erwin Ratz, *Einführung in die musikalische Formenlehre*. Vienna: Österreichischer Bundesverlag, 1951, pp. 201 ff.

visible to everyone, even to those who cannot recognise what exactly the lines depict. But what do they actually depict? Anyone, presumably even someone with no musical gifts whatever, can analyse musical form with some success, provided he is taught how to follow certain intellectual mechanisms. Tracking down the character, the psychological process of the music, however, demands talent. Beethoven's pupil Ferdinand Ries reports as follows about the master's piano instruction:

> If I missed something in a passage, or played wrongly the notes and leaps he often
> wanted me to bring out strongly, he rarely said anything; but when I fell short
> as regards expression, crescendos, etc., or the character of the piece, he got exas-
> perated because, as he said, the first was an accident, but the other was a lack of
> judgement, feeling or attentiveness. The former happened to him quite often too,
> even when he played in public.

It is indicative that composers of the past were much more inclined to talk about 'expression and gusto' (Mozart), about character, atmosphere, the poetic idea and similar matters, than about the formal aspects of musical craftsmanship.

Let us look at the start of the last movement of Op. 10, No. 3. There are themes in which a lot, if not everything, depends on what the performance brings to light beneath the surface of conventional performing habits. One can play the rondo theme of Op. 10, No. 3 with academic strictness or in the spirit of an apparently improvised game of musical hide-and-seek that determines, with two important exceptions, the further sprightly progress of the piece. The first of these exceptions is the false recapitulation beginning at bar 46, which leads us to a question ('Is all this really just a joke?')

followed by a big six-bar question mark

that is resolved in the true recapitulation.

We heave a sigh of relief: it was a joke after all. But after the second energetic out-burst of the movement, which seemed like an ultimate triumph of joy, serious doubts begin to crop up again fourteen bars before the end:

Then the last eight bars unite the opposing sentiments: we feel happily freed from a burden, yet we sense that our doubts were not unjustified. These two episodes give the movement a poetical background that makes the torment of the slow movement legitimate in retrospect; we are assured that the torment was not suffered in vain.

As a second example, let us take the Minuet of the same sonata. We shall con-sider it separately at first and disregard its context within the work. We have before us a little piece in which graceful freshness alternates with sections of rustic vigour. Now let us put the four movements of the sonata together again, experiencing the bright-as-day energy of the first movement followed by the Adagio's melancholy night, which ends when the great elegy slowly dies away, and then attempt, not mechanically but with emotional involvement, to hear the Minuet grow out of it.

Is this still the healthy, unconstrained piece we said it was just a moment ago? What sen-sitive performer will expose us immediately to the full light of day? Will he not rather evolve the beginning of the Minuet with circumspect gentleness from the darkness of the general pause between the movements? What is the function of that general pause, anyway? Does it break the continuity between the two movements? Can the audience be permitted to move around in its seats, to relax and cough before the Minuet begins, as though nothing had happened? The purpose of the general pause seems to me to create a moment of motionless silence, after which the Minuet drops like balm on the wounds.

An example of a similar kind is the last movement of the Sonata Op. 26. Taken purely on its own terms, the piece reminds us of the 'Clementi-Cramer passage style,' to which an unproblematic performance with emphasis on technical elegance would do justice. Within the 'psychological composition', to use the phrase Edwin Fischer applied to this sonata, the finale takes on a completely altered meaning. We would brand Beethoven a bungler or a cynic if we were to launch a brilliant *étude* after the moving coda of the familiar funeral march.

As we know, Beethoven toyed with the idea of publishing a complete edition of his works with descriptive titles. It is hardly surprising that he did not do so after all. I recall a statement from an English newspaper, the *Daily Mail*: 'When I glimpse the backs of women's knees, I seem to hear the first movement of Beethoven's "Pastoral" Symphony.' I am afraid that many comments on musical character are not much more illuminating, but less amusing. There was probably another reason that caused Beethoven to drop the plan. The later his style, the more he tries to prevent psychological misunderstandings, the more he confirms the psychological process by procedures of form and texture up to the point where they disclose each other mutually.

A particularly good example of this is the first movement of the Sonata Op. 54. There is no conventional form to lull us. The movement begins like a minuet, with a *dolce-grazioso* theme that is emphatically feminine in nature.

The sharply contrasted second theme, with its masculine stamping octave triplets, coincides with the beginning of the trio.

In its rage it gets out of all control, winds up in A flat major to its amazement, makes a rather subdued modulation to F major and a transition to the gracefulness of the beginning. Beauty, however – I am referring to Richard Rosenberg's christening of the movement 'La Belle et la Bête'[20] – Beauty has not remained completely unaffected by the Beast's wild behaviour: the recapitulation of the minuet has lost a bit of its naïveté; the lady puts on airs and figurations.

The trio, that is to say the triplets, appears a second time; now it is shorter and does not leave the tonic, something the Beast finds noticeably difficult – but then he must also pay his tribute to Beauty. His truculent rattling on the dominant leads straightaway to the second recapitulation of the minuet.

The minuet has further gained in experience, and not only as regards figuration, for the bass progression has also changed since the beginning. Now the minuet does not begin from the repose of the tonic, but from the third – the theme, so to speak, has been shaken to its foundations.

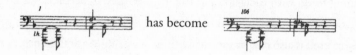 has become

Passing minor harmonies cast little sad shadows on the comedy. Beginning at bar 128, the recapitulation expands into a foreshortening that faintly reminds us of the trio's stamping sequences, without, however, taking on the rhythm of the quaver triplets.

The sequences resolve into a chain of trills that runs out in an improvisatory passage. The lovely coda unites the feminine and masculine elements. Beauty's face appears transformed: from a motive of the minuet a new lyrical idea emerges.

Of the Beast, however, nothing more than the triplet rhythm remains, and we hear it rumbling quietly in the bass. Not only has the Beast been tamed, but he has become part of Beauty. There is, however, one last outburst of beastliness, as a result of which the Beast finally loses his identity. Triplets are resolved into duplets. The movement's end is feminine.

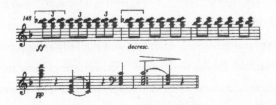

What has happened in this strange piece of music? The two principles that would have nothing to do with each other at the beginning have become inseparable at the end. As we see, the psychological process establishes the form of the movement, but the form itself is also cast in such a way that one can deduce from it the psychological process. Again we detect an antagonism between Beethoven and Schubert. Schubert trusts the directness of his emotions so much that he makes the weight of his formal organisations as light as possible. In contrast, Beethoven creates the firmest intellectual basis imaginable, so that the emotions can emerge from it more clearly, distinctly and unequivocally.

This intellectual basis would be unthinkable without the technique of foreshortening. I should like to draw attention to precisely this aspect of Beethoven's form, and for two reasons: first, so far as I know, it has been noticed only in a rudimentary way, and with no general application; second, it can be of great practical value to the performer.

The principle of foreshortening progressively tightens the musical texture. It can achieve this in several different ways and combinations of ways. Whole sections can be foreshortened; there are foreshortened phrases or parts of phrases, foreshortened successions of rhythmic values or rhythmic sections, foreshortened harmonic progressions (often combined with rhythmic foreshortening), tightened melodic structure and tempo, tightened accents and dynamic progressions. It usually happens that several foreshortening processes are superimposed, that they interlock or overlap. The continuity of the total process is determined by the combination and symbiosis of various foreshortenings, so that in the course of a whole movement, except for a few significant caesuras, one or another of the foreshortening elements is constantly intensified. As a rule, subsidiary themes are more foreshortened than principal themes; the rhythmic subdivisions are often denser, the motive components briefer, or the harmonic progression is closer. This does not mean, however, that the character of the subsidiary theme is necessarily more agitated than that of the principal theme. The reverse can as easily be the case. When I talk about continuous foreshortening, tightening or intensification, I do not mean to suggest a crescendo of any kind (although such foreshortening may occur too, for example in the inversion of the Fugue in Op. 110). The variety of the elements that make up the foreshortening process means that there is room for every change of mood, every contrast, every conceivable emotion.

I should like to explain the mechanism of two foreshortening factors in more detail. The rhythmic organisation gets tighter when notes on strong beats are followed by syncopations (or vice versa), when duplets are followed by triplets, minims by crotchets, quavers by semiquavers, and so on; the last step in rhythmic foreshortening is the trill. The melodic organisation can tighten in roughly the following order, assuming that the rhythmic values remain constant: 1) broken chords; 2) diatonic neighbouring notes; 3) chromatic figuration; 4) repeated notes. Repeated notes, however, lead a kind of Jekyll and Hyde double life. If we listen to the energy of each separate note, there is a high degree of tension; if we hear the repetition as one sustained note, there is minimum tension. In that case one could place repeated notes at the head of the list. The function of repeated notes, then, can be given a new interpretation: it can be the end of an evolution and the beginning of a new one at the same time. (Reinterpretations play an important part in the foreshortening process altogether.) We can study rhythmic and melodic aspects of foreshortening quite clearly in the last movement of the Sonata Op. 109. The first half of variation 6 is filled with rhythmic foreshortenings; the last half is devoted principally to melodic tightening in constant demisemiquaver motion. As an introduction to the general foreshortening process I shall give a brief analysis of the first movement of Op. 2, No. I.[21]

The application of the foreshortening technique is not limited to sonata forms. I should like to end with two examples, one from a fugue, the other from a set of variations, thus showing how Beethoven bent this technique also to his psychological purposes.

Let us look first at the Sonata Op. 110. Here, the Arioso dolente and the Fugue form a unit which finds its analogy on another level, a half-step lower, in the *Ermattete Klage* ('Exhausted Lament') and the inversion of the Fugue. The Arioso's falling from A flat to G is as expressive of exhaustion as is the lamenter's short, fitful breathing; he can no longer summon the strength to span an extensive melodic phrase. We are led to the brink of death and then witness 'the gradual resurgence of the heartbeat' (Edwin Fischer) in the crescendo on the repeated G major chords. *L'istesso tempo della Fuga poi a poi di nuovo vivente* is written over the inversion of the Fugue. Editors of the sonata have interpreted this in several ways. Some apply it to the tempo of the Fugue, others to the dynamics. For me, however, these words draw attention to the compositional process; from here to the end of the work, as it happens, the Fugue is constructed as one continuous foreshortening. And something else happens too: as the foreshortening progresses, the fugal bonds are gradually shaken off; polyphony is transformed into homophony. Vincent d'Indy called the Fugue of Op. 110 an 'exertion of will to banish suffering'.

Now let us turn to the conclusion of the Sonata Op. 111. Its two movements are thesis and antithesis. Whether one speaks in terms of the real and the mystical world, of Sansara and Nirvana (Bülow), of resistance and submission (Lenz), or of

---

21   See 'The Process of Foreshortening in the First Movement of Beethoven's Sonata Op. 2, No. 1', p. 58.

the masculine and feminine principle – in any event we have the impression of a
final statement.

The polarity of motion and repose is reflected in the choice of forms. The forms
with the greatest tension and activity are sonata and fugue; the first movement of
Op. III is a sonata form interlaced with fugal elements. The form of repose and
steadfastness amid change is the variation form – or at least it was until Beethoven
developed a new concept of variation form in his *Diabelli Variations*. The Adagio of
Op. III is a set of variations in progressive rhythmic foreshortening – that is, each
variation is rhythmically more tightly organised than its predecessor. (Variation
movements of this kind have been known since the Baroque chaconne. I would just
mention two of Mozart's finales, namely those of the Piano Concertos in G major,
K.453, and in C minor, K.491.)

Only once does the Adagio of Op. III move away from the tonic C major. This
occurrence coincides with the inner climax of the movement. At the same time, the
foreshortening process is suspended and then begun again. I am talking about
the cadenza-like passage that grows out of the fourth variation, after the material of
this variation has been so foreshortened that it has had to resolve into a trill (bar
106). With the modulation to the dominant of E flat major we reach the focus of
mystical experience. The *sf* entrance of the B flat in the bass (bar 106) starts a new
foreshortening process which leads into variation 5 as though into a recapitulation,
and lasts until the end. The fifth and sixth returns of the theme make possible further foreshortenings in comparison to the fourth. Schenker's sketch of the rhythmic
intensification of the variations demonstrates this:

Variation 5 keeps up the motion of 27 notes to a bar, but the demisemiquavers are
now moving the bass line and bringing about closer changes of harmony. The last,
transfigured vision of the theme is accompanied by a trill. An epilogue of six bars
leads to the closing chord; its entrance on a weak beat, and the foreshortenings that

led all the way to it, hardly permit an idea of finality. This chord does not close something off; rather it opens up the silence that follows, a silence we now perceive to be more important than the sound that preceded it.

(1970)

The Process of Foreshortening in the First Movement of Beethoven's Sonata Op. 2, No. 1

I N MY ESSAY 'Form and Psychology in Beethoven's Piano Sonatas' I mentioned that the opening theme of the Sonata Op. 2, No. 1 consisted of two two-bar units, two one-bar units and three half-bar units leading to a fermata (see example on p. 45). The next six bars foreshorten the eight-bar opening. First we have two bars of C minor harmony, in which a fourth crotchet is added to the melody at the end of the triplet turn.

This crotchet leads on from where the phrases of the theme had previously broken off, and enhances the intensity by repetition. The next four bars bring fragmentation:

In the first two bars the upper two voices imitate the final fragment of the theme; in the last two only the 'soprano' has the fragment and the harmonies follow each other more closely. (While in bars 11–12 the harmonies are still connected by appoggiaturas, bars 13 and 14 have separate harmonic weight.)

In the next bars (15–20) the sound is smoothed out further. One could say that between bars 9 and 20 the staccato and separate melodic units of the theme have been gradually transformed into legato and continuity. Syncopation is introduced into the melody.

We hear two different subdivisions at the same time: minim (left hand) and crotchet (left plus right). A statement repeated twice with more and more emphasis arouses expectations. The omission of the *crescendo-diminuendo* sign in bar 19 conveys the message that the syncopation is no longer a major event. The crotchet rhythm now dominates, helped by a *forte* marking and octave doublings.

This crotchet rhythm leads into the left-hand quavers of bar 20 ff. These quavers are, however, a case of Dr Jekyll and Mr Hyde: their detailed intensity soon gives way to the impression of a sustained pedal point. And they prove to be disguised two-part writing: the bass carries on the preceding minims, now foreshortened into crotchets,

while the middle voice can be understood as syncopated quavers.

If we play the left hand in a simplified manner, we notice at once how the fore-shortenings are organised.

Schematically we have the *ostinato* first:

The bass now starts to move, while the pedal point is retained.

It then moves more quickly, tying pairs of harmonies together.

The last three harmonies stand separate.

What happened in the right hand after bar 20? The seemingly new melodic idea
in A flat is in fact related to the first subject as a free inversion.

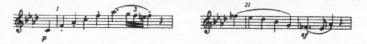

It insists on making its statement three times. (The second section, beginning at
bar 20, is indeed full of repeated notes and phrases.) During the third statement,
however, the bass line starts to move and the statement remains unfinished. The
right hand now breaks up into ascending syncopations.

From bar 27, where the left hand is further subdivided, the figurated syncopations
of the right hand give way to exclamations in which each note has melodic importance; these exclamatory groups are also dynamically emphasised.

During the further harmonic subdivision in which the left-hand harmonies stand
separate (bars 31–2) instead of being linked in groups of two (bars 28–31), the right
hand is again split up in ascending syncopations, and the left hand underlines their
emphasis with four E flats, thus linking the changing harmonies. The ascending
syncopations lead to a new idea which transforms the broken-up fragments of melody into a continuous flow of quavers. We now have two sets of four bars of similar
construction. Each of the four-bar phrases contains foreshortening: in the first, as
a point of departure, we have two bars of descending scale,

then one figuration of the E flat,

and finally two figurations of the E flat.

The foreshortening of the second phrase will be understood in conjunction with the left hand.

In bar 33 the left hand had introduced syncopations. (Even though the value of the notes is much greater than in the preceding bars, the syncopations have a marked effect within the foreshortening process. Here, their importance is stressed by *sforzandi*.) In bars 36 and 40 the syncopations give way to crotchets.

Whereas from bar 33 onwards the harmonies have moved bar by bar, from bar 42 they start to change twice in a bar. During the closing idea (bars 42–9) the syncopated chords of the left hand help to indicate the exalted intensity of feeling (*con espressione*).

The right hand makes three nearly identical statements, the last of which arises to a higher register of the piano and culminates in a *fortissimo* chord. This chord derives additional impact from the fact that it is a dissonance and a kind of written-out fermata.

The development (bar 49 ff.) starts a new foreshortening process. Its first fourteen bars relate to the opening twenty-seven bars of the movement. The exposition of the first theme is now condensed into six bars in two units of three, each of which is subdivided into two plus one, again a foreshortening.

In the second unit the left hand abandons its comparatively passive role to take the initiative: the crotchets lead into a quaver rhythm of broken octaves while the right hand, instead of rising one step, insistently repeats its fragment of the theme at the same pitch, thus increasing the tension.

Beethoven has also written a *crescendo* sign. (Even in his early works, dynamic markings are usually tied to structural events.)

The three-bar units are now succeeded by the two-bar units of the second idea. Bars 55–62 are directly related to bars 20–27. In bars 61–2 the player has to be aware of the rhythmic subdivisions that are required.

When the pedal point on F in the middle voice is abandoned, each of the quavers is given equal importance.

The following five-bar unit (63–7) relates to the foregoing eight-bar phrase, but omits its fragmented ending. The insistent melody moves from the soprano into the bass, signifying an increase of tension.

Three-part writing turns into four-part: there is the added excitement of the right-hand interjections

which greatly influence the further course of the development. They appear split up in syncopations in bars 73–80,

while the left hand strips away the insistent melodic idea: only an octave skeleton in syncopations remains. In the last bar the motion has narrowed down to a familiar rhythmic figure:

We recognise the opening theme's accompaniment. This rhythm is pursued in the middle voice of the left hand,

while the lower voice persists on the dominant in fast syncopations – a foreshortened consequence of the preceding syncopated minim rhythm. The melodic line of the middle voice is foreshortened,

and the corresponding foreshortenings in the right hand are easy to detect. The middle voice leads into repeated notes (bar 93); they bring continuity to the flow of crotchets which has so far been inconsistent in both the preceding melodic voices. In spite of the very low dynamic level, the rhythmic intensity of each repeated note commands our attention.

But again Jekyll turns into Hyde. The introduction of a second and third voice in bar 95 changes the hearing pattern; we now perceive two extended beats per bar rather than four. And the platform of the first two bars, 93–4, gives way to descending bar-by-bar steps in the overlapping voices. The interjections of the right hand are reminiscences of the fierce syncopations (bar 73 ff.) which precede the little thunderstorm in the development. At the same time, they prepare the recapitulation; we know these triplet turns form the initial theme. The left hand also paves the way for the recapitulation; its three-voiced chords in bar 100 foreshadow the accompaniment of the theme and bring back the impact of the crotchet rhythm. The theme, after such masterly introduction, appears with overwhelming self-confidence. All reminders of conventional grace are swept away in the bars that follow, where the left-hand chords are firmly placed on the beat.

This simple firmness after so much syncopation is marvellously effective. Even the anguished question at the end of the theme (bar 8) is turned into defiance in bar 108.

The rest of the movement proceeds on the lines of the exposition. Broadly speaking, the movement consists of two foreshortening series; the first extends from the beginning to the development, the second from the development to the end.

(1970)

Musical Character(s) in Beethoven's Piano Sonatas

E ACH SONATA BY Beethoven has its own particular character. But is this really anything more than a platitude? Should we still be clinging to such concepts as 'character' and 'atmosphere'? Aren't the musical cognoscenti interested primarily in understanding 'structure', leaving something as vague as 'poetic associations' to amateurs? And haven't the post-structuralists long since exposed 'character' as a mere illusion?

Arnold Schoenberg, whom no one would accuse of being an amateur, recommended that

> in composing even the smallest exercises, the student should never fail to keep in mind a special character. A poem, a story, a play or a moving picture may provide the stimulus to express definite moods. The pieces which he composes should differ widely.[22]

When the concept of character first began to emerge in writings about music around 1795, it was intended as a corrective to Kant's relative deprecation of instrumental music. In his *Critique of Judgment* (1790), Kant had declared that music took 'the lowest place among the fine arts', because 'it plays merely with sensations.'[23] Music, according to Kant, was an agreeable (*angenehm*) rather than a fine art. Writers like Christian Gottfried Körner and Christian Friedrich Michaelis subsequently came to the aid of music and in the process consistently drew on the sonata to support their arguments.

Eighteenth-century listeners perceived the sonata as a remarkably private genre, in comparison with the Baroque suite. In place of a succession of more or less formal dances, sonatas now appeared to be 'like studies of the various attitudes and passions of man.'[24] Even the minuet – the only one of the suite movements to find

---

22   Arnold Schoenberg, *Fundamentals of Musical Composition*, edited by Gerald Strang and Leonard Stein (London: Faber & Faber, 1967), p. 95.

23   Immanuel Kant, *The Critique of Judgment*, translated by James Creed Meredith (Clarendon Press/Oxford University Press, 1952), p. 195 (section 53).

24   Noel Antoine Pluche, *La Spectacle de la nature*, 2nd edition, Vol. 7 (Paris: Chez les Frères Estienne, 1745), p. 116.

its way routinely into the symphony, string quartet and sonata – was capable of taking on a variety of characters, whether gracious or impetuous, solemn or humorous. This distinctive element of what could be called the humane, the personal or the individual characterises the sonata more aptly than the presence of any so-called 'sonata-form movement.' After all, there are plenty of sonatas without even a single such movement.

From works on aesthetics written just before 1800, we know that musical character was perceived as consisting of 'psychological' and 'moral' components, and as mediating between these two supposedly contrasting spheres. Körner's essay 'On the Representation of Character in Music', which appeared in 1795 in Schiller's journal, *Die Horen*, goes beyond this to speak of what amounts to a masculine and feminine Ideal.[25] (We might recall the report of Anton Felix Schindler, Beethoven's secretary and biographer, that Beethoven himself spoke about the 'two principles' – masculine and feminine – in music.)[26] Körner goes on to say that 'the concept of character presupposes a moral life, diversity in the use of freedom, and in this diversity a unity, a rule within this arbitrariness.'[27]

Carl Czerny, Beethoven's pupil, tells us that every one of Beethoven's compositions 'expresses some particular, consistently maintained mood or perspective to which the piece remains true, even in its smallest details.'[28] This assertion would have found favour with Schoenberg. That Schoenberg himself adhered to this advice in his own compositions can scarcely be doubted. His String Quartet Op. 7 is based on an amazingly detailed psychological programme that he set down in the early stages of its composition. It lists 'Rebellion; defiance; longing; rapture; depression;

---

25   See Christoph Khittl, '*Nervencontrapunkt': Einflüsse psychologischer Theorien auf kompositorisches Gestalten* (Vienna: Böhlau, 1991), pp. 85–6.

26   See Anton Schindler, *Beethoven as I Knew Him*, translated by Donald W. McArdle (Dover, 1996), p. 406. Schindler is of course a highly unreliable witness; his report nevertheless reflects the continuing power of this image throughout the period. See also Arnold Schmitz, *Beethovens 'Zwei Prinzipe': Ihre Bedeutung für Themen- und Satzbau* (Berlin: Dümmlers Verlagsbuchhandlung, 1923).

27   Christian Gottfried Körner, 'Uber Charakterdarstellung in der Musik', *Die Horen* (1795): p. 604. For a commentary and English translation of Körner's treatise, see Robert Riggs, ' 'On the Representation of Character in Music': Christian Gottfried Körner's Aesthetics of Instrumental Music', *MQ81* (1997), pp. 599–631.

28   Carl Czerny, *Uber den richtigen Vortrag der sammtlichen Beethoven'schen Klavierwerke* (1842), edited by Paul Badura-Skoda (Vienna: Universal, 1963), p. 25; the English translation was published as *On the Proper Performance of All Beethoven's Works for the Piano*, edited by Paul Badura-Skoda (Vienna Universal, 1970), p 21.

despair; apprehension of sinking; unfamiliar emotions of love; desire to be engrossed; solace; relief (she and he);' and so on. And this is only part of the first movement.[29] Like the titles for the movements of his Piano Concerto, this programme remained unpublished during Schoenberg's lifetime.[30]

In a radio broadcast, Schoenberg once remarked about his musical works: 'I cannot disclose their spiritual background[s], and I would have to assert that I am inclined to be at some pains to disguise them.'[31] This strangely twisted formulation reveals Schoenberg's conflicting emotions, or more precisely, the conflict of his emotions with a musical rationality that presupposes a work of music to be convincing without the aid of any descriptive device. Czerny's comments on Beethoven's Piano Sonata Op. 81a – 'Les Adieux' – are very much along these lines: 'Moreover', Czerny writes, 'this sonata … may and indeed should be of interest even to those who are willing to enjoy it as pure music, without regard to the titles.'[32] Yet Beethoven's goal, in this sonata, had also been to set to music, as clearly as possible, feelings or sensibilities – *Empfindungen* – evoked by Farewell, Absence and Return, the titles of the individual movements. The titles provide clues towards understanding the music's character, not only for the listener but above all for the performer. (They also made it possible for the dedicatee, Archduke Rudolf, himself a musician, to judge whether Beethoven had successfully expressed feelings associated with the titles.) Rather than deny the element of character in the music of Beethoven or Schoenberg, we should be thankful for these kinds of verbal aids. If Schoenberg conceived the first movements of his Piano Concerto under the rubric 'Life was so easy', then this will perhaps deter performers from playing the piece all too dreamily. And even if the composer covered up the 'background' to his compositions and wished to leave no psychological clues, it must be granted that there is occasionally a kind of musical coherence that is above all psychologically motivated. One of the most delectable tasks of the interpreter is to sense such motivations, even if they are not to be captured in words.

29 Christian Martin Schmidt, *Schönbergs 'Very definite – but private' Programm zum Streichquartett Op. 7.* In *Bericht über den 2. Kongress der Internationalen Schönberg-Gesellschaft* (Vienna: Elisabeth Lafite, 1986).

30 See Arnold Schoenberg, 'Werke,' part VI, series B, vol. 20, *Streichquartette I: Kritischer Bericht*, edited by Christian Martin Schmidt (Mainz: B. Schott's Söhne, 1986), pp. 109–10.

31 Arnold Schoenberg, *Stil und Gedanke: Aufsätze zur Musik*, edited by Ivan Vojtech (Frankfurt: S. Fischer, 1976), p. 273.

32 Czerny, *Über den richtigen Vortrag*, p 55; On the Proper Performance, p. 51.

Like the essays by Körner and Michaelis, Beethoven's first piano sonata, Op. 2, No. 1, in F minor, was published in 1795. The need for 'Unity in Variety', as expressed by contemporary writers on aesthetics, is fulfilled in this work in a pointed manner. Compared with the plethora of ideas in the other two sonatas of Opus 2, the variety in this first sonata seems to be rather tightly reined in. By contrast, the unity of deriving all the themes from the motifs stated at its beginning is clearly established in Op. 2, No. 1. So, too, is the Beethovenian technique of foreshortening, a device that progressively breaks down harmony, rhythm and melodic elements to create long spans of tension.[33]

Directly or indirectly, all the themes of all the movements in Op. 2, No. 1, are derived from its very beginning. Beethoven did not aspire to such concentration in every sonata. A work like Op. 26, for example, appears to be so loosely constructed from a thematic point of view that one can speak justifiably of a 'psychological composition', as Edwin Fischer put it, a work that reveals itself as a whole through an understanding of the relationships among the characters of all movements.[34] On the other hand, the musical materials in some of the most ambitious and moving sonatas, like Op. 10, No. 3; Op. 31, No. 2; Op. 57 ('Appassionata'); Op. 106 ('Hammerklavier'); and Op. 111 display a particularly strong sense of economy.

In Beethoven's music, the motifs on which a work feeds are almost always stated at the very beginning; in keeping with this, a movement's fundamental character can be found in its first few measures or lines. The Sonata in D minor, Op. 31, No. 2, begins with a theme whose three different motifs correspond to three different tempos. Seldom has musical material been presented to the performer and listener so clearly. The tripartite structure of this theme contains at the outset a (solemn) broken chord, at the end an (expressive) embellishment, and in the middle a layered figure on the notes A-F-E-D, which contains something like a genetic code for all the themes of all the movements, and which reappears repeatedly, either openly or in disguise.

The two other motifs are also to be found in all the themes of the D minor Sonata.

---

33   For detailed discussions of this technique, see 'The Process of Foreshortening in the First Movement of Beethoven's Sonata Op. 2, No. 1', pp. 58–65, and William Kinderman, *Beethoven* (University of California Press, 1995), pp. 30–35.

34   Edwin Fischer, *Beethoven's Pianoforte Sonatas: A Guide for Students and Amateurs*, translated by Stanley Godman (London: Faber & Faber, 1959), p. 58.

Only the opening theme of the third movement dances out of line: the embellishment is omitted here. But it soon reappears in the second theme of the movement with a persistence that is downright obstinate.

The concentration of materials in the 'Hammerklavier' Sonata, Op. 106, is perhaps even more astonishing. Everything in this gigantic work seems to be related to the interval of the third: the construction of the themes as well as the most important tonalities of the work are all based on this interval. Charles Rosen has pointed out how the harmonies in sections of the first movement, as well as in the development of the Adagio, progress through a series of descending thirds.[35] In the Adagio, we find no fewer than sixty-five progressions by a third, along with another twenty in the Largo introduction to the fugue. From such examples, it is easy to see that the motifs binding a work do not establish the character of that work. The character (or characters) of the 'Hammerklavier' Sonata obviously cannot be derived from the interval of a third. Motifs can contribute substantially to the unity of a work, but they usually do this in an abstract sense. The impression of coherence establishes itself – even if only indirectly – when the listener's unconscious perception is presented with recurring motifs. But musical 'expression' – to which Jean-Jacques Rousseau devoted no fewer than six pages in his *Dictionnaire de musique* of 1768 – is not dependent on motifs or constellations of motifs.[36] Rather, expression makes use of them.

The fundamental character that is presented at the beginning of a movement dominates throughout. Later themes or episodes are scarcely capable of threatening its hegemony, even when they provide contrast and variety. One could perhaps point to Beethoven's Piano Sonata in F major, Op. 54, as an exception. This little-loved, highly original work establishes two contrasting characters at its very beginning. Here is a prime example of what used to be called contrasting masculine and feminine principles; or, to put it in more contemporary terms, *animus* and *anima*. But even here, *anima*, which starts the piece, has the last word, while the second, concluding movement of this sonata synthesises both principles.

It is the interpreter's responsibility to play the roles of different characters. Like

---

35   Charles Rosen, *The Classical Style: Haydn, Mozart, Beethoven*, 2nd ed. (New York: Norton, 1997), pp. 404–34.

36   Jean-Jacques Rousseau, *Dictionnaire de musique* (Paris: Veuve Duchesne, 1768; rpt. Hildesheim: Olms, 1969).

every person, it would seem, every sonata has distinct qualities and potentialities. Each character lives and breathes as a sum of its attributes. If the interpreter goes beyond the boundaries of these attributes, a character would be falsified and ill-portrayed. Sometimes this character is marked by contradictions, through two or more souls dwelling in the same breast. (In the writings of Anton Reicha, one of the principal theorists of sonata form, the sections of a sonata-form movement bear the wonderfully dramatic designations of 'exposition', 'intrigue' and 'dénouement'.)[37] In the three or four movements of a sonata – provided they do not traverse the excep-tionally consistent emotional terrain of a work like Beethoven's Op. 31, No. 3 – a wide range of conflicts can arise, yet the finale usually confirms the character of the first movement, albeit somewhat modified. Even in sonatas with a contrasting mid-dle movement, like Op. 27, No. 2 ('A flower between two chasms', as Liszt is said to have called it), or Op. 31, No. 2 (an angel between two demons, as it might be called) – in other words, in sonatas whose outer movements are entirely in minor and whose middle movement never leaves the sphere of the major – we experience the bright major mode as the complement that reinforces all the more powerfully the darkness of the minor-key movements.

An exception to this pattern may be found in the two-movement sonatas whose movements suggest opposites. In the case of Op. 111, we have turmoil and peace, or the real and mystical worlds. In the Sonata Op. 90, we have the comment attributed to Beethoven himself about a 'Conflict Between Head and Heart' that is followed by a lyrical 'Conversation with the Beloved.'[38]

The idea of 'character' can also be understood in a broader, less personal sense. Rather than 'human attitudes and passions', some sonatas appear to reflect elements from nature surrounding us – nature seen through a temperament. In the 'Waldstein' Sonata, Op. 53, the impression of space and three-dimensional depth is produced by several factors: the extended harmonic perspective, which now incorporates the mediants as a matter of course; the extraordinary ambit of the principal themes, which incorporate distinctive and unusual intervallic leaps; the broad, liberal use

---

37   Anton Reicha, *Traité de haute composition musicale ou Cours de composition musicale*, vol. 2 (Paris: Rich-ault, 1826), p. 299.

38   According to Schindler, Beethoven made this comment to Count Lichnowsky, to whom the sonata is dedicated (Schindler MacArdle, p. 210). Again, even if the attribution to Beethoven is inaccurate, the comment nevertheless reflects the aesthetics of Schindler's time.

of repeated notes, resonances and sequences; the new manner of handling sounds that suggests the qualities of being near and far, high and low, clear and obscure; and finally the extended panorama of dynamics. Exceptionally, a motivic idea also contributes to this impression: the leap of twenty diatonic tones (a twelfth plus an octave) in the opening theme. The performer should present this gigantic interval as the ascent of one *single* voice; in this manner, our perspective as listeners will be expanded from the very beginning.

The external movements of the 'Waldstein' Sonata seem to me like landscapes that unfold before the musical eye. Perceiving this, I would like to let my fantasy run free and imagine for myself how, in the first movement, the horizon lies low with a great deal of sky above it, whereas in the rondo, we find ourselves high in the mountains, listening to a mountaineer's song, a *chant montagnard*. In the valleys, there is dancing: both episodes of the rondo are imbued with the character of a Russian dance, like the kind we know from the 'Rasumovsky' Quartets, Op. 59, and from the coda of the 'Appassionata' Sonata, Op. 57. The outer movements of the 'Waldstein' reach out into brightness; we step outside of ourselves in these movements, whereas the Adagio turns us inward, into the darkness of our natures.

The 'Waldstein' Sonata is often perceived as a bravura work. Here, I would like to suggest that a more careful reading of Beethoven's notation can help lead us to a better understanding of the composition's psychological elements. The 'Waldstein' is the only one of Beethoven's piano sonatas in which all of the movements begin *pianissimo*. And perhaps there is no other sonata prior to those of Schubert in which the cumulative span of *pianissimo* sections plays such an important part. Granted, Beethoven's *pp* is not Schubert's *pianissimo espressivo*, but rather almost always a *pianissimo misterioso* (to borrow formulations from Rudolf Kolisch), and only occasionally a *pianissimo dolce*, as we have in the opening theme of the 'Waldstein' finale.

The pedaling Beethoven specifies for this rondo, which has precisely the effect that was forbidden during children's piano lessons – a lack of harmonic clarity – is all too happily ignored by grown-ups. Without it, the rondo theme takes on a banality worthy of a music box. I am now convinced that the point of this heavily pedalled pedal-point is not primarily the audible maintenance of the bass note, but rather those delicately confused harmonic contours that create an atmosphere of tonic and dominant flowing in and out of one another. To be sure, the result of this should not be opaqueness, but transparent opalescence.

The Sonata in D major, Op. 28 (which not coincidentally has come to be called 'Pastoral'), points in two different directions. An introverted Andante in D minor interrupts the listener's affectionate enjoyment of country life, which in turn incorporates two thunderstorms. The three-part psychological layout of this Andante deserves closer consideration. The first and third parts (the latter of which is an embellished repeat of the first) alternate between stern composure and sighing lamentations. The middle part, by contrast, surprises us with a bucolic scene in the major mode; in this section, the quality of innocence remains wholly untouched by melancholy or fear.

It is therefore all the more disturbing that such naïveté is turned into anxiety and horror in the coda. What does Beethoven do to lead us into the daylight after the bitter resignation of this movement's conclusion? Gradually, cautiously and humorously, he opens our eyes. The entire scherzo is devoted to the restoration of the major third: it persists with the note F-sharp, which had been the object of near fixation throughout forty measures of the introductory Allegro movement's development section.

In the Sonatas Op. 28 and Op. 53, the performer and the listener are invited to share in the composer's musical communion with nature. But there are also pieces that confront us like a superior power – more elemental than personal, more angelic than human. Both are to be found in the D minor Sonata Op. 31, No. 2. The outer movements are for the most part elemental, while the Adagio is angelic. Czerny, who clearly knew this sonata better than most of the others, speaks of the 'tragic character' of the work but also notes 'the romantic-picturesque quality of the entire tone-painting.'[39] To me, Czerny's own story about the finale having been inspired by riders galloping past Beethoven's window seems more revealing than Schindler's notion of its affinity with Shakespeare's *Tempest*, an idea that Czerny ignores. For a performer of the piece, nothing could be more suggestive about matters of rhythm and tempo than the 'continuously passionate motion' – as Czerny puts it – of horse and rider.[40]

Czerny's indication of the 'picturesque quality of the tone-painting', the painterly and painted effect of Op. 31, No. 2, is also useful. Of Op. 31, No. 3, Czerny claimed

---

39 Czerny, *Über den richtigen Vortrag*, p. 47; *On the Proper Performance*, p. 43 (translation modified).

40 Czerny, *Über den richtigen Vortrag*, p. 48; *On the Proper Performance*, p. 44 (translation modified).

that 'this sonata is more declamatory (*sprechend*) than picturesque.'[41] In this work, in fact, only the minuet is lyrical, in its second half even sighing a bit.

What about the first sonata of this group of three? When Beethoven gathers three sonatas under a single opus number, he always wants to show just how different sonatas written within the latest phase of his style can be. Alongside the al fresco, painterly D minor Sonata and its eloquent, indeed wittily garrulous sister in E♭ major, the G major Sonata, Op. 31, No. 1, strikes me as dancing, as an expression of bodily movement by dancers or mimes with a distinct tendency toward the grotesquely comic.

The connection between character and structure in this sonata is particularly striking. In and of itself, the structure might appear to be full of inexplicable shortcomings. Only when we take into account the comic character of this work does all the apparent structural nonsense make sense. If one were to grasp merely the character, however, then the formal and structural expectations that the piece violates would remain incomprehensible. Whoever denies the ability of 'absolute music' to incorporate comic intentions and effects must necessarily give a poor grade to this piece (an evaluation that has in fact been made repeatedly in critical commentaries). There are plenty of indicators of a comic character in the first two movements. The unique designation of the slow movement – 'Adagio grazioso', almost a contradiction in itself – gives some indication of Beethoven's ironic treatment of the kind of *galant* style found in the two early Rondos, Op. 51, or in the Violin Romances, Op. 40 and Op. 50.

Assigning qualities like 'speaking', 'painting' or 'dancing' can be helpful in understanding other sonatas as well. To these we should add a fourth possibility, 'singing'. This is applicable to those pieces in which singing outweighs speaking, or in which speech is entirely absorbed by song.

Basically, the performer should welcome anything that supports our understanding of the musical characters or characteristics in a given work. One useful concept is that of the four natural elements. The finale of Beethoven's Sonata in C# minor, Op. 27, No. 2, can easily be related to fire, as can the finale of his Sonata in E♭ major, Op. 31, No. 3, marked 'Allegro con fuoco'. The Rondo of Op. 2, No. 2, and

---

41 Czerny, *Uber den richtigen Vortrag*, p. 49 'Diese Sonate ist mehr sprechend als malend'; *On the Proper Performance*, p. 45.

the second movement of Op. 54 could be perceived as flowing. The first movement of the Sonata Op. 109 hovers a few inches above the earth: the bass line follows the upper voices as weightlessly as possible. In contrast to this, the bass line of the second movement scrapes into the earth, as it were. The third movement, then, unites earth and air: it both hovers and rests at the same time. Every good performance of a work, incidentally, needs its breath of fresh air, so that the music does not suffocate as if under a bell-jar.

Combinations of natural elements are entirely possible in music. In the fugue theme of the 'Hammerklavier' Sonata, we can discover other elements alongside the flaming, darting, flickering: the impetus of the stream, the stormy air, and the rootedness of the bass. In a sense, this finale is the most elemental movement that Beethoven ever wrote. It unleashes the elements and yet holds them under strict structural control. This is just one example of how structure and character need not necessarily conform but can rather relate to each other as contrasting features. Not only the fugue, but also the first two movements of the 'Hammerklavier' Sonata are manic, the great Adagio by contrast singularly depressive, with ecstatic outbursts.

In attempting to grasp at least a few expressions of a work's characteristics, its mood, its atmosphere, it helps to be alert to the nuances of language. A great deal – including perhaps the most essential – must remain unspoken. And yet language can stimulate perception and support psychological memory. An awareness of contrasting pairs can clarify a good deal. Opposites like calm/agitated, stiff/flexible, opaque/translucent, active/passive, real/unreal, public/private, resisting/conceding, pious/witty or sublime/profane help to sharpen our discrimination. In the Sonata Op. 110, for example, the sublime third movement grows out of the profane second. It is always the goal of such exercises in consciousness to go beyond similarities and analogies and perceive the peculiar and unusual elements of any given work.

In this regard, let us return to Schoenberg once again. In the chapter 'Character and Mood' in his *Fundamentals of Musical Composition*, we read the following: 'It is fallacious to think that the tempo indications determine character. In classical music, at least, this is not true. There is not one Adagio character, but hundreds; not one scherzo character, but thousands.'[42]

This is a highly judicious criticism of what Schoenberg's friend, son-in-law and

---

42   Schoenberg, *Fundamentals of Musical Composition*, p. 93.

interpreter Rudolf Kolisch tried to demonstrate twenty-four years earlier in his controversial essay 'Tempo and Character in Beethoven's Music.' In that music, according to Kolisch, 'There are typical categories of tempo ... corresponding to categories of expression.'[43] Kolisch, as is well known, associated Beethoven's surviving metronome indications, along with indications of meter and tempo, with such expressive 'types.' Kolisch maintained that the 'Allegro ma non troppo 6/8' category, for instance, has a 'sombre and passionate character. Motives in 16th-notes alternate with trochaic formations.' Among the examples he gives for this are the finale of Op. 28 and the fugue of Op. 110.[44]

To perceive these movements as 'sombre and passionate', however, would scarcely be acceptable even for Kolisch's most unreserved admirers. I count myself among those who cherish his early quartet recordings; but his comments on tempo and character must be approached with a degree of scepticism. When I visited Kolisch in his old age, he himself seemed not altogether free from doubt on this point. Already on 16 November 1943, Theodor W. Adorno had written to him: 'I believe that it is not possible to construct Beethovenian "types" on the basis of an isolated aspect such as tempo, and that this often brings together heterogeneous elements...'[45] Kolisch's pupil and long-time assistant David Satz would later point out that 'for Kolisch, as for any other serious musician, tempo was only one aspect of performance; no element of performance was to be neglected at the expense of another.'[46] Thus no matter how important tempo might be as an element of character, one cannot determine the character of a given work without carefully taking into account all the other aspects of that work. In Beethoven's music (as, incidentally, in Schoenberg's), the metronome indications are not infrequently to be adjusted according to these other 'elements of performance'.

Structure and character relate to one another: they may work hand-in-hand, or

---

43   Rudolf Kolisch, 'Tempo and Character in Beethoven's Music', *MQ29* (1943), p. 176; revised German version in Rudolf Kolisch, *Tempo und Charakter in Beethovens Musik* (Munich: text + kritik, 1992) (Musik Konzepte 76/77), p 9.

44   Kolisch, 'Tempo and Character', p. 291; ibid., *Tempo und Charakter*, p. 42.

45   Theodor Adorno to Rudolf Kolisch, November 16, 1943, in Adorno, *Beethoven: Philosophie der Musik*, edited by Rolf Tiedemann (Frankfurt: Suhrkamp, 1993), p. 256; translated from Adorno, *Beethoven: The Philosophy of Music*, edited by Rolf Tiedemann and translated by Edmund Jephcott (Stanford University Press, 1998), p. 180.

46   David Satz, 'Nachwort' to Kolisch, *Tempo und Charakter*, p 168.

they may have a relationship of fruitful tension. But interpreters should never assume that understanding the structure of a work might automatically give them insight into the work's character, atmosphere or spiritual state. The interpreter would do well to concern himself with structure and character as two functions that emanate, as it were, from different sides of the same work, in the hope that he might one day unite the two at a point where the pain of interpretation can be transformed into the relief of a satisfying experience. That the character of music (or at least of Beethoven's music) incorporates psychological and moral components, as contemporary writers on aesthetics maintained, is an idea that confirms itself for the performer today. One can talk or argue about the psychological components; about the moral ones, it is better to remain silent. At most, one can attempt to demonstrate them.

(2000)

Beethoven's New Style

BEETHOVEN'S LATE STYLE still strikes me as unexpected and prodigious. Everything by way of preparation, all the various portents and new departures apparent in works like the Opp. 74 and 95 Quartets or the Sonatas 'quasi una fantasia' Op. 27 hardly mitigate the astonishing impression made by the two great Piano/Cello Sonatas Op. 102. They still come as a violent shock, as they did to Beethoven's contemporaries – the beginning of a new style so diverse as to elude definition.

Until 1812, Beethoven's output had continued without interruption; the B flat Piano Trio Op. 97, the Seventh and Eighth Symphonies (Opp. 92 and 93) and the Op. 96 Violin Sonata had brilliantly signalled the end of an era in instrumental music, during which the transition from early to middle-period Beethoven – insofar as such simplifications are acceptable at all – had proceeded smoothly and, as it were, of its own accord. The years 1813–14 mark a pause. Besides the revision of *Fidelio*, they are taken up with those unworthy showpieces *Wellington's Victory* and *Der glorreiche Augenblick*, which represent the summit of Beethoven's public fame. The only instrumental work belonging to these years, apart from the Polonaise Op. 89, is the intimate Op. 90 Piano Sonata, at once a throwback and a forerunner. The following year, after his brother's death from consumption, Beethoven plunged with tragic zeal into a new role as his nephew's guardian. The pain associated with this relationship remained with him to the end of his life. Illness and real or imaginary money troubles helped to increase the effort required to complete a work. The cello sonatas of 1815 in particular seem to have been a threshold painful to cross. In 1816 the final rupture of relations between Beethoven and Therese Brunswick's sister Josephine (von Stakelberg, formerly Countess Deym) contributed towards making this a singularly trying time in Beethoven's life. Yet the influence of biographical events on Beethoven's manner of composition should not be exaggerated; the slowing down in his working procedures may well be explained by the greater density and complexity of his later style. Works like the Sonata Op. 106, the *Diabelli Variations*, the *Missa solemnis* or the Ninth Symphony needed extended planning and preparation. They concentrate Beethoven's entire composing experience into huge, bold syntheses while, at the same time, requiring new means of expression to be developed and tested.

Synthesis and expansion of resources – that is where a description of Beethoven's late style would have to begin. Direct opposites are forced together. A new intricacy is matched by its antithesis, a new naïveté. Apparent exaggeration is juxtaposed with apparent artlessness, abruptness with a novel, relaxed lyricism. Simple, primitive, popular and vulgar elements all find their place in the music without damaging its structure. Martin Cooper has pointed out the use of two popular songs, 'Unsa Kätz häd Katzln ghabt' ('Our cat has had kittens') and 'Ich bin lüderlich, du bist lüderlich' ('I am draggletailed, you are draggletailed'), in the second movement of Op. 110.

The complexity of Beethoven's late style may be broken down into a new delicacy and density of detail, and a new rigour and refinement of its polyphonic part-writing. Diversity of detail now complements the spacious grandeur of the 'Waldstein' and 'Appassionata' Sonatas, the *Emperor* Concerto, or the 'Archduke' Trio. But there is also a new attitude towards the miniature: as with the slow introduction to the finale of Op. 101 or the scherzo of Op. 106, extremely concise forms are incorporated within the context of large ones, though they may also be left on their own, as in the late Bagatelles. (Incidentally, it was precisely these pieces which were grossly misunderstood by some of Beethoven's contemporaries, as shown by Schindler's contemptuous remarks about the Op. 126 set.)

The new polyphony which, even in the most homophonic sections, now pervades Beethoven's part-writing is a first indication that, in his late works, Baroque influences are more evident than ever before. This polyphony 'turns the bass into melody' (Walter Riezler) and provides in some of his late sonatas, his B flat Quartet, the *Diabelli Variations*, the *Missa solemnis*, and the finale of the Ninth, climaxes with the aid of fugal form. Other Baroque features that have left their mark are the recitative, the (sometimes richly ornamented) aria, and the chaconne. As for Beethoven's new polyphony, it makes his music not only more refined, but also a great deal more radical and uncompromising. Even Hans von Bülow, who used to play all the last five sonatas in one evening and possibly did more than anyone else to popularise them, found it necessary to 'dilute' a few instances of the 'Hammerklavier' fugue. It took Schoenberg and Bartók to carry on where Beethoven's late polyphony had left off.

One of Beethoven's uncompromising traits is his predilection for clashing seconds (as when the basic note and the suspension are sounded together). This had already been apparent in the 'Lebewohl' Sonata Op. 81a ('Les Adieux'), where the telescoping of the horn-calls which so graphically depicts the disappearance of the coach aroused misgivings well into the nineteenth century. Nor is Beethoven afraid of writing false relations. Another feature is the wide separation of the registers, of treble and bass. Finicky listeners have blamed Beethoven's deafness for all this. If it was indeed his deafness that brought out the use of such artistic means, we should be grateful for it.

With this exploitation of extreme registers goes a new 'geographical' awareness of sound – not of spatial depth, as in the 'Waldstein' Sonata, but of 'deep down' and 'high above', or indeed of 'subterranean' and 'stratospheric'. Here, the fourth variation from Op. 111 provides a magical example.

Apart from clashing seconds, false relations and suspensions, the characteristics of Beethoven's late style include syncopations, bold leaping intervals and chromatic transitional harmonies. Perfect cadences are, wherever possible, avoided or 'veiled' (Riezler), while church modes mysteriously expand tonality. Like the 'open endings' of the last three sonatas, they are among those attributes of Beethoven's late music that have aroused religious associations. Did Beethoven, in his late works, progress from the personal to the universal? His *Missa solemnis*, and the grand invocations to the 'Creator' and 'Dear Father' in the Ninth, have certainly provided powerful arguments to support this assumption. The roughly opposing view, however, has also found its adherents; resting on the observation that Beethoven showed less regard than ever for the 'wretched fiddles', the wretched throats or wretched ears of his contemporaries – that is to say, the accepted usages of listening and playing – it suggests that Beethoven retreated from the universally accessible into subjectivity. Simplifications of this kind cannot possibly do justice to the richness of a style that embraces past, present and future, the sublime and the profane.

Sonata Op. 101

Dorothea Ertmann's incomparable performance of the rondo from Op. 90 was praised by Schindler. In dedicating the A major Sonata Op. 101 to the Baroness, Beethoven was doing more than merely repaying a debt of courtesy. Having been a pupil of Beethoven's for many years, she became a personal friend and one of the best interpreters of his piano music. (And how much Op. 101 in particular needs a confident and initiated player!) To some, she even seemed to qualify as a candidate for Beethoven's 'Immortal Beloved', a notion dispelled by recent scholarship. It is interesting, however, that another masterpiece of 1816, the song cycle *An die ferne Geliebte*, shares with Op. 101 the characteristic of recalling its opening theme at a later stage.

In the sonata, the tenderly questioning phrase that opened the first movement reappears between the Adagio and the finale with a visionary quality. This kind of harking back to earlier movements, as also practised in the Cello Sonata Op. 102, No. 1 and the finale of the Ninth, was later beloved of the Romantics. Altogether, this sonata had great impact on Romantic composers; the second movement affected Schumann's style more than anything else by Beethoven, and the *cantabile* lyricism of the first not only left clear traces in Mendelssohn's Sonata Op. 6 but also caused Mendelssohn's musical opponent Wagner to remark that his own ideal of 'unending melody' had here already been realised.

Op. 101 marks a fundamental change in Beethoven's sonatas. Formerly, the sum of the movements resulted in a perfect balance. Now, the dynamic, developmental aspect of his composing takes hold over the entire work; the last movement becomes the climax to which everything leads; it gathers together the forces which in the earlier movements have been pulling in different directions, or surpasses the first movement by the conviction of a superior, and opposite, position, as in Op. 111. The rondo form, unsuitable for this kind of intensification, is now abandoned. The scherzo, when present at all, moves to second place before the slow movement; so far has it shifted from the conventional scherzo pattern that Beethoven from now on grants this title only to the second movement of Op. 106. Even sonata forms no longer appear without some element of strangeness: they may do without contrast (Op. 101); or contain development sections simpler than those of Mozart's most serene sequences (Op. 110); or they unite, as composite forms, with scherzo and fugue. Final movements are now reserved for strict counterpoint or for a set of slow variations. Although the finale of Op. 101 is a sonata form, its imitative polyphony is agglomerated, in the development section, into a fugue.

Op. 101 is not an exuberant work. In it, as Wagner observed, passionate outbursts are out of the question. It does not belong to the line of spiritual dramas that 'wrestle with the elements' or 'quarrel with fate'. All the happiness, all the power and assurance with which the sonata is imbued are imparted with supreme composure. It does not overwhelm and compel like Op. 106, nor does it release mysterious sources of feeling with the immediacy of the last three sonatas. The brief Adagio does not sing out its melancholy like the ariosi of Op. 110 – played *una corda*, it communes with itself in a whisper, reticent and clear-sighted. As may be gathered from Beethoven's indications, the tempi avoid extremes throughout: the Allegretto not too flowing, the Adagio not too slow, the last movement 'fast, but not too much so'; and the 'march-like' second movement, which was marked 'ziemlich lebhaft' (lively enough) in the autograph, lost its 'ziemlich' in the first print.[47]

Sonata Op. 106

Even today, this work shows up the outer limits of what a composer of sonatas can accomplish, a performer can control, or a listener can take in. In a magnificent exertion of will, it combines grandeur and delicacy, the grand sweep and extreme density of detail. The player should muster endurance as well as boldness, fierce intensity as well as the cool grasp of a panoramic overview.

Czerny, who had played the sonata for Beethoven, describes the tempo of the first movement as 'uncommonly fast and fiery'. The initial theme relates to the rhythm of the words 'vivat, vivat, Rudolphus'; it was the Archduke Rudolf to whom the sonata was dedicated. Two elements, the tension between the keys of B flat major and B minor, and the interval of the third, are decisive in the unfolding of the vast design. The intrusion of B minor (the 'black key', according to Beethoven) into the recapitulation of the first movement has grave consequences: not until the final fugue is this conflict resolved. In the coda of the scherzo, eerie juxtapositions of B flat and B natural bare the problem to its bones. We encounter the 'black key' once more at a declamatory climax of the Adagio ('con grand'espressione') and, finally, in the cancrizans of the fugue. For both B flat major and B minor, the related thirds are G and D; these are the only tones the two keys have in common. In G major, there is the second thematic group of the first movement, and the inversion of the fugue. The 'religious' D major sphere is given to secondary themes of the Adagio and the fugue.

---

47   In this context 'ziemlich' does not suggest moderation. Beethoven himself, in *An die ferne Geliebte*, translated 'ziemlich geschwind' as *assai allegro* (suitably/sufficiently fast).

Beethoven's special contribution as a fugal composer is the turbulent and frenzied fugue that nearly, but only nearly, defies the strictures of the contrapuntal writing. Boundless energy and intellectual rigour have never been coupled at a higher pitch of excitement.

The slow introduction of the fugue resembles in its psychological situation the final movement of Beethoven's Op. 110: after its 'exhausted lament' vital forces gradually reappear. The Adagio itself, a 'mausoleum of collective suffering' (Lenz), is the depressive counterpart to the manic agitation of the fast movements. Its alternating sections of *una corda* and *tre corde* turn out to be different regions of sound and grief. (On Beethoven's pianos, the quality of sound produced by the soft pedal was more shadowy and fragile than it is today, a sphere of whispering and subdued *mezza voce* singing.) To join the end of the Adagio and the beginning of the Largo in performance seems to me a psychological mistake; listeners and players ought to have the chance to draw breath.

Two contentious issues challenge the performer to a decision. The first relates to whether A natural or A sharp should be played before the start of the recapitulation. I have never doubted that A natural is what Beethoven wanted. It seems obvious that Beethoven, on the evidence of the harmonic progression, forgot to put in the natural sign. In Tovey[48] we find a very good collection of arguments for the natural, the most important being Beethoven's own harmonic sketch for this passage and the downright orthographical improbability of A sharp and F in the same bar. Furthermore, Paul Badura-Skoda[49] has shown that, on this particular page of the first edition, a host of mistakes and omissions has remained uncorrected. A psychological point should be added: anyone who rejects the reasonable and expected in favour of the 'audacity of genius' embodied in the A sharp should consider whether, at this moment of the piece, such a surprise move in the bass serves any useful purpose. Should not the resounding entry of the recapitulation lull us into a sense of security? Should we not think we have returned home before the modulation via G flat major to B minor destroys our illusion? This can only be imparted by a bass progression that does not skip the leading-note A, and with it the whole cadence.

The second bone of contention concerns Beethoven's metronome marks. I must

---

48　*A Companion to Beethoven's Pianoforte Sonatas*, p. 218.

49　*Musik, Edition, Interpretation, Gedenkschrift für Günter Henle* (1980), pp. 58–9.

confess that to me they do not, even in conception, seem wholly appropriate to the character of the movements, with the possible exception of the Largo introduction to the fugue. The indication ($\downarrow$ = 138) for the first movement is – by any player, and on any piano – simply unworkable; not for nothing did Beethoven himself change his mind about the original Allegro *assai*, deleting the *assai*. Let us, by all means, play this movement 'fast and fiery' yet leave enough room for its wide range of colour and dynamics to emerge.

The first London printing, which appeared almost simultaneously with the Viennese edition by Artaria, offers by comparison several interesting corrections, additions and alternatives. It may be mentioned as a curiosity that in the English edition the Adagio comes before the scherzo. In a letter to his pupil Ferdinand Ries in London, Beethoven himself allowed the option of interchanging the inner movements at will or even omitting the Largo before the fugue, suggestions that seem to defy sanity.

Sonatas Opp. 109, 110 and 111

The last trilogy of sonatas (1820–22) was written in conjunction with Beethoven's work on the *Missa solemnis*. All three have in common a new way of ending. Where the last chords of Op. 106 had finished off the work in an unequivocal manner, Op. 109 withdraws into an inner world, Op. 110 ends in euphoric self-immolation, while Op. 111 surrenders itself to silence.

Two movements in sonata form precede the superb variations of the E major Sonata Op. 109. They are fundamentally different in character. The quasi-improvised, dreamlike first movement suspends gravity; the second is an excitable outburst veering between anger and fear. In the first movement the bass hovers in syncopation behind the notes of the melody, hardly touching the ground. In the second it makes itself all the more clearly felt: clinging to the ground, yet unable to impose stability as it remains almost entirely rooted in the dominant. The first movement glides along in a single rhythmic pattern, interrupted by the declamatory second theme in a new tempo and time-signature; it has light colours, long breath-spans and undulating contours. On the other hand, the second movement is dark, flickering and jagged, jerky and short-winded; within the 6/8 time the rhythm is diverse; the subsidiary ideas offer no contrast, but in the main theme itself there is competition between the melody and the bass, which dominates the development section on its own.

The final movement combines the essence of the first with the aspirations of the second; it both floats along and brings repose. Czerny wanted it played 'in the style of Handel and Seb. Bach' (see 'Notes on a Complete Recording of Beethoven's Piano Works', p. 22.). Indeed, Handel's influence reveals itself at once in the sarabande-like variation theme – if we disregard Beethoven's extremely sensitive dynamic indications.

In 1821 Beethoven wrote: 'From last year until now I have been ill all the time, over the summer I also caught jaundice … now, thank God, it is going better and good health finally seems to want to put new life into me …' The experience of abating and returning powers had left its mark on works both earlier and later than the A flat Sonata Op. 110. Already the 'Hammerklavier' Sonata had gathered up new musical energy in the introduction to its fugue, and in the 'Heiliger Dankgesang' from the Op. 132 Quartet we read 'Feeling new strength'.

As with the Op. 101, 109 and 111 Sonatas, the thematic fundamentals of Op. 110 are the space of six adjacent diatonic notes (a hexachord) and the intervals of a third and a fourth which subdivide it. Whether the motifs rise or fall within the sixth remains important throughout the piece. In the caressing *cantabile* of the first movement it is not the slender development section but the subsidiary theme that imparts a notion of excitement; here contrary motion combines ascending and descending lines. The apparently static development section shows the opening theme in a crisis – unable to rise to the sixth, its first two bars wander around in regions of minor tonality. The restoration of the theme in the recapitulation then gives the impression of breathing freely again; here, its left-hand answering phrase even manages to overreach the hexachord.

The second movement, a piece in the style of the late Bagatelles, is dominated entirely by contrary motion. D'Albert tried to read into it a gavotte with accents on every second bar, yet the capricious character of the piece and the justification for the 2/4 notation both stem precisely from its frequent changes of accentuation, and from the fact that the bar pattern before the trio and coda becomes confused in a manner half burlesque and half mysteriously modal. The obdurate right-hand figuration in the trio may be construed as a sequence of thirds and fourths within the smallest possible space.

The third movement is Passion music – a complex of Baroque forms in which ariosi and fugues are interwoven. The sections are arranged as follows: (1) *Recitative* (modulating from the F major close of the scherzo to A flat); (2) *Arioso dolente* (A flat minor); (3) *Fugue* (this part of the fugue remains an exposition; it does not leave the key of A flat major); (4) *Return of the Arioso in G minor* ('wearily lamenting'); (5) *Inversion of the Fugue* ('gradually reviving' – a new start, but also a continuation of the first fugue as its modulating section, in which entries follow in close succession); (6) *Homophonic conclusion in A flat major.*

In a movement for which Beethoven has left us such specific and meaningful instructions as 'wearily lamenting', one may assume a large psychological context. What is the relationship of ariosi and fugues? The first part of the fugue attempts to counteract the 'lamenting song' – which, it has been noted, bears a resemblance to the aria 'It is finished' from Bach's *St John Passion*. There is no immediate healing effect; the second arioso shows this not only by its abrupt semitone drop but also by the way in which the melodic line becomes porous, expressing, with its continual sighs and pauses for breath, the reduced resistance of the sufferer. (In the Cavatina of the Op. 130 Quartet the singing line in the 'beklemmt' (stifled, constricted) return of the arioso is similarly fragmented.)

Ten gently swelling, syncopated G major chords emerge from the closing bar 'like a reawakening heartbeat' (Edwin Fischer). The inverted fugue theme then appears, as unreal as a mirage. The ensuing process reluctantly leads back to reality. Its path is not made easy for the listener – and it obviously did not come easily to Beethoven. Stretti, progressive diminution of the theme, and tempo changes all obey the law of continual foreshortening; they are musical symbols of returning vitality, but also stages in a dissolution of fugal constraints. Polyphony becomes a burden to be shaken off. The opening theme, augmented and syncopated, vainly resists the collapse of polyphony. Its augmentation is gradually reduced to the initial outline of the theme, which enters in the bass when the return to A flat major is accomplished. At last, the dominance of fugal polyphony is broken, the goal of revival attained. The remainder of the movement is a lyrical hymn. In a last euphoric effort, its conclusion reaches out beyond homophonic emancipation, throwing off the chains of music itself.

Beethoven's C minor Sonata Op. 111 leaves a dual impression – it is the final testimony of his sonatas as well as a prelude to silence. Its two movements confront each other as thesis and antithesis. We recall attempts at interpretation, such as 'Samsara and Nirvana' (Bülow), the 'Worldly and Otherworldly' (Fischer), 'Resistance and

Submissions' (Lenz) or the masculine and feminine principles which Beethoven himself was so fond of expounding.

In the context of musical form this contrast is one of animation against repose. The forms with the most compelling animation are sonata and fugue; the Allegro of Op. III is a sonata form suffused with fugal elements. The form representing tranquil constancy within change is a set of variations; the Adagio of Op. III is again a variation movement, its progressive rhythmic foreshortening even more consistently realised than in the finale of Op. 109.

Once more, the beginning of the first movement immediately determines its basic character, one of angry revolt. At the same time it provides a thematic seed for the whole sonata: E flat – C – B natural in downward motion. Psychologically and materially, Schubert's setting of Heine's 'Der Atlas' is closely akin to it. The *maestoso* introduction and the main Allegro relate to one another as dominant and tonic. With his tempo marking *Allegro con brio ed appassionato*, Beethoven makes clear that he is not enthroned on Olympus. In the Adagio the words *semplice e cantabile* aim to show performers the way. What they imply is not ingenuousness or simple-minded sweetness, but simplicity as a result of complexity – distilled experience.

(1976)

Must Classical Music Be Entirely Serious?

I · THE SUBLIME IN REVERSE

IN A REMARKABLE essay on Schubert, Antonín Dvořák[50] makes it clear that he cannot consider Schubert's masses ecclesiastical, even though he concedes that the feeling for what is truly sacred music 'may differ somewhat among nations and individuals', as does the sense of humour.

I own a cartoon from Czechoslovakia. In it a pianist is shown sitting on a concert platform. But instead of performing the piece on the music stand in front of him, he is helpless with laughter. The composition that provokes his amusement bears the title 'A. Dvořák – Humoresk'. In the cartoon the faces of the audience are all completely serious; they appear quite unmoved by the mirth of the pianist, who must surely have been the first to discover that Dvořák's *Humoresque* should be a matter of laughter. Of course, a pianist's audience is not supposed to laugh, but neither is the pianist.

Humoresques are notoriously unfunny. In the German-speaking countries and Central Europe the word 'humoresque' was applied to a literary genre: a short, good-humoured and amiable story that avoided the grotesque or satirical. Schumann's beautiful *Humoreske* differs from the later ones in being a piece on a much grander scale, in both size and emotional scope; if it aims for a 'felicitous blend of rapture and wit' (to use one of Jean Paul's formulas for humour), what it mainly achieves is to be capricious, lyrical and unpredictable.

For those who claim that music cannot be truly comical without the assistance of words, or without relating to visible reality, humoresques from Schumann to Rachmaninov and Max Reger seem to provide ample proof. So, I am afraid, does Mozart's *A Musical Joke*, usually regarded as a prize example of musical wit. It is a work in which, as far as I can see, a catalogue of musical blunders is distributed with little kindness, along with some blatantly wrong notes that the performers are made to play on purpose.

Where, then, does one look for the comical in music outside the realm of opera and song? There are, of course, pieces with funny titles. 'Ouf! Les petits pois' or

---

50 See p. 149.

'Prélude inoffensif' show that Rossini, in those late compositions that are called *Sins of Old Age*, refused to take himself as seriously as the Romantic composers did. This man, who throughout his life suffered discomfort from several illnesses, kept up the appearance of a musical buffoon; his delightful non-operatic music, unusual in its time, casts no shadows. Some of Rossini's pieces make me laugh even without their titles, whereas nearly all of Erik Satie's melancholy miniatures are funny mainly on account of their titles.

For me, the most convincingly comical absolute music has been written by the Viennese classical masters and by some twentieth-century composers. György Ligeti's *Aventures et Nouvelles aventures*, even on records, should make almost anybody laugh – and much more so if you *watch* the singers and players produce all those lovely noises in the concert hall. The work qualifies as absolute music because it does not employ words, and it is not basically theatrical. It is reminiscent of human utterance, action and behaviour, which to me remains one of the legitimate effects of music even if, in the past, it used to be achieved in a far more stylised fashion.

I do not know whether the public in Haydn's time ever laughed during, or at the end of, a performance. For perfectly good reasons, there is an understanding between a civilised audience and the performers that the music should be played, and listened to, without too many additional noises. There is no shortage of evidence that at least some of Haydn's and Beethoven's contemporaries had a musical sense of humour, and admired it in the works of the two composers. In one of the most important early essays on Haydn, Ignaz Ernst Ferdinand Arnold[51] made an acute comment on Haydn's comic style:

> Being in command of all artistic means, this play of easy imagination endows even the smallest flight of genius with a boldness and audacity [*Keckheit und Dreistigkeit*] that expands the area of aesthetic achievement into the infinite without causing damage or anxiety … The last Allegros or Rondos consist frequently of short, nimble movements that reach the highest degree of comicality by often being worked out most seriously, diligently and learnedly … Any pretence at seriousness only serves the purpose of making the playful wantonness of the music

---

51   'Joseph Haydn', *Bildungsbuch für junge Tonkünstler*, Erfurt, 1810.

appear as unexpected as possible, and of teasing us from every side until we succumb and give up all attempts to predict what will happen next, to ask for what we wish for, or to demand what is reasonable.

According to George August Greisinger, an early biographer of Haydn, 'a sort of innocent mischievousness, or what the British call humour, was a principal trait of Haydn's character. He easily discovered what he preferred – the comical side of things.' Haydn himself confessed (to Albert Christoph Dies) that there is a frame of mind in which, to quote Dies, 'a certain kind of humour takes possession of you and cannot be restrained'. He also thought this was a quality which stemmed from an abundance of good health. About Beethoven, Friedrich Rochlitz writes: 'Once Beethoven is in the mood, rough, striking witticisms, odd notions, surprising and exciting juxtapositions and paradoxes occur to him in a steady flow.'[52] If we apply this statement to Beethoven's comic music, we have a valuable list of characteristics that bear musical scrutiny.

Before I present some musical examples I should like to draw attention to the fact that there is widespread confusion about the meaning of humour, irony and wit. Not only does it differ from language to language; in the sense of Dvořák's remark quoted above, it turns out to be a deeply personal matter, as indeed religion should be. (According to another of Jean Paul's definitions, humour is 'the sublime in reverse' – *das umgekehrte Erhabene*.) I can therefore only submit a choice of pieces that I personally find funny, amusing, ludicrous or hilarious, and I have settled for the word 'comic' to signify an ingredient that is common to all of them. Whether oddities and incongruities of a purely musical nature will strike the listener as hilarious, strange or disturbing must depend on the psychological climate of each piece, but also on the psychological disposition of each listener.

Let me start with a piece by Haydn. Before taking in the complete third movement of Haydn's late C major Sonata Hob XVI:50, I would ask you to read, or play, through an edited version of it. In the musical text I have indicated where four bars of the first part, and thirty of the second, should be left out.

---

52   *Für Freunde der Tonkunst*, Leipzig 1868, IV, p. 235.

Comparing the edited and the complete version, I would already call the shorter one a burlesque. The teasing avoidance of classical four- or eight-bar patterns, the abortive storm in D minor that peters out almost before it begins, and its laughing and bouncing staccatos contribute towards making it comical. The complete version of the piece, however, is ludicrous to a much greater degree. By introducing the 'wrong' B major chords as the most memorable surprise, it presents the listener with an intriguing problem. How should we 'understand' these chords? How many explanations can we find for them? And which of these explanations prevails?

The listener's initial impression of the first B major chord must be that of a *faux pas*. When we try to verify this impression we soon get into trouble. How would a player of a C major piece behave who has stumbled into a B major chord by mistake? He could, like Sir Adrian Boult in the first performance of Tippett's Second Symphony, turn to the audience, say 'Sorry, my fault', and start again. More probably, he or she would try to cover up the blunder.

In this way, the offence of the B major chord would be 'rationalised'; a mistake would be turned into an advantage, *Schadenfreude* into admiration for the player's quick reaction. The listener would, ironically speaking, laugh not *at* the player but *with* him.

The second-best way out for the imaginary player would be to pretend that nothing had happened. Somebody slips on a banana skin and suddenly finds himself sitting on the ground; it will take him a few moments to pick himself up and proceed, *come prima*, with an innocent face. That is what Haydn *seems* to have done. A second hearing, though, may reveal that the 'wrong' B major chord does not come completely out of the blue. The piece that had started, and continues, in purely dia-tonic writing brings in, as a little warning, a C sharp in the bar before. A C natural here would sound downright harmless, as indeed it is supposed to sound four bars later when the same figure returns.

Is, then, our B major chord a premeditated challenge that is not accepted? After all, Haydn could have stayed within the means of musical propriety and continued in the following fashion:

We know more about the B major chord when it has reappeared in the recapitula-tion. It reasserts itself, almost menacingly, with the help of a ritardando, after a short digression into C minor has ended on the Neapolitan D flat (bars 58–65). More than anything else, the indicated ritard underlines the fact that this is not simply a reproduction of the 'memory lapse' or 'slip of the tongue' that had occurred earlier. This is not just a mistake obstinately repeating itself. The proximity of the Neapoli-tan harmony makes the B major chord all the more provocative. Again, there is no apology afterwards; neither is there any sign of unease. The piece continues in high spirits, laughing at us at the end.

I am aware that there is some sort of harmonic resolution to the B major irritant four bars later. In the recapitulation (69, 73) it is resolved into the dominant seventh. As I feel it, these cheerful resolutions do not calm the psychological seas completely. They do not, and should not, remove the final suspicion that these B major chords are arbitrary and unjustified, an insult veiled by apparent innocence, an act of splen-did nonsense that is all the more delightful because it cannot be explained away. As Schopenhauer said in his analysis of laughter: 'It is diverting to see the strict, untir-ing, troublesome governess, Reason, for once convicted of inadequacy'.

Summing up the comic traits in Haydn's piece, I find: (1) breaches of convention; (2) the appearance of ambiguity; (3) proceedings that masquerade as something they are not, for instance as lacking professional knowledge or skill; (4) veiled insults; and (5) nonsense. All of these distinctions belong to the stock-in-trade of the comical in general.[53]

A comic feature that is specific to music is the evocation of laughing and leaping, familiar manifestations of playfulness and high spirits that can be musically suggested by short staccato, leaps of large intervals, and short groups of fast notes separated by rests, as in the scherzos of two A major sonatas: Beethoven's Op. 2, No. 2 and Schubert's D.959. In Kandinsky's late painting *Scherzklänge* ('Jocular Sounds'), such musical effects become visible by means of abstract art: short staccato is represented by wedges, while hopping or skipping is suggested by arched shapes. Though musical laughing and leaping may not be sufficient to make a piece of music comical, it can greatly contribute towards setting a mood from which comic surprise will emerge.

To become apparent, breaches of order need a framework of order. In other comical contexts, the framework is given by words and their meaning, by human situations and reactions, and by the kind of thought that is connected with language. In music, the framework relies on the established musical forms and expectations, and on the logic of purely musical thought. Such a framework is indeed available to the musical layman; the musical experience that is needed is comparable to the verbal experience a child needs to understand a joke. Of course, there are also sophisticated jokes for grown-ups.

Why does classical music lend itself so readily to comic effects? Because it seems to me to reflect, in its solid and self-sufficient forms and structures, the trust of the Enlightenment in rational structures that rule the universe.[54] The spirit of classical music seems to imply the belief that the world is good, or at least that it could become so. For the Romantics, there was no sense of order to rely upon; it had to be found and created in oneself. The open and fragmentary structures of Romantic music, as epitomised by the fantasy, aimed to be as personal, and exceptional, as

---

53 I am especially indebted to D. H. Munro's survey of comical tendencies in his book *Argument of Laughter*, Melbourne University Press, 1951.

54 'A sense of humour develops in a society to the degree that its members are simultaneously conscious of being each a unique person and of being all in common subjection to unalterable laws,' W. H. Auden, 'Notes on the Comic', in *The Dyer's Hand* (Faber & Faber, 1963).

possible. Where, as with Berlioz, surprise becomes the governing principle of composition, and music a succession of feverish dreams, comic effects have little chance; they have to be achieved as an assault on what is proper and predictable.

Cadenzas of classical concertos were allowed, and supposed, to be unpredictable. The final trill, however, traditionally leading from the dominant seventh into the tonic and the orchestral *tutti*, was something that could be relied on, for listeners and orchestral players alike. Beethoven, one of the supreme musical architects, wrote cadenzas that make Mozart's look like models of restraint. In the marathon cadenza for his own C major Concerto, the trill is the special target of his mockery. It never happens as it should. After some hundred bars that run amok through various keys and wreck classical conventions right and left, the cadenza appears to come to an end. The dominant of C major is reached, the trill has begun. But why has there been a diminuendo that deflated the tension? And why is there no dominant seventh chord? If this was to be the proper conclusion, the situation has been mishandled.

Again, we are in an area of ambiguity. We may have the impression of heroic bravura running out of steam; but also of turning in a new, poetic direction indicated by a trill that is not brilliant but lyrical. For a moment, time stands still. What is the composer going to do? Nothing happens that we expect.

We have been plunged, rather cruelly, from a 'higher emotional level' to a 'lower' one. Instead of a lyrical episode, or an orchestral *tutti*, we get a parody of the third theme in

G major, a key that sounds provocatively out of place because Beethoven did not modulate there. Soon the unreality of the harmonic situation makes room for the harmony we were missing; throughout the considerable remainder of the cadenza, the presence of the dominant seventh remains unchallenged. Another ironic attempt at a final trill proves useless because the chord is in the wrong position (that of the second):

Ultimately, when the dominant seventh has been let loose in a frenzy of vehemently repeated scales, there is a last, truly bizarre surprise: the two final chords are, 'unnecessarily', interrupted by a soft, short, arpeggiated one. Playing the end of the cadenza without this soft chord and leading directly into the orchestral *tutti* helps us to realise the degree of Beethoven's mischief.

If this chord could speak an aside to the public, or the orchestra, we might well make out something like: 'Are we really coming to an end?', 'Wouldn't you like the cadenza to be over?', 'What a ridiculous frenzy!', 'Heavens, didn't we forget the trill?', 'As it didn't work before, why should it work now?', or simply 'Am I fooling you well?'

Comic irreverence in classical music has a rational and an irrational significance. The rational side may be illuminated by a quotation from Francis Hutcheson: 'Nothing is so properly applied to the false Grandeur, either of Good or of Evil, as ridicule.' And, according to Schiller, the comic writer has 'continuously to amuse reason', 'shun pathos' and 'defend himself against passions'. Comic music has no other use for the solemn, the rapturous, the pastoral, the heroic or the frenzied than to make fun of it. On the other hand, irrationalism, which had started to undermine the 'certainties' of reason, is musically manifest as a mockery of what is normal, worthy and well behaved. What rationalism does to grand emotions, irrationalism does to the civilised procedures of musical form. Diderot likened great artists, in their defiance of rules, to great criminals, and he conceded that the dark forces in man had their share in the creation of works of art. Nowhere have these dark forces surfaced more cheerfully than in several of Haydn's finales, and more disquietingly than in some of his works in minor keys.

It needs to be said that any formal peculiarities are not sufficient evidence for the comic leanings of a piece. Form and psychology have to interact. Two hallmarks of Haydn's eccentricity, his sudden rests and fermatas at unlikely places and his extended repetitions of the same soft chord, or note, over several bars, can have a very different psychological impact on the listener in pieces of different character. To suspend, interrupt or freeze the flow of music can be purely hilarious, or purely disturbing. If it is both at once, or oscillates between the two, the effect may be called grotesque. (Ligeti's *Aventures et Nouvelles aventures* is grotesque music, and so is much of the comic music of our time.) Generally, the same devices that make music amusing can also make it strange, eerie, disturbing and macabre. The psychological climate of a piece will finally decide whether they are one or the other, or both. In classical music, they are likely to be one *or* the other. Incidentally, the colloquial use of the word 'funny' takes care of both the comical and the strange.

The basic key of a basically comic piece is a major key. There is, outside the field of opera or song, only one comical example in a minor key that comes to mind: Beethoven's C minor Bagatelle from Op. 119. The piece is comical because a cheerful dance that should be in a major key is used to express grim resolution. Communication of comic resolution or comic anger is generally reserved for episodes in Beethoven's earlier rondo movements. A well-known example is the A minor section in his C major Piano Concerto.

This seems a good moment to introduce another area of comic music: that of the excessive and obsessive, of overstatement and *idée fixe*. There is an 'as if' character about such music. It may resemble comic acting, caricature and *opera buffa*. The composer seems to imply: 'This is not really me. I am just turning into somebody choleric or absent-minded, into a pedant, a naughty child, or a very, very innocent child, to amuse you'.

At the beginning of Beethoven's Variations Op. 35 there is a juxtaposition of excessive contrast: *pianissimo* and *fortissimo*.

One may call it an alternation of whispering and stentorian laughter, or of tiptoeing and stamping. Other comic elements are in evidence: the bass alone pretending to be the complete theme (that in effect is only presented later); the rests before and after the *fortissimo* B flats; and the following B flat, marked *piano*, that appears to me like an actor putting a finger to his lips, and going 'Shhhh'.

In the course of these variations, Beethoven plays with the contrast of soft and loud, of changing and repeated notes. In Variation 1 he makes fun of the loud strokes, brings them in too soon, and thereafter cunningly subdues the middle section. In Variations 9 and 13 the loud B flats take over the whole variation as furious grunts, or tear it apart as hysterical shrieks. In Variation 7 there is a series of grim belly-laughs in the bass register, while the rest of the piece is provided with odd accents.

Odd, misplaced, bizarre, obsessive accents are another tool of the composer in a comic frame of mind. The rondo of Beethoven's Second Piano Concerto starts with accents against the grain which later, before the coda, are misplaced in a parody.

The alternation of fast and slow can also generate results of a comical, and highly theatrical, kind, like two different characters who speak *to* one another, or *past* one another. In Variation 21 of Beethoven's *Diabelli Variations* the utterances of the two characters, one coarsely energetic, the other whining, remain incompatible, and the unity of musical context is startlingly broken up. Before the end of Beethoven's G major Sonata Op. 31, No. 1 there is a succession of different tempi, with adagios almost too slow, and rests almost too long, for comfort – only to be followed by a presto that tries to make up for the wasted thirty seconds by comic haste. The pianist who has not succeeded in making somebody in his audience laugh at the end of this sonata should become an organist.

The sarcastic Hans von Bülow once shouted to a female pupil who tried to play the third movement of Beethoven's 'Lebewohl' ('Les Adieux') Sonata: 'Stop! In the joy of reunion, you rush off, get entangled in the train of your dress, crash down, and smash all the flowerpots in the garden!'[55] I think certain classical pieces should communicate a whiff of such a state of mind, with the player in ironic command. Musicians like Bruno Walter, Edwin Fischer and Artur Schnabel had more courage to turn such movements into an exhilarating romp than most of us today.

One of the pieces that can only be appreciated in terms of the obsessively comical is the first movement of Beethoven's Sonata Op. 31, No. 1.

If one looks at this piece from a purely formal perspective, and without any psychological insight, one might dismiss it as incompetent, repetitious, and unworthy of Beethoven. It would, however, be naïve to assume that Beethoven, in the course of

---

55   Theodor Pfeiffer: *Studien bei Hans von Bülow*, Berlin, 1894, p. 55.

this movement, brought in the same opening idea seven times in the same G major, and in an identical position, without doing so on purpose.

There are further clues to his comic intentions: the two hands that seem unable to play together; the short staccato; the somewhat bizarre regularity of brief spells of sound interrupted by rests. The character that emerges is one of compulsive, but scatterbrained, determination. The piece seems unable to go anywhere except where it should not. What a nice surprise to find oneself, at the start of the second theme, in B major instead of the dominant, or in E major instead of the tonic; a surprise that, within a sonata form in a major key, must have been a novelty of an almost exotic flavour. Only Beethoven's String Quintet Op. 29 had made use of the mediant – the related third – before, but in its exposition alone. What, in Op. 31, No. 1, sounds jocular and provocative must have signalled to some of Beethoven's contemporaries a delicious disregard of rules, while simply bewildering others. (It took Beethoven's later 'Waldstein' Sonata, as Tovey has pointed out, to establish the same harmonic progressions as a natural part of widely extended harmonic perspectives.) The coda indicates to anybody who may have missed the point that nothing in this piece was meant to be taken at face value.

As for the second movement, Adagio grazioso, here is a version of the theme that I have simplified to make it unfunny.

And here is Beethoven's own version.

I think, of the two versions, Beethoven's original sounds like a parody of early Beethoven produced by Rossini – who, when this sonata was completed, was ten years old. In Beethoven's Adagio, a complicated balance is achieved between sympathy and mockery, the graceful and the bizarre, nostalgia and anticipation, lyricism and irony. What is Beethoven being ironic about? His own style of the early rondos? The manner of coloratura embellishment? The demeanour of a prima donna on stage? Or the slightly grotesque suppleness of a Taglioni or Fanny Elssler, indicated by the well-oiled mechanism of trills, staccato quavers and musical pirouettes? One might call this movement the first neoclassical piece of music. It is an irony in itself that Op. 31, No. 1 seems to have been the only Beethoven sonata Stravinsky did not enjoy.

The combination of incongruous elements is generally regarded as a distinguishing feature of wit. In another example of musical wit, Beethoven's F major finale from the Sonata Op. 10, No. 2, the solemn technique of fugal writing is 'abused' for burlesque purposes.

Adolf Bernhard Marx likened the movement to 'a child that plucks an old man's beard'. Of course, there is never a serious attempt to present a proper fugal exposition and the listener is left wondering what the composer's intentions were, wittily torn between counterpoint and homophony, sonata and rondo, bristling energy and musical laughter. Already Haydn had been commended (by Griesinger) for his ability 'to lure the listener into the highest degree of the comical by frivolous twists and turns of the seemingly serious'. Devices of musical style that were supposed to suggest such elevated emotional states as 'magnanimity, majesty, splendour, rage, revenge, despair, devotion, delight or virtuousness' (to quote from C. P. E. Bach's friend Christian Gottfried Krause, whose book *Von der musikalischen Poesie* impressed Lessing) were applied by Haydn to the lowest category of poetics, the comical. The 'mescolanza di tutti generi' of which Salieri spoke in connection with Haydn's masses is evident also in his comic music. There is a strong theatrical element in some of Haydn's works, not surprising in a composer who over a period of fifteen years organised performances of opera at Esterháza, and was acquainted with all comical genres of the musical theatre, marionette opera included. Haydn himself turned his incidental music to Jean-François Regnard's *Le distrait* into a capriciously humorous symphony in six movements known as 'Il distratto'. The success of this symphony shows how fluid the borderlines were, how readily such music was appreciated without the stage, and how eagerly the contemporary public, particularly in France, tried to find out what music 'expresses' or 'represents'.

The promotion of the comical in string quartet, sonata and symphony is one of Haydn's great innovations. Carl Friedrich Zelter explains in a letter to his friend Goethe (9 March 1814) that Haydn's art was criticised in earlier years 'because', as

he says, 'it immediately made a burlesque of the deadly seriousness of his predecessors', J. S. Bach and C. P. E. Bach. Haydn certainly did not set out to parody
C. P. E. Bach, whom he revered,[56] in the way early *opéra comique* had parodied
some works of Lully. Rather, the listener was stimulated to take the comical more
seriously, and accept it as part of one's own life. The term 'the elevated comical' (*das
hohe Komische*) had been used, and may have been coined, to characterise Haydn's
music, including even, as the *Musical Almanach of 1782* states, the Adagios, 'during
which people actually, and properly, are supposed to weep'.

Beethoven's F major finale from Op. 10, No. 2 starts with what one may call a
'laughing theme', and the dominating impact of the movement remains that of
laughter. (Nobody seems to doubt that music can 'sigh', metaphorically speaking,
but I have read denials that music can 'laugh'.) To some people, the noise of laughter
is contagious. To the depressive, laughter may be painful and unavailable. To others, laughter is vulgar, seriousness a sign of maturity, and everything that is hilarious
a desecration of loftier states of mind. To step down from one's elevated platform
would mean to lose one's self-respect.

The Austrian Emperor Joseph II disapproved of what he called 'Haydn jests'.
Laughter poses a danger to state and religion. Plato wanted to ban it. Laughter is
incompatible with the holy and the absolute. Or rather, it is the privilege of the
Deity, whether sardonic (as in Indian mythology, and the *Iliad*) or serene (as in
Hegel's 'unquenchable laughter of the Gods'). Umberto Eco, dealing with the significance of laughter in his novel *The Name of the Rose*, quotes Pliny the Younger:
'Aliquando praeterea rideo, iocor, ludo, homo sum' ('Sometimes I laugh, I joke, I
play, I am human'). The laughter of man is not the laughter of gods. Anybody who
has witnessed a little child recognizing a parent, revelling in a new toy or embark-
ing on an exciting adventure knows that there is laughter that does not originate in
catastrophe, or represent superiority.

In a German musical encyclopaedia of 1875[57] I found an admirable article on

---

56   From C. P. E. Bach, Haydn adopted not only some exemplary qualities of the early sonatas ('clear formal
     disposition, unity of emotion and thematic material in each movement, consequent motivic develop-
     ment', in the words of the German keyboard player and scholar Andreas Staier) but also the inclination
     to be unpredictable. If C. P. E. Bach, in the 'bizarrerie' that was to become characteristic of his style, ever
     tried his hand at suggesting the comical, he was bound to fail. With surprise as the governing principle,
     humour could not be accommodated – a situation later repeated in Berlioz.

57   *Musikalisches Conversations Lexikon* (Verlag R. Oppenheim).

humour (the *New Grove* has none); it sets humour apart from other modes of the comical in that it is a world view, a complete outlook on life. 'For the humorist', the article says, 'there are no fools, only foolishness and a mad world'. (This, again, is a formula borrowed from Jean Paul.) 'He will therefore perceive man and the world to be not ridiculous or revolting but pitiable'. Humour relates to the dark undercurrent of life, and prevails over it. If we understand humour in this comprehensive sense, Beethoven's *Diabelli Variations* are one of its musical paradigms.

The reader may have noticed that the name Mozart has hardly been mentioned. In looking for examples in his works, I found myself to be the victim of prejudice. I wrongly assumed that his absolute music should be a mine of the comical because his letters abound in hilarious wordplay and nonsense and because the music of his operas makes such superlative use of all comical resources. Haydn and Beethoven, with all their love of *cantabile*, were predominantly instrumental composers; sensual beauty of sound was not an innate quality or a primary concern. The imagination of Mozart or Schubert, however, was predominantly vocal, even in their instrumental works, and the style of Mozart's symphonies had been castigated accordingly by Nägeli as too operatic. Singing, like sensuality, is hardly funny. It constitutes an area of beauty that opens itself to the comical only by means of words and comic acting. Singing itself can become comical where it turns into grotesque utterance; the music of our time has seized upon such sounds or noises, suggestive of the absurd and the crudely physical.

Mozart's beauty of *cantabile* is matched by the beauty of his musical proportion and balance, that singular illusion of complete formal perfection at any time. Next to Mozart's truly classical sense of order, Haydn often appears whimsical. Where Mozart somehow manages to surprise us with what we expect, Haydn excels in the unexpected. The sudden *fortissimo* chord in the Adagio of his 'Surprise' Symphony is only one of many examples.[58]

Writing about 'The Comical in Music', Schumann claims that Beethoven and Schubert were able to translate any state of mind into music. 'In certain *Moments musicaux*', so he says, 'I imagine I recognise unpaid tailor's bills'. This would undoubtedly

---

58   I have changed my mind: I do now find some of Mozart's final rondos very funny and associate their sound less with the human voice than with wind instruments.

have come as a surprise to Schubert, who, according to Eduard Bauernfeld, asked a certain Josef Dessauer whether he knew any funny music when Dessauer pronounced one of Schubert's songs to be too melancholy.

Whatever 'lustig' may have meant to Schubert, his music bears out the fact that it hardly aspires to be comical. Schumann's sometimes does; of the important Romantic composers, he was the only one to be influenced by those German Romantic writers to whom humour and irony were a major concern. But Schumann's 'Humour', wherever indicated in his music, is too good-humoured and warmly lyrical to be comic, and his capriciousness does not come from a light-hearted disposition. I cannot find a trace of humour in the music of Chopin or Liszt. And Wagner is reported to have turned Schiller's line 'Ernst ist das Leben, heiter die Kunst' on its head: art must be serious, while life may be cheerful. The only excuse for the Romantic composer to write funny music seems to have been the use of a funny text, in opera or song.

For most performers and virtually all concert audiences of our time, music is an entirely serious business. Performers are meant to function as heroes, dictators, poets, seducers, magicians or helpless vessels of inspiration. The projection of comical music needs a performer who dares to be less than awe-inspiring, and does not take him- or herself too seriously. Comic music can be ruined, and made completely meaningless, by 'serious' performance. It is much more dependent on a performer's understanding than an Allegro di bravura, a nocturne or a funeral march. To manage to play a piece humorously is a special gift; yet, I am afraid, it is not enough: the public, expecting the celebration of religious rites, may not notice that something amusing is going on unless it is visibly encouraged to be amused.

I admit that to expect a player to radiate amusement while performing is a tall order. The trouble is that many performers, on account of their concentration and nervous tension, look unduly grave or grim, no matter what they play. The first bars of a classical piece set its mood. To sit down and start Haydn's last C major Sonata with a tortured look is even worse than to embark on the so-called 'Moonlight' Sonata with a cheerful smile. Nobody will mistake the first movement of the 'Moonlight' for a cheerful piece, whereas the hilarious beginning of Haydn's C major Sonata can easily sound wooden and pointless. Before the first note, a discreet signal has to pass from the performer to the audience: 'Caution! We are out for mischief.'

When the English notion of 'humour' arrived in Germany, Lessing translated it as 'Laune'. *Laune*, according to Kant, means, in its best sense, 'the talent voluntarily to put oneself into a certain mental disposition, in which everything is judged quite differently from the ordinary method (reversed, in fact), and yet in accordance with certain rational principles in such a frame of mind'. This sounds to me like an apt description of the quality that a performer of comical music should be able to summon up. 'But this manner', as Kant further says, 'belongs rather to pleasant than to beautiful art, because the object of the latter must always show a certain dignity in itself...'[59] For my part, I am perfectly happy to enjoy the 'sublime in reverse' and leave Kant's dignity behind where Haydn and Beethoven took such obvious pleasure in doing so.

(1984)

---

59   Immanuel Kant: *Critique of Judgment* (1790) § 54.

Must Classical Music Be Entirely Serious?

DESPITE THEIR VAST range of different emotions – serious, lyrical, mysterious and depressive, withdrawn and brilliantly extroverted – Beethoven's *Diabelli Variations* reveal themselves to be a humorous work in the widest possible sense. Beethoven's first biographer, Anton Schindler, says – and for once I am inclined to believe him – that the composition of this work 'amused Beethoven to a rare degree', that it was written 'in a rosy mood', and that it was 'bubbling with unusual humour', disproving the belief that Beethoven spent his late years in complete gloom. According to Wilhelm von Lenz, one of the most perceptive early commentators on Beethoven's music, Beethoven here shines as the 'most thoroughly initiated high priest of humour'; he calls the variations 'a satire on their theme'.

The theme itself – which Diabelli had sent to fifty fellow composers, asking them to contribute one variation each – is comical because both halves are so stubbornly alike, and because it seems to be trying to be something it is not. It is not a genuine waltz of any kind. If one disregards the dynamic markings and tempo indication *vivace*, it rather resembles an old-fashioned minuet. With its markings, on the other hand, the piece tries a bit too hard to mimic a modern bagatelle; indeed, Konrad Wolff has asked whether all these thoroughly un-Diabellian crescendos and *sforzandos* might not be additions by Beethoven himself.

Compared with any of Beethoven's previous variation works, the *Diabelli Variations* are highly unorthodox. An unwritten rule of classical variation practice stipulated that the first variation should remain close to the character of the theme. Beethoven counters such expectations, and the unreality of the 'waltz', immediately with a march. (In his splendid monograph on the *Diabelli Variations*, William Kinderman[60] has shown that this was an afterthought; while the majority of the pieces were composed in 1819, the march is one of ten variations added by Beethoven after the completion of his last three sonatas, and the *Missa solemnis*, in 1822.) Later in the set, at least eight of the variations laugh or giggle; some others take on an air of the grotesque, of diablerie – if the pun is permitted.

---

60   Clarendon Press/Oxford University Press, 1987.

But apart from its sense of comedy, there is relatively little in the theme that informs the set as a whole. The theme has ceased to reign over its unruly offspring. Rather, the variations decide what the theme may have to offer them. Instead of being confirmed, adorned and glorified, it is improved, parodied, ridiculed, disclaimed, transfigured, mourned, stamped out and finally uplifted.

Even the more innovative of Beethoven's sets had adhered to some 'classical' component as a matter of principle: the Prometheus Variations Op. 35 to the bass, the Op. 34 set to the melody. In the *Diabelli Variations* the components Beethoven makes use of are variable, and a matter of choice. Some variations are dominated by one motif while leaving others in the background: variations 2, 6, 9, 11, 12 and 25 employ the initial embellishment figure; variations 7 and 19 the broken chord; variations 27 and 28 the sequential motif of bars 9–12 of the theme. In their unprecedented freedom of choice, the *Diabelli Variations* always retain enough of the motivic material to make their connection with the theme sufficiently clear. As in Beethoven's sonatas, the motivic components of the opening theme are more important than the theme itself in providing the unifying threads for the whole work.

If there is one feature of the theme that is most consistently honoured, if modified and refined, it is its build-up of foreshortenings in both halves. Otherwise, the basic design is often called in question. Even its phrase lengths are frequently ignored: no fewer than ten variations shorten or augment its layout or change its proportions (not to mention the fugue, and those variations in which some or all repeats are missing for good reason).

Apart from the urge to make fun of the theme, there is another evident explanation for such liberties. In a work of this unique size and scope, the listener who remains exposed to the key of C major (and, very sparingly, C minor) for little less than an hour needs to be stimulated in novel ways. In addition to the unending variety of texture and temperament there is the variation of the formal scheme itself.

Only the fugue in E flat (Variation 32) leaves the home key. It calls to mind Handel's lapidary style, but it also conceals the maximum aggressive tension. In its almost boundless energy, it presents an example of what must have been Beethoven's most personal contribution to contrapuntal writing: the explosive fugue. Not that Beethoven, as is so often assumed, had to wrestle desperately with the fugal idiom. This notion has already been gloriously refuted earlier on in the Fughetta (Variation 24), a piece of otherworldly purity, and one of those few variations in the set that reach into the mysterious and sublime. (If humour, according to Jean Paul, is 'the sublime in reverse', then variations such as nos. 14, 20 and 24 offer the contrast of sublimity in full view.)

Three variations in C minor (nos. 29–31) prepare the ground for the fugal eruption. The third of these elegies combines again the old and the new: a Bachian aria fused with almost Chopinesque figuration. The closing variation begins as a tribute to Mozart. From a distance of thirty-three variations, its 'tempo di minuetto' lifts the mask from the original theme with irony and affection. What had started out as a satire ends as a work of humour in Jean Paul's comprehensive sense.

To my mind, it has not been sufficiently stressed that Beethoven's greatest set of variations leaves a good many conventions of classical variation practice behind. In his title Beethoven uses the German word 'Veränderungen' (alterations, rather than variations), although elsewhere in the work he adheres to the standard Italian terminology. The boldest of these alterations are structural. 'To interpolate a digression, or to alter the phrase-lengths of a variation, is to incur a risk which the great masters of classical variation form hardly ever venture,' says Tovey. It is a pity that Tovey did not pursue this train of thought any further, instead of asking himself whether Beethoven, in two or three variations, might not have 'inadvertently omitted a bar'.[61]

Let me give you a survey of those variations which shorten, or extend, the theme, or change its organisation. In the first half of Var. 4, and the second of Var. 11, one bar is missing where, almost imperceptibly, two phrases are pushed into one another. In Var. 21 there is an excess of eight (4+4) bars, to comical effect. Var. 22 parodies the theme with the help of 'Notte e giorno faticar' from the beginning of Mozart's *Don Giovanni*. Two bars are added to give Leporello[62] the chance to find his way back into C major, whereas the 'German dance' of Var. 25 feigns incompetence by 'losing' the last bar of its first half.

In Var. 29 there are a couple of excess bars in each half:

61   Donald Francis Tovey: *Beethoven* (Oxford, 1944) pp. 125, 129; *The Forms of Music* (Oxford, 1944) p. 244.

62   It has been said that Beethoven's relationship to this theme, like Leporello's relationship to his master, was critical but faithful. To me, a classical borderline of faithfulness has been overstepped.

Without these bars, the structure of the variation falls into place if we understand that every two bars of the theme correspond with one of the variation. No. 30 repeats its last four bars only. Var. 31 compresses the first eight bars of the theme into two, whereafter its foreshortenings take their own time, multiplying their coloratura of grief. We encounter irregular halves of six and five bars respectively in which each last bar consists of twelve quavers instead of nine.

While some of these 'deformations' easily escape notice, anomalies such as missing repeats are quite obvious, if less significant. In other works by Beethoven, the occasional irregular repeat always expands the structure, adding repeats where the theme had none. This has never been deemed offensive, whereas the breaking of pattern in the *Diabelli Variations* by infrequently leaving out repeats indicated by the theme has irked some musicians, who feel cheated in their most basic expectations of proportion. (Artur Schnabel, in his celebrated recording, repeated the first half of Var. 2, contrary to Beethoven's intention.) Beethoven's priority here is psychological, not formal: where repeats are missing, he counteracts monotony in variations which are based on short, recurring rhythmic figures and contain little rhythmic variety. Vars. 2, 11 and 12 offer no first-part repeat. Vars. 20 and 29 skip both repeats, suggesting intense concentration. In Var. 30 a sighing coda of desolation is created by repeating the final four bars only. But why, it has been asked, did Beethoven not proceed similarly in those other variations which are also steeped in one short rhythmic idea? Let me submit my answers. In Vars. 1 and 9 the insistence on recurring patterns is comical, a stubborn demonstration of muscular power. In Var. 25 the missing bar has to be verified: one needs to hear it missing twice to believe what the player has done. In Var. 26 the very wide compass of pitch makes up for the rhythmic uniformity of semiquavers. Var. 28, again, is obsessed with its own manic energy, a paroxysm of comic rage or laughter.

It is interesting that those 'un-Diabellian' crescendos mentioned by Konrad Wolff remain the single element of Diabelli's theme that Beethoven discards. (Which shows that he could not have inserted them in the first place.) They are not structural enough to be of strictly musical value. Yet Beethoven takes up their psychological cue – the licence to proceed grotesquely in his own structural way. If the ludicrous, drastic and weird juxtaposition of highly disparate elements is characteristic of the grotesque, then the *Diabelli Variations* are a remarkably grotesque work. From Var. 13 on, the set offers an almost unbroken succession of sharply defined contrasts. Nothing seems to be more indicative of the prevailing comical spirit than the fact that the most sublime seriousness in Vars. 14, 20 and 24 is immediately followed by light comedy, or farce. The suddenness, on the other hand, with which the depressive minor key sphere takes hold of the piece after the frenzy of Var. 28 recalls an unforgettable visual image from Alain Resnais's *Last Year in Marienbad*: a bedroom is shown in whiter and whiter light until its whiteness gives way, within an instant, to the near-black view of the garden.

For grotesque surprises *within* variations, examples abound. Let me pick out three. In Var. 13 short bites of sound are startlingly juxtaposed with silence. Var. 15 jumps into the bass in bar 22, confounding anybody who looks for amiable logic and euphony, yet making, to my ears, a great deal more sense than the 'corrections' attempted since Moscheles. Var. 21 breaks up the unity of each half by splitting it into two different metres, paces and characters.

Another overstepped borderline is exemplified by the much-discussed mysterious Var. 20. The enigmatic harmonies of bars 9–12 are 'fairly easily explainable', or so Hans von Bülow believed.

To me, Bülow's explanations, or anybody else's, illuminate little except the fact that Beethoven commentators wanted Beethoven's music to remain explicable. (If there is any logical clue to this passage we shall find it in its motivic organisation: Jürgen Uhde[63] speaks of 'frozen motifs contained in a crystal'.) I cannot see why this mysterious passage should not have been so conceived as to remain mysterious forever. Liszt must have had this passage in mind when he called the variation 'Sphinx'. Like Haydn's B major chords in the finale of his C major Sonata Hob. XVI:50, these harmonies are musically unreasonable. But their effect could not be more different. By misbehaving, Haydn provokes the listener's sense of humour. What Beethoven provokes is our sense of awe.

Among all the twenty-odd contrasts following one another, that of Vars. 20 and 21 must be the most striking; it sets hypnotic introspection against vaudeville. Kinderman sees in Vars. 19–21 a group that shares canonic features as well as the structural opposition of its halves. I would, nevertheless, plead for a separation of Vars. 20 and 21 in performance. As the centrepiece of the *Diabelli Variations*, its inner sanctum, Var. 20 also marks the midpoint of their duration. A moment of silence, to savour the sublime, seems appropriate.

As Tovey says, Beethoven 'could not have made an enormous set of variations out of the sublime themes which he treats in variation form in his sonata works.

---

63   *Beethovens Klaviermusik* (Reclam, 1968), Vol. 1, p. 542.

Diabelli's theme is as prosaic as the hard-shell businessman who wrote it, but it does mean business ... It is a theme which sets the composer free to build recognisable variations in every conceivable way'.

Thanks to the variety of the material and the clarity of its presentation, Beethoven was propelled to extend his task beyond measure. Allegedly, Beethoven asked Diabelli[64] (who came to urge him finally to deliver the promised variation for Diabelli's volume): 'How many contributions have you got?' 'Thirty-two', replied Diabelli. 'Go ahead and publish them', said Beethoven. 'I shall write thirty-three all by myself'. In Beethoven's own pianistic output, the figures 32 and 33 have their special significance: 32 sonatas are followed by 33 variations as a crowning achievement, of which Var. 33 relates directly to the thirty-second sonata's final Adagio.[65] Looking back at Beethoven's outstanding independent variation works, one could point out yet another, playful reason for the composer to have been attracted by the figure 33. There happens to be, between the 32 Variations in C minor and the sets Opp. 34 and 35, a numerical gap. The *Diabelli Variations* fill it.

Of course, Beethoven must have been perfectly well aware of the musical components entrusted to him by Diabelli. Here is my list of the *motivic elements* offered by the theme:

1) The upbeat embellishment, changing note, or appoggiatura;

2) The interval of the fourth and fifth;

3) The repetitions of single notes or chords, as well as the pedal point (usually on the dominant G);

---

64 According to Beethoven's friend Karl Holz, who related the story to Lenz (see Wilhelm von Lenz, *Kritischer Katalog sämmtlicher Werke L. von Beethovens*, Vierter Teil, p. 138).

65 See Michel Butor: *Dialogue avec 33 variations de L. von Beethoven sur une valse de Diabelli* (Gallimard, 1971) pp. 33 ff., and Kinderman, p. 118.

4)   The broken chord (bars 1–4, 5–8, etc., right hand and left hand);

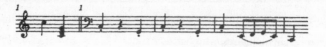

5)   The dance rhythm

and its variants;

6)   The sequential figure;

7)   The melodic curve in the last four bars of each half.

In addition, two *structural elements* should not be overlooked: the series of *foreshortenings* in both halves; and the *melodic direction*, with descending intervals, or motion, in the first half, and ascending ones at the start of the second half. (Diabelli's theme starts its first half with descending fourths and fifths, its second half with an ascending fifth.)

While Beethoven's use of motivic components is capricious, the two structural features mentioned above have, on the whole, earned Beethoven's respect – with the exception of four variations in which motivic or melodic direction as defined above is ignored, namely vars. 12 (which also makes its foreshortening almost imperceptible), 22, 28 and 29. In Var. 18 the descent is maintained in the relation of bars 1 and 3, 5 and 7; the ascent in bars 17 and 19, 21 and 23. In Fughetta and Fugue, the (main) theme enters alternatively with a fourth and a fifth.

One more element which I have listed among the motivic components has its structural implications. It is the tone repetition (or pedal point) on G, spread out over the first eight bars of both halves; in the melody of bars 1–8, and the middle voice of bars 17–24. It acts as a spine holding the harmonies together, particularly emphasised in the repetitions of vars. 1, 10, 15, 16 and 21, or contained as a latent idea in the background in Vars. 12 or 26. Of the variations that depart from this component of the theme, the most discreet is Var. 8 (bars 5–8), the most demonstrative Var. 9 (bars 1–24), while the funniest are Var. 13, with its (wrong) beginnings to both halves, and Var. 22, which goes astray after the double bar. In the *minore* variations 29–31, the structure of the theme disintegrates, and harmonic emphasis is gradually shifted further and further away from the dominant.

Another element that is carried into many variations is what I should like to call a spirit of dance. The theme itself is a dance, if not clearly a waltz; its initial left-hand rhythm leaves its mark on at least sixteen of the variations. Some of them are touched by it only indirectly; in Var. 26 the continuous semiquaver motion needs the underlying dance rhythm to come alive.

The turning of this 3/8 variation into a 2/8 triplet piece I can only take as a misunderstanding.

Beethoven's humorous variation works are triggered by 'funny' themes. (To my mind, they include not only his Variations Op. 35 and the 'Kind, willst du ruhig schlafen' set, but also – may the British forgive him! – the bizarre one on 'Rule, Britannia'.) There are works such as Bach's Goldberg Variations, whose pensive aria is followed by a succession of diverse character pictures; on the other hand, in Mozart's Duport Variations, Beethoven's *Diabelli Variations* or Liszt's Variations on *Weinen, Klagen, Sorgen, Zagen* the character of the theme remains decisive. In the *Diabelli Variations* there is room for a number of sublime and depressive pieces; yet, psychologically, the theme determines the course of the entire work.

It is not difficult to discover those variations that laugh or leap. (To spot the laughing, giggling or cackling, just apply the syllables ha-ha, hey-hey, hee-hee to the music and see whether they fit.) But there are also variations of a latent humour: they display, as in vars. 1 and 9, characters deeply serious but slightly lacking in brains, or, as in 23, 27 and 28, one-track minds in an excited state. In the context of this work, they should be taken, and delivered, with more than a grain of irony.

I have devised a series of titles for the *Diabelli Variations* to amuse myself, but also for practical purposes. In a cycle of variations or other shorter pieces, the switch from one character to the next has to be prompt and secure, the characters themselves sharply defined and clearly set apart from one another. In a song cycle or Liszt's *Années de pèlerinage*, the performer is guided by poems and other literary allusions. Where they are missing, or composers are unwilling to operate with extra-musical images, the performer may find it useful to develop an acute verbal awareness of contrast, character and atmosphere to aid his psychological memory. Chopin's Preludes – pieces by a composer who always steered clear of poetic 'associations' – have inspired pianists such as Anton Rubinstein and Alfred Cortot to invent titles which undoubtedly helped them to sustain a great performance. Uhde, in a stimulating list,[66] has defined the *Diabelli Variations* in the manner of Bartók's *Mikrokosmos*, a different approach that tries to encompass the variety of characters mainly in musical terms. In his titles, descriptions like 'Invention', 'Imitation', 'Accents' or 'Relaxed Upbeats' remain on strictly musical ground, while images like 'Columns', 'Cascades', 'Loop', 'Crystal' or 'Swirl' are used more rarely. In addition to the titles, Uhde specifies the sound of each variation as being that of a string quartet, an orchestra, an organ, a wind ensemble, a mixture of groups or the piano itself.

I could also imagine a view of the variations that employs the four Classical elements – earth, air, fire and water – as tools for differentiations. Variations 1 and 9 are clearly terrestrial, Var. 20 is subterranean. Fire blazes in vars. 16–17 and 23. The gentle flow of water informs vars. 12 and 26, while vars. 2 and 33 suspend gravity and float in the air. In some of the variations, elements appear combined (the impossible becomes true, if only in music): in vars. 6 and 27 there is a fusion of fire and water, in Var. 13 of earth and air. Var. 10 shows simultaneously characteristics of air, fire and water; and the fugue, which starts as an amalgam of earth and fire, turns into water at the entrance of its third subject.

While these verbal crutches share the feature that they are contrived in all seriousness, Wilhelm von Lenz's titles of 1860 – the first ever to be printed – bear witness to this Tsarist privy councillor's quirky mind and sense of humour. Var. 1 is called 'The Mastodon and the Theme – a fable'; Var. 7 occurs 'In the Tyrol'; and the facetious word 'Raptus' (tantrum) is applied to vars. 6, 23, 26 and 27. My own titles, written down before I encountered those by Lenz, try in similar spirit to illuminate Beethoven's 'rosy mood' or, rather, to hint at his own degree of seriousness and amusement.

---

66   pp. 554–5.

Theme. Alleged waltz

Var. 1. March: gladiator, flexing his muscles

   2. Snowflakes

   3. Confidence and nagging doubt

   4. Learned ländler

   5. Tamed goblin

   6. Trill rhetorics (Demosthenes braving the surf)

   7. Swivelling and stamping

   8. Intermezzo (to Brahms)

   9. Industrious nutcracker

  10. Giggling and neighing

  11. 'Innocente' (Bülow)

  12. Wave pattern

  13. Aphorism, biting

  14. Here He Cometh, the Chosen

  15. Cheerful spook

16–17. Triumph

  18. Precious memory, slightly faded

  19. Helter-skelter

  20. Inner sanctum

  21. Maniac and moaner

  22. 'Notte e giorno faticar' (to Diabelli)

  23. The virtuoso at boiling point (to Cramer)

  24. Pure spirit

  25. 'Teutscher' (German dance)

  26. Circles on the water

  27. Juggler

  28. The rage of the jumping jack

  29. 'Stifled sighs' (Konrad Wolff)

  30. Gentle grief

  31. To Bach (to Chopin)

  32. To Handel

  33. To Mozart; to Beethoven

'To Beethoven'? In the coda of the concluding variation, Beethoven speaks on his own behalf. He alludes to another supreme set of variations, that from his own last Sonata, Op. III, which had been composed before the *Diabelli Variations* were finished. Beethoven's Arietta from Op. III is not only in the same key as Diabelli's 'waltz', but also shares certain motivic and structural features, while the characters of the two themes could not be more disparate. One can hear the Arietta as yet another, more distant, offspring of the 'waltz', and marvel at the inspirational effect of the 'cobbler's patch'.

How do the ten variations of 1823 fit into the corpus of pieces composed four years earlier? What do they add? Vars. 1 and 2 give a broader base to the 'group of ascent' which, if we follow Uhde, incorporates the first ten variations in a gradual increase of speed or density, a group that contains Var. 8 as a well-nigh Brahmsian 'intermezzo'. Vars. 15 and 25 are inserted to remind us, as 'parodies' (Kinderman), of the initial theme. Vars. 23–6 extend what Uhde calls the 'scherzo group' (vars. 21–8), introducing into it the contrast of the Fughetta (Var. 24) as a sublime sort of 'trio' (Uhde). At the end of this group, Var. 28 provides the final climax of agitation before we are plunged from extroversion into inner darkness. Here, with the addition of vars. 29 and 31, the single C minor variation of 1819 (30) now becomes part of the larger C minor area. The expanding grief and desolation of these pieces corresponds to their remoteness from the theme's structure. But these elegies also fulfil another, large-scale need. A great set of variations, Tovey tells us, has 'the enormous momentum of something that revolves on its axis or moves in an orbit. The highest problem in the art of variation-making is to stop this momentum'.[67] In the *Diabelli Variations*, the slow *minore* variations act as a brake to which the reinvigorating fugue responds, not as a finale (being in E flat major) but as an elemental experience, a purifying ordeal from which the 'waltz' emerges transformed, 'reborn'. Do I detect a touch of Orphean mysteries and Masonic initiation rites? I shall, rather, turn to Heinrich von Kleist's wonderful essay 'On the Marionette Theatre'. Near the end, there is a sentence that reads like an outline of the *Diabelli Variations*: 'When perception has passed through infinity, gracefulness reappears'. I wonder whether Beethoven knew it.

(1989)

---

67 *Beethoven*, p. 125.

The Text and Its Guardians:

I F MUSICAL ERRORS drag on, those performers responsible can be said to fall into three groups. The first, enthralled by printer's ink, read music as uncritically as most people read their newspaper: they simply believe what they see. For the second type, the composer is an object of loathing. What they want is not a father-figure but some kind of musical parthenogenesis. Did the composer actually exist? And assuming he did, what does it matter today? Did he really know what he was doing? At any rate, we know better.

Somewhere in the middle are those musicians who do not take the trouble to ascertain that their text is correct. For them, life is too short for the fine print. They are happy to play the large print, whatever that may be, and with no matter what distortions it has arrived on the page.

Because of musicians like these, some fundamental misunderstandings in Beethoven's piano concertos linger on. Another reason is that a modern *Urtext* edition of these works has long been overdue. Bärenreiter has now remedied the situation; the editor is Hans-Werner Küthen.

The delay in the availability of a new edition has been connected with the strange fate of the autograph of Beethoven's C minor Concerto. After 1945 it was considered lost. But many years later it turned up in a Polish library, and was finally handed back to the Deutsche Staatsbibliothek in East Berlin. In the autograph the metre of the first movement is **C**, not the habitual *alla breve*. This, of course, will not come as a surprise to anybody who has consulted Franz Kullak's edition for two pianos (1881) or Carl Czerny's essay 'On the Correct Performance of all Beethoven's Piano Works' in his *School of Piano Playing* Op. 500 (1842). Unfortunately, the *alla breve* marking appears in the old Breitkopf & Härtel complete edition (1862), and their scores and orchestral parts of the Beethoven concertos are still in general use. Since then, most editions have adopted it. In the Eulenburg pocket score it is just one of many contestable features, but the Kinsky-Halm Beethoven catalogue has it too, and so does the cadenza volume of the new complete edition by Henle. All original sources read **C**.

Why so much fuss about a vertical stroke? Is it not more important to have 'the proper feeling' for a piece? Certainly, but the performer – for all the liberties he is entitled to claim – must be able to answer to the composer for that 'feeling'.

The difference between ¢ and ₵ can, on occasion, be great enough to move mountains. It has an influence not only on the beat (the placement of stresses within the bar) and the character but definitely also on the tempo; Beethoven demonstrated in his original metronome markings elsewhere – whether or not we wish to take them literally – that two tempo categories are indeed intended. We need hear no more than the first few bars of the C minor Concerto to realise what damage is done by an *alla breve*; the quavers of the opening theme lose their rhythmic footing. A chair that needs four legs is made to stand on two.

The men responsible for this misdeed are those in charge of the old complete edition: Gustav Nottebohm and Carl Reinecke. The second movement of the Fifth Concerto did not escape their blue pencil either; here, the authentic ₵ was altered to ¢. (This was the more frequent procedure. In the old Mozart complete edition several concerto movements are 'corrected' in such a manner.)

Playing the Adagio un poco mosso of the Fifth Concerto as solemnly as possible has become an impressive habit. Again, Czerny and Kullak are the only ones to give the correct metre, *alla breve*; Czerny does so quite specifically with the words 'the Adagio (alla breve) should not drag' (darf nicht schleppend gehn). It was Czerny, after all, who gave the first Vienna performance in 1812 under Beethoven's eyes.

Czerny's comments on Beethoven's piano works are available, in German and English, in an annotated edition by Paul Badura-Skoda (Universal Edition). They remain the most important source of information that has come down to us about the performance of these works. Czerny's metronome figures for the first movements of the Concertos Opp. 15, 19 and 37 strike me as a convincing product of practical experience; they can at least be taken as approximate values. Although the three movements have the same tempo marking, *allegro con brio*, they are given metronome figures corresponding to the individual character: Op. 15, $\downarrow$ = 88, or more correctly $\downarrow$ = 176; Op. 19, $\downarrow$ = 152; Op. 37 $\downarrow$ = 144. With brisk activity and an alert intentness in common, they do have different things to say. The driving tempo of the C major Concerto counteracts any feeling of *maestoso*; it makes sense if the pianist is not afraid to see the development as a piece within a piece – a more restrained, and romantic, sphere from which the listener is suddenly propelled by the *fortissimo* octave run before the recapitulation. I do not recall any other Beethoven Allegro in which the development has been placed so noticeably in parenthesis.

In the slow movements, however, Czerny's sometimes rather hurried speeds remind me of the late Hans Schmidt-Isserstedt's pun: 'Spielen Sie flüssig, aber nicht überflüssig' ('Be fluent but not superfluous').

Three more textual corrections should be mentioned:

1) In the Adagio of the B flat Concerto the demisemiquaver in bars 76 and 79 must be read as a semiquaver.

2) In the first movement of the C minor Concerto there are three 'new' bars in the timpani part (334–6).

3) In the cadenza of the C minor Concerto the bass octave G1–G, two bars before the double trill, is missing in both complete editions although it looms large in the autograph. (A facsimile edition of Beethoven's cadenzas was published by Eulenburg in 1979.)

In the G major Concerto, I make use of a few alterations and corrections by Beethoven himself, published by Paul Badura-Skoda in *Österreichische Musikzeitschrift*, October 1958. I also recommend looking through the solo part of the Fifth Concerto in Clementi's London edition which, as we have learned from Alan Tyson, was published simultaneously with the Leipzig first print. May I assure all doubting Thomases that the cadenza I play in the first movement of the Fourth Concerto is indeed Beethoven's own; the autograph has the superscription *Cadenza ma senza cadere*, an allusion to its pianistic pitfalls. I have often been asked why I should waste my time on this bizarre piece when another more lyrical, and plausible, cadenza is available. I think that the Cadenza ma senza cadere adds something to our knowledge of Beethoven. It shows almost shockingly how Beethoven the architect could turn, in some of his cadenzas, into a genius running amok. Almost all the classical principles of order fall by the wayside, as comparison with Mozart's cadenzas will amply demonstrate. Breaking away from the style and character of the movement does not bother Beethoven at all, and harmonic detours cannot be daring enough. No other composer has ever offered cadenzas of such provoking madness.

The warning 'ma senza cadere' reminds me of another tendency of Beethoven the virtuoso – that of stretching the player's bravura to new limits. In a few cases these limits are, either mischievously or erroneously, overstretched. The brilliant broken octave triplets in the first movement of the Sonata Op. 2, No. 2 (bars 84 ff.) are provided with a fingering that flies in the face of reason: it is in any tempo impracticable, and in the prescribed *allegro moderato* unplayable. (Even such a literal-minded Beethovenian as Heinrich Schenker recommended the use of both hands.)

Another case that amounts almost to a practical joke is his four-hand setting of the 'Grosse Fuge', in which he simply keeps the violins for the primo player and leaves the viola and cello for the secondo, regardless of all crossings between the voices.

Then there is the octave passage immediately before the recapitulation in the first movement of the C major Concerto. What Beethoven wrote down is doubly confusing: there are *fortissimo* semiquaver octaves in the right hand, but also a bass note G in the left. This note is marked *forte*, whereas the strings coming in at the same downbeat have *pianissimo*. The editor of the Bärenreiter score suggests in his critical comments that, in order not to lose the bass note, 'fast legato octaves' should be played by the right hand. I have heard a performance (and pitied its conductor) where the soloist had decided on a kind of snail's pace for the whole movement in order to give those octaves their due. If this is faithful to the maxim that every note has to be played in the way the composer wrote it down – a maxim I would not accept without reservations – it is quite damaging to the exhilarating spirit of this piece. Furthermore, fast octaves were evidently not part of Beethoven's technical equipment; unlike Weber or Schubert, he never used them at all – unless they are glissando octaves indicated by slurs. Our octave run is slurred, and so are the runs in the stretta of the 'Waldstein' Sonata. Czerny refers to both as glissando passages.

What does the musical situation demand? The dreamy atmosphere of the organ point, sustained by the horns and surrounded by diminished-seventh chords in a haze of pedal, is brusquely terminated. With the entry of the first *fortissimo* octave, two bars before the actual recapitulation, the initial character returns: brisk, witty and wide-awake. The *pianissimo* in the strings seems to indicate that Beethoven intended a *fortissimo* to appear only two bars later. When (subsequently?) writing down the solo part, Beethoven may have forgotten to adjust the dynamics.[68] If this adjustment is made, and the strings played forte, the pianist's bass note becomes redundant. But there is an even better solution, albeit a less literal one: Edwin Fischer started the passage an octave higher and played, from there, a double glissando, beginning after the bass note. While this surpasses the compass of Beethoven's instrument, and ignores the printed semiquaver rhythm, it seems to suit the psychological idea to perfection and blends admirably with the pre-Lisztian piano style of the (later) grand cadenza. It might well have amused Beethoven to know that there have been pianists who, perplexed by the notation of these bars, decided to stay away from the concerto altogether. Perhaps it would have pleased him to have dumbfounded performers whose trust in the composer's infallibility lacked the counterbalance of imagination and critical scrutiny.

(1983)

---

68 Unfortunately, the autograph does not bear out this assumption; the octave run was evidently written first.

SCHUBERT

❧

Schubert's Piano Sonatas, 1822–28

I T I S O N L Y recently that Schubert has been recognised as one of the great piano composers and one of the supreme masters of the sonata. We are indebted for this to Artur Schnabel and, in Germany, to Eduard Erdmann, who, as performers and influential teachers, opened the road to future generations. But they were isolated cases within their time. In 1928, the year of the centenary of Schubert's death, Rachmaninov, the celebrated pianist, admitted to Cesar Saerchinger that he had not realised sonatas by Schubert existed. Even today, some older musicians continue to show a surprising amount of ignorance, doubt and contempt where Schubert's sonatas are concerned. Thus, it seems fitting to examine certain of the prejudices that still prevail against these works, in the hope of providing clues as to their neglect.

Prejudice 1: Schubert's style did not develop

The reason for this belief can be found in the fact that, in spite of O. E. Deutsch's catalogue, many people have still not discovered the chronology of Schubert's output. The order in which Schubert's works were published and provided with opus numbers has little or nothing to do with the order of their composition. With the exception of his four-hand music, for which the contemporary demand must have been astounding, only a few of Schubert's major instrumental works were published during his lifetime: not more than three of the sonatas (Op. 42, 53 and 78), along with the C major Fantasy, the *Moments Musicaux* and the first two of the Impromptus. The rest of the Impromptus were not published until ten years after Schubert's death, when the publisher changed the key and time signature of No. 3, transposing it from G flat to G, and omitted a couple of repeats in the opening Impromptu of the second set, Op. 142.

One can distinguish roughly two main periods in Schubert's instrumental music. The first ends in 1819 and contains the first six symphonies and fifteen piano sonatas, eleven of which remained fragments. There follows a three-year gap in Schubert's instrumental production, during which time he concentrated mainly (and unsuccessfully) on composing *Singspiele*, a kind of German opera, while, of course, the flow of Lieder never stopped. Apart from sketches for an E minor symphony, the only instrumental work composed during this time was the movement for string quartet in C minor of 1820, which already foreshadows his later, 'mature' style – that of the period starting in the autumn of 1822 and terminated by his death. The masterpieces of this period are the last eight sonatas, the last three string quartets, both piano trios, the Octet, the String Quintet, and the Unfinished and Great C major symphonies, as well as all the important four-hand works.

With the exception of a few pieces written for virtuoso display in the concert hall, such as some of the violin music and the Variations on 'Trockne Blumen' for flute and piano, nearly all of these compositions are on the same high level of accomplishment. By comparison, the compositions of the earlier period are of lesser importance, although they include such delightful works as the earlier symphonies, the *Trout* Quintet and the smaller of the A major sonatas, which has sometimes been mistaken for a later work of 1825. In these works, Schubert can be seen as a young composer gradually and playfully exploring large forms. He has not yet come to terms with Beethoven and he sees no necessity to rush his fences. When one looks at the Unfinished Symphony and the *Wanderer* Fantasy, which he composed in the autumn of 1822, the impression is strikingly different. That his venereal disease supposedly started at the same time may well be a coincidence, and I do not wish to add new myth to old prejudice; but it is not too difficult to imagine that the shock of this illness made Schubert gather his forces with almost desperate intensity, faced as he was with the possibility that the span of his life might be limited.

The later sonatas start with the rigidly concentrated A minor, Op. 143, in three movements, which closely follows the *Wanderer* Fantasy. Then we have a middle group of four sonatas, composed between 1824 and 1826, comprising the C major Sonata (the last two movements of which were not for nothing left unfinished); the great four-movement A minor, Op. 42, the D major, Op. 53 (with the strange, not completely convincing innocence of its finale) and the dreamy G major, Op. 78. Finally, the three sonatas of 1828, in C minor, A and B flat.

Let me give a few general characteristics of Schubert's later sonatas.

The first movement is always composed in sonata form and covers a wide emotional range. The tempo is more often moderate than fast. In the works of 1824 and 1825 the subsidiary theme is conceived as a variant of the principal theme.

Sonata in C major (D 840), first movement

Sonata in A minor, Op. 42 (D 845), first movement

Grand Duo in C major (D 812), first movement

The idea of monothematic composition, more fully realised in the *Wanderer* Fantasy, influenced Liszt and found its consequence in the dodecaphonic technique.

Expositions and recapitulations are nearly identical. To observe the repeat of the exposition is therefore in some cases not only superfluous, but positively damaging. There is only one sonata, the D major, where the repeat is indispensable; in three others it is optional, because the presentation of the material is more terse (A minor, Op. 143; A minor, Op. 42 and C minor).

The arbitrariness of some classical repeats will already be familiar to those who are acquainted with Haydn's sonatas. Beethoven, in some of his *Diabelli Variations*, leaves the most obvious considerations of proportion aside and omits repeats where the music is based on uniform patterns of rhythm sustained throughout the whole variation. I wonder how the experienced master felt about his much earlier work, the Sonata Op. 10, No. 2: he may have found the opening movement's second repeat unnecessary on account of the extreme simplicity of the material in the development.

The player at home may happily indulge in repeating the exposition of a Schubert sonata a dozen times for his private pleasure. In the concert hall he will be wise to consider that the perception of the audience, as well as his own concentration, should not be overtaxed.

That repeats are inevitably a matter of proportion is nothing more than a fashionable belief. Nor does it always follow from the inclusion of new material in those bars which especially lead back to the beginning that the composer counted on the execution of the repeat. In the case of the B flat Sonata, which is the most frequently lamented example, I am particularly happy to miss those transitional bars, so utterly unconnected is their jerky outburst to the entire movement's logic and atmosphere.

Recapitulations are followed by important codas which sum up the essence of the piece.

The second movement is most often an andante. It moves forward with the step and spirit of an idealised dance. This dance-like character is missing in the adagios of the *Wanderer* Fantasy (brooding) and the C minor Sonata (quiet, hymn-like), and in the *Con moto* of the D major Sonata, which is so often played at a funeral pace. If not in variation form, the second movement invariably follows the same scheme: it has three or five sections (ABA, ABABA); the contrasting section is always more agitated – in the late works sometimes as if shaken by fever. The motion of section B is usually continued in the reprise of A. Towards the end of the movement at least part of the opening theme may be stated in its initial simplicity.

The third movement is a scherzo or fluent minuet, the trio being a *Ländler*. Only the last two sonatas abandon the Viennese character of the trio. The Sonata Op. 143 makes do without such a movement. The motion of the finale may be graceful, sprightly or frighteningly macabre. This last type is a Schubert specialty; we find these dances of death in the D minor and G major string quartets and in the A minor, Op. 143 and C minor sonatas. The rhythm of many of Schubert's finales shows Spanish or Hungarian influence. The final movements of the last three sonatas are more expansive and contain literal recapitulations, while the idiom of their slow movements has ceased to be 'alpine'. There are, in fact, only two instances in these works where the local colour is identifiably Viennese: the trios of the minuets of the C minor and A major sonatas.

Prejudice 2: Schubert modelled his sonatas on Beethoven's and failed

Schubert worshipped Beethoven. On his deathbed, he asked his friends not only for more of James Fenimore Cooper's books, but also for a performance of Beethoven's Quartet in C sharp minor, Op. 131, which had been published the previous year, but had not yet been performed. To hear this work must have been Schubert's last deep joy. And later, in his delirium, he was reported to have said, 'Take me away from here, from under the earth. Beethoven does not lie here'. But though he venerated Beethoven, Schubert was not overwhelmed by Beethoven's greatness. He admired the master far too much to challenge him on his own terms. And he must have been keenly aware of the basic differences in their temperaments, minds and backgrounds. As I have written elsewhere, compared to Beethoven the architect, Schubert composed like a sleepwalker. In Beethoven's sonatas we never lose our bearings; they justify themselves at all times. Schubert's sonatas happen. There is something disarmingly naïve in the way they happen.

Yet I do not want to imply that Schubert's music is primitive, let alone amateurish. Schubert's naïveté leaves room for a good deal of sophistication, as did Haydn's, and for a marvellous variety of mood, colour and texture. Therefore, to accept all-out simplicity as a cardinal virtue of the Schubert player is to accept an oversimplification; it would turn the music of a great composer into minor music. Just in case a warning is needed, let me quote Tovey: 'Nothing is more false than the doctrine that great music cannot be ruined in performance'. This prejudice belongs to the family of popular statements like 'There are no bad pianos, only bad pianists' or 'There are no bad orchestras, only bad conductors'.

It may well be that this 'accidental' quality in Schubert's sonatas is one of the main reasons why they are so dearly loved by present-day musicians and have been so much more readily accepted by the public within the last decades, along with Mahler's symphonies. The music of these two composers does not set self-sufficient order against chaos. Events do not unfold with graceful or grim logic; they could have taken another turn at many points. We feel not masters but victims of the situation. This reflects for many of us the experience of living in a world in which the exponential growth of problems seems to defy all conceivable solutions. Mahler, by the way, is known to have played one of Schubert's A minor Sonatas for his friends in Leipzig in 1887. The second idea in the last movement of Schubert's D major Sonata, bars 30–32, strikes us as typically 'Mahlerian'.

If we look in Schubert's sonatas for Beethoven's virtues, we shall find them full of flaws; they will seem formless, too long, too lyrical and harmonically overspiced. We should, instead, concentrate on the basic differences of their styles.

In my essay 'Form and Psychology in Beethoven's Piano Sonatas' I have already examined some evidence of Beethoven's logical energy as compared to Schubert's more random and episodic writing. Beethoven seems determined to create the firmest intellectual basis in order to make all matters of emotional character as unmistakable as possible. Schubert puts more trust in the directness of his emotions. Economy to him is hardly a matter of prime importance. And over all its prodigious emotional range, his music remains mysteriously episodic.

The resemblance of the beginning of Schubert's C minor Sonata to Beethoven's theme for his C minor Variations has often been quoted as proof of Beethoven's influence on Schubert. Yet it seems to me that the similarities of these two openings are less revealing than their differences.

In Beethoven's theme the opening bars give rise to expectations which, by the use of foreshortening, the concluding bars precisely fulfil. Schubert disappoints our structural expectations as early as bar 6. From here to bar 12 the music tries, but does not manage, to leave the ground. Schubert's bass is tied to the basic C until the transition which precedes the subsidiary theme in E flat starts to move away from reality to illusion. If Schubert has set out to create foreshortening in Beethoven's manner, he has failed. The question is, however, whether the foreshortening was meant to succeed, or whether its failure gives us a psychological clue. If we look at the course of events in this movement, we find that the initial feeling of despair is maintained. The structure of the theme justifies itself in retrospect. It gives the impression less of majestic grandeur than of panic. The leading character in this tragedy is being chased and cornered and looks in vain for a way of escape.

Whenever Beethoven attempted to convey a similar atmosphere of panic – we might think of his 'Sonata Pathétique' – he would, at the same time, offer consolation by adhering to his structural logic. Even in his most chaotic moments Beethoven chose (or could not help) to represent order, whereas the music Schubert composed in the middle section of the Andante of the great A major Sonata comes amazingly close to being chaos itself.

The same A major Sonata's last movement is strikingly related to the Rondo of Beethoven's Op. 31, No. 1. As both Charles Rosen and Edward T. Cone have observed, Schubert made very accurate use not only of Beethoven's general formal design, but also of many individual details of construction. Yet the result does not easily give its secret away. Schubert has significantly changed the proportion of sections, and his finale is distinctly different in atmosphere and a great deal wider in its emotional range.

In 1828 Schubert must have felt secure enough to learn from Beethoven without losing his identity. Any listener to Schubert's Rondo who did not know Beethoven's would by no means be reminded of Beethoven's style; he would probably consider it a particularly pure example of Schubert's instrumental lyricism. The listener to Beethoven's Rondo, on the other hand, unfamiliar with Schubert's, and unaware of the chronology, might find this movement more 'Schubertian' than anything this composer wrote, with the possible exception of the Rondo from the Sonata Op. 90. As it happens, this is the only other of Beethoven's pieces whose layout Schubert seems to have deliberately used as a model; his A major Rondo for piano duet, also of 1828, follows its formal pattern with similar liberties, and results.

Where Schubert modelled his music on Beethoven's, he succeeded.

Prejudice 3: Schubert's music is like the soft, comforting contours of the Austrian landscape

Whoever invented this description seems to have missed the bizarre, majestic and forbidding aspects of the Austrian countryside. The image of Schubert's music as being genial, pleasing, mellow and sentimental stems from the times when his melodies were misused in operettas. Schubert could be all these, though he seems to me very rarely sentimental. But he could be so many other things besides. Like all truly great composers, he defies pigeon-holing. It was Artur Schnabel who, in an article for the *Musical Courier* in 1928, pointed out that Schubert was no mere melodist, but a composer of intensely dramatic sonatas. Schubert's range of expression was miraculously wide. His dynamic indications alone belie the mellow lyricist: not only in his piano works does he expand previous dynamic limits to *ppp* and *fff*, following the example of Weber, whose E flat Polonaise of 1808 has *fff*, also songs like 'Der Doppelgänger' give evidence of Schubert's craving for the extreme, encompassing mere whisper and frenzied cry. His emotional scope as a sonata composer leads us from the severe determination of the Sonata Op. 143 to the roaming, quasi-improvising freedom of the first two movements of the great A major, which culminate in the feverish paroxysm of the Andante's middle section, leaving conventional construction so far behind that it needed Schoenberg to surpass its degree of anarchy in the third of his Piano Pieces, Op. 11.

Prejudice 4: Schubert's piano works are 'unpianistic'

An accusation like this seems slightly ludicrous to me at a time when pianists have accepted *Petruschka* and the unsurpassable pianistic perversions of Brahms's Second Piano Concerto. Who, in all seriousness, would compare such challenges to the few pages of the D major, C minor and C major sonatas, where Schubert forces onto the piano ideas which would be more comfortably executed on other instruments? Schumann, by the way, was full of praise for Schubert's sonorous piano style, which 'seems to come from the depths of the pianoforte'. However, his piano music neither idolises the facile performer nor respects the limitations of the instrument. Schubert himself was not a very brilliant player; he does not seem to have owned a piano and would hardly have had the time to practise anyway. Nevertheless, his instinct for the possibilities of the instrument was powerful, though it was rarely used for its own sake. I recall a recital at New York's Carnegie Hall, where a piano student said to his girlfriend, after a performance of the G major Sonata, 'I don't dig it. It's all music'.

Schubert's piano style is no less orchestral than it is vocal. In the *Wanderer* Fantasy, the piano is turned into an orchestra much more radically than had ever been done before; not only the individual colours of orchestral instruments are evoked, but also the full blast of the *tutti*. If you try to play the *Wanderer* Fantasy and Beethoven's Sonata Op. 106 on a piano of the 1820s, you will realise how much more Schubert's piece depended on the instruments of the future to come alive. Much the same applies to his Great C major Symphony in comparison with Beethoven's Ninth. The *Wanderer* Fantasy influenced Liszt decisively, not only in its approach towards piano sound and its demands on the stamina of the player, but also in its monothematic construction. The sonatas of 1823 to 1826 continue an orchestral style of writing which employs tremoli, fast octaves and repetitions. The first movement of the Unfinished C major Sonata comes closest to a piano reduction of a symphonic movement; and the D major Sonata suggests to us the possibility that the great C major Symphony in a first version may also have been composed at Gastein in 1825. The last three sonatas, on the other hand, seem more like disguised string quintets, and they were written in the year of the String Quintet, 1828, shortly before Schubert died.

We must ask ourselves whether these are works destined for another medium which found their way to the piano by mistake. We find the answer when we compare Liszt's transcription of the *Wanderer* Fantasy for piano and orchestra with a good performance of the original version: the latter is the more convincing. Schubert evokes an orchestra, a chamber music group or a Lieder singer on the piano, but he does it in pianistic terms. The opening of the second movement of the B flat Sonata may serve as an example.

One could imagine this opening played by a string quartet with pizzicato bass notes, and indeed I have heard a pianist who tried to perform it that way. But this is a misunderstanding: the pedal has to give the mild glow to the *pp* cantilena of the two violins (or singers), which would otherwise sound rather pale and unsustained, while the accompanying figure adds to the *cantabile* quality and makes it dynamically more vibrant. Even if Schubert in his manuscript had not given one of his rare pedal indications at the beginning of the line, we would know from the layout of the sound that the pedal has to maintain the harmonies through each bar There are many other instances of short bass notes held by the pedal, as for example in this passage from the second movement of the *Wanderer* Fantasy:

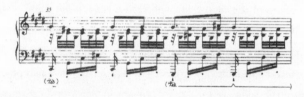

In Schubert's piano music – as also in Liszt's – Anton Rubinstein's assertion that the pedal is the soul of the piano comes true. Without the controlled, generous and inspired use of the pedal, Schubert's music remains buried within the conventional self-containment of the piano which he left behind. Unfortunately, Schubert's notation is often misunderstood in this respect. There are two possible methods of notation: either the composer writes down how long the note should sound, or he indicates how long the finger should or can be kept on the key. We could call these the musical notation and the technical notation. The two can, but do not have to, be identical, because the pedal can make the sound continue after the finger has left the key. Schubert's notation is technical. The value of the notes, as Schubert wrote them down, does not always apply to the duration of sound as musically necessary.

As Schubert's pedal markings are a good deal sparser even than Beethoven's, it is left to the imagination of the player where the pedal has to help the notation. If I were to play, for instance, bars 33–4 from the second movement of the C major Sonata (D.840)

without the necessary pedal, it would introduce an alien character to the context it would sound grotesque rather than grand and it would lose its orchestral richness. Now this is a fairly clear case of sustained bass notes where the fingers could not hold the keys. The opening of the second movement of the D major Sonata is an example of where the fingers *should* not hold the keys, even though they would be available to do so.

Its staccato chords have probably to be understood plus pedal: Schubert wrote the word *legato* on top of the first bar. It may be surprising to those who are not experienced pianists to learn that it makes a difference whether we play staccato, portato or legato within the pedal: but it does colour the sound differently and retains some of the characteristics of *secco* articulation. Generally, however, when Schubert wants detached notes tied by pedal, he puts dots *and* slurs: ⌢ ⌢.

Among the innovations Schubert introduced into piano literature is the expressive use of string tremoli, as in the second movement of the *Wanderer* Fantasy,

or in the first of the Posthumous Piano Pieces D.946. Schubert writes them down in the simplest possible manner. But his notation should not be more than a point of departure for the imagination of the player. It is essential to adapt the tremolo figures in the first movement of the Sonata Op. 143, for instance, so as to bring out their musical meaning and orchestral colour. Here, as so often, the performer should imagine himself to be a conductor rather than a pianist.

Renderings of tremolo figures that are all too literal may be the reason for the belief that tremoli are badly suited to the piano. It should be remembered that Liszt delighted in tremoli all his life, whether he used them in an orchestral manner in 'Vallée d'Obermann', as an imitation of the cimbalom in his

Eleventh Hungarian Rhapsody or as a poetic evocation of water in *Les jeux d'eau à la Villa d'Este.*

Schubert was still a young composer when he died. He was not used to hearing his instrumental works performed. To quote John Reed: 'The piano sonata had an old-fashioned air about it. Public performance of a piano sonata was a very rare event (only one of Beethoven's sonatas, it is said, was performed publicly in his lifetime), and in the domestic market the demand was all for fantasies, dances, duet pieces ('brilliant, but not too difficult') and trivial salon pieces'. Schubert's notation did not always develop the practical clarity of that of Beethoven's middle and late years. Like Mozart's, his notation is that of a *cantabile* composer, a string player or singer. Mozart and Schubert have in common the trait that their melodic invention is often vocal. Mozart was criticised by Nageli, one of the leading writers on music at the beginning of the nineteenth century, because his instrumental music was not, like Haydn's, purely enough instrumental; Nageli called it too operatic. In Schubert's music we hear the Lieder singer (in the last movement of the A major Sonata, D.959), the narrator (in the opening of the A minor Sonata, Op. 42) or the rather strange combination of a narrating male choir (in the opening of the second movement of the D major Sonata).

It is not enough to imagine Schubert's melodies sung or fiddled: we have to translate their *cantabile* into pianistic terms. The main problem is the understanding of accents. *Cantabile* accents often cannot be played on the piano as positive accents, that is, as isolated louder notes. They usually have to be prepared, and lend some, or even most, of their emphasis to the upbeat; or they can be made meaningful by a change of colour (balance); or an accompaniment figure can discreetly suggest an increase in intensity within the accented note. Schubert was an accent maniac. Some of his accents are negligible: I prefer the beginning of the Great C major Symphony without obvious accents in the horn.

Some of Schubert's notation habits are surprisingly old-fashioned. His writing of appoggiaturas in his songs has fortunately been taken care of since Friedländer's edition and cannot do much more harm. But there is hardly a composer after the Baroque age whose rhythm is so frequently 'misspelt'. Whenever Schubert wants to use triplets in a quadruplet time scheme he writes not ♩ ³♪, but ♫. This rhythm, then, has often to be adjusted to its rhythmic surroundings in the Baroque manner.

Neither the manuscript nor the first print of the song 'Wasserfluth' from *Die Win-terreise* leaves the slightest doubt that the polyrhythm usually produced is wrong: the dotted rhythm has to be adjusted to the triplets where they occur together and, I should like to add, most probably where it stands alone as well.[69]

From my experience of Schubert's works, and my knowledge of manuscripts and first prints, I am inclined to think that the adjustment of dotted rhythms, even in slower tempi, is the rule, and polyrhythm the exception. (If there is any evidence for soft contours in Schubert's music, here it is.) In the middle section of the slow movement of the B flat Sonata, the dotted rhythm has to go with the sextuplet.

There are, however, a fair number of exceptions and doubtful cases. One of the exceptions seems to be in the Adagio of the C minor Sonata, where an adjustment

---

69 No composer in a sane mind would have written down the last right-hand chord in bar 3, as well as bars 17 and 45, in such a way if the semiquavers needed to be played after the triplet.

of the demisemiquavers in bar 29 ff. would diminish the feeling of continuity established before, and weaken the sinister impact of the following octave leaps,

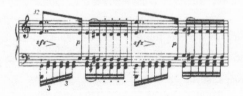

whereas the later episode after the first recapitulation of the opening theme (bar
62 ff.), with its continuous triplets, demands adjustment for as long as the triplets
last (bar 78), again for the reason that greater continuity is thereby suggested until
the accompaniment switches to demisemiquavers and gives the signal for the dotted rhythm to take over.

Schubert was not the last composer to write 'dotted triplets'. There are plenty of
them in Schumann's first Novelette and particularly in Chopin's *Polonaise-Fantaisie*.

For the musician dealing with Schubert's sonatas, another practical hazard is that
some of the editions are full of mistakes. The necessity of using a text which cleanly
reproduces Schubert's original manuscripts, or the first prints where they are relevant, or both, can not be stressed enough, even if this text at some points is only
raw material for the performer. The Lea pocket scores, which have the word *Urtext*
on the cover, are in fact merely a reproduction of Breitkopf & Härtel's old 'Complete Edition' with its abundance of alterations and mistakes.

The problem starts with Schubert himself. If Beethoven has been called a bad
proofreader, Schubert, in the case of the first print of his *Wanderer* Fantasy and
his Sonata Op. 42, appears to have been no proofreader at all. After the rediscovery of the manuscript, at least the text of the *Wanderer* Fantasy has been restored
in recent editions. The manuscript of Op. 42 unfortunately is missing: it thus
remains our not too demanding task to recompose the four bars which were left
out by mistake in the first variation of the second movement, as they are still
missing in all modern editions. Paul Badura-Skoda was the first to comment on
these bars; he has also pointed out a missing bar of rest in the finale, after bar
154, and I should like to add to the list of mistakes a wrong octave in variation 4
(bar 114) of the Andante, where the fourth octave in the left hand should read
G instead of F.

In the second movement of the G major Sonata, manuscript and first edition differ in one important point: of eight turns which adorn the theme and its recapitulations in the manuscript, seven are omitted in the first print. Is it fair to blame the engraver for so many omissions? It seems much more likely that Schubert had second thoughts before the sonata went into print – it was one of the three published during his lifetime – and left out the turns where they are unnecessary. Once one becomes familiar with the unadorned version of the theme, these turns sound irritatingly conventional. Only the extensively ornamented first recapitulation asks for turns, and only here, so I believe, has the engraver omitted the first of the two (bar 82) by mistake. If I had not checked the first print, I would never have discovered the discrepancy: two modern *Urtext* editions present all the turns according to the manuscript. One edition omits any reference to the matter, while the information provided by the other is incomplete and misleading.[70]

Most texts of the later A major Sonata give a wrong reading of bars 7 and 8 of the Scherzo, owing to errors in Schubert's manuscript; a sketch for the movement in the Vienna Municipal Library shows the right notes.

should read

Most performances of the D major Sonata, including Schnabel's, follow the distortions of the Breitkopf & Härtel edition, with its two excess bars, one in the second and one in the fourth movement, apart from the large number of wrong notes and wrong or missing dynamic markings.

---

70   Recently, Tirimo's edition (Wiener Urtext Ausgabe) has put it right – or very nearly, as it erroneously gives a turn to bar 164.

Finally, I should like to go back to my starting point and ask: Why has Schubert been neglected as an instrumental composer? Here is a short list of reasons.

1)   The neglect originated in Schubert's lifetime. Schubert's personal appearance was unprepossessing. There was no visible sign of the genius.

2)   Schubert was neither a solo concert performer nor a teacher who would pass on a tradition of performance.

3)   Apart from his four-hand music, most of his instrumental works were not published and performed until long after the composer's death. The Great C major Symphony (if we are to believe John Reed) was rehearsed in Vienna in its first version in 1826, but put aside because of its length and difficulty. In 1839 another performance was attempted, but at the first rehearsal the musicians refused to carry out the necessary number of rehearsals for the whole work. In the same year, in Mendelssohn's Leipzig performance, the work was considerably cut. The first complete performance took place in Vienna in 1850.

4)   Vogl, the singer, convinced the audience of the Schubertiads of Schubert's genius as a Lieder composer. The view of Schubert as a miniaturist, and his youth, seemed to preclude the ability to master big forms. Franz Grillparzer's text for the inscription on Schubert's tombstone can be taken as the opinion of Schubert's friends: 'Music buried here a noble property, but far more beautiful hopes'.

5)   The Classicism of music lovers. Schubert's expansive and often unpredictable music contradicted Beethoven's structural power, or Mendelssohn's easy clarity.

6)   The Romanticism of music lovers. They mistrusted the use of apparently conventional musical forms.

7)   Schubert's piano works often surpassed the possibilities of his instruments, as the Great C major Symphony surpassed the size and performing habits of contemporary orchestras. To play many lines of difficult and 'ungratifying'

accompaniment in its final movement caused a wave of protest among the
second violins.

8)   The Vienna of the 1820s indulged in a Rossini craze and adored the easy-going.
     Later, in 1839, when two movements of the Great C major Symphony were
     finally played, there was an aria from Donizetti's *Lucia di Lammermoor* per-
     formed in between. Of the important Schubert pioneers, only Brahms was
     connected with Vienna; Schumann, Mendelssohn, Liszt, Dvořák, George
     Grove – none of them was Viennese. To see four of the great composers of the
     nineteenth century among Schubert's most faithful admirers ought to impress
     those who persist in the belief that Schubert, though gifted, was not sufficiently
     professional. As a fitting conclusion, I should like to quote Liszt, who said of
     Schubert:[71] 'Such is the spell of your emotional world that it very nearly blinds
     us to the greatness of your craftsmanship.' (Fast lässest Du die Grösse Deiner
     Meisterschaft vergessen ob dem Zauber Deines Gemütes.)

(1974)

---

71   In a letter to Sigmund Lebert, 12 February 1868.

A cast of Schubert's life mask.

Photograph © John Batten, London (Collection Alfred Brendel)

Schubert's Last Sonatas

SCHUBERT'S DEATH DEPRIVED us of a wealth of possible masterpieces, though hardly, as Franz Grillparzer s epitaph suggests, of even fairer accomplishment. The last three sonatas should not be taken as a final message. As far as we know, they were composed in the brief period between May and September 1828. The fair copy was made just a few weeks before Schubert died of typhoid, his constitution already weakened by syphilis and by a burst of productivity frantic even by his standards. Since the death of his mother, he may have had to come to terms with a growing awareness of his mortality. Yet, when he completed his last sonatas (and most probably also the C major Quintet) in the autumn of 1828, it seems to me that he had no intimation of imminent death.

The style of Schubert's last year is not in any sense the kind of late style which I can perceive (*pace* Wolfgang Hildesheimer) in late Mozart. Admittedly, in the first two movements of Schubert's B flat Sonata, in the Adagio of the C minor Sonata and in the slow movement of the String Quintet, a new gentle, serene, hymnic facet can be identified; but this is less surprising if we consider the Mass in E flat, a major achievement of the same period, which left its mark on the instrumental music composed during those hectic months, just as it in turn was marked by the expressionism of the Heine songs. Plagal harmonies, like those which conclude the Gloria and 'Et incarnatus' of the Mass, can be found not only at the close of some sonata movements but also at the heart of the A major Sonata's first subject which, in the first draft, was conceived without the energetic left-hand leaps, in the manner of a chorale:

Many other themes in Schubert's sonata trilogy are based on or contain plagal harmonies as well.

The opening of the B flat Sonata also belongs in this 'sacred' sphere. Schubert offers solemn introspection, while Mozart's Piano Concerto K.595 in the same key seems to suggest, in its deceptive simplicity, childhood regained. There is, however, common ground: in the vocal character of the melodies, in the undemonstrative calm with which both works unfold and in their all-pervading melancholy.

The reappearance of a B flat major theme in the remote musical perspective of B minor, at the beginning of the development of K.595, reminds us of Schubert's passion for chromatic neighbouring keys. In his B flat Sonata, Schubert himself brings off an unforgettable harmonic projection of a very different kind: at the end of the development he quotes, *pianississimo*, his main theme in the tonic key of B flat – yet we experience it, in relation to the surrounding D minor sphere, as if from the remotest distance. When, only a few lines later on, the theme is restated in its original guise, our standpoint has changed completely; by now the theme, in its gentle serenity, has come so close that the listener can sense it as if from within.

Our perception of this theme is crucial for understanding the whole movement. Its trill (bar 8) has been described as a 'disturbing foreign element' (Dieter Schnebel)[72] or as a '*Movens*'; in contrast to the '*Quietiv*' of the calmly soaring melody (August Halm).[73] I prefer to see it as the disclosure of a third dimension.

---

72   Dieter Schnebel, 'Schubert: Auf der Suche nach der befreiten Zeit', *Denkbare Musik*, 1972.

73   August Halm, *Beethoven*, 1927.

The pause allows the sound to disappear as if into infinity. There is no break in continuity – the dominant chord easily carries the tension through the pause to the next tonic; rather, a rapport is established between music and silence. (The timpani roll in the Sanctus of the Mass in E flat is a comparable case.) Schubert's first draft, which consists almost entirely of the melody, already contains this trill; but it also contains the notes G–F in the fourth bar, to which the trill relates.

The G flat trill could be called a darkened reflection of these notes. The major and minor second and their combination G–G flat–F continue to remain prominent. In the bass, F and G flat determine much of the exposition. A variant of the first subject reappears almost immediately (bar 20) in G flat: it seems as if, over a distance of eleven bars, the first trill has caused the second one to descend. Later a new, pleading theme is introduced in F sharp minor, and the development begins a fifth higher, in C sharp minor, which is also the key of the second movement. C sharp and F sharp are again present, as D flat and G flat, in the scherzo.

Time after time the final movement recalls its opening G octave, forcefully emphasised in the manner of a *fp* horn accent. Here G flat is present only, as a passing note between G and F; if this descent signifies a sigh, then it suggests comic relief rather than suffering or fatigue. In the touching epilogue, which seems to suspend time before the final stretta, the three-note descent emerges as a serious question. The ensuing bars subtly make us aware that G flat has ceased to pose a problem, and the sonata's *Dolens* (as I would call it) is finally overcome.

A brief presto coda exults in this achievement. Altogether, I find this movement distinguished by playful, graceful energy rather than by 'sighing fatigue' (Schnebel). Here, as in certain other points, Beethoven's last work, the B flat Rondo, written as an afterthought for his Op. 130 Quartet to replace the 'Grosse Fuge', offers a parallel.

Artur Schnabel and Eduard Erdmann were, to my knowledge, the first to play Schubert's sonata trilogy in one evening. After one of my performances of this wonderful, if strenuous, programme, a Viennese newspaper pronounced that even if I, who had turned my back on Vienna, were to deny the fact, I must have 'experienced' these works while resident in Schubert's city. How these sonatas, *Die Winterreise* and the Heine songs, the Mass in E flat or the String Quintet could be 'experienced' in present-day Vienna was not disclosed. Not that Schubert had ever been the kind of provincial musician that a cosmopolitan like Busoni chose to see in him. His music shows no shortage of elements from far beyond the city gates: in the finale of the B flat Sonata we detect, perhaps, a Hungarian flavour; in the third of his Posthumous Piano Pieces D.946 there are Bohemian dance rhythms (polka and sousedská); and the macabre finale of the C minor Sonata turns out to be a tarantella, which, like the whole work, is spiritually much closer to the black fantasies of Goya than to Schubert's painter friends Kupelwieser and Schwind.

What is a 'Viennese composer'? (Besides Schubert, the critic mentioned Gustav Mahler and Alban Berg.) A composer – penalised for failing to imitate Johann Strauss – whose music was so disquieting that it had to be inflicted on the Viennese belatedly and with great effort? In a letter of 1827, Schubert describes Metternich's Vienna: 'It is certainly rather big, but makes up for this by an absence of warmth, of openness, true thought, sensible words, and, in particular, of spirited deeds'. Even today, Vienna may be the right place for musicians to learn what a Strauss waltz is about. But it would be wishful thinking to claim that a Viennese Schubert tradition ever existed or still exists. Who in nineteenth-century Vienna, apart from Brahms and the Hellmesberger Quartet, took any interest in Schubert's instrumental music? (The Schubert enthusiasts Schumann, Mendelssohn, Liszt, Anton Rubinstein, Dvořák and George Grove were all occasional visitors.) How many of the great Schubert singers or conductors came from his home town or country? Where, until quite recently, were the Viennese pianists who championed Schubert's sonatas? For Sauer, Rosenthal and Godowsky they were of no consequence; they owe their discovery to Schnabel and Erdmann in the Berlin of the 1920s. True, Schnabel did study in Vienna, but, even if he had been advised to look at the unexplored Schubert sonatas, his teacher Leschetizky would scarcely have told him how they ought to be played.[74] Significantly, Schnabel's enormous influence as a teacher did not permeate Vienna at all.

Today, Vienna offers no more clues about Schubert than any other city. The panorama from the Belvedere may have remained unchanged since Schubert's time. But do people still live in one-room apartments – as Schubert's family did – and give birth to their children in an alcove which also serves as the kitchen? Do adults still play blindman's buff? Do manuscripts have to be submitted to the censor? Is the country governed by the secret police? Is that popular and suburban music which Schubert found so charming still a living musical presence, or just a beautiful relic of 'better days'? Even the Viennese assertion that 'Vienna remains Vienna' is no more than a Viennese delusion.

Schubert's last sonatas did not appear in print until eleven years after his death. Johann Nepomuk Hummel, a Mozart pupil and leading pianist, was Schubert's intended dedicatee; however, as Hummel died in 1837, the publishers decided on Schumann, who had warmly praised the E flat Piano Trio, the D minor Quartet and the piano sonatas in A major (D.845), D major and G major in his *Neue Zeitschrift für Musik*. Regrettably, the last sonatas disappointed him. He criticised their 'much greater simplicity [*Einfalt*] of invention' and Schubert's 'spinning out of certain musical ideas, where usually between one period and the next he interweaves new threads'. If Schumann intended to imply a greater concentration of musical material and the use made of it – if, that is, we were to interpret *Einfalt* as 'unity' – we could

---

74 The Viennese element in the scherzo of Schubert's D major Sonata is grossly exaggerated in Schnabel's recording.

agree and, unlike Schumann, approve. Alas, he also speaks of Schubert's 'voluntary renunciation of shining novelty, where he usually sets himself such high standards', and concludes: '[These pieces] ripple along from page to page as if without end, never in doubt as to how to continue, always musical and singable, interrupted here and there by stirrings of some vehemence which, however, are rapidly stilled'.

It is to be hoped that Schumann, in later years, became better acquainted with the works, and regretted his verdict. Not even from him will I accept that Schubert's sonatas 'ripple along'. The occasional 'stirrings of some vehemence' amount, not infrequently, to the grandest of dramatic developments if not, as in the C minor Sonata, the impetuosity of entire movements. As for a 'voluntary renunciation of novelty', the middle section of the A major Sonata's second movement alone should suffice as a striking refutation. Even today, this eruption of the irrational must rank among the most daring and terrifying pages in all music.

'As if without end' – Schubert's 'length', which Schumann, writing two years later of the Great C major Symphony, considered 'heavenly', came to be deemed his principal weakness. When Mendelssohn conducted the C major Symphony in Leipzig, he felt obliged to make cuts; in the early twentieth century the pianist Harold Bauer produced an abridged version of the B flat Sonata. Growing familiarity with Brucknerian and Mahlerian dimensions has since relaxed our perception of musical space. Aesthetic appetites have changed. We experience marathon concerts, huge television serials, the six-hour *Hamlet* in Berlin – whispered and in slow motion – while neo-Expressionist painters savage oversized canvases. Art is expected to forget all constraint, mix up disparate elements, be unreasonable, want more than it can achieve and achieve more than anybody can want. Boundless is beautiful. (The novel, on the other hand, which formerly encompassed entire worlds, has shrunk to something fragmentary, a dialogue between the writer and his obsessions.)

Schubert's music, which used to appear excessively long, is suddenly not long enough. Where some earlier pianists took the first movement of the B flat Sonata at an almost nervous *alla breve* (two beats to a bar), nowadays, in extreme cases, it is counted in eight, with the exposition repeat thrown in for good measure, making for a movement longer than the sum of the other three.

If I understand Schubert rightly, his tempo indication *molto moderato* calls for neither approach. *Moderato* or *mässig*, a term used by Schubert more often than by other composers, seems to imply the calm flow of a measured *allegro*; *molto moderato* would then correspond to a none too dragging *allegretto*. Schubert's avoidance of this word in the B flat Sonata or the first of his Impromptus may be explained by the fact that *allegretto*, like *largo* or *grave*, signifies not only a certain speed but also a certain character. Just like its amiable sound, the word suggests a graceful tripping or strolling. (Moreover, Schubert's first-movement tempo indications refer to the opening; except for the stable *allegro giusto* of the A minor Sonata D.784, the initial tempo of all these movements is modified during the course of the exposition to a more flowing or more measured pace.)

On the question of repeats, let me quote from an article by Antonín Dvořák,[75] which has so far gone unnoticed in the Schubert literature. One of the most affectionate and sensible statements about Schubert, it offers a number of critical insights that appear almost modern. Dvořák, while sharing the view that Schubert sometimes did not know when to stop, writes of the symphonies: 'If the repeats are omitted, a course of which I thoroughly approve, and which indeed is now generally adopted, they are not too long.' Dvořák loved Schubert and knew the classical masters. It would be as silly to accuse him of thoughtlessness or incompetence in questions of form as to accuse Brahms, of whom Edwin Fischer reported:

> How composers themselves sometimes feel about repeats is illuminated by what Johannes Brahms told a young musician who showed surprise that, in a performance conducted by Brahms, the exposition of the Second Symphony was not repeated. 'Formerly', explained Brahms, 'when the piece was new to the audience, the repeat was necessary; today, the work is so well known that I can go on without it.'

My intention is neither to 'improve' on Schubert nor to abolish repeats altogether. What Dvořák suggested (that Schubert is not too long, provided he is not made longer than necessary) seems particularly valid in the case of some sonata expositions. Repeat marks should not be taken as a command and obeyed unquestioningly, as if the section had been written out in full by the composer. Before deciding how to proceed, one should consider a number of points:

---

75   Antonín Dvořák (in co-operation with Henry T. Finck), 'Franz Schubert', *The Century Illustrated Monthly Magazine*, New York, 1894.

Does a repeat, within a work or movement, appear necessary, desirable, possible, questionable or harmful?

Was the repeat a concession to those listeners who, conditioned by preclassical dance forms, expected to be led back from the dominant to the tonic – a concession similar to that of incorporating minuets into symphonies and sonatas as an area of repose for sluggish ears?

How extensive is the exposition of a sonata movement, and how tersely or generously laid out is its musical material? (The exposition of Schubert's A major Sonata contains more than twice as many bars as that of Beethoven's 'Appassionata'; 'it exceeds even that of the 'Hammerklavier' Sonata, which, moreover, moves at about twice the speed, while presenting its material at the highest degree of density.)

How far does the exposition differ from the recapitulation? (In Schubert they are usually almost identical. Except for a few significant modulations and transitions, interrupted only by the development, the listener is allowed to wander twice through virtually identical musical landscapes.)

Are the movement's themes distinctly different in character (as is generally the case with Beethoven), or are they intimately connected (as sometimes with Schubert)?

Do the first two movements present a marked contrast (as with Beethoven's Allegro and Adagio), or do they inhabit neighbouring areas of tempo (as often with Schubert's Moderato and Andante)?

What are the consequences of a repeat for the equilibrium of all movements within the work? (In Schubert's last sonatas the final rondos adopt features of sonata form; their symmetrical scheme, with a central development section, seems to me much more happily matched if the first movement repeat is not taken.)

Finally, repeats should be considered in conjunction with the structure of a whole recital. In the case of a performance of the last three Schubert sonatas in one programme, they are ruled out.

Beethoven's repeats are immediately compelling, with very few exceptions. In Schubert, psychological considerations often overrule formal ones. In music, as with food, quantity can be an important factor. As the British critic Bernard Jacobson has wittily pointed out, both gourmand and gourmet, glutton and restrained epicure, have their musical equivalents. Some musicians seem quite unable to stop making music, unless they fall asleep. Similarly, there are critics – and Jacobson, with admirable candour, counts himself among them – who cannot have enough of a piece

they love. I side with the gourmets: my appreciation of food has not been tainted
by Marco Ferreri's notorious film *La grande bouffe*, in which a few gentlemen gorge
themselves to death. True gourmands avoid seeing it.

The great A major and B flat major Sonatas have stirred the repeat enthusiasts
more than other works: did Schubert not write out a few bars which lead back to
the beginning? To omit any original music by Schubert, we are told, is unforgivable;
it would be equally unjustified to make cuts elsewhere.

I beg to differ. Both expositions end in ways that do not permit a simple return
to the beginning. In certain external matters of form and notation, Schubert was
much more old-fashioned than Beethoven, and for this reason he wrote down the
disputed bars. Beethoven would doubtless have gone straight into the development;
in his 'Appassionata' the F minor exposition ends in A flat minor, while the development follows in the unexpected key of E major. It is intriguing to speculate on
how Beethoven, with Schubert's harmonic means, might have led back to the F
minor of the opening:

Whether in this or any other manner, Beethoven did not see fit to do so. Evidently
he was able to resist the pressures of convention where his music called for it.

Another argument advanced by the guardian angels of the B flat Sonata repeat
emphasises the amazing novelty of the transitional bars: they are supposed to add
something to the piece which would otherwise remain unsaid, and alter our perception of its character. Even if there were not so many counter-arguments – the
generosity of the exposition, the literal recapitulation, the lyric character of all themes

(and of the following Andante), the balance between movements – I would, for once, have to disagree with Schubert's judgement. An irrational explosion, such as occurs in the Andante of the A major Sonata, does not come out of the blue. It has its psychological bearing on the bleak melancholy of the movement's opening as well as on the chromatic episodes of the preceding Allegro. But which elements in the B flat Sonata justify the emergence of the transitional bars in question? Where are they announced? Should they be allowed to upset the magnificent coherence of his movement, whose motivic material seems quite unrelated to the new syncopated, jerky rhythm? Is the material or atmosphere of this transition taken up anywhere in the later movements? Should its irate dynamic outburst rob the development's grand dramatic climax of its singularity? Most painful to me, however, is the presentation of the trill in *fortissimo*: an event which elsewhere remains remote and mysterious is here noisily exposed. Schubert's first draft, in which the exposition was relatively brief, presents the trill in *pianissimo*.

Schubert could be admirably concise, not only in his *Moments musicaux* and countless songs but also in such a work as the A minor Sonata D.784. I hardly see him among the musical gourmands, anyway. Sketches for his last sonatas show – if one had not surmised it already – how self-critically he proceeded. They also reveal that Schubert's 'length' only appears obsessive where the music is intended to express an obsessive state of mind. In order to move freely, Schubert needs space. In some of his earlier sonatas certain ideas did not receive the ample treatment they deserved. In the sketches for the later sonatas, Schubert's expanding interpolations are particularly convincing. It may be hard to believe, but this is how the lyrical first subject of the A major Sonata appears in the first draft:

Schubert subsequently elaborated on it as follows:

Classical forms define boundaries. The space which Schubert requires in order to move freely has little to do with Classical definitions. Haydn did not need such space, although his desire to surprise, his tendency to wander, his naïveté as well as his daring may at times resemble Schubert's. (Haydn springs surprises, while Schubert, I think, allows himself to be surprised.) Mozart's forms give constant evidence of a perfection seemingly without aim or constraint. For Beethoven, form is the triumph of order over chaos, a triumph furthermore of its concord with whatever has to be 'expressed'. Schubert's forms are a matter of propriety, a 'veil of order' – to quote Novalis – which barely conceals the most beautiful chaos music has ever seen.

As early as 1827 the Leipzig *Allgemeine Musikalische Zeitung* wrote of the first movement of the G major Sonata that 'within its not unusual formal layout, everything internal [*alles Innere*] is uncustomary and full of fantasy'. Gustav Mahler spoke of

Schubert's 'freedom below the surface of convention',[76] and Hans Költzsch, the author of a book which for several decades remained the only (and largely dubious) investigation of Schubert's sonatas,[77] offered the view that Schubert's particular quality as a 'Romantic' lay in his having dissolved the classical legacy from within by preserving much of its outer shell. According to Költzsch, 'isolated deviations from the scheme indicate how far removed the new forces are from tradition', while, at other times, 'the same effect is achieved by an all too schematic compliance with formal usage'.

In his larger forms, Schubert is a wanderer. He likes to move at the edge of the precipice, and does so with the assurance of a sleepwalker. To wander is the Romantic condition; one yields to it enraptured (as in the finale of the A major Sonata), or is driven and plagued by the terror of finding no escape (as in the C minor Sonata). More often than not, happiness is but the surface of despair. Suddenly, the mind is overcast. Nothing is more typical of Schubert than these febrile afflictions of unease and horror, which in the most extreme case (the second movement of the A major Sonata), hardly attempt to maintain any 'veil of order': apart from its chromatic bass line, the only remnants of organisation are a few of those motivic particles common to all three sonatas, which I shall discuss later.

Order, even when only an adornment through which the chaos of emotion shines, is decisive because it makes the work of art possible. Such order, however, is never complete. Modern science seems to have moved away from the idea of a rigorous master plan behind the evolution of nature. The concept is no longer that of an engineer strictly realizing a design but of a tinkerer, as François Jacob has suggested, who uses the available components as best he can, mending and combining them, producing intentional or random mutations. The 'natural' process of composition is similar. The composer limits himself to the available basic material, which is usually provided at the beginning of a piece; he sifts, rearranges, varies, develops or comments, with the aid of hypothetical working schemes which leave a small but important area open to chance – and whim.

Among the concepts of order which left an imprint on Schubert's sonatas is that of the interconnection of themes, the cohesion of movements. Just how verifiable is this? The 'inner unity' of a cyclic composition has been much discussed, with rather

---

76 'ungebundene Anlage unterhalb des Üblichen'.

77 *Franz Schubert in seinen Klaviersonaten*, Leipzig, 1927.

more reliance on interpretative notions than on evidence provided by the musical material. The first to mention a 'substance common to all movements' was, to my knowledge, Walter Engelsmann (*Beethovens Kompositionspläne*, Augsburg, 1931). According to him, each Beethoven sonata is 'developed from one single principle subject or motif in all its sections'. It is scarcely surprising that Engelsmann did not manage to present convincing proof for his ambitious thesis.

The pipe-dream of a system into which everything can be crammed and by which everything can be evaluated is a temptation analysts can rarely resist; it is all too easy to see what is hardly there while overlooking what should be self-evident. In Rudolph Réti's over-complicated motivic analysis of Beethoven's 'Sonata Pathétique', there is no mention of the significance to all themes of the fourth and fifth, or of their summation as an octave.

Masterpieces never betray all their secrets, not even those of craftsmanship. Invariably, only a few threads are disclosed. It is considerably more profitable to pursue the thread of motivic connections than opinion in Europe and in the USA would acknowledge. The word 'analysis' is sometimes held to stand for a process of dissolving the whole into its component parts, while it ought in fact to guide us from specific details towards the whole. Long before the advent of twelve-tone technique, motivic and thematic cross-references provided the most unequivocal hallmarks of musical cohesion. When Hans Keller sought to unearth the latent elements of unity in the manifest contrasts of a work, however, I asked myself whether such elements had necessarily to be latent. Is manifest proof of musical unity not widely overlooked? I am not, of course, referring to such patently audible ones as the dotted rhythm of the *Wanderer* Fantasy, Berlioz's *idée fixe* or those transformations in Liszt and César Franck which leave the notes of a theme easily recognisable while its character changes. (In Liszt's B minor Sonata, the background of Beethovenian motivic relationships is considerably more interesting than the evident metamorphosis of Mephisto into Gretchen.) A hidden connection, says Heraclitus, is stronger than an obvious one (*Fragments*, 54). It is the more subtle motivic coherence which in the long run leaves the deeper mark, provided that a certain measure of musical common sense, a firm ground of verifiable fact, is not abandoned. Let me explain the motivic connections in Beethoven's so-called 'Appassionata'. My awareness of such connections stems from my own experience in dealing with all the Beethoven sonatas, even if my findings tally with some of Réti's. I have gratefully adopted his term 'interversion', a word that signifies those variants of motifs or motivic groups in which only the sequence of notes is changed.

The opening of Beethoven's Sonata Op. 57 contains:

1)   A (broken) triad;

2)   An octave (as octave leap or area or transposition of a phrase);

3)   A second as appoggiatura or trill, most frequently in its simplest form of three notes, and in the degree of the dominant;

4)   The area of a third, filled in by the combination of the simple trill (C-D-C) with the fast trill (D-E-D);

5)   Note repetition.

Of lesser consequence, and not included in this survey, are the intervals of a fourth and fifth.

The D (D flat)–C of the trill reappears before long as a 'drum-tap' appoggiatura in the bass (3′).

In the further course of the variation theme, the central pitches Db-C-Db appear as
a variant of the 'drum-tap' theme, returning three more times in its second part.
(I use the term 'central pitches' for notes which recur prominently throughout the
whole work.) The theme's triadic component indicates that the idea of the triad,
whether broken or chordal, is a constituent element of the piece; in variations 2 and
3 we find the triad dissolved in figuration.

The larger structure of some themes is permeated by the changing note (3). In
bars 3 and 4 of the first subject, the first note can already be heard as the beginning
of the changing note, as Schenker and Réti have shown.

The harmonic scheme of the opening

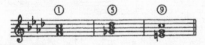

recurs in the third subject as well as in the principal subject of the finale. In the case of the Andante, the Neapolitan harmony is transformed into a subdominant chord with *sixte ajoutée*.

In the coda of the finale, what appears to be a new theme is derived from the first subsidiary theme of the first movement or, more precisely, from its reappearance in bars 239–41, linking one stretta with the other.

Not every work proceeds with such rigour. Some are assembled playfully around a principal idea, as is Beethoven's Op. 10, No. 3, which revolves around a short motif with its inversions and interversions.

Other works go back to a number of basic formulas at random or develop new materials as they proceed. Groups of works can also be interdependent. Beethoven's last three sonatas (Opp. 109, 110 and 111), for instance, make use of the area of the sixth as a combination of third plus fourth (and six-four chords). Within this hexachord, steps of thirds and fourths occur more frequently, a succession of six neighbouring notes more rarely, as in the second movement and Arioso of Op. 110. A zigzag of thirds and fourths distinguishes not only the fugue theme but also the beginning of the first movement of Op. 110 (here the left hand assists the right).

Analogously, Var. 5 of Op. 109 features melody and bass together.

Var. 2 already seems to move in Op. 110 territory.

At the beginning of Op. 109, the zigzag of thirds and fourths is similarly evident.

Here the six notes of a hexachord between tonic and third are simultaneously provided by the bass. They characterise the bass line of all principal themes in this sonata.

Another hexachord area is that between G sharp (III) and B (V) in the middle
voice. We find it recurring not only in this sonata

but also figuring prominently in Op. 111.

The fugato theme in the development of Op. III offers a chromatic zigzag variant.

While the composition of Beethoven's Opp. 109, 110 and III was spread out over three years (1820–22), that of another famous trilogy, Mozart's final symphonies, appears to have been completed in a matter of months (in 1788). In this respect, and in their musical magnitude, these symphonies are comparable to Schubert's last sonatas. Here the question arises: what happens when a great composer creates a series of works virtually side by side? Their individual characteristics will certainly be strictly defined. But what of the thematic-motivic material? Is it to be rigorously specified or will there be give and take? In both Mozart and Schubert I find a freely communicating common property of motivic, thematic and harmonic elements, which lends Schubert's original titles (*Sonate I*, *Sonate II*, *Sonate III*) a significance well beyond that of accidental juxtaposition or commercial viability. We encounter a family of pieces.

Looking at Mozart's last symphonies, one is struck first of all by the astonishing similarity of two themes.

It may take longer to realise that both are derived from the slow introduction of K. 543.

This opening contains the same three- or fourfold note repetition which figures in

every movement of all three symphonies (more frequently in its threefold form).
The beginnings of K.550 and K.551 are likewise infused with the threefold beat.

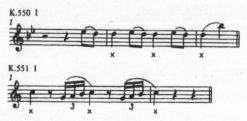

The opening of the *Jupiter* Symphony offers a premonition of the opening bars of
its finale.

This is only one of at least eight statements of these bars within the whole work. In
the minuet, the first six notes of the finale theme are stated in retrograde.

The second part of the finale theme (bars 5–8) is anticipated in the trio section of
the same minuet

and, most elaborately, in the ten-bar theme of the preceding Adagio.

The first four notes, or more extended portions, of the finale theme already feature frequently in the other two symphonies, as in the second movement of K.550

or in the last movement of K. 543.

In the first movement of K. 543, the opening of the Allegro presents the initial motif of the *Jupiter* finale no fewer than three times.

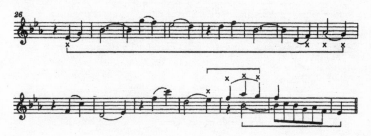

Bars 27–9 introduce another striking familial trait of all three symphonies: the melodic use of the six-four chord, often ascending and sometimes, significantly, starting with a leap of a sixth.

Its position is usually in the tonic, less frequently in the subdominant. In the *Jupiter* Symphony, all principal subjects relate to the subdominant sixth of C major, C-A. The beginning of the G minor Symphony's second movement sounds to my ears like a combination of the six-four chord and the initial notes of the *Jupiter* finale, which also appear in the first four bars of the K.551 Adagio as a complement to the melody.

Most of the significant note sequences and note areas in Schubert's sonata trilogy are provided by the first lines of the C minor Sonata. Like a large quarry, this rugged theme contains building material for future use.[78] Two figures in particular are of far-reaching consequence: those of bars 7–8 (*b, c* and example 40) and 14–15 (*h*). The first moves within the compass of a minor sixth, the second within a diminished fifth; I shall refer to them as the *Sixth* and *Fifth formulas.* The first five notes of the Sixth formula (*h'*) are related in retrograde to the Fifth formula (*h*). Both formulas are stressed within the theme by being repeated and varied.

In all three sonatas, formula *h* proves to have the greatest impact. It is taken up in the same key in C minor II (ex. 2).[79] The beginning of the minuet (6), abbreviated by one note and in the minor key, looks back to the lyricism of the Adagio and of the Allegro's second subject. The same note area, as we can see in exx. 4, 6, 7 and 9, can be harmonised in major as well as minor. Exx. 9–13 are distinguished by the same 'A major position', even when located in the B flat Sonata (12, 13).

---

78   On pp. 166–80 I have assembled a series of examples which will demonstrate the motivic coherence of the three works.

79   For the sake of conciseness, movements are denoted by Roman numerals.

The G-F appoggiatura in the first subject of the B flat Sonata, which I mentioned above, is ambiguous. It belongs to the middle voice, legitimizing the 18-bar melody of the soprano voice as an extended version of formula *h*. At the same time, it is an integral part of this melody which, without these two notes, sounds trivial; at the beginning of the scherzo and in the coda of the finale, 'both voices' are thoroughly amalgamated (21, 22). Another amalgamation precedes the third subject of the first movement, following the notes F-G-F with the initial notes of the work, a terse statement of the opening material which clears the way for the new theme (24).

The effect of the beginning of the C minor Sonata (formula *a*, 25) is pursued in exx. 26–34. The opening melody of the finale has its roots in the Sixth formula *b* and its continuation formula *f* (35, 36), if one is willing to accept the workings of interversion. Schubert changed the first two bars twice; the final version comes closer to formula *d*, while the original had varied figures from the first and third movements.

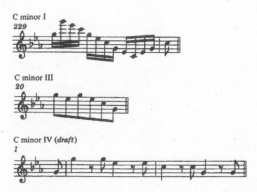

From this opening Schubert had distilled the beginning of the episode, which also takes up the rhythm of the preceding chordal blows.

Along with the plausibility of such motivic relations, the harmonic connection of the initial version with the minuet has been lost.

Examples 1–8

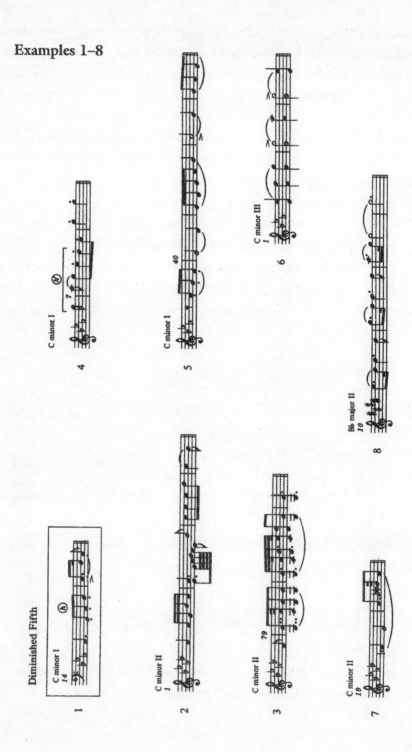

Examples 9–15

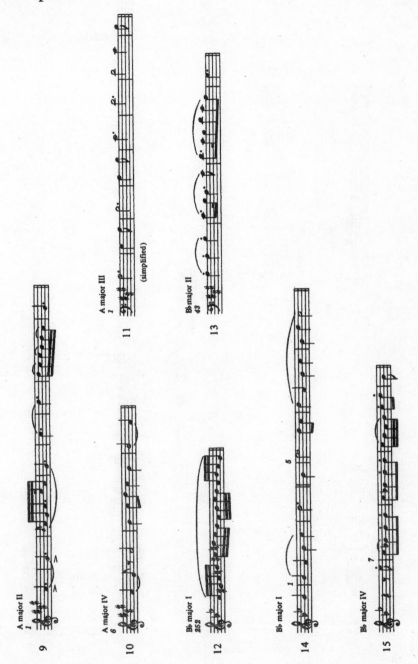

Examples 16–20

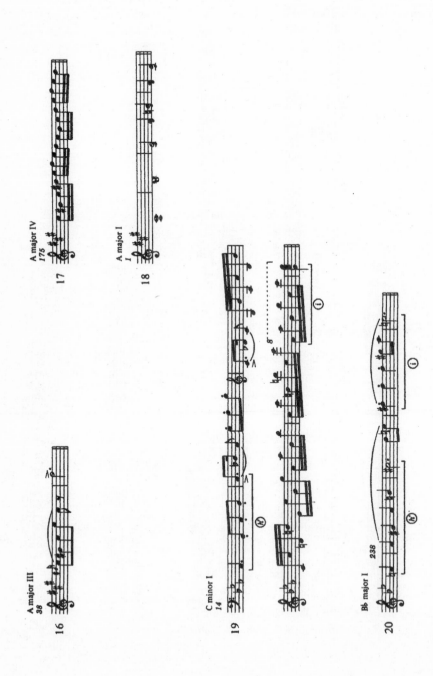

Examples 21–24

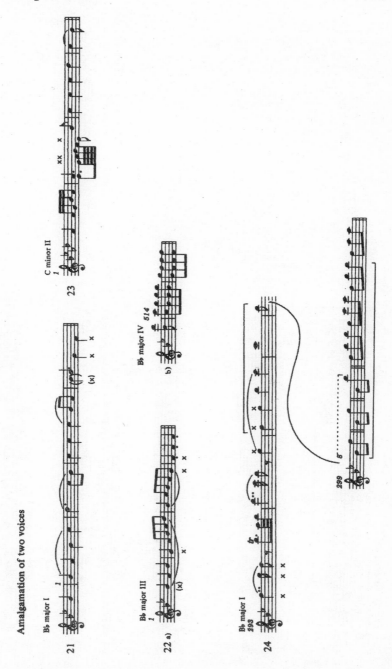

Examples 25–30

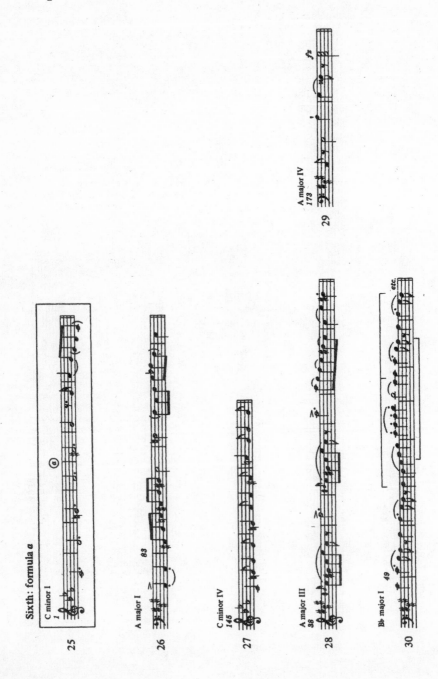

Examples 31–37

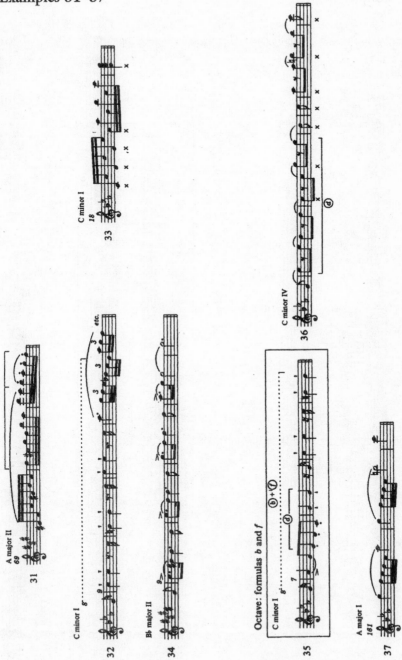

Examples 38–42

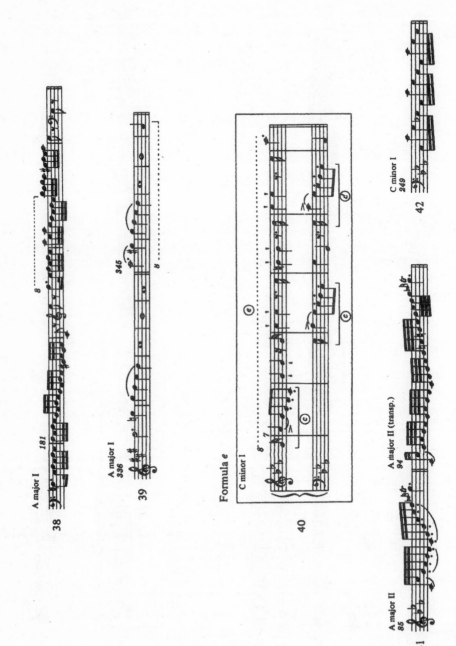

Examples 43–54

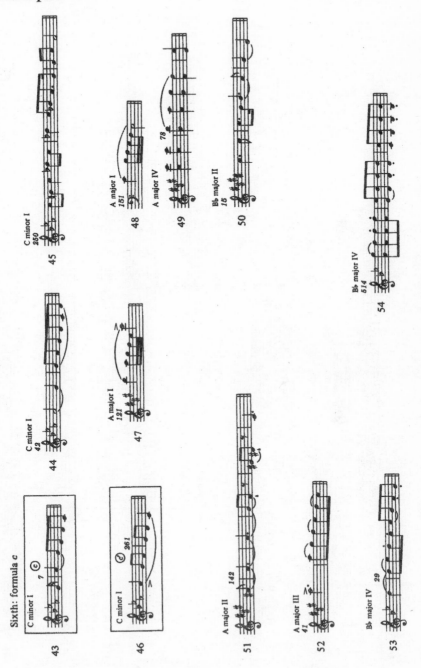

Examples 55–63

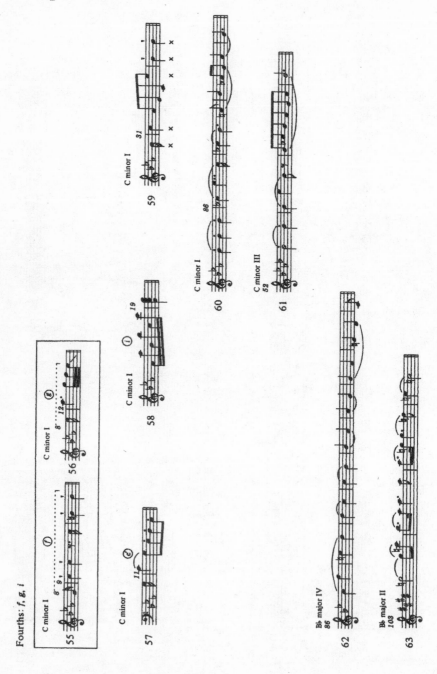

Examples 64–71

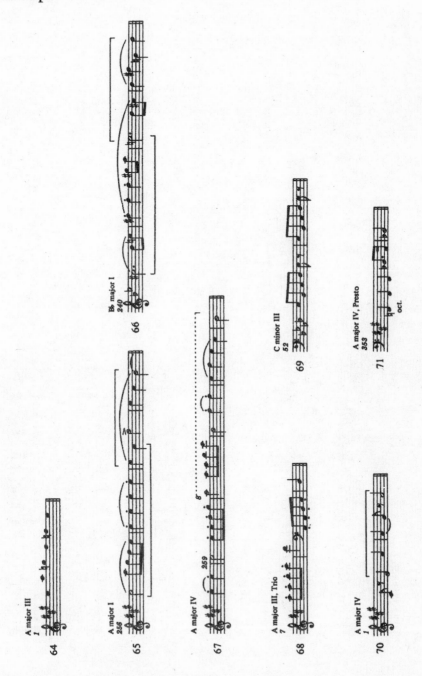

Examples 72–79

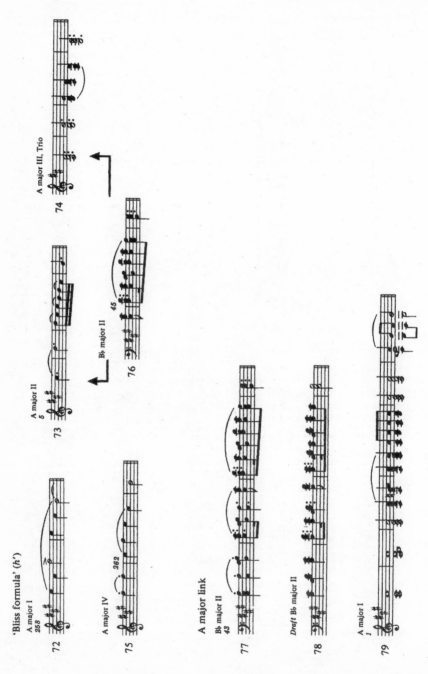

Examples 80–82E

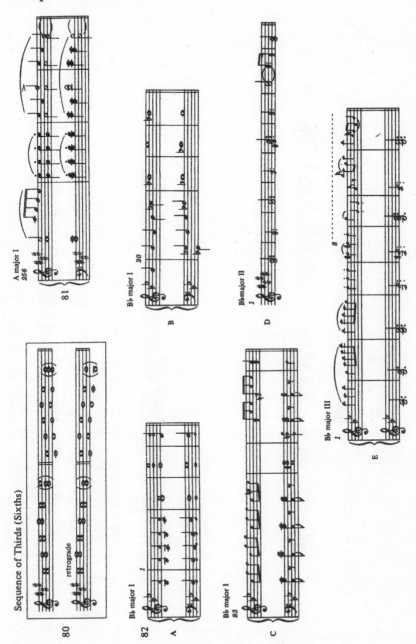

Examples 82F–83

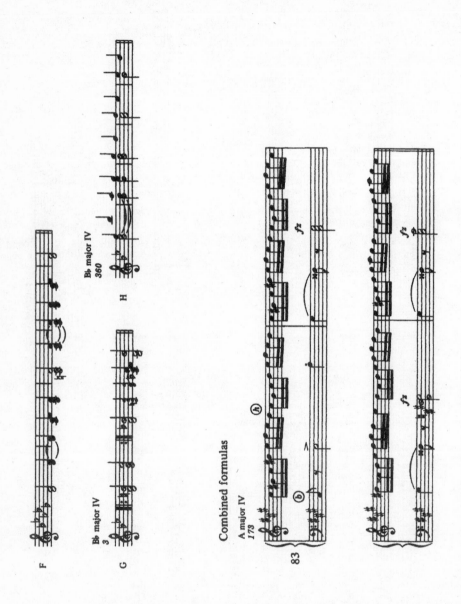

Examples 84–87

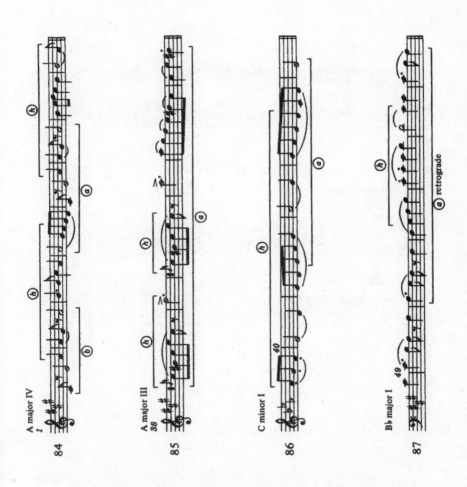

Examples 88–91

C♯(D♭) – F♯minor link

Rhythmic connections

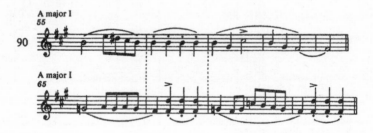

(Arthur Godel, p. 162)

The melody at the end of the episode combines the arpeggio of the movement's original opening with the revised harmony.

Later I shall hint at the psychological cause and effect of Schubert's far-reaching correction.

Examples 35–54 deal with the Sixth formula *b*, *c* and *d* and their continuations *e* and *f*, a group of motifs which hardly has any bearing on the B flat Sonata. It is remarkable that the F sharp minor Andantino (A major II) points back in its turbulent middle section to the distant key of C minor and the compass of formula *e* (40–42); for a few bars, not only the key but also the character of the C minor Sonata make an impressive appearance.[80]

In ex. 40 a variant of the Sixth formula *c′* (bar 11) now contains the leap of a fourth, as a reaction to the fourth in the melody two bars earlier. Exx. 55–71 concentrate on the *Fourth* motifs contained within the opening of the C minor Sonata (*f*, *g*, *I* and *c′*). The effect of motifs *f* and *g* in particular can be traced in both other sonatas. Ex. 64 simplifies the line of the highest notes in the scherzo theme of the A major Sonata. In exx. 65–7 two elements succeed one another: a lyrical variant of the Fourth formula and, derived from *h′*, a figure of unselfconscious bliss between the sixth and second note of the scale which, although a constituent element of the A major Sonata, turns up in the B flat Sonata as well. Even there, the 'bliss formula' reappears in keys of the A major sphere. Within the key of F sharp minor, in A major II, bliss turns into melancholy (73).

Combining features of the A major and B flat major Sonatas, the A major theme in the middle section of B flat major II emerges as a mediating factor between the two works, and as a focal point of motivic orientation within the trilogy. In its melodic sequence of sixths, it comes close to the B flat Sonata's beginning (77). The

---

80 As William Kinderman has pointed out to me, 'One could argue that the shadow of the C minor Sonata is not only cast on the middle section of the Andantino but on the Andantino theme itself, and beyond into the F sharp minor episode of the B flat Sonata.'

version in the first draft (78), however, makes it sound very much like the opening of the A major Sonata (79). Clearly, it was this degree of similarity which caused Schubert to reformulate the theme. The version in the draft, as well as the first, purely chordal version of the A major Sonata's beginning, should open our ears to another crucial harmonic-melodic factor common to the three works: the *sequence of Thirds* (or Sixths) (80) which is inherent in nearly all themes, if sometimes modified or latent. The opening of the C minor Sonata is no exception:

Exx. 82 A–G pursue the sequence of Thirds in the themes of the B flat Sonata.

The combination of formulas is examined in exx. 83–6. The fusion of Sixth formulas with the Fifth formula *h* in A major IV may draw our attention to the fact that this theme's innocent predecessor in the second movement of Schubert's Sonata D.537 did not reach down to the third.

The second subject of the B flat Sonata (87) has been placed beneath that of the C minor Sonata (86), as they are related in retrograde.

A *Seconds* formula should be added to the list:

A first hint of it can be discovered in bars 5–7 of the opening of C minor I. The return of the theme brings the variant:

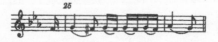

Bars 119–52 of the development are guided entirely by the Seconds formula, from its melodic constellation, harmonic consequences are drawn. There are areas of harmonic twilight: are we in the tonic or the dominant?

In the A major Sonata we encounter the same ambiguity on three occasions.

Here Schubert has taken his cue from the first movement of Beethoven's 'Sonata quasi una fantasia' Op. 27, No. 2.

In B flat major IV the development section is fired by a Seconds formula (bar 256) which had previously brought the first subject brusquely to its close (bars 30–32).

The same formula marks the entire layout of C minor IV: its most important sections begin in the keys of C minor-D flat major (beginning of episode)-B major (middle section)-C minor.

In B flat major III the second subject seems to reach back to C minor IV (exx. 88–9). Even the keys, C sharp minor (D flat major)-F sharp minor, remain the same. Of these, C sharp minor and D flat major have their say in all three sonatas, whereas F sharp minor and G flat major appear mostly in the C minor and A major Sonatas. A major II is in F sharp minor, B flat major II in C sharp minor.

More easily discernible, and therefore not included in the musical examples, is the *Octave leap*. We find it in bar 4 (ascending melody) and bars 8 and 10 (descending bass) of the C minor opening. It figures prominently in every movement of the A major Sonata but also in C minor IV where, in the initial sketch, the ascending octave dominated much of the movement. It further appears in the episodes of C minor II and, less significantly, in three movements of the B flat Sonata (I, bar 301 and development; II, accompaniment; III, bars 5–8).

The use of motifs is not generally tied to specific keys. There are some special cases, however, where motifs appear in fixed positions, with or without octave transposition. Such a tone constellation can be noted in exx. 9–13, 20, 30, 77 and 82D; it remains fixed in the A major-F sharp minor sphere within the compass of G#-D' or one octave lower, and is confined to the sonatas in A and B flat major. A first glimpse of this position is provided by C minor II (if such chronological reckoning makes any sense within these works). One of Schubert's most personal modes of expression is his shifting the basic key by a semitone; the appearance of A major in this A flat major movement (bar 56)

C minor II

is an event whose reverberations remain evident in the coda.

The same Adagio presents, for the first time, a note constellation C sharp-B sharp-E, fixed in C sharp (D flat) minor. We discover it in the bass of the second subject:

Other instances of the C sharp minor constellation can be found in exx. 16, 17 and 34.

The opening of the C minor Sonata includes a succession of chromatic notes (bars 3–7)

which remains effective as the *Chromatic constellation*.

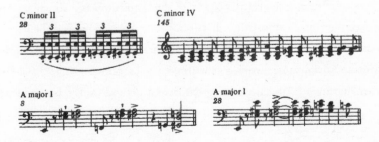

See also ex. 64.

It seems remarkable that, in all three first movements, chromatic developments begin their ascent on the note E.

'Transgressions' of motivic material are mainly, as in Beethoven, those of note sequences, note areas and note constellations. In comparison with Schubert's preceding sonatas, the significance of rhythmic motifs has diminished. Rhythmic variety is now more important than rhythmic unity.

In the first subjects of C minor I and A major I, as well as in the accompanying figure of B flat major II, there is a unifying rhythmic formula: ♪♩♩ (♪♩♩). The rhythm of C minor IV evolves from its upbeat beginning as a variant at approximately double speed: (♪) ♫♪ ♫♪ etc. B flat major refers to this rhythm in bars 65–6 and 284–5 (♪♩♩♩), while IV dwells on it extensively in its *ff* episode, where the key of F minor mediates between the keys of the two sonatas, B flat major and C minor. (B flat major IV refers to the C minor Sonata in yet another way: it simply insists, as it were, on opening in C minor. It does so, stubbornly, no fewer than nine times; only before the stretta is the C minor spell finally broken.)

A major I derives its main rhythmic impulses from two formulas

(*a*) ♩ ♩ (on the beat), (*b*) ♪ ♪ ♩

which, in succession, in conjunction or in opposition, steer its course and hold it together. In Schubert's draft, the opening formula *a* was not used from the outset; it surfaces later, during the further course of the exposition, and contributes to the initial chords in the recapitulation. In his fair copy, Schubert added the rhythm by analogy to the very beginning of the work. The first-movement coda, after dwelling exclusively on formula *a*, surprises us with a formula *b* close.

Other rhythmic connections are given in exx. 90 and 91, the latter devised by Arthur Godel.[81]

---

81   *Schuberts letzte drei Klaviersonaten*, Baden-Baden, 1985.

While a basic repertory of note sequences and note areas supplies the majority of themes in the three sonatas (least plausibly in C minor IV), the character of each individual work and movement is set clearly apart. (I believe that, for the player, definition of musical character can be of the greatest value. On pp. 204–205 I have tried to tease out the characters within the trilogy or put my feelings about them into words.)

One could say that the Fifth formula leans towards lyricism, whereas the Sixth formulas are mostly propelled and excited (except the descending formula *e*, which tends to be gentle and lyrical). The Fourth formula is open to both possibilities. Yet if one compares themes of gentle solemnity based on the Fifth formula – the second subject of C minor I and the beginnings of C minor I, B flat major I and II (middle section) – distinct, if discreet, differences of temperament become apparent.

Besides the gentle and solemn, there is a disturbing and menacing side to Schubert's last music. Its classical poise is sometimes undermined by anxiety, exploded by nightmares or shaken by despair. In such moments the music exposes neither passions nor thunderstorms, neither the heat of combat nor the vehemence of heroic exertion, but assaults of fever and delusion. Chromaticism raves in the opening movements of the C minor Sonata (development) and A major Sonata (strette); the episodes of the Adagios in the C minor Sonata and the String Quintet are darkly affected by fever; the middle section of A major II almost destroys itself in a frenzy of anguish. I shall refrain from connecting such states of mind with the reality of Schubert's illness, something Fritz Lehner, in his fictional Schubert film of 1986, unfortunately did not avoid. Is it not sufficient to feel that, at certain moments in this music, demons descend to strangle or mercilessly to chase? It is precisely the obsessional quality of the C minor finale which makes this movement convincing – in a good performance.

Until recently, Schubert's macabre side has been largely ignored, suppressed or restricted to what was seen as its epitome, 'Der Erlkönig'. Walter Dahms, in his Schubert biography of 1912, found these words for the C minor finale:

> Light-winged, the coquettish six-eight theme flutters upwards. It offers plenty of opportunity for hide-and-seek, and for extensive gossip ... Thanks to the speed with which the changing pictures pass by, one does not notice the movement's length. Suddenly: dominant, tonic, the end.

Taking Dahms's lead, one could perceive 'Der Erlkönig', without the corrective of its text, as a cheerful gymnastic exercise. According to Költzsch, the C minor finale reveals 'simple technical incompetence' and offers 'little more than rhythmic sound-motion'. As for the A major Sonata's Andantino, he asks himself whether 'the strangely eruptive caprices' of its middle section might not be 'partly artificial'.

Arthur Godel has described the main section of this Andantino as a 'peaceful barcarole' and the C minor finale as 'moderate', devoid of any 'manic dimension … The playfully and generously unfolded C minor theme with its optimistic brightening into the major (bar 67 etc.) lacks the vehemence of syncopated accents and the awkward minor-major alternation of the G major Quartet's finale'. This may be so but, given the restriction of its comparative monotony, the movement manages to be all the more tortuous. As mentioned above, Schubert altered the first two bars of the initial theme; by eliminating the onslaught of its broken chord, which had dominated large portions of the movement in the manner of an *idée fixe*, and by providing a necessary minimum of melodic variety (at the expense of reducing the logic motivic cohesion), he prevented the monotony from becoming unbearable.

In contrast to Dahms, to whom the C minor finale is 'light-winged', and Godel, who finds it intermittently optimistic, the composer Dieter Schnebel detects in the comparatively light-hearted finale of the B flat Sonata 'strength that peters out – an ominous image of impending death … For the time being, cheerful music no longer seems to work – it may not ever again'. According to Schnebel, the whole movement represents a 'hidden diminuendo', containing 'musical symbols which anticipate Mahler in the hammer strokes of his Sixth'. In the first movement of the B flat Sonata, where Dahms made out a 'flowering, momentous main theme' and 'genial lyricism', Schnebel sees the 'document of a disintegrating life'.

I feel little inclination to quarrel with a man of such stimulating intelligence, but there is no option. Is it impossible to imagine that Schubert, even as a sick man, might have been able to convey in his music emotions of well-being, teasing, excitement, euphoria, a happiness conjured up by his imagination (if not founded on fact) which would try to ease what he called his 'dismal awareness of a miserable reality'? Is it not likely that a depressive composer, instead of letting himself sink deeper into despair, would take advantage of the act of composing as a lever with which to lift himself out of his inertia? Is it frivolous to conceive that even a syphilitic may have some lighthearted notions a few months before he dies? Where Schubert was once labelled genial and sentimental, he has recently been construed as desolate and relentlessly depressive. The protagonist of *Lilac Time* wreaks belated vengeance, while the aura of what had been termed 'Schubert's last compositions' adds a shiver of awe. In the A major Sonata's finale, Schubert sounds joyfully transported; in the scherzo I hear laughter and see hats thrown into the air. The 'optimistic' episodes of the C minor finale, on the other hand, turn out to be chimeras, insinuations of the Erl King.

Comparison between fair copies and first drafts reveals a change in Schubert's perception of musical space. In the sketches, certain ideas or sections are already laid out in their entirety, while others appear all too condensed; only in the revision are they given the space they deserve. Such a flowering of the original seed provides an amazing glimpse into the workings of an imagination at once fertile and critical. Proportions are rectified, details start to tell, fermatas suspend time. Rests clarify the structure, allowing breathing space, holding the breath or listening into silence. (In the sketch, C minor II contains not a single fermata, the minuet not a single bar's rest!) Some ornaments are added, others deleted, such as the trill on E in the third bar of the C minor Sonata, or the turn between C sharp and D in bar 49 of the A major scherzo. Where ruggedness is moderated, the music is not weakened but clarified. Occasionally Schubert takes a risk which he felt compelled to tone down in the final version: I note with regret that in bar 73 of A major II he softened the staggering G major chord by turning it into a G sharp appoggiatura.

Skizze

I	II
C MINOR	
Allegro	*Adagio (A flat)*
At once heroic and anxious, nervous and determined, threatening and threatened. Sections in major keys (second theme) in parenthesis: vistas of unattainable bliss as seen from harsh, inhospitable surroundings. Coda of despair.	Spiritual, tenderly solemn, devoid of pathos, intermittently gripped by surges of fever.
A MAJOR	
Allegro	*Andantino (F sharp minor)*
Kaleidoscope of ideas and feelings (approximately: 1. Credo, ma con fuoco; 2. Capriccioso con grazia; 3. Dolcissimo innocente; 4. Delirando). Seemingly improvised; in the development section, poised, transfixed stasis, and wide, lyrical-dramatic arch. Mystery coda.	Desolate grace behind which madness hides, from which it erupts, into which it sinks back quivering. Expiring coda.
B FLAT MAJOR	
Molto moderato	*Andante sostenuto (C sharp minor)*
In its basic character: composed, gently hymnic. Grand musical context that is broken up towards the end of exposition and recapitulation, blissfully fatigued. Coda of humility.	Clear-sighted melancholy, with middle section singing praise.

III	IV
Menuetto: Allegro	*Allegro*
Anti-minuet, at once nervous and determined, without firm ground under its feet. Suburban trio.	Dancing dervish; or death gallop, with Cerberus barking, and the B major lure of the Erl King.
Scherzo: Allegro vivace	*Rondo: Allegretto*
High-spirited, frolicsome, with dolce French horns (or male choir) in the trio.	The big daydream of bliss, with thunderstorm development and multifariously fragmented coda: first hesitating, then storming, finally recapitulating.
Scherzo: Allegro vivace con delicatezza	*Allegro ma non troppo*
Soaring, playful. Trio: muffled and obstinate.	'Fatigue and resignation'? No, rather: graceful resolution, playful vigour. Ironic twinkle; generous signing line; stubborn pugnacity. Surmounting of C minor fixation after the ninth assault: precious moment of self-abandonment. Assertive coda.

This G major harmony communicated at one stroke the hallucinatory quality of the new section, and initiated the pedal G that gives support to the following twelve bars before being resolved into C minor. Significantly, this movement assembles all three dark keys – F sharp minor, C minor and, at the climax of the central section, C sharp minor – as the utmost concentration of the trilogy's depressive forces.

Portraits of Schubert, it seems to me, often show him idealised, as if trying to produce a face harmless enough to match the sounds of *Rosamunde*. A more realistic Schubert is presented by the 1826 portrait without glasses (Gesellschaft der Musikfreunde, Vienna) and particularly by the life-mask, copies of which are preserved at the Curtis Institute in Philadelphia and the Vienna Conservatory.[82] This mask, evidently suppressed by Schubert's friends, has at last received due recognition thanks to the efforts of Eva Badura-Skoda.[83] (I agree with her assumption that it can hardly be a death-mask, as which it was previously identified.) What we see is not a 'Biedermeier face' but powerful, sensuous, robust and propulsively energetic features, more akin to those of Beethoven than to Grillparzer's or Johann Nestroy's. Similarly, the musical image of an idealised, harmonious Schubert has long determined the taste of performers and listeners. Even today, he remains for some largely a source of lyrical, genial, mellow and elegiac pleasure. The 'well-known timidity and phlegm' ascribed to him by Schindler is unhesitatingly applied to the character of his works. (According to the recollections of Schubert's friends, he was far less timid than Schindler made him out to be; and what could be phlegmatic about the temperament of a man who produced nearly a thousand compositions in a short lifetime?)

'A gentle melancholy pervades Schubert's music', writes Godel (p. 254). The crisp enthusiasm of the Great C major Symphony, the vitality of many a scherzo, the fury of certain finales, the acute despair of *Winterreise*, the terror of 'Der Doppelgänger' are all as far removed from gentleness as Goya is from Schubert's Viennese painter friends. Kupelwieser or Schwind never painted the equivalent of what Schubert called his 'gruesome songs'. To be sure, Schubert, that most immediately moving of all composers, offers beside his chill dances of death also something of the warmth and shelter of death,

---

82   Reproduced in the entry on Schubert in *The New Grove Dictionary of Music and Musicians*.

83   Eva Badura-Skoda: 'Eine authentische Porträt-Plastik Schuberts', *Österreichische Musikzeitschrift*, November 1978.

its sweetness and enticement, its siren voices and lure to surrender. After the death of his mother, her memory seems to have merged into an image of death. But here as well, the word 'gentle' will not do. The singer who observes the dynamic markings of *Winterreise* (written predominantly in the piano part) will be bound to startle those listeners who consider an evenly beautiful sound and a nobly shaped phrase the quintessence of Lieder singing, and *Winterreise* the musical portrait of a resigned old man.

Schubert's dynamic markings are extreme, indeed far more so than those of Beethoven. (The same applies to his daring harmony, with his fondness for juxtaposing chromatically neighbouring keys.) Experience teaches the player, however, that Schubert's dynamics are frequently incomplete; he tends to omit intermediate steps, as for instance in bars 184–224 of the B flat finale: literally, a decrescendo is supposed to begin after nineteen bars of *pianissimo*, followed eight bars later by another decrescendo which after four bars, in its turn, leads into a diminuendo that prevails for the last eight bars. Even as an idea, this hardly makes musical sense. Schubert evidently left it to the player to take corrective action, such as starting each phrase (upbeats to bars 202, 210, 216) at a slightly stronger dynamic level. In his notation Schubert takes too much for granted: I wonder whether he ever had the opportunity of hearing his piano works played by others, and of reacting to performances.

Another source of misunderstanding is Schubert's use of accents. In his autographs they vary considerably in size and graphic emphasis, so that an accent may sometimes look like a diminuendo. (The new Bärenreiter complete Schubert edition simplifies the problem unduly: instead of adhering as closely as possible to Schubert's own ambiguity, leaving decisions to the player, a very small accent has frequently been used.) On the keyboard the matter is particularly precarious. Schubert's mania for accents calls for discretion; otherwise the pianist may sound pedantic and run the risk of overemphasizing isolated notes in *cantabile*.

In recent years Schubert's old fashioned triplet notation has justly received some publicity. Here I should like to correct myself and announce that, in the Adagio of the C minor Sonata, I have now come to adjust the dotted octave leaps (bar 32, etc.) as well – a long look at the autograph (Floersheim Collection, Basle) has taught me that polyrhythm seems out of the question. In his fair copy Schubert replaces the single dots of his sketch with double dots, a fact which serves as an argument for, not against, adjusting the triplets: only the shorter rhythmic value may be adjusted.

For yet another reason, examination of Schubert's autographs proves essential:

his use of ties is casual, incomplete and sometimes indecisive. I have come to treat such ties in secondary voices *ad libitum*, following my ear.

Three quotations from the Schubert literature:

> His pianistic style is demanding enough, even sometimes in his songs. But it hardly goes beyond Beethoven in the exploration of technical possibilities, and would seem to have been determined by the light touch and bright tone of the Viennese instrument of this period.
>
> (Hans Gal, *Franz Schubert and the Essence of Melody*, 1974)

> Little tension, but an even sweetness and a deficiency of tempo.
>
> (Carl Spitteler, *Schuberts Klaviersonaten*, 1887)

> The permanence of the theme as a theme is guaranteed in the potpourri, adding one theme after the other without having to draw consequences from any modification ... assortment of themes blindly embarked on ... Just as there is no constitutive history between the entry of one Schubertian subject and the next, life is not an intentional object of his music.
>
> (Theodor W. Adorno, *Schubert*, 1928)

A musicologist-composer in the most conservative mould, a music-loving Swiss poet and a composing thinker offer statements that need to be questioned.

Schubert's piano style is by no means that of Beethoven; in its part-writing and disposition of sound, it seems to me often fundamentally different, while its rapid octaves, tremolos and note repetitions prepare the way for Liszt. To me, Schubert's piano style is determined far more by vocal and orchestral colour than by the timbre of contemporary Viennese keyboard instruments. The influence of string quartet or quintet sonority is as evident in his last sonatas as that of his sacred choral music. Only a number of his lyrical piano pieces (Impromptus, etc.) show a more directly 'pianistic' approach, and only there should the player's inner ear immediately imagine piano sound.

It is easy to deduce from Spitteler's comment that he had never heard good performances of the Schubert sonatas. It is to his credit that he paid heed to them at a time when nobody else seemed to care.

As for Adorno, his assumptions about the 'potpourri' nature of Schubert's music, its random arrangement of beautiful themes without inner connection or development, do not bear scrutiny. After introducing the second subject in F sharp minor in the first movement of his B flat Sonata—a theme which Adorno cites as an example of unrelatedness—Schubert leads up to the third subject with a twenty-bar motivic development. The area of the sixth inhabited by the F sharp minor theme (ex. 87) is modified to that of a diminished fifth.

The next step brings out elements of the first subject.

Finally, from a shorthand version of the first subject, the third subject emerges (ex. 24).

The highly unorthodox first movement of the A major Sonata begins with two successive heterogeneous ideas. I have tentatively called them 'Credo, ma con fuoco' (bars 1–7) and 'Capriccioso con grazia' (bars 7–16). They immediately begin to interact (bars 16–22). The second idea is propelled through an extensive development, arriving at the third, the actual subsidiary theme (bar 55), which is itself intimately related to the beginning of the piece: the initial harmonies are now supplied with a *cantabile* melody in the soprano. Again there is no sign of an abrupt change of scenery. The music which follows the subsidiary section, growing out of its final rhythm, could easily be taken for the actual development section. (The unwitting listener expects it to lead into the recapitulation and may, indeed, have the erroneous impression that it has arrived there – if the player does not skip the repeat.) In contrast to this exposition full of development, the beginning of the actual development section seems to suspend time and activity; it is a product of the exposition's codetta, generously laid out in *cantabile* style, a variant of 66. Later on, the Credo character, with its octave leaps, gradually takes the lead, preparing the entry of the recapitulation with symphonic grandeur.

Potpourri-like exposition, interchangeability of themes, developments lacking conflict – these are much less Schubert's than Mozart's hallmarks. In the exposition of the Piano Concerto K.595 Mozart presents an array of at least eight different melodic sections in the manner of an 'unending melody', and seemingly without constructive commitment. The result is phenomenal and seamless.

Of Schubert's last three sonatas, the one in B flat has, in our century, cast the strongest spell. One could call it the most beautiful and moving, the most resigned and harmoniously balanced, corresponding most clearly to the concept of a gently melancholic Schubert.

The first two movements sound valedictory. Farewells are not necessarily composed in the face of impending death. Beethoven had a penchant for farewells far beyond his 'Lebewohl' ('Les Adieux') Sonata: from the Andante favori to the Adagio of Op. 111 and the final minuet of the *Diabelli Variations*, 'Lebewohl' pervades some of his codas, both in the sound of its syllables and as an emotional hue.

Everything in the B flat Sonata seems controlled and considered. The F sharp minor theme that so startled Adorno, far from appearing out of the blue, has its harmonic and motivic roots in the lines which come before, while the aggressive episodes of the finale are preceded by a silence of the kind that anticipates the storm. Only those transitional bars in the first movement, an intrusion from the feverish regions of the other two sonatas, ignore the newly acquired countenance. Carried over from an earlier phase of conception, they seem to me no less ill-advised than the execution of the repeat which they instigate.

If the B flat Sonata is the most beautiful, the one in A major must be the most astonishing and comprehensive. Here, the brightest of worlds confronts its darkest counterpart. Between movements which, luminously, bring together certitude and adventurous flight of fancy, sweetness and mystery, wit and abandon, stillness and chromatic uproar, stands the Andantino, spelling out the most acute emotional disturbance. The first movement maintains a precarious balance between improvisation and construction, operating with changing degrees of weight, varying its narrative pace and disclosing only with hindsight the highly unusual formal scheme. The coda quotes the movement's initial idea in a different light: not with confident timpani strokes but in a whisper; not in public but in secret. Its final arpeggios combine elements of both initial characters – broken chord and octave leap – in reverse direction, descending, no longer ascending. The first pianist to give the sonata its due was Artur Schnabel. Even today, his 1937 recording transmits the freshness of an exhilarating discovery.

Seekers after comforting musical beauty will be taken aback by the C minor

Sonata: predominantly sombre, passionate yet icy, it may well be the most unsensual, uninviting and, behind its classical façade, the most neurotic sonata Schubert wrote.

Schubert helped to carry Beethoven's coffin. One year later, he evokes the memory of Beethoven and the classical style – but not as a docile follower. On the contrary, his familiarity with Beethoven's works taught him to be different. Dvořák noticed that Schubert had from the outset little in common with Beethoven except 'in the vigour and melodious flow of his basses', already found in his early symphonies.

The idea that Schubert tried to model his sonatas on Beethoven's and failed has nevertheless confused many a listener; all the more so in the earliest decades of this century, when it became fashionable to break away from the pathos and musical idealism of Beethoven. In 1927 Maurice Ravel explained Beethoven's fame as resulting mainly from his deafness, from the legend of his life and from the magnanimity of his social ideas! Neoclassicism, 'Neue Sachlichkeit' and protest against the dominance of 'German' instrumental music combined to belittle not only Beethoven's but also some of Schubert's achievements.

Arnold Schoenberg knew better. In a short text drafted for the centenary of Schubert's death[84] he emphasises Schubert's 'inconceivably great originality in every single detail next to a crushing figure like Beethoven', which has either remained unnoticed or been denied. No wonder this originality was not fully appreciated, even at a time when its boldness had almost ceased to be disturbing. Schoenberg's admiration for Schubert's 'self-respect' is boundless: 'Close to such crushing genius, Schubert does not feel the need to deny its greatness in order somehow to endure. What self-confidence, what truly aristocratic awareness of one's own rank which respects the equal in the other!'

Schubert relates to Beethoven, he reacts to him, but he follows him hardly at all. Similarities of motif, texture or formal pattern never obscure Schubert's own voice. Models are concealed, transformed, surpassed.

Beethoven's influence on the finale of Schubert's great A major Sonata is hidden (or would have remained so but for Charles Rosen and Edward Cone), although the movement adheres to the formal example of Beethoven's Op. 31, No. 1 finale. Schubert's C minor Sonata seems more overtly Beethovenian in its key, its character of sombre determination, its sublime Adagio which replaces the usual graceful Andante,

---

84   The Schoenberg Institute, Los Angeles.

and in the contribution of sonata form to its rondo. There are also thematic resem-
blances; for instance, the theme of Beethoven's C minor Variations seems to have
triggered off the opening of the Schubert C minor Sonata. However, while Beethoven
organises his theme within the stringent logic of 'foreshortening', Schubert allows
his foreshortenings to go astray. The character Beethoven presents is one of defiance
based on firmness of musical proportion. Schubert presents an energy that is nervous and unsettled, avoiding four- and eight-bar patterns; his pathos is steeped in fear.

The player who, at the beginning of the A flat Adagio from the C minor Sonata,
is reminded of Beethoven's Op. 10, No. 1 Adagio or, rhythmically closer, of the Largo
from Beethoven's C major Concerto, should be aware of the different emotional
situation: where Beethoven offers tenderly enraptured declarations of love, Schubert
embarks on his movement in 'holy sobriety' (*heilignüchtern*, to borrow Hölderlin's
word). The emotional climate of the D flat theme is thoroughly modified in comparison with the first subject of the Adagio cantabile of Beethoven's 'Pathétique',
from which it may be derived. A second glance at the Adagio and the minuet – an
anti-minuet in the manner of Haydn – reveals that these movements owe more to
Haydn than to Beethoven, and to the string quartet more than to pianistic predecessors. (The fingers of every pianist will have noticed that the finale also incorporates
some ideas which could be more painlessly executed with the string bow.) Schubert's
Adagio seems in spirit to be only a small, albeit highly personal, step removed from
the slow movement of Haydn's B flat Quartet Op. 76, No. 4. We easily forget that the
solemn Adagio – also that of earlier Beethoven – originated in Haydn, and that the
first of all great C minor piano sonatas was Haydn's. Even more perfunctory are
reminiscences of Beethoven's Op. 31, Nos. 2 and 3 in Schubert's C minor finale, the
controlled frenzy of which adopts a novel, almost pathological course.

Schubert's last sonatas belong together. A succession of musical examples – mostly
beginnings of themes – should make this even more obvious. The examples are
arranged as a chain of developing variations and transposed, where necessary, into
the same A major/F sharp minor range, to facilitate comparison (see pp. 199–200).
Another chart shows (simplified) melodic connections in the two inner movements,
both within the same work and in relation to the other sonatas. Not that the three
works cannot be played separately; yet, as they illuminate one another, they seem
to me more interdependent than Beethoven's sonata trilogies. A thesis of menace
and destructive energy (C minor), followed by an antithesis of positive, luminous

activity (A major), is concluded by a synthesis of resigned composure. The finale of the B flat Sonata shows a kind of gaiety that is neither innocent, like that of the *Trout Quintet*, nor tooth-gnashing, as in the finale of the String Quintet. Its territory lies somewhere between the humour of Jean Paul and the well-known Viennese saying that life is 'hopeless but not serious'. It is comforting to know that the composer of *Winterreise* should have been able, shortly before his death, to make light of his suffering. Nothing, however, could reconcile us to the cynicism of a fate which was to take his life away at the age of thirty-one.

(1988)

Succession of examples – mostly beginnings of themes – from Schubert's last three sonatas, arranged as a chain of developing variations, and presented within the same A major/F sharp minor range, starting with the Fifth formula (*h*).

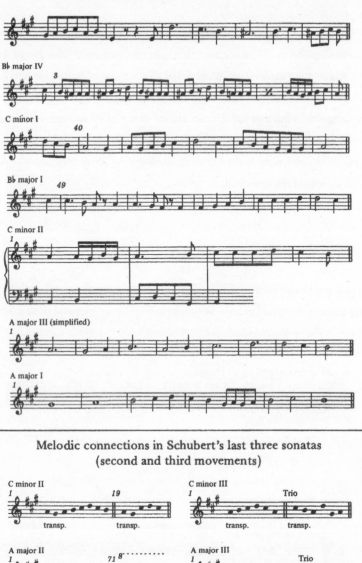

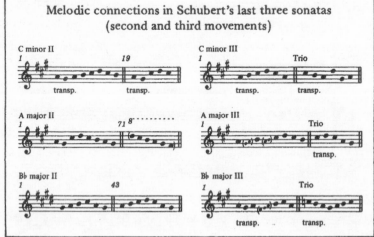

Melodic connections in Schubert's last three sonatas
(second and third movements)

A Footnote on the Playing of Schubert's Four-Hand Works

THE PLAYING OF four-hand music on one piano poses problems different from any other duet combination. During a performance I once became entangled in the evening suit of Daniel Barenboim because we had spent all our rehearsal time in shirtsleeves. Apart from the benefit of some extraordinary physical contortions – the result of crossing or overlapping of voices, and not without a pleasure of their own – four-hand playing seems to be designed to make discriminating players, if not their audiences, unhappy; it tends to sound either stiff or sloppy. The reasons for this are partly technical. What would pass as good ensemble in a violin and piano duet might still sound casual when produced by four hands on a keyboard. Comparable to a photographer who tries to get a clear picture, the players have to focus all musical contours with perfect acuteness.

That induces the imagination to shrink or to get stale. Stay in time and you'll be safe. Play as evenly as possible and you will avoid mannerisms, since you will not have to synchronise matters of declamation.

Another factor to stifle the imagination is the customary clinical use of the right pedal. It seems to be taken for granted that the left player operates the pedal in order to keep harmonies and accompaniments clean. An experienced two-hand pianist, all by himself, will often employ the pedal to enhance the sonority of the upper registers; they need atmospheric support. It therefore seems more sensible to me that, in four-hand playing, the player on the right should have control over the pedalling; he will be less inclined to act like those whom Busoni accused of treating the pedal 'in much the same way as they might try to force air and water into geometric shapes'.

The player on the right-hand side, then, would need to be more than dimly aware of what his colleague on the left is playing. In this he is hardly helped by the common layout of a four-hand score which is, alas, not that of a score; it presents the two parts separated as *primo* and *secondo* on adjacent pages.

While testing the performers on all these counts, Schubert's glorious four-hand music adds some hazards particularly of its own. Schubert's piano sound is that of a singer and orchestrator, but it is also, in a highly novel way, that of a painter. Suggestive of light, colour, atmosphere and vast space, it sometimes abandons the requirements of strict part-writing. We are, musically, reminded of clouds moving over a landscape, or shadows cast over the mind. Octave doublings are switched on and off within a melodic phrase, governed not by considerations of polyphony but by the composer's spontaneous ear. The true Schubert player sits, so to speak, on the edge of his (or her) seat, reacting to changes of texture and mood, concentrating his attention on the peculiarities of an instrument, balancing each chord for its own expressive sake. And he will have to extend dynamics to extremes, in order to do justice to Schubert's disturbing emotional power. Is there any other composer who so often tests the limits of intensity? Schubert's music disintegrates into silence as well as violence. Feverish nightmares lead to the brink of madness. We are reminded that Francisco Goya y Lucientes, another dark visionary, died, like Schubert, in 1828.

Schubert's alleged remark, 'Do you know any jolly music? I don't,' complements the impression of manic energy which some of his music conveys. While his words should by no means be applied to every bar he ever composed, they do point to the depressive core of his personality. For Schubert as well as for his faithful performers, music is a matter of life and death in a rather literal sense – life and death seem, in many of his masterpieces, close to one another, occasionally merging into one.

(1978)

Testing the Grown-Up Player: Schumann's *Kinderszenen*

'EASY PIECES FOR the pianoforte' – what Schumann himself presented as easy, simple and childlike proves to be, for the performer, a trying task. In this music nothing can be concealed. Each note must speak with its particular significance, neither taken too lightly nor buried in 'meaning'. There seems to be a prevailing attitude in the performances of Schumann's *Scenes of Childhood* which, if I had to put it in one sentence, would read: 'As naïveté cannot be forced, let us improvise and trust in God'. The results of such trust can be deplorable. What these miniatures need is affectionate care, loving detachment, an appearance of directness. The player should not turn himself into a child.

Where the artist mobilises childlike qualities in himself, he does so with artistic means to serve his artistic purpose. Alban Berg censured Hans Pfitzner for seeing in 'Träumerei' the prime example of 'inspiration', a melody sent down from heaven, rendering the analyst speechless. In Berg's brilliant account of the compositional process of 'Träumerei', its motivic connections with other pieces in the cycle are not discussed. Before I try to deal with these connections, let me examine another area that links the pieces.

Over a few weeks during February and March 1838, Schumann composed 'nigh on thirty quaint little things', thirteen of which he put together as *Scenes of Childhood*. In this arrangement a magnetic cohesion seems to have taken hold of the pieces, pointing out relationships and turning them into components of a lyrical world bigger than the sum of its parts.

Among performers, perceiving series of pieces as a complete whole is a relatively recent notion. Busoni seems to have been one of the first pianists to play Chopin's Preludes and Etudes complete. Liszt, in his Leipzig performance of *Carnaval*, restricted himself to a selection of the pieces, and Clara Schumann in the same work simply left out 'Florestan', 'Eusebius' and 'Chiarina' – too intimately connected with her private life, according to Tovey.

Of the *Scenes of Childhood*, 'Träumerei' has achieved notoriety around the globe. I remember a villa in Buenos Aires which bore the inscription 'Reverie'; it fulfilled the promise of its name by providing a musical-box performance of 'Träumerei' while the visitor entered the house. Standing on its own, the mauled piece seems to have changed its identity: it is strangely different from those thirty-two bars that occupy the central position (No. 7) in *Kinderszenen*. There, after the comic excitement of 'Wichtige Begebenheit' (Important Event), 'Träumerei' comes as a surprise in F major, an island of peace, a small domain of suspended breath and intangibly dislocated rhythmic emphasis, a delicately polyphonic dream, before the lively motion of 'Am Kamin' (By the Fireside) transfers the listener back to reality.

Within the whole course of *Kinderszenen*, 'Träumerei' is the first crucial turning-point. The reign of sharps during the first six pieces, in keys gathered around D major, has now been broken; only the next turning-point, No. 10, will bring them back. Here G sharp minor abruptly follows the C major close of 'Ritter vom Steckenpferd' (Knight of the Hobbyhorse, No. 9) – an event gently introduced yet traumatic in its impact. The new emotional state – ironically intimated by the tide 'Fast zu ernst' (Almost too serious) – is maintained in all the remaining pieces. It manifests itself as nervous sensitivity in the increased complication and irregularity of musical phrases; as the inner unrest of syncopations and fermatas in 'Fast zu ernst'; and as wavering between F minor and G major in 'Fürchtenmachen' (Frightening) – which, in spite of its soothing G major ending, remains rooted in its parallel E minor: the next piece, 'Kind im Einschlummern' (Child Falling Asleep), makes this evident. But here again the conclusion is not on the tonic E minor on which the piece started, more awake than asleep; it stops on a wonderful, truly romantic A minor chord that opens up like a mouth opened by sleep.

This mouth, to pursue the analogy, now begins to speak with the voice of the poet. In the last piece, 'Der Dichter spricht', the poet provides an epilogue, and answers the unresolved A minor question by leading back into the initial key of *Kinderszenen*, G major. We have come full circle: while in the preceding pieces the poet had seemingly turned into a child, the epilogue turns the child, as it were, into the poet.

A cycle of smaller pieces challenges the performer to reconcile two points of view: the acute characterisation of the single piece and the pull of the whole. Cortot's recording of Chopin's Preludes is a perfect model. In it, each prelude instantaneously shows its own, unmistakable face. One follows the other almost without interruption, a credit to Cortot's truly phenomenal command of character. The fact that each piece inhabits its own world, and the voyage through all the keys, become hallmarks of the Preludes' organisation. In other cycles, constant looking back to the theme (variation form) or the common denominator of motifs may tie the complete work together. Usually in cyclical works the momentum of musical events is such that a quiet intake of breath between pieces is a rare occurrence. In *Kinderszenen* tiny separations before 'Träumerei' and after 'Fast zu ernst' are required. All the other pieces should lead into, or follow, one another without pause.

Motivic Connections

As usual, the very beginning presents the crucial motivic material. (My reference to the lovely opening phrase of the first piece as 'motivic material' will offend only those who believe that poetry and intellect are opposites; Romantic aesthetics should show them otherwise.)

The *basic motif*

'VON FREMDEN LÄNDERN UND MENSCHEN' (OF FOREIGN LANDS AND PEOPLES)

reappears in the pieces that follow in a variety of shapes, always related to the notes of the melody but not to its rhythm. These notes are B-G-F sharp-E-D; we find them plain or in disguise, transposed or untransposed, varied in their order of succession (which Rudolph Réti[85] calls 'interversion') or provided with additional notes ('auskomponiert', to use Schenker's term). Two shapes of the basic motif may be distinguished by name. In the *Original* (OR) our motif recurs on its initial pitch independent of key – regardless of octave transpositions or added accidentals. The *Transposition* (TR) puts the initial notes into different keys and/or different degrees of the scale.

From an ample number of examples, I should like to offer the following selection.

In the openings of the second and third pieces there is an interaction between TR and OR.

---

85   In Réti's *The Thematic Process in Music* (Faber & Faber, 1961) *Kinderszenen* is presented as a 'theme with variations'. This seems to me to exaggerate the closeness of its pieces. As so often, Réti gets carried away by the notion of a near-complete motivic coherence. The results of my own independent investigation are, I think, more modest.

'KURIOSE GESCHICHTE' (A DROLL STORY)

'HASCHE-MANN' (CATCH ME IF YOU CAN)

The fourth piece, 'Bittendes Kind' (Entreating Child), has the OR, without any melodic change in the key of D major.

After various transpositions in the fifth piece, the OR appears as its conclusion:

'GLÜCKES GENUG' (HAPPY ENOUGH)

The beginning of the sixth piece combines two transpositions:

'WICHTIGE BEGEBENHEIT' (IMPORTANT EVENT)

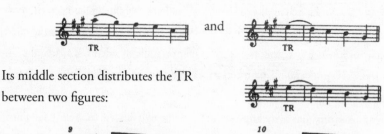

Its middle section distributes the TR between two figures:

In the theme of 'Träumerei' the TR is easily audible.

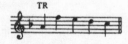

The eighth piece contains, next to transposed interversions of the basic motif, the OR twice.

'AM KAMIN' (BY THE FIRESIDE)

In the first four bars of the ninth piece there is a TR in the background.

'RITTER VOM STECKENPFERD' (KNIGHT OF THE HOBBY-HORSE)

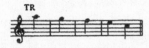

With the tenth piece the situation becomes more complex. The change of emotional climate has its motivic implications.

'FAST ZU ERNST' (ALMOST TOO SERIOUS)

Starting with the two G sharps in bars 1 and 3, I hear their continuation in the fifth bar.

The figure returns very similarly later on.

At the beginning of the eleventh piece there is, again, an opportunity to 'listen ahead'.

'FÜRCHTENMACHEN' (FRIGHTENING)

A later version of the OR reads:

The penultimate piece distributes the OR between two voices.

'KIND IM EINSCHLUMMERN' (CHILD FALLING ASLEEP)

In the last piece the perspective has changed. The basic motif almost disappears. Four-note fragments can be spotted in the initial phase and, somewhat more distinctly, in the recitativo, while the complete transpositions are barely noticeable.

'DER DICHTER SPRICHT' (THE POET SPEAKS)

Here the player should observe the part-writing with loving care; the ascent of the G sharp up to the E of the appoggiatura can easily remain obscure. I am still waiting for the edition that will visually clarify the matter and refrain from printing that last note of the turn underneath the anticipated E. Where Schumann's notation errs, we are entitled to correct it. The entry of the appoggiatura, by the way, has to coincide with the C of the bass if the ascending interval of the sixth is to become clearly audible. In bars 18 and 23 we can detect two intertwined transpositions in the upper voice and one in the middle voice. Whether, and to what degree, such motivic procedures are produced intentionally is open to speculation.

To me, devices of musical order are no less impressive if generated, or adopted, by the workings of the unconscious.

Metronome Figures: A Digression

In *Kinderszenen* Schumann makes do without conventional tempo indications, although he elsewhere, whether in German or Italian, invariably adheres to them. Instead there are descriptive titles – 'of course devised later', as Schumann explains, 'and actually nothing more than subtle hints at performance and conception' – as well as metronome marks. The latter are contained only in subsequent editions of the first print, which has none. Malcolm Frager kindly told me about a copy of this *Urtext* of all *Urtexts* (in the Staatsbibliothek, East Berlin) in which its owner, a certain Otto Boehme, had written: 'The metronomes of *Kinderszenen* are neither by Schumann nor made with his knowledge and assistance ... I got this information from the music dealer Friedrich Whistling of Leipzig (13.9.46), who in turn got it from Schumann himself.'

On the other hand, there is a comment by Brahms which refers to the preparation of a complete edition of 'Schumann's works (Breitkopf & Härtel); in a letter to Clara Schumann of April 1879, Brahms writes: 'Notify Härtel that the pedal and metronome markings in *Kinderszenen* have to remain. The volume delivered to me shows that Schumann himself owned such copies and had them bound'. (Brahms's advice was not taken.) When we look at Mr. Boehme's own insane metronome figure for 'Träumerei', ♩ = 132, we can quickly disregard him as a musical authority – unless he has mistaken quavers for crotchets. Whether authentic or not, I feel obliged to examine Schumann's 'original' metronomes and try to make sense of them.

I confess that I am more comfortable with the *idea* of a tempo, even if rather vaguely expressed by words like 'allegro' or 'andante', 'sehr rasch' or 'mässig', than with the outstretched finger of the metronomic prescription. Is the information conveyed by a figure really more precise? Does a minutely described fictional character come to life more vividly than one that leaves enough room for the imagination to fill in the details? I have met only one musician who possessed the equivalent of absolute pitch, an absolute memory for tempo. The ability of the late conductor Paul Paray to reproduce, and retain, a certain tempo evening after evening seemed unfailing even at the age of ninety. Other musical mortals, composers not excluded, are prone to considerable fluctuations in their perception of tempo, owing to hall, instrument, weather and well-being. (I shall not consider here the practice of modifying an initial tempo.) The player or listener may have very different memories of performances of the same piece, even if the stopwatch guaranteed that the duration was identical to the second; what dragged along yesterday seems fluent enough today. Otto Klemperer in his old age hardly realised how slow his tempi were and how much they had slowed down since his earlier years. Béla Bartók, one of the most meticulous masters of notation, attended rehearsals of his works with the pocket metronome on alert, yet played in his commercial record three of the four movements of his Suite Op. 14 at least twenty beats faster than he himself had stipulated. And how embarrassing for conductors to learn after thirty-five years that the printed metronome figure for the second movement of Bartók's Concerto for Orchestra – desperately adhered to against their better judgement – reflected the composer's wish as little as did the verbal tempo indication (Allegretto scherzando $\Downarrow$ = 74, instead of the authentic Allegro scherzando $\Downarrow$ = 94). According to Leonard Stein, Schoenberg's assistant in Los Angeles, Schoenberg's as well as Stravinsky's notions of tempo varied greatly over the years. In Schoenberg's Piano Concerto Op. 42, judging by Eduard Steuermann's performances, some metronome marks are 'correct' while others, ignored by Steuermann, are absurd and unplayable. On a tape of a performance by Steuermann and Hermann Scherchen (Frankfurt, 1955) the work lasts nineteen minutes and not twenty-eight – the preposterous figure put down by Schoenberg. A literal execution of Schoenberg's metronome indications would render it even quicker.

The 'right tempo', fixed in figures, is hardly the key to the 'right' performance. Rather, the tempo will be a result of all factors combined: the formal and emotional attributes of the composition; its markings which, to a certain extent, regulate articulation, dynamics, character and atmosphere; the descriptive and programmatic indications, if at hand; the (at least approximate) playability; and, finally, the necessary degree of clarity and transparency within the acoustic surroundings of a concert hall.

That said, I should point out that I am not the sort of performer who would disregard the composer's metronome marks untested 'because they don't work anyway'. I am already quite pleased if some of them sometimes do. In the case of *Kinderszenen* I do find a majority of the early metronomes convincing; I adhere to them, at least approximately, in nine out of the thirteen pieces. (Users of the Clara Schumann edition should realise that the metronomes offered in it, which rarely tally with the earlier ones, are of Clara's own invention.) The quick tempo of 'Hasche-Mann' (♩ = 138) is more than justified by bars 15–16: here the sforzando octave in the bass has to be sustained by the pedal, which, if this were done in Clara's ♩ = 120, would produce a clumsy blot. Equally indispensable is a fluent pace for 'Bittendes Kind' if one wants to take the ritards in bars 9–12 seriously. (Clara surpassed herself in reducing the 'original' ♪ = 138 to ♪ = 88!) In 'Wichtige Begebenheit' as well, ♩ = 138 seems to me nearer the mark than ♩ = 120, which makes the middle section sound unduly pompous. When children come to relay some important news, they rush in and blurt it out.

The lively tempo of 'Am Kamin' (♩ = 138, slowed down by Clara to ♩ = 108) appears to me, after 'Träumerei', just right; instead of dozing off in a corner we enjoy the glowing fire, and manage to get the natural feel of the little retards in bars 16 and 22. Technically, a well-oiled player is needed to execute jumps, accents and polyphony with elegance.

One of Clara's most wilful infringements is her correction, in 'Fast zu ernst', of ♩ = 69 to ♪ = 104. Nothing could be less appropriate than to measure the pulse in quavers. Even Schumann's crotchets appear to be an inadequate solution in a piece whose extended phrases reach over several bar-lines and steer towards its closing pause. (However, it is only at the repeat of this piece that I approach ♩ = 69, a tempo too agitated for its beginning.) The fluency of 'Fürchtenmachen' is also welcome: instead of an amiable idyll with scary episodes, a character is at once presented whose very timidity makes it liable to succumb to fright.

Four of the 'original' metronome figures have remained, to me, thoroughly implausible. The speed of the first piece, 'Von fremden Ländern und Menschen' (to which, in a rare feat of unanimity, Clara also subscribes), makes it scurry along with the industry of an ant; there is no time to relate to, take in or marvel at anything those unfamiliar shores may have to offer. (According to her best-known pupil, Carl Friedberg, Clara Schumann took it considerably more slowly in performance.) Equally mysterious remains ♩ = 100 for 'Träumerei'. I am the last person to want this piece to reel in pink-and-purple affectation or collapse under the weight of its own 'depth'. But even Clara's ♩ = 80 sounds hurried and superficial. The cycle's centrepiece and heart deserves better. In 'Kind im Einschlummern' the feverish speed of ♩ = 92 does not permit the child to breathe quietly. (Here Clara's ♪ = 80 is preferable.) And the poet ('Der Dichter spricht', ♩ = 112) is prevented, even at Clara's more moderate pace (♩ = 92), from accommodating the turns and syncopations of his epilogue poetically. My own approximate tempi for these pieces are: 'Von fremden Ländern und Menschen' ♩ = 76; 'Träumerei' ♩ = 69; 'Kind im Einschlummern' ♪ = 72; 'Der Dichter spricht' ♩ = 82.

Irony: A Brief Epilogue

'Glückes genug' – a title that ironically contradicts the music. What happens in this composition rather reminds me of the line from the Swiss poet Conrad Ferdinand Meyer: 'Enough can never ever satisfy' ('Genug kann nie und nimmermehr genügen'). Ceaselessly, the same motivic symbol of rapture reappears in all voices. And there is more to follow: a da capo of the entire piece. But even boundless happiness can overreach itself – within that da capo, I insist on skipping the repeat, which Clara Schumann, in her edition, chose to write out.

Irony creates distance. In *Kinderszenen* there is an ironic distance between the child and the grown-up in ourselves. We do not identify with the child, and do not want to be hurtful. Schumann's irony in this work is lovingly lenient. With Schumann we observe how a sheltered world turns vulnerable, or 'fast zu ernst', as he put it. If, in irony, things are not what they seem to be and do not mean what they seem to say, then 'Fast zu ernst', by its title and its music, strips the mask from an illusory security. With irony, we look back to 'Glückes genug'. What appeared naïve proves to be, in Schiller's distinction, sentimental. The Romantic humour of Jean Paul and his disciple Schumann betrays its dark core.

(1981)

THEME AND VARIATIONS

∾⤳

Schumann and Beethoven

S TRICTLY SPEAKING, A 'symphonic étude' is a contradiction in terms. However much he admired Chopin's, Henselt's or Moscheles's 'poetic' études, Schumann was striving for something beyond what he felt was the 'narrowness' of the genre. He was equally dissatisfied with the thoughtless, 'clumsy' assembly-line production of variations by many of his contemporaries. 'The really brilliant epoch of the variation', he wrote, 'is clearly coming to an end and giving way to the capriccio. May it rest in peace...' (He called his own Variations on a Theme by Clara Wieck 'Impromptus'.) To coerce étude, variation and the 'the symphonic' into a single work – that is the goal the printed versions of the 'Symphonic Etudes' set out to accomplish.

The versions of 1837 and 1852 were preceded by at least three very different sequences of etudes or variations in the manuscript. These also contained a further five wonderful pieces which were only published posthumously. Their withdrawal caused almost the entire Eusebius to be deleted from a work whose original title had read 'Etüden im Orchestercharakter von Florestan und Eusebius'. (Subsequent titles – 'Fantaisies et Finale sur un thème de M. le Baron de Fricken', 'XII Etudes Symphoniques' and 'Etüden in Form von Variationen' – tell us something about the difficulty encountered in arriving at a definitive concept.) It hardly speaks for Clara Schumann's musical judgement that she thought little of these posthumous pieces, so little that she had them published only at Brahms's insistence; but resentment against Schumann's former fiancée, Ernestine von Fricken (whose foster father was responsible for the theme), may also have played a role. In any event, Schumann here displays an eroticism of sound which is rare indeed elsewhere in his work. The fourth of these 'Etudes' is much closer to Chopin than the 'Chopin' portrait in *Carnaval*, written at about the same time.

Not all the études of Opus 13 actually deserve to be called variations; not all the variations, if we count the posthumous ones, are really études. Romantic licence to the contrary, it is certainly not enough for a variation (Etude No. VII) merely to quote briefly the beginning of the theme twice in its middle section. Schumann eliminated Etudes III and IX in his second version ('Etudes en forme de variations') because they had no relevance to the theme apart from free fantasy. But he retained the no less peripheral No. VII as a variation, and this is confusing. The finale, too, has only a tenuous connection with the funeral march theme; in it, Schumann – with a sidelong glance at William Sterndale Bennett, to whom the work is dedicated – makes use of the romance from Heinrich Marschner's opera 'Templer und Jüdin'. (The words set by Marschner are 'Wer ist der Ritter hochgeehrt' – 'Who is the honoured knight' – and 'Du stolzes England, freue dich' – 'Proud England, rejoice'.)

Compared to the first version, the second has several minor textual variants and a larger alteration in the finale, but to speak of a 'stylistically strongly divergent … fundamental revision', as Wolfgang Boetticher, the editor of the Henle Urtext edition, does, is nonsensical and misleading. A third version, by DAS (Dr A. Schubring, 1861), puts the two eliminated études back in, as does Clara Schumann's edition, which presents the textual variants of the printed versions for the player to make a choice.

That keyboard music can be 'orchestral' has been nothing new since Bach and Mozart. With them, the orchestra hidden in the piano often remained latent, while Schubert, Schumann and especially Liszt knew how to make it manifest. The spectrum of timbres is expanded, as is the volume of sound, which now threatens to overflow the hall. It is perhaps a pity that Schumann used the somewhat vague term 'symphonic' rather than merely pointing towards an orchestral quality of sound. But 'symphonic' probably aims here at tautening the work in a big span or sweep such as holds Beethoven's Op. 35 and Op. 120 together – works to which Schumann nowhere refers. It also brings about the virtual absence of lyrical contrast. After many years of working with Schumann's 'symphonic' version, I would not want to go any longer without the five posthumous pieces; it is their inclusion that makes Schumann's Op. 13 one of his finest compositions. Alfred Cortot was the first to reinstate them. In my performance, they are placed within the canon of the other études according to my own judgement.

Two sets of variations on this recording, Beethoven's Op. 34 (1802) and 'Nel cor più non mi sento' (1795), belong to the species of the melodic variation: all the variations retain the complete melody. In his set on a duet from Paisiello's opera 'La molinara' Beethoven proceeds in a strictly classical fashion, never departing from the theme's 6/8 metre and never leaving the sphere of innocent freshness. The combination of

Beethoven's own kind of gracefulness with Mozartian limpidity is wholly admirable. The Variations in F, Op. 34 also grow out of song-like melodiousness, but to the tender lyricism is added an experimental feature. Beethoven announced Op. 34 to his publisher, along with the 'Eroica' Variations, Op. 35, as 'worked out in a manner that is truly entirely new'. What is novel about Op. 34 is that the variations are set off from one another by different tempos, metres (after the first variation) and keys. The layout of work is as follows: Theme in F major, Variation I in D major, both *Adagio* 2/4; Variation II in B flat major, *Allegro ma non troppo* 6/8; Variation III in G major, *Allegretto* ¢ Variation IV in E flat major, *Tempo di Menuetto* 3/4; Variation V in C minor, Marcia, *Allegretto* 2/4; Variation VI in F major, *Allegretto* 6/8. The richly embellished return of the theme after the sixth variation actually creates a seventh variation with the marking *Adagio molto*. The work's unique feature is its consistent change of key, first at the interval of a third and finally at the interval of a fifth – and that within a form which makes a principle of adhering to the key of the theme. This was Beethoven's delightful exception to the rule; no similar tonal experiments were to follow.

Alongside these works, which are stereotypically feminine in their deportment, the Variations on 'Rule, Britannia' exhibit an almost provokingly masculine behaviour. Part of their masculinity is mockery, for Beethoven treats this patriotic song [86] with a broad wink. Here, too, the composer has something new to offer. Already the first variation, which customarily should bear a close resemblance to the theme, changes the metre. The melody has simply vanished; but it is subliminally present and could easily be added. In Jürgen Uhde's view, this highly peculiar set of variations is a stylisation of the sea ('Britannia, rule the waves') in its various ruffles and wind speeds. Only gradually, in Variations II and III, does something of the melody emerge from the surging and lapping. In the fourth variation the theme has finally surfaced, but in a fierce B minor – Admiral Nelson swathed in gun smoke! The coda of the finale presents the naval hero, for a number of hilarious bars, as losing his grip over his boisterous sailors.

(1991)

---

86   Incidentally, the tune comes from Thomas Arne's masque of 1740, *Alfred*.

From Mozart to Brahms

VARIATIONS CAN RELATE to their themes in a variety of ways. The dependence needs to be one of musical material: bass, melody, harmony, individual motifs and formal layout of the theme can all contribute to generating a recognisable kinship. But there can also be a psychological dependence. The four sets of variations discussed here share the feature that they are motivated by the character of their themes. Unlike Bach's Goldberg Variations, whose pensive aria is followed by a succession of diverse character pictures, each of these themes gives a signal that determines the psychological course of the entire work.

The Minuet by Jean-Pierre Duport, Friedrich Wilhelm II's court composer in Berlin, is graceful, and so are Mozart's lovely variations of 1789. Their superb finish remains apparent in spite of textual problems: no autograph has survived, and the best-known sources – the edition published by Artaria in 1792 after Mozart's death, and an old Viennese copy – are obviously corrupt. Furthermore, there seem to have been two versions of the piece, as Mozart's own catalogue of works lists only six variations instead of nine. Fortunately, a better text has recently come to light: the edition of J. J. Hummel (Berlin, 1791), now considered to be the first print. Although not without mistakes and omissions, it clarifies certain details and rings stylistically true.

In Mendelssohn's *Variations sérieuses*, his outstanding piano composition, the theme's latent pathos becomes increasingly manifest. Mendelssohn described the work humorously to a friend as being 'in D minor, and peevish'. For the Classical masters, a set of variations in a minor key used to be the exception, and one that did not end in the major even rarer. Independent variation works had to entertain, and to serve as a vehicle for instrumental proficiency. (Even Haydn called his glorious F minor Variations 'Un piccolo divertimento'). The *Variations sérieuses* have a forerunner in Beethoven's 32 Variations in C minor; other sets undoubtedly known to Mendelssohn, and showing the penchant of Romantic composers for minor key variations, were those in Schubert's D minor String Quartet ('Death and the Maiden'), published in 1831, and Schumann's 'Etudes symphoniques' (1837). While Mendelssohn's tide is a reaction against the multitude of 'Variations brillantes' that were the fashion of the day, the work does not renounce bravura but manages to fuse it with a deeply personal expression. The adherence to the theme is strictly Classicist; at the same time, disturbing passions are unleashed. This most composed of composers seems to be haunted by demons in the 'witches' sabbath' (Cortot) of the finale until the turmoil finally collapses in quiet despair.

The theme of Liszt's variations is a brief basso ostinato taken from Bach's Cantata No. 12 which has also been used by Bach in the Crucifixus of his B minor Mass. Its sighing chromatic descent symbolises the suffering implicit in the Cantata *Weinen, Klagen, Sorgen, Zagen sind der Christen Tränenbrot*. Also adapted from Bach's Cantata is the idea of redeeming this suffering: both works are concluded by the chorale 'Was Gott tut, das ist wohlgetan'. The death of his beloved elder daughter Blandine stirred Liszt to compose, in 1859, one of his most deeply felt, concentrated and uncompromising pieces, an example of programme music at its most emotional and least pictorial.

The work is impressive on three levels: experimental, psychological and religious. One may call it experimental for its use of chromaticism and for its combination of intellectual rigour with a free flow of associations. As so often, Liszt starts with an improvisatory introduction which leads into the actual variations in F minor, a passacaglia consisting of forty-eight sections. There is nothing stereotyped, however, about the use of the bass motif; Liszt counteracts any hint of repetitiveness by spreading 'unending melodies' over it, by blurring its edges and, where convenient, by extending its final cadence. The passacaglia is followed by a recitativo and a fantasia after which the chorale appears, so to speak, from heaven.

On a psychological level, the work encompasses a wide range of grief, terror and despair. The extended lament which opens the fantasia is entirely given to three-note groups: their declamation recalls the name Blandine. Juxtaposing sombre chromaticism (which stands for suffering and insecurity) and 'pure' diatonic melody and harmony (which represent the certainty of faith), Liszt takes us into the sphere of his own religious belief. As in Haydn's *Creation*, though with very different musical results, chaos and darkness are annihilated by light. In the compositions of his later years, Liszt refrained from consoling the listener, and himself. As his own music moved farther away from functional tonality, the analogy between religious faith and the imperishable power of the triad ceased to ring true.

In arranging the Andante from his first string sextet for the piano, Brahms apparently fulfilled a wish by Clara Schumann who, in a letter, confessed to being overjoyed when she received the variations as a present for her forty-first birthday in 1860. The transcription remains faithful to the original (which occasionally makes for piano writing that seems to ask for a three-handed executant) without trying to suggest the characteristic glow of its string sound. Instead, different pianistic colours are mobilised to convey the same heroic mood.

The work's attitude is neo-Baroque. Indeed, it offers a musical parallel to the striving of German Romantic writers to evoke a mythical, 'medieval' past. The theme, stern as well as passionate, shows young Brahms in his balladesque D minor mood: the defiant intensity of its forte is carried on by no fewer than four variations before tenderness, as if by a stroke of magic, takes over.

(1990)

LISZT

∽∾∽

Liszt Misunderstood

I KNOW I AM compromising myself by speaking up for Liszt. Audiences in Central Europe, Holland and Scandinavia tend to be irritated by the sight of Liszt's name on a concert bill. If one should happen to play a Beethoven sonata in the same programme, they are apt to shut their ears, as it were, and project onto that performance all the prejudices they have against Liszt: his alleged bombast, superficiality, cheap sentimentality, formlessness, his striving after effect for effect's sake. For, so the audience reckons, a pianist who champions Liszt cannot be taken seriously as an interpreter of the Classics. People forget that Liszt himself was the foremost Beethoven interpreter of his century. It would be more to the point if they were to adopt the opposite approach and accept as an outstanding Liszt player only a pianist who had proved his competence in the interpretation of Classical masterpieces.

So pianists tend to warn one another to avoid performances of Liszt in Amsterdam or Vienna, Munich or Stockholm. Yet in the rest of the world, east and west alike, his piano music continues to cast its spell, although even so one still finds a weakness for a certain type of virtuoso who, unmindful of Classical rules, seems to be at his best whenever – to put it bluntly – the greatest possible number of notes has to be crowded into the shortest possible space of time. Composers as dissimilar as Liszt and Rachmaninov are sometimes mentioned in the same breath, as if genius and the art of elevated conversations were only one step apart. When the difference between a great man and a *grand seigneur* is so lightly ignored, one must regard any enthusiasm for Liszt with caution.

Liszt's musical idiom has been claimed as part of their own by the Hungarians, Germans and French. His love of French poetry and culture – at one time personified by Marie d'Agoult – is as familiar to us as that passion for the Romantic vision of Hungary which addressed his senses chiefly through its gypsy music. Though it would be an exaggeration to say that the Hungarian Rhapsodies occupy as central a place within his *oeuvre* as do the Mazurkas and Polonaises in Chopin's life work, the role played by the gypsy scale in Liszt's compositions from the Weimar period onwards should not be underrated. The musical language of both Berlioz and Chopin also had a significant influence on this style. All three had in common an admiration for Italian *bel canto*. The essential Liszt, however, emerges when we look on him as the pupil of Czerny; as the youth who in Paris discovered for himself and for the public the works of Beethoven and Weber; as the editor and transcriber of Schubert, whose friend, Franz von Schober, was for a time Liszt's secretary, providing him with material for an (unwritten) Schubert biography; and as the elder musical brother of Richard Wagner. Add to this the Saint-Simonian and philanthropist; the kindest and most incorruptible of colleagues; the world-weary Catholic, as well as the man of the world who, even in his old age, was not averse to the adulation of ladies from all circles, particularly the highest – and the picture is rounded off in human, all too human, dimensions. Images such as 'Abbé Liszt at the Villa d'Este, thundering through the Waltz from Gounod's *Faust* while his cassock flutters about him' have circulated long enough. Our critical faculty should guard itself against anecdotes. In the Faustian seriousness of the B minor Sonata there is no room for ambiguities. One has to take Liszt seriously in order to play him well.

It is a peculiarity of Liszt's music that it faithfully and fatally mirrors the character of its interpreter. When his works give the impression of being hollow, superficial and pretentious, the fault lies usually with the performer, occasionally with the (prejudiced) listener, and only rarely with Liszt himself.

Liszt's piano music depends to a great extent on an art that makes us forget the physical side of piano playing. Yet it tends to be a vehicle for players of mere manual ability who lack any deeper musical insight. (In places where Liszt is viewed with disfavour, the conservatory students give themselves over with the same blind zeal to the demolition of Prokofiev sonatas.) The spell of 'technique for its own sake' will soon kill off the weaker brethren, and in the end it may well be Liszt himself who gets the blame for the whole epidemic.

In reality, Liszt stood in angry opposition to the drawing-room virtuosity of his time. He was first and foremost a phenomenon of expressiveness – Schumann called him 'Genie des Vortrags' ('a genius of interpretation') – so much so that he is said to have infused even Czerny and Cramer studies with radiant life. The frenzy and poetry of his music-making, allied to the new-found daredevilry of his technique, must not only have amazed the general public, but also dumbfounded his fellow pianists in the early years. Clara Wieck wrote to Robert Schumann, describing how Liszt's recitals had affected her: 'My own playing seems so boring and haphazard to me now – I've almost lost the inclination to go on tour again. After hearing and seeing Liszt's bravura, I feel like a student'. And again: 'Sometimes you think it's a spirit sitting there at the piano'. Technique served Liszt as a means of opening up new realms of expression. Anyone who is of the opinion that there is even one work by Liszt where gymnastics is the principal aim, had better keep his hands off this composer.

A word about Liszt's form. One must not expect perfection in the Classical sense. The sonatas of Schubert, when measured by the yardstick of Classical form, already reveal nothing but flaws and shortcomings. There is something fragmentary about Liszt's work; its musical argument, perhaps by its nature, is often not brought to a conclusion. But is the fragment not the purest, the most legitimate form of Romanticism? When Utopia becomes the primary goal, when the attempt is made to contain the illimitable, then form will have to remain 'open' in order that the illimitable may enter. It is the business of the interpreter to show us how a general pause may connect rather than separate two paragraphs, how a transition may mysteriously transform the musical argument. This is a magical art. By some process incomprehensible to the intellect, organic unity becomes established, the 'open form' reaches its conclusion in the infinite.

Anyone who does not know the allure of the fragmentary will remain a stranger to much of Liszt's music, and perhaps to Romanticism in general.

This music, therefore, in no way 'plays itself'. One has to interpret it, and interpret it intelligently. Often, it is only one step from the sublime to the ridiculous.

The pianist should be careful not to take that step. It is up to him whether pathos turns into bathos, whether Liszt's heroic fire freezes into a heroic pose, whether his rapt lyricism is smothered under perfumed affectation. He should give the passages of religious meditation simplicity, bring out the devilry behind the capriciousness, and convey the profound resignation behind the strangely bleak experiments of his late works.

He should be sure to use the best modern *Urtext* editions, the first prints or the Breitkopf & Härtel Collected Works, and consult the *Liszt-Pädagogium*.[87] Special attention should be paid to Liszt's pedalling instructions. They provide important information about declamation, colour and atmosphere; they create pedal points, underline harmonic connections. They should be observed, not literally, but in the

---

87 See 'The Noble Liszt', p. 228.

spirit in which they were conceived: that way, the pedalling will not drown the music, but will let it breathe. The pianist should beware of dismissing out of hand pedal marks that seem to endanger clarity where there are numerous secondary notes. It is his job to create transparent textures with the aid of minute pedal vibrations. (Wilhelm Kempff's masterly Decca recordings are a perfect illustration of how this can be done.) Anyone who misconstrues the cadenzas at the start of *Totentanz*, with their chaotic agglomerations of tone masses, and insists on rattling them off *secco*, had better play Stravinsky.

Speeds should be kept in check – as far as the performer's boundless exuberance will permit! It has become virtually obligatory to play Liszt as if he knew only one tempo indication: *prestissimo possibile*. The poor E flat major Concerto in particular has become the target of sporting ambitions. What is the present record – fourteen minutes' playing time? Or has it been bettered to thirteen? The performing style of the mature Liszt tended rather towards majestic breadth; this is borne out, in spite of all necessary scepticism about metronome figures, by the tempo indications in Siloti's edition of *Totentanz* and in the *Liszt-Pädagogium*. As a conductor of Beethoven symphonies too, Liszt is said to have taken slower tempi than was usual – 'with surprising advantage to the overall effect', as even a conservative Leipzig journal could not help but recognise.

Another danger to be avoided is excessive rubato. Of course, it is as unwise to insist on strictness of tempo as it is to lapse into anarchical freedom. Rhythm should be firm yet without constraint, masculine as well as elastic. It should be remembered that Liszt transcribed the First Mephisto Waltz and other piano pieces for large orchestra, so the player should restrict himself in general to tempo modifications that could be achieved by a first-rate orchestra under a first-rate conductor. Liszt's music asks for refinement without pettiness. Works like the Sonata and the Piano Concertos are not patchworks, but symphonic organisms.

Liszt was one of the most amazing revolutionaries in the history of music, and the pianist should prove this both to himself and to others. He should present Liszt's daring harmony with such freshness as to make the listener forget that new harmonic thresholds have been crossed in the intervening hundred years. How 'modern' his late compositions seem! It is no accident that the great pioneers Busoni and Bartók vigorously defended the music.

We are all of Liszt's line. He created the type we aspire to: that of the universal performer of grand stature. To him also we owe our aural imagination and our technique.

It would be nice if some of my fellow pianists were to acknowledge this. It would be nice if the public were to shed a few prejudices. A rehabilitation of Liszt is overdue.

(1961)

Liszt and the Piano Circus – An Afterthought

THE DENIGRATION OF Liszt has long since passed its peak. Today one almost has to defend him from those admirers who tend to see the whole nineteenth century as a kind of pianists' circus and would gladly subscribe funds for research into the achievements of Friedrich Kalkbrenner.

Yet the extent to which the circus is reflected in concert-giving should not be underestimated. The interpreter puts himself on display: a juggler, tightrope-walker and trapeze-artist of piano playing, he performs tricks which even the supremely assured amateur would not believe himself capable of, and although he is not literally risking his neck, he does hazard his prestige for effortless security. It is this security of smoothly working reflexes rather than the communication of musical essentials which even today draws many deeply serious listeners to the concert hall, unaware of their motivation.

The engraving on the title page of Liszt's paraphrase of Halévy's *La Juive* (see p. 226) provides visible evidence of the fact that Liszt himself has contributed to the pianistic spectacular. Of course, his mastery of the instrument practically knew no bounds. But what musical daring underlies the pyrotechnics! How far removed Liszt's display is from the antics of the musical lightweights of his century whose bravura concertos have become the recent passion of a limited group of specialists! And, leaving the circus arena behind, how naturally did Liszt's music react to the Swiss countryside, to Italian works of art or to the deaths of Hungarian friends! While it is being debated whether Henselt, Scharwenka or Moszkowski is to be preferred, even the best works of Smetana – whose Polkas had a similar place in the music of his native country to that of Chopin's Mazurkas and Polonaises in Polish music – still remain virtually unknown.

That some of Liszt's own major piano works have fared no better is exemplified by the neglect of his Variations on *Weinen, Klagen, Sorgen, Zagen*. To me this is one of his most moving masterpieces. The stature of his original piano version – so vastly superior to the subsequent version for organ – is emphasised by the dedication to Anton Rubinstein, the century's other pianistic genius. Young pianists who played the work for Liszt in his last years were ironically informed by the master that 'this piece is a total flop'; how could anyone play such sombre 'hospital music' when art was supposed to be cheerful? Liszt produced a superb example of programme music at its most emotional, and least pictorial. A very wide range of human suffering is suggested with almost austere concentration. Chromaticism stands for suffering and insecurity, while 'pure' diatonic harmony, introduced at the conclusion of the piece, represents the certainty of faith. We are reminded of the opening of Haydn's *Creation*, where Chaos and Light follow one another in a comparable way. In Liszt's work 'Light' is identical with the chorale 'Was Gott tut, das ist wohlgetan', which, incidentally, also closes Bach's Cantata. Liszt succeeds in offering relief without a trace of triviality: the entry of the chorale is a miracle of tenderness.

Liszt does not appear as the most self-critical of composers. Yet he realised sooner than anyone where the development of musical harmony would lead, and he adhered to this perception with admirable integrity. Consequently, his later pieces leave tonality and consolation behind. The analogy between the religious faith and the faith in the imperishable power of the triad had ceased to ring true.

(1976)

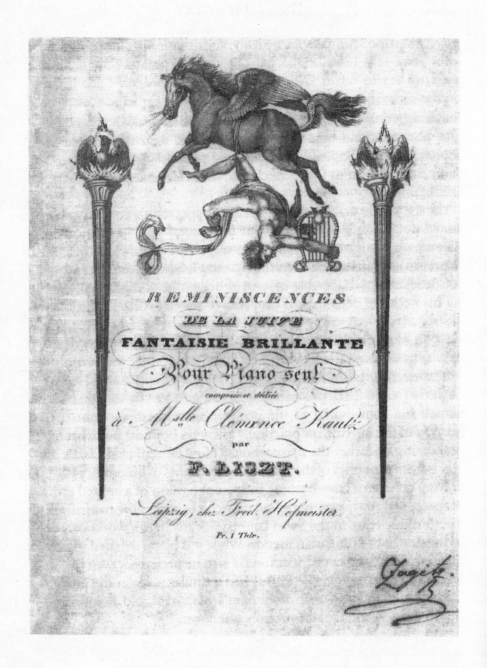

The title page of Liszt's paraphrase of Halévy's La Juive.

The Noble Liszt

D O COMPOSERS GAIN from posthumous anniversaries? If their greatness is well enough established, the playing of their lesser-known works may further enhance their reputation; if unduly neglected, they may be helped out of their oblivion. Those afflicted by a history of chronic misrepresentation, pervasive malice and lingering doubt stand the slimmest chance. Celebrating the 100th anniversary of Liszt's death and the 175th of his birth, a plethora of Liszt festivals, marathons and competitions may well prove to have further obscured the stature of a man who has to be defended on several fronts: against some of his champions and partisan admirers, against the crowd of sceptics and adversaries, and, to a lesser extent, against himself.

When Liszt died, he made the mistake of leaving behind an unusual legacy of envy. There is a relation between envy and posthumous fame. Liszt's early European success as virtuoso and improviser equalled that of Mozart; a few years later, his 'genius of expression' (Schumann) and boundless pianistic skill made him, as a player, superior even to Chopin, Mendelssohn or Clara Schumann. The combination of a lively mind, personal magnetism, masculine beauty, the social triumphs enjoyed by a privileged parvenu and a love life bordering on scandal turned out to be, within one human being, barely forgivable. There was a conspicuous absence of mitigating circumstances, such as Mozart's or Schubert's early death, Mozart's alleged impoverishment and 'unmarked pauper's grave', Schubert's syphilis, Beethoven's deafness, Chopin's consumption or Schumann's mental disorder – features that make the fame of a genius a great deal more gratifying, and guarantee its solidity. (Wagner's monstrous egotism and merciless promotion of his own ends, while not stimulating compassion or malicious glee, present a frame of mind many people enjoy sharing.)

Arguably, Liszt and Haydn are the most frequently misunderstood among major composers; their biographies afford little food for pity. (The insufferable bigotry of Haydn's wife and the senility of his last years do not, it seems, sufficiently atone for his achievement in being the first great symphonist and the grand master of the string quartet.) In old age, Haydn reigned over the musical world as its undisputed leading light. For this, the nineteenth century punished him – as it punished Liszt for his undisputed supremacy as a performer. Haydn was branded the ingenuous

Classicist (something he rarely was), 'the family friend who is always welcome but has nothing to say that is new' (Schumann). Liszt, in his compositions, was seen as a poseur and charlatan (which he only occasionally was), the embodiment of a superficial and bombastic Romanticism. Not until our century did a greater number of composers – from Richard Strauss, Ravel and Busoni to Schoenberg, Bartók and Boulez – appreciate Liszt by taking him seriously.

One of the more interesting recent German contributions to Liszt scholarship is the belated publication of Lina Ramann's *Lisztiana* (1895),[88] a collection of reminiscences by Liszt's official biographer. 'Alas', exclaims Miss Ramann after listening to some of Liszt's classes, 'none of our masters is so dependent on performances that make sense of their compositions ... and only too few players manage to get through to the core of his music! There is a lack of either poetry, or intelligence, or wealth of feeling'. In Liszt's case, performance is less a matter of quality than of existence: a 'to be or not to be' of a work, its spark of life. Possibly Liszt entrusted his musical executants with too much power; his demands upon them reflect the transcendent authority of the greatest performing musician of his day.

Most leading pianists of the later nineteenth century had been, at least briefly, among Liszt's disciples; yet, despite all claims to the contrary, no convincing tradition of Liszt playing developed. Of course Liszt, after his virtuoso years, hardly ever performed his own works himself, and did very little to promote them. (Rather, he helped others, notably Wagner.) In the *Liszt-Pädagogium*, a valuable set of comments on the performance of some of Liszt's works by his pupils, recently republished by Breitkopf & Härtel, the editor, again Lina Ramann, counters certain misconceptions about Liszt's style. According to Miss Ramann, Liszt should be taken as a lyrical tone poet first and foremost – as a rhetorician, rhapsodist and mime. The poetic essence of a piece explains its form; the musical spirit creates its technique.

But poetic freedom is not, 'as the practice of immature virtuosos may suggest, distortion of form', nor is it 'autonomy of virtuoso fingers'. The *grosse Stil* (grand style) becomes possible only through Liszt's 'periodic execution' that prevails over bar-lines and metric stereotypes. The *melos*, or melodic spirit, in Liszt no less than in Wagner, permeates everything; it contains Liszt's 'profundity [*Innerlichkeit*] and passion' – which brings us to qualities that, alongside the grand style, should be

---

88   Published by Schott (Mainz, 1983).

mandatory for Liszt players. Passion and introspection, daring and nobility by no means exclude one another. Nobility need not be pale or academic. Neither should passion have to be vulgar. Miss Ramann warns against mistaking 'passage-work' for an invitation to technical bravura, and stresses the importance of rests and pauses – a point later taken up by Busoni in his *Outline of the New Aesthetic of Music* – telling us they may be of 'longer or shorter duration' (than their written value) and have to be determined 'precisely by the character of each transition'.

For Liszt, the much-maligned programme musician, music was fundamentally a tool of poetic expression, and the piano an object to be transformed into an orchestra, turned into the elements, lifted into the spheres. In lesser hands, his extraordinary pianistic demands risk becoming an end in themselves. Chopin's strictly pianistic music provided the ideal medium for a concept of sound that limits itself to a certain idea of beauty, and specialises in maintaining the most ravishing timbre. In Liszt's piano style, the concept of a 'beautiful' sound is superseded by that of an expressive one. Subservient to the desire to encompass every facet of experience, and freed from classical restrictions, the piano is made to release the whole gamut of colour, dynamics and nuance, and encouraged to forget its own boundaries.

Liszt's 'poetic' imagination relied no less on the sensations of the surrounding world than on those of the world within. Their musical transmission is often amazingly subtle and precise – a feat the performer should demonstrate to his audience, and himself. Those who conceive music as 'absolute' and autonomous should find plenty to admire in Liszt's B minor Sonata, the one major work that makes do without any programme or motto; but, even here, they will lose a large domain of Lisztian expression. Without its poetic core, Liszt's music easily degenerates into a vehicle of *Effekt*, which, in its German sense, has been defined as 'effect without cause' by Wagner. On the other hand, it would be a grave mistake to overlook, or underestimate, Liszt's musical intellect even if it was not always employed to full advantage. In the end, response to poetic images may come more easily to many than the insight into Liszt's professional mastery of part-writing (often dissolved in figuration), and the coherence of the musical whole.

Liszt's music, unlike that of Mozart, projects the man. With rare immediacy, it gives away the character of the composer as well as the musical probity of his executant. Hans von Bülow, Liszt's favourite pupil and the first pianist to offer a complete Liszt recital, taught his students to distinguish between *Gefühl* (feeling) and *Dusel* (giddiness, sentimentality). Likewise, one might add, the Liszt player should keep pathos and *Schwulst* (pomposity) firmly apart. When playing Liszt's superb variations on Bach's *Weinen, Klagen, Sorgen, Zagen,* he or she should make the music weep, lament, worry and despair without lapsing into howling, or chattering of teeth, and, at the work's conclusion, whether a believer or not, prove capable of demonstrating certainty of faith without producing a wrong gesture. To a good mime, nothing should be unattainable.

'Good taste is a barrier to an understanding and appreciation of the nineteenth century', writes Charles Rosen. For Busoni, who stunned Berlin audiences with his series of Liszt recitals in 1905, feeling had to be linked to taste, and style. According to him, the popular concept of feeling ignores taste, and therefore relishes sentimentality and over-projection. In the matter of taste, no composer could be more vulnerable than Liszt. In contrast to Charles Rosen ('To comprehend Liszt's greatness one needs a suspension of distaste, a momentary renunciation of musical scruples'),[89] I consider it a principal task of the Liszt player to cultivate such scruples, and distil the essence of Liszt's nobility. This obligation is linked to the privilege of choosing from Liszt's enormous output works that offer both originality and finish, generosity and control, dignity and fire. Where Liszt has been casual and uncritical, the player, and listener, must come to his rescue. After eliminating many a lesser piece, there still remains a rich harvest, at least within his piano music. It is bound to include his Sonata, the *Années de pèlerinage,* the *Weinen, Klagen* variations, late pieces like *Mosonyi Mihály,* and a selection from the Etudes – works I feel to be on a par with the best of Chopin and Schumann.

Though enjoying, once in a while, some of the Hungarian Rhapsodies and operatic paraphrases, I wince at Charles Rosen's assertion that 'only a view of Liszt that places the Second Hungarian Rhapsody in the centre of his work will do him justice', or at the kind of praise he gives to Liszt's *Réminiscences de Don Juan*:

> With his international reputation for erotic conquest already set, Liszt must have known that the public would take his fantasy as a self-portrait, just as everyone had assumed that Byron's *Don Juan* was an autobiography. As Mozart, in *The*

---

89 'The New Sound of Liszt', *The New York Review of Books* (12 April 1984).

Magic Flute, had used coloratura brilliance as a metaphor for rage and power, so Liszt uses virtuosity here as a representation of sexual domination.

Once again virtuosity and sexuality are in the spotlight. With such distinguished support, the argument whether Liszt's niche should be in the pantheon or in a bazaar of oddities and monstrosities may well drag on.

It is difficult to find, for Liszt's music, a fitting national identity. In the end, not even Hungary laid claim to it after Liszt made the mistake of equating the native folklore of his country with gypsy music. Instead of 'specializing in himself', Liszt presents a panorama of style. His skill in appropriation resembles that of his beloved gypsies. Already the intellectual poets of German Romanticism had half adopted, half created a manner of folk poetry; and later nineteenth-century architects made unhesitating use of past styles. Not until Stravinsky, however, did another composer emerge who elaborated on the most varied musical material without losing himself.

Liszt's variety extends from the sacred to the utterly profane, from the lavishly sumptuous to the ascetic – and from the careless to the masterly. His music was deemed lacking in 'Germanity' as long as instrumental music was taken to be a German monopoly. For European purists of the twentieth century, on the other hand, only original compositions were admissible until recently, and preferably those which avoided rhetoric, apotheoses and arpeggios. While much of Liszt's music assimilates material from elsewhere, the use he makes of it is not uniformly felicitous. Melodies by his operatic contemporaries, folk tunes and Gregorian chant lend themselves more readily to Liszt's handling than does Mozart's or Schubert's idiom; this is not a question of Mozart's or Schubert's tunes being too good for Liszt but of Liszt's treatment clashing, to my ears, painfully with their style and character. (An exception is Schubert's *Wanderer* Fantasy, which Liszt understood well enough; here his error was to 'set free', in an orchestral score, qualities that are supposed to turn the piano itself into an orchestra.)[90] These days, arrangements have regained respectability. If Liszt, however, had left nothing but his Lied tran-

---

90   Liszt's *partitions de piano*, his straight piano transcriptions of orchestral scores such as Beethoven's symphonies or Weber's overtures, are an entirely different matter; what they require from the player is not a 'Lisztification' of style but a faithful reproduction, as far as the piano permits, of their original orchestral colour.

scriptions and operatic paraphrases, he would hardly be better remembered than his erstwhile rival Thalberg.

It is upon some of his original compositions that his fame most durably rests. To deny Liszt a melodic style of his own would be unfair, even if the quality of its invention wavers. (Among Liszt's occasional shortcomings are facile melody, the compulsion to say something two or three times, lack of formal economy and a reliance on the glorious and idealistic.) The B minor Sonata shows none of his weaknesses; none of the themes is disappointing, patterns of repeated phrases help to articulate the structure, the grand design is impressively controlled and the projected *fortissimo* ending has been replaced by a moving and mysterious lyrical coda. Altogether, this is the most satisfying sonata written after Beethoven and Schubert, two of the three composers Liszt most ardently admired. (The third, at least in Liszt's earlier years, was Weber.) It has remained the only one of Liszt's large-scale works that, to the last bar, shows him in complete command; all the others, whether orchestral or vocal, suffer, if intermittently, from a lack of economy, direction, thematic distinction or freshness. (Liszt was not, like Busoni, a natural orchestrator unless he used his own instrument as an orchestra; and he is, to me, more convincing in some of his religious piano pieces – a genre he created – than in his church music.)

Liszt's works show various degrees of finish. Some were published in several versions; in others, optional variants (*ossias*) testify to restlessness and indecision. In the case of the Transcendental Studies and many pieces from the *Années de pèlerinage* (a few have remained unaltered), the final versions are almost invariably the most satisfying. It was one of Liszt's great achievements during his Weimar years to have made some of his potentially finest compositions playable, if only by a few, and to have clarified their musical purpose. Sometimes a new version amounted to a new piece. The player may permit himself, here and there, to adopt a detail from an earlier version as long as it fits into the definitive one without altering its formal design.

In the only version of his B minor Sonata, Liszt has achieved the same practical clarity of notation that we have learned to respect in Beethoven or Brahms. It is a myth that Liszt needs the kind of extemporizing performer he himself is known to have been on occasion. But was he really, as Harold C. Schonberg maintains, invariably bored if he could not prove his alertness by adding something to the pieces he played? Even if this were so, he would be better served by ardent, if critical, devotion than by performers pretending to be another Liszt. Some of his improvised *ossias* can be attributed to a lack of practice time; his activities as composer, virtuoso, conductor, teacher, writer of essays and letters, reader, lover, society figure, supporter of colleagues, abbé, tireless traveller, whist player and cigar and cognac addict make it evident that he must have been used to either sight-reading or relying on his memory.

Liszt would surely have been the first to object to others meddling with his texts unless he had given the player an *ad libitum* authorisation, as in the cadenza of his Second Rhapsody. (One wonders what he would have made of Horowitz's recorded performance of 'Vallée d'Obermann', which, among various changes, omits several bars of its stormy middle section.) In his *Memories of Liszt* (1877) Alexander Borodin writes:

> In spite of having heard so much, and frequently, about his playing, I was surprised by its simplicity, sobriety and severity; primness, affectation, and anything that aims only at surface effects, is completely absent. His tempi are moderate; he does not push them or become hot headed. Nevertheless, there is inexhaustible energy, passion, enthusiasm and fire. The tone is round, full and strong; the clarity, richness and variety of nuance is marvellous.

Liszt's supposedly arbitrary handling of the music of others is uncorroborated by his editions of Beethoven's concertos, and Beethoven's and Schubert's sonatas,[91] while his pupils hardly dared to touch up his own texts, so that obvious writing or printing mistakes have lingered on to this day. As Liszt confessed, he was a good proofreader where others were concerned but a bad one for himself.

Modern chroniclers of the piano like to call Liszt a showman. That he was capable of behaving ostentatiously during the most hectic years of his virtuoso career, throwing his kid gloves to the floor of the stage, and staring at the ladies while playing, is undeniable. As a general characterisation of his art and personality, however, the label is undeserved. Liszt was the first to depart from the salon. To the displeasure of some contemporaries, he democratised the concert by occasionally performing for an audience of thousands in large theatres like Milan's La Scala. This required a

---

91   The sonatas by Weber, however, are a different matter; in Liszt's questionable elaboration of these works, his own promise that the large print would reproduce Weber's authentic text while all of Liszt's additions would appear small in print, was not kept. I counted nearly a hundred errors and changes in the large print of the first movement of the A flat Sonata alone.

different projection of music, one based on a physically freer and more demonstrative treatment of the piano that, when we take account of the feeble instruments of the 1830s and 1840s, may well have gone through three pianos during one evening. He also inaugurated the 'recital', a concert presented by one single player, and was promptly castigated for his self-sufficiency.

The personal life of Liszt, like that of Paganini, soon became the subject of myth and calumny. Neither his alleged noble origin nor the 'evidence' of his unofficial children bears scrutiny. Liszt inhabited a world peopled by women writers and fascinated by *romans à clef*. George Sand and Marie d'Agoult parted company over private indiscretions revealed in Balzac's *Béatrix*. The Countess d'Agoult, under the pen-name Daniel Stern, then gave vent to her resentment against Liszt in her novel *Nélida*; in the guise of a painter, Liszt is accused of being unable to produce works in a large format, a charge he once and for all refuted with his B minor Sonata a few years later.

The pinnacle of malice was reached by Olga Janina, who, as we are told by Dezsö Legány and Alan Walker, was neither a countess nor a Cossack but a pathological impostor. It is significant that Ernest Newman, the respected biographer of Wagner, was taken in by her books because they represent Liszt, in accordance with his own view, as a weak character. If Liszt was thought in the English-speaking world – at least until the publication of his letters to the Baroness Meyendorff (1979) – 'to be vain, duplicitous and, above all, a showman, given to the tawdry and bombastic in life as in art' (Robert Craft), this was due mainly to Newman's *The Man Liszt*, a book ungenerous to the point of defamation while always priding itself on its 'objectivity'. It was, to Robert Craft,[92] a 'complete and welcome surprise' that Liszt emerged from the Meyendorff correspondence as genuinely modest, sincere in his religious convictions, commonsensical, wise and full of understanding of human nature. Newman's distorted portrait rests on his musical scepticism: where access of Liszt's music is clouded by prejudice, or lack of sympathy, the outline of Liszt's personality easily becomes shaped according to the writer's distrust. Eduard Hanslick, Vienna's ruling critic, was a remarkable exception: he esteemed Liszt highly as a man and as a performer, although he despised his compositions.

---

92   'The New Liszt', *The New York Review of Books* (5 February 1981).

During his lifetime, Liszt must have had his portrait painted more frequently than any other celebrity in Europe. In a new pictorial and documentary biography that should for many years set a standard for accuracy and splendour (Ernst Burger, *Franz Liszt*, List Verlag, Munich, 1986), an oil sketch shows him being painted by three painters at once. But Liszt's vanity was counterbalanced by his selflessness, his urge to dominate held in check by his humility. Has there been another musician as generously helpful, as magnanimously appreciative? Liszt bore the *amertume de cœur* (bitterness of heart), the personal and artistic disappointments of his later years, with imposing self-control. He mustered the strength to react against the hysteria surrounding a triumphant virtuoso career by leaving the concert platform at the age of thirty-five; he did penance for a superabundance of notes by carrying music, in his uncompromising and spare late pieces, to the brink of silence.

To be sure, the excess of worship bestowed on him by blind admirers, and the biographical semi-fiction fabricated by his mistress Carolyne Sayn-Wittgenstein in conjunction with Lina Ramann, was bound to provoke criticism. Here Liszt must take some of the blame. At the end of a questionnaire submitted to him by Miss Ramann before she completed the first volume of her biography, Liszt, to her bewilderment, volunteered the advice: 'Don't get too entangled in details. My biography has to be made up rather than made out.' ('Meine Biographie ist weit mehr zu erfinden als nachzuschreiben.') Meanwhile, even his renunciation of public concerts (except for charity) and his taking minor orders have been turned into acts of Lisztian self-pro-motion. To steer clear of the devotional figure on the one side, and the vulgarian of films and gossip magazines on the other, one needs precise information, and good will. The most urgent requirement, however, is that of musical fairness. A musical charter of human rights, if there were such a concept, would grant any composer the basic privilege of being judged by his finest works, and their worthiest perfor-mances. Whether this Liszt year has brought us any nearer to such an ideal state of affairs remains the question.

(1986)

Franz Liszt. Bust, possibly by Ludwig von Zumbusch, from the estate of the pianist Josef Pembaur.

Photograph © John Batten, London. (Collection Alfred Brendel)

Liszt's *Années de pèlerinage* I and II

NEXT TO THE B minor Sonata, Liszt's *Années* seem to me one of his finest achievements. The first two *Années* combine a youthful direct-ness – the material for most of the pieces comes from his late twenties – with the advanced clarity and control of the Weimar period, while the Third Year offers generous examples of Liszt's late style before it shrank into fragmentary, and enigmatic, brevity.

The B minor Sonata should convert all those who have chosen to see Liszt mainly as an assimilator of styles and tunes not his own, and as a composer who could never truly finish a piece. The *Années de pèlerinage*, on the other hand, draw for their inspi-ration on a reservoir of diverse impressions – nature and musical folklore, art and religion, craving for freedom; above all, on poetry and literature.

Arriving at the final version was not always easy. Liszt, the improviser, composed at an awesome speed that hardly allowed time for reflection. The sometimes chaotic and overwritten music of his virtuoso years needed to be organised and purified. It became Liszt's habit to amend at least some details of his earlier works when he returned to them later on, unless he preferred to recompose whole sections. (In the case of the 'Chapelle de Guillaume Tell', barely a faint memory of one theme has survived.) Invariably, it is the poetic idea of each piece that continues to fire Liszt's musical imagination. It would be a mistake to assume that the greater transparency and fluency of the later versions involves a sacrifice of such pianistic obstacles as are musically relevant; rather, monstrosities are purged, or reduced to human scale.

Of the nine pieces that make up the Swiss Year, two ('Au lac de Wallenstadt' and 'Eglogue') have remained virtually untouched. A third one, 'Orage', was composed at a later date (1855). Of the rest, Liszt's Weimar versions are clearly superior, or at least, as in 'Pastorale' and 'Le mal du pays', equally successful. Only in the open-ing of 'Les cloches de Genève' has Liszt's slimming resulted in anaemia; the piano writing of the early draft is so much more seductive that I have decided to retain it, along with some details from the original 'Vallée d'Obermann'.

The early versions of the Swiss Year had been published in Liszt's *Album d'un voyageur*. To be a wanderer and pilgrim, not belonging anywhere, and looking for a place to belong, was a central concept of Romanticism. George Sand's *Lettres d'un voyageur*, Byron's *Childe Harold's Pilgrimage* and Schubert's various 'Wanderers' must have contributed to Liszt's frame of mind, as did E. P. de Sénancour's *Obermann*, in whose footsteps Liszt and Marie d'Agoult roamed through Switzerland, just as their Italian route followed that of Goethe, Chateaubriand and Madame de Staël in the footsteps of Montesquieu. The writers who inspired Liszt's Swiss Year shared a disdain for convention while oscillating between ecstatic lyricism and a sceptical (Sénancour) or cynical (Byron) outlook on life.

Of Beethoven's developmental approach to composition which permeates Liszt's B minor Sonata, the *Années de pèlerinage* show no trace; the first two Years are much closer to Berlioz and Franco-Italian opera[93] than to the Austro-German masters. What united most Romantics, however, was the disavowal of predictable forms on one side and the striving for an ultimate simplicity on the other.

Première année: Suisse

The First Year of Pilgrimage (Switzerland) deals with nature in a twofold sense: as nature around us, and as the nature within. Liszt's own nature was full of compassion; his charitable disposition had a direct bearing on his revolutionary sympathies. In 'Lyon', a piece later discarded, Liszt commemorates the uprising of textile workers. Visiting the 'Chapelle de Guillaume Tell', he is reminded of the Swiss struggle for liberation. In the central section the signals of revolt reverberate through the mountainside until 'freedom' is achieved. Three different kinds of dotted rhythm make for diversity within the unity. (Appropriately, Schiller's well-known line 'Einer für Alle, alle für Einen' – 'One for all, all for one' – is the motto.) Musically, the piece is close to Bellini, whom Liszt had transferred to the piano in some of his grandest paraphrases.

Byron's lines which preface 'Au lac de Wallenstadt' contrast the stillness of the lake with the 'wild world'. Should one not 'forsake Earth's troubled waters for a purer spring'? The beginning of the piece rivals Schubert's ability to distil the essence of a song in an initial figure; here it is the movement of the oars, the gliding over the lake and the melancholy of twilight that are established before a yodelling melody comes in. In the first of his *Moments musicaux*, Schubert had provided a mountain tune as well as its musical mountain range. Liszt's *chant montagnard* is, on its later

---

93   Rossini's *Guillaume Tell* had been first performed in Paris in 1829.

appearances, embellished with echoes and spiky contours. The elegance of 'Au lac de Wallenstadt' is Mendelssohnian, with the added bonus of *plein air* painting. As in 'Pastorale' and 'Eglogue', Liszt demonstrates the high art of being natural, and makes it hard to decide whether such delicious simplicity should be taken as the reverse of Romantic *raffinement* or, rather, as its very peak.

In contrast to his impressionist descendants, Liszt experienced nature through the eyes of literature. 'Pastorale' may be an exception: in it, without any accompanying words, an ancient alphorn melody is presented in a straightforward manner. The only whiff of artifice is the alternation of veiled and distinct areas of sound.

After these two vignettes of rural life, two splendid poetic études follow. 'Au bord d'une source' (Allegretto grazioso, dolce tranquillo) creates the illusion of a shimmering multitude of drops by means of delicately clashing or suspended seconds. Again, the printed words give the player valuable information: Schiller tells him that the 'games of young nature' begin in 'murmuring coolness' – which may prevent him from turning the piece into a fountain of perfume.

In relation to 'Orage', some lines by Byron speculate on the nature of tempests. 'Are ye like those within the human breast? Or do ye find, at length, like eagles, some high nest?' There is certainly no 'high nest' for the storm unleashed here in torrential octaves; it remains an elemental uproar in the blackest C minor.

In 'Vallée d'Obermann', a superb fantasy on the first three notes of its opening theme, the gates of the human breast are again wide open, yet this is less a passionate symbol of surrounding nature than a vehicle for grandiose introspection and personal confession. Thanks to Sainte-Beuve's recommendation, Sénancour's *Obermann* became a favourite of a whole generation of French Romantics. Liszt called it 'the monochord of the relentless solitude of human pain', but also 'the book that soothes my sufferings'. For Obermann, the intellectual drop-out and radical sceptic, every cause is hidden, every purpose deceptive, and nature remains impenetrable. The opening of 'Vallée d'Obermann' paints a musical picture of solitary despair. As it turns into major keys, however, the piece adopts Sénancour's belief that the only dependable truth is in one's own feelings: 'to feel, to exist – only to be consumed by irresistible desire, to become intoxicated by the spell of an unreal world, and finally to perish in its beguiling deception'.

In utmost contrast, 'Eglogue' is all lightness and graceful perfection. Byron describes the morning, 'with cheek all bloom, laughing the clouds away with playful scorn'. The title of the piece refers to Virgil who, in his bucolic poetry, had erected a vision of an Arcadia that is removed from reality, an elevated land of blessed being into which Liszt introduces us with the help of a Swiss shepherd song.

Another long quotation from *Obermann* muses on the Romantic effects of nature in the unspoilt countryside: they are 'the sounds of a primeval language not intelligible to all people'. In a footnote, Liszt himself calls such 'hidden sanctuaries' 'the last refuge of a free and simple mind'.

'Le mal du pays' is based on a *ranz-des-vaches* (herdsman's melody) from the Appenzell that had been mentioned as early as 1710 in an essay on the impact of homesickness. This impact, according to Rousseau, was so devastating that the playing of *ranz-des-vaches* among Swiss mercenaries had been forbidden on pain of death. While the first version of 'Le mal du pays' treats its rhapsodic alphorn tune (and some other Swiss melodies) without comment, as it were, the second version adds the psychological connotations of homesickness: within the E minor melancholy, brief episodes in major keys open up like visions of an unattainable paradise. 'Happiness is where you are not' – this statement of a fundamental Romantic experience had been composed by Schubert in his song 'Der Wanderer'.[94]

The last piece of the Swiss Year, 'Les cloches de Genève', makes do, in its final version, without any dedication or motto. It moves away from the literary sphere and into a private one – a song of love in the expansive style of Liszt's 'Cantique d'amour' or 'Bénédiction'. Only the definitive version contains this cantilena: by then, the Princess Sayn-Wittgenstein had supplanted Marie d'Agoult (and the newborn Blandine to whom the first version was dedicated) as the mistress of Liszt's emotions. The introduction of the piece projects the sounds of distant nocturnal bells, dreamlike and beguiling. According to Liszt, the player should surprise himself, and play the beginning as if 'unprepared'.[95]

Deuxième année: Italie

The Second Year (Italy) of the *Années* focuses on works of art and literature. 'Sposalizio' (after Raphael's *Betrothal of the Virgin* in Milan) manages to employ highly

---

94 In a less Romantic mood, Liszt called the same statement 'la maxime du bonheur conjugal', according to his daughter Cosima (*Franz Liszt, ein Gedenkblatt von seiner Tochter*, Bruckmann, 1991).

95 Wilhelm Jerger: *Franz Liszts Klavierunterricht 1884–86*, Gustav Bosse, 1975, p. 147.

sophisticated harmony in order to create an aura of elated innocence. Its initial melodic figure – pentatonic, undulating and seemingly improvised – turns out to be of greater significance than the *cantabile* themes; increasingly, it casts an exotic spell over the piece that looks forward to Debussy.

'Il pensieroso' stunningly anticipates Wagnerian harmony. It refers to a sculpture and a poem by Michelangelo whose quatrain 'The Speech of Night' serves as a clue to the music: 'I am grateful to be asleep, and more grateful to be made of stone, as long as injustice and shame remain on earth. I count it a blessing not to see or feel; so do not wake me – speak softly!' The sculpture is a statue on the tomb of Lorenzo de'Medici in Florence. Liszt wanted this piece, in an augmented orchestral version, to be performed at his own funeral.

'Canzonetta del Salvator Rosa', a carefree marching song, is a later addition to the set. Its allusions seem threefold: to Salvator Rosa the adventurer, who wrote its words ('While I often change my place of being, the fire of my love remains unchanged'); to Salvator Rosa the Baroque painter, whose self-portrait in the National Gallery in London reveals a remarkable physical likeness to Liszt himself; and, unwittingly, to Giovanni Bononcini, who wrote the tune. (This is the only arrangement of somebody else's music within the set.)

The three Petrarch Sonnets are very free transcriptions of songs Liszt wrote before 1839. Both the early piano versions and the songs were extensively reworked in the Weimar years. In his 'Sonetto 47' Petrarch blesses the hour when Laura cast her first glance upon him, in spite of the longing, the pain, the tears and the 'resonance of sighs' that it has brought in its wake. 'Sonetto 104' evokes the ambivalence of love. The poem tells of its freezing glow, its seeing blindness and its weeping laughter. 'While I hate myself, I ardently love others'. Liszt's treatment of this array of oxymorons is intensely powerful, and on an almost constant level of *forte*; only the epilogue gives in to resignation – 'This is what you, my mistress, have done to me'.

'Sonetto 123' lifts us into an unearthly state: Laura is seen as an angel. Her sighs and words are capable of softening stones and stopping rivers. The heavens hold their breath, and no leaf dares move. The final expiring of the piece seems to conclude all conclusions, and brings the sequence of the first six pieces to a close.

'Après une lecture de Dante' has adopted the title of a poem by Victor Hugo that begins with the line 'The poet who paints Hell paints his own life'. The relation between the A flat of the preceding 'Sonetto 123' and its own key of D minor is that of a tritone: *diabolus in musica*. The opening theme of the Dante Fantasy is based on tritones as well; according to Liszt's pupil Stradal, it does *not* represent the inscription above Dante's gate of Hell, but should be understood as a call to the spirits of the damned to rise – 'Step out, shadows, from the realm of misery and distress!' The chromatic theme (Presto agitato assai) then suggests the approach and wailing of the damned – their contours blurred by Liszt's direction to maintain a continuous five-bar pedal – while the first appearance of the chorale (F sharp major, *fff*, double octaves) is a portrait of Lucifer.

After the return of the rousing tritones, the music depicts the Francesca da Rimini episode: 'Nessun maggior dolore, che ricordarsi del tempo felice nella miseria' ('There is no greater sorrow than to remember happy times while in misery'). Later on, in Stradal's view, the damned mock, split up and trivialise their themes of grief. The piece is as near to Berlioz as anything Liszt ever wrote, yet strikingly original. It is rightly subtitled 'Fantasia quasi sonata' and not, as in Beethoven's Op. 27, 'Sonata quasi una fantasia'. The concept of the fantasy remains variable; while relating to the familiar forms, it makes free use of them, calls them into question, tears them apart or amalgamates several at once. Not until the B minor Sonata did Liszt compose a large-scale work in which the psychological cohesion is matched by the cohesion of musical structure.

(1986)

Liszt's B Minor Sonata

I F, A S I believe, the B minor Sonata represents the exception among Liszt's works, what is the rule? For me, Liszt is a master of the shorter format, the creator of the religiously inspired piano piece, the magical transformer and unchallenged orchestrator of piano sound, the generous musical poet, visionary and revolutionary. Pieces the size of 'Vallée d'Obermann', 'Funérailles' or the Variations on Bach's *Weinen, Klagen, Sorgen, Zagen* show his command of an often innovatory idiom. His musical imagination is nourished by a large variety of intellectual and emotional food; literature and the arts, religion and nature, personalities and ideas, the political struggle for freedom and an awareness of death all contribute to it. The B minor Sonata, on the other hand, the most original, powerful and intelligent sonata composed after Beethoven and Schubert, is a work of absolute music, and it exemplifies total control of large form. Its blend of deliberation and white heat, unique in Liszt's output, remains all the more astonishing as it was achieved in the face of a most demanding task: a one-movement sonata of half an hour's duration.

Themes, Characters

What, in comparison with Liszt's 'Faust' Symphony, becomes immediately evident is that none of the themes is a disappointment. Six strongly individual characters are introduced – I shall call them themes, and ignore the controversial aspects of this term. The first impression produced by these themes, their initial character, remains, despite all later metamorphosis, the main source of information for the listener who does not want to lose his bearings.

The first three themes are presented one after the other. They could be called an introductory group. (Whether one perceives the Sonata to contain four, five or six themes depends on one's view of this group; one could also subdivide it into two, separating the passive Lento theme from the two active Allegro characters.)

The *First Theme* (Lento, sotto voce, quasi G minor, bars 1–7) relates sound to silence. Syncopations are preceded by 'accented' rests. Musically, the theme is representative not of speech or singing, but of thinking. Interspersed between short, muted blows on G – quasi timpani plus pizzicato – one hears two descending scales, the Phrygian and the gypsy scale. Questions are posed, doubts arise. Harmonic expectations, if any, point towards C minor.

I have come across two commercial recordings of the Sonata that omit the first bar. The sound engineers, apparently assuming that the pianist had not seriously started, edited it away. Little did they know that a good sonata exposes its basic material at once. Thus the repeated notes of this beginning are among the motifs that are important to the whole work. (Each of the themes takes off from, or is introduced by, repeated notes.) Other motifs to remember are the intervals of the seventh and the second, as well as the opening rhythm.

In the *Second Theme* (Allegro energico, B minor, bars 8–13) an actor makes his grand entrance on stage. His attitude is a mixture of defiance, despair and contempt. May I call him Faust? Not before the angry octave triplets in bar 10 do we realise that B minor may be the basic key.

The *Third Theme* (Marcato, bars 14–18) follows suit. It counters Faust's questions with its own. The character, instigating subversion, is Mephistophelean. Faust and Mephisto join, fifteen bars later, to produce what could be called a symphonic main idea (sempre forte ed agitato). With the initial group the presentation of motivic material comes to an end. All remaining themes now belong to major keys.

The *Fourth Theme* (Grandioso, D major, bars 105–13) is derived from the first in rhythm and melodic substance. It is preceded by a transition on a pedal point that is as gripping as anything the work has to offer. The word 'grandioso' is appropriately chosen for a theme that carries the conviction of omnipotence.[96]

---

96   I cannot reconcile myself to recent religious interpretations of the Sonata. Surely any religious view of the work must stand or fall by assessment of the so-called 'Cross motif'. If its use in the amorous B major tune of the E flat major Concerto, or the grotesquely exuberant march from the same work with its cymbal crash, marks these themes as religious, then all music might well be called religious, in the manner in which all art was deemed political not too long ago.

The Grandioso theme of the Sonata is, to me, ruled out as a theme of religious character by the imperious gesture of its ending, which suggests, to a psychologically inclined listener, megalomania rather than omnipotence.

Having played a good number of Liszt's religious pieces, I have found them to be distinguished by a specific poetry, a devotional aura, rather than by intervals of a motif the use of which is as little confined to the religious sphere as Liszt's religious music can be defined by it. For me, the Faust-Mephisto-Gretchen constellation does better justice to the Sonata as I understand it. However, it remains a working hypothesis, and my personal luxury. The B minor Sonata does not need a programme.

The *Fifth Theme* (Cantando espressivo, D major, bars 153–70) sets out as a lyrical variant of the third: Mephisto turned into a vision of Gretchen – if, for the sake of enlivening the terminology and simplifying description, one agrees to accept such verbal crutches in a work that makes do without them. Nine bars later we discover Faust to be under Gretchen's spell; there is no doubt about it that we experience the events of this work from his point of view. The first eight bars of the theme are clearly based, in its bass line, on Theme 1 (seventh and descending scale).

The *Sixth Theme* (Andante sostenuto, F sharp major, bars 331–46) is, musically, less a matter of character than of idea. To stay with Goethe, I am reminded of 'the eternal feminine that transports us to higher spheres'. Although the Sixth Theme appears independent, it does relate to previous themes. Its beginning paraphrases the climax of the Grandioso theme, projected into a transparent distance. In its later course, the First Theme (tone repetition and descending minor scale) is lovingly enriched by the ascending major seventh. The use of the seventh in this sonata would deserve an essay of its own; nothing may be more indicative of the work than the expressive quality of this interval.

A multitude of emotions, contrasts, colour and texture is mobilised to justify the dimensions of the piece. Within its vast area of tension, the unity of its motivic material seems to me of more than little importance. What I am hinting at is not the transformation of themes, rather typical of Liszt, which leaves them clearly distinguishable while their character and atmosphere change. It is Beethoven's much more subtle technique of relating all themes and movements to one another through common motivic denominators that, in this work, is also applied by Liszt.

Another procedure inherited from Beethoven is the technique of foreshortening. If Liszt, as impatient critics have claimed, chose in this sonata to 'say everything twice', he used this pattern to clarify the structure. Where the pattern is broken, usually a foreshortening process has come to an end. The possibilities of saying things twice are diverse enough; they comprise variants (First Theme), sequences (Second and Third Themes), varied (Fifth Theme) or elaborated sequences (Sixth Theme), and identical repeats ('symphonic main idea').

Form, Structure

Liszt's amalgamation of first-movement form and the movements of a sonata within one structure must have been inspired by the finale of Beethoven's Ninth Symphony and Schubert's *Wanderer* Fantasy, both of which Liszt knew intimately. In the B minor Sonata, the F sharp Andante stands for the slow movement, while the fugato has some features of a scherzo, though not the usual one in 3/4 or 3/8; its short staccato and rhythmic layout are reminiscent of the unorthodox 'scherzo' in Beethoven's Sonata Op. 31, No. 3.

A brief outline of the B minor Sonata may be content to show that a fiercely modulating exposition is based, as much as necessary, on the keys of B minor and D major; that the F sharp major Andante occupies the space of the development; and that, depending on Catholicism of taste, the fugato, or else the return of the 'symphonic main idea', indicates the beginning of the recapitulation. In its course, all the themes that previously did not have a chance to appear in the basic tonality are permitted to do so. Is it really as simple as that? Let me try to investigate some of the events of the work in greater detail.

(a) Exposition. First Development. First False Recapitulation. There are plenty of development sections in this sonata. The themes themselves, instead of being, in Liszt's well-known style, merely clad in different garments or presented in a different light, are given to all manner of developments and combinations. The exposition of the Fifth Theme is followed by a modulating section that, in spite of lacking a clearly defined onset, could well be mistaken for the main development: it does lead back into the First Theme in such a grand way that we may ask ourselves whether the recapitulation has started at bar 277. We expect the Second Theme to reappear in B minor, confirming recapitulation and basic key. Instead, this theme is chiselled into the piano in the 'wrong' key of F minor (deciso, bar 286). Our harmonic expectations have been surpassed. We find ourselves not in the recapitulation but in a

(b) Recitativo section, rugged and punctuated by rests, that starts with C sharp minor chords (*fff* pesante, bar 297). The opening of the Fourth (Grandioso) Theme now sounds merciless and monumental: it brings the propulsive drive of the exposition to a halt. Faust reacts in a free variant of the retrograde. His argument with fate should never be allowed to degenerate into hysterical or whimpering self-pity. Liszt's *forte* markings, indicated in both hands, are all too often ignored. During a long, Mephistophelean pedal point on B the fire of Faust's defiance burns down. The whole section ends on the dominant of E minor.

(c) 'Slow Movement' (Andante): Middle Section with Second Development. Again, Liszt surpasses our harmonic expectations. The surprise of F sharp major and a new, Sixth Theme strikes us like a vision of a better world. The air is pure: during the exposition the key of F sharp had been left out. After a sustained spell of rapture that includes the Fifth (Gretchen) Theme in its entirety, the actual development takes up the declamatory gesture of the recitativo section. Its drama, however, is now chan-nelled into symphonic continuity. The magnificent climax it leads to, thematically identical with the beginning of the middle section (Sixth Theme), is dynamically its opposite: the 'eternal feminine' overwhelms us with all-embracing power. It is one of the most moving moments of the work, and one of the most demanding for the player, when triumph suddenly turns into sweetness. Gradually tension gives way to calm; the key of F sharp major is never left. During thirty-eight bars, time stops. The audience forgets to breathe – or so the pianist hopes. The First Theme appears in F sharp, bringing the middle section to a close and, at the same time, leading into the fugato. Having returned to the origin of the piece, we expect to renew our acquaintance with Faust and Mephisto.

(d) Fugato; simultaneously Second False Recapitulation, Third Development and 'Scherzo'. I do not know what to admire most: the introduction of a fugato at this point; the anticipations it fulfils or ironically disappoints; how three-part writing gradually grows back into 'symphonic' texture; the Mozartian effortlessness of its polyphony; the originality that sets this fugato apart from Baroque stereotypes that held sway well into the nineteenth century; or its manifold connotations that recall a picture puzzle.

Faust and Mephisto reappear; the fugato theme makes room for both of them. The constellation of the Sonata's very beginning has once more materialised, and everything bodes well for the recapitulation. But why are Faust and Mephisto leaping around on tiptoe? Why do they talk in a sarcastic whisper? The 'spirit of negation' seems to have taken hold of both of them; but is there, musically speaking, an object of negation? It is, so we begin to realise, the basic key of B minor in which the reca-pitulation, according to Classical rules, should have started. Actually, the fugato proves to be in the 'wrong' key of B flat minor, one semitone too low.

What is the purpose of this dislocation of a section that could also be called the Third Development, and a contrasting section with scherzo character? The clue is in the long, transfixed dwelling on F sharp that precedes it, and the tonal solidity of the recapitulation that follows. The fugato, harmonically scintillating and extraterritorial, separates both stable sections and postpones the takeover of the basic key.

(e) Recapitulation and Epilogue. It is only where the Second and Third Themes are fused together (bar 533) that we reach the key of B minor; we shall not seriously move away from it again. For the rest of the piece, light (B major) and darkness (B minor) fight against one another, with the light eventually triumphant. Compared with the exposition, the recapitulation is considerably more terse as a result of the limited harmonic scope. Not only the Fourth and Fifth Themes, but also both false recapitulations are brought home into the basic key (the second one first, from bar 569 on, then the first from bar 673). The domination of B major is frantically underlined by a tornado of rapid octaves and vibrating chord repetitions – an extrovert climax that hardly challenges the true, inner climax of the work in the central section of the Sonata.

Enthusiasm switches, after an extensive silence, to sudden introspection: the coda brings back the quiet Sixth Theme in the key of B major. Peace is found. A few bars before the end, the First Theme makes a final appearance, at last in the home key. With the last bass note, all tension is resolved.

We cannot thank Liszt enough for deciding against a projected *fortissimo* ending. The seven lines that took its place have enriched the Sonata beyond measure. In toto, this work is beautifully finished. Neither *ossias* nor suggestions for cuts betray improvisatory haste. The performer should, wisely, avoid treating the piece as a bizarre and feverish dream. One thing has to lead inevitably into the next. Each note has its place. The markings, similar to those of later Beethoven or Brahms, indicate the essential with admirable clarity.

Liszt's B minor Sonata was finished on 2 February 1853. It is dedicated to Schumann in return for Schumann's dedication of his C major Fantasy to Liszt. In 1854, when the Sonata appeared in print, Schumann had retired from the world into an asylum. Neither his wife Clara nor her friend Brahms, for whom Liszt had played the Sonata in Weimar, was able to appreciate it. Wagner was the only one to accept it with joy. As late as 1857, Hans von Bülow premiered the piece in Berlin.

(1981)

Liszt's Hungarian Rhapsodies

TWO PRINCIPAL WAYS of approach have helped to make Liszt, or at least parts of his personality, more accessible to the modern listener. The first proceeds from new music, seeking in Liszt those elements which pointed towards the future – his drive towards experimentation, his revolutionary achievements that directly paved the way for the disintegration of tonality. The other path leads to Liszt's poetic-religious Romanticism, thus running the risk of giving preference to the Franciscan at the expense of the gypsy.

This brings us to the Hungarian Rhapsodies. These are the pieces we perhaps have the most to make restitution to. One must defend them on two fronts: firstly, against musicians of the 'serious' breed who look down on them as showpieces, and secondly, against the piano maniacs who abuse them as showpieces. One must also contend with recollections of salon orchestras and bar pianists. Where is the masterpiece that is able to survive a bar pianist? It is above all the Rhapsodies that come to life through the improvisatory spirit and fire of the interpreter; they are wax in his hands like few other pieces in existence.

Not only Liszt, the Hungarian, was fascinated and inspired by the tunes from neighbouring Hungary, but also Brahms (and Haydn and Schubert before them). Liszt and Brahms even had an 'informant' in common, the violinist Reményi. There is still some confusion about the term 'Hungarian music'. It is not an entirely simple matter to draw a clear dividing line between three areas: that of the gypsy musical style, that of the folk melodies of the eighteenth and nineteenth centuries, which derived for the most part from the aristocracy and the middle class, and that of the actual folklore that was first brought to light through the research work of Bartók and Kodály. What the nineteenth century knew as Hungarian music seems to have been principally a conglomeration of gypsy style and 'urban' folk music. The gypsies helped themselves to the melodies of an Elemér Szentirmay or a Kéler-Béla and assimilated them into their style of performance, a style which aimed at the spontaneous and improvisatory. In that respect, gypsy music-making is related to jazz – which, incidentally, has exercised for some time a stimulating influence from its position on the fringe of 'art music', an influence similar to that exercised by 'gypsy music' a century earlier. Liszt made the mistake of crediting the gypsies for Hungarian national music; Hungary did not forgive him that for a very long time. Bartók and Kodály rectified the error, but in doing so they possibly went a little too far; they stigmatised the gypsies as mere imitators of a general Hungarian style, without granting them any creative identity whatever. All the same, the so-called gypsy scale (minor scale with altered fourth and major scale with altered second and sixth, respectively) was probably brought by the gypsies to Hungary from the Orient. In Hungarian folk music of the nineteenth century, however, it plays a lesser role than in Liszt's later works.

Strictly speaking, then, Liszt's Hungarian Rhapsodies belong to his paraphrases. Like Brahms in his Hungarian Dances, Liszt made use of 'urban' folk music melodies; standing quite apart from the phenomenal peasant folklore of Hungary, they have retained a freshness and charm in their own right. As to their working-out by Liszt, I quote Bartók, who did not care for the 'material' used, but who was forced to admit that 'the Rhapsodies, especially the Hungarian ones, are perfect creations of their own kind. The material Liszt uses in them could not have been treated with more genius and beauty'. This treatment takes possession of the principles of the gypsy style: the roving freedom, the romantic exaltation, the curious modulations, the volatility and abruptness, the renunciation of metrical fetters – all these elements were bound to awaken feelings of congeniality in Liszt. A multiplicity of pungent, darkly glowing and delicately languishing shades of tone colouration awaits rediscovery in the Hungarian Rhapsodies, in addition to characteristics that the public at the turn of the century can hardly have appreciated and possibly did not even notice: the Mephistophelian humour, the inclination to grotesqueness, the readiness to indulge in irony, mocking one's own intoxication.

Not all of the Rhapsodies contrast *lassú* (slow) with *friss* (fast), as does the famous, indestructible Second. The Eighth and Thirteenth, for example, combine the three basic characters of this kind of music: a defiantly or melancholically declamatory introduction, a coquettishly frisky Allegretto, and a fiery, whirling Presto. The delightful Thirteenth begins, incidentally, with a theme of somewhat Hebrew strain and develops from the Allegretto a marvellous climax in the style of Bellini. In the Third Rhapsody the *Friska* is lacking; the work is limited to the first two characters, which as B flat minor (close up) and G minor (far away) contrast poetically with one another. The sound of the cimbalom can be heard in the G minor episode, as in the beginning of the Eleventh. The Fifteenth Rhapsody is one of Liszt's three versions of the Rákóczy March, which Liszt first introduced to Berlioz.

Chopin paid musical tribute to his native country in a very different way from Liszt. While Liszt toys with chance, Chopin, in his Polonaises and Mazurkas, builds organisms. About the *Polonaise-Fantaisie*, one of Chopin's finest and most elusive works, Liszt made the following comments in 1851: 'An elegiac sadness dominates, interrupted by confused gestures. Melancholy smiles, unexpected tremors, awe-inspiring silences suggest the emotions of someone caught in a trap, enclosed from all sides'. Liszt speaks of 'despair which puts the mind into a state of near-delirious sensitivity', of 'groaning cramps of agony', and concludes that these are 'images of little convenience of art ... lamentable aspects which should be granted access to the territory of artistic production only with the utmost reluctance'. These lines may, of course, be inspired or even written by the Princess Sayn-Wittgenstein. Yet it seems surprising that a man who was to become so openly involved with the blackest sides of Romanticism in his own late compositions would lend his name to such views.

The last four of the nineteen Hungarian Rhapsodies, along with pieces like *La lugubre gondola* (in two versions), *Unstern* ('Disaster'), the *Csárdás obstiné* and the *Csárdás macabre*, exemplify this trait. In his own words, Liszt's late music is to his earlier music as *l'amertume de cœur* is to *l'exubérance de cœur* (as bitterness of heart is to exuberance of heart). During his lifetime, Liszt's late compositions must have been considered as products of senility, insofar as they were known at all. Tonality is undermined; the harmonic consequences of the gypsy scale are drawn. The sonorities become bleak and dwindle until only that which is indispensable remains, and sometimes less. Often, only the skeleton – not to say the ghost – of a piece is left. *Ostinato* figures heighten the torment of their monotony. Understanding for these death sighs and *danses macabres* has been found only in our time, a time which has become more accustomed to seeing the macabre with open eyes.

(1968)

Liszt's Bitterness of Heart

I T WAS LEFT to our time to discover Liszt's late piano pieces. They establish the Mephistophelean abbé as a founding father of the music of our century, a fact some experts had noticed before. But these works were considered suitable for reading, not for performance. Only recently, almost a hundred years after they were written, have they emerged as music that can be played and conveyed to a listening public.

It is not, however, from the nineteenth-century concert stage, from the pomp and intoxication of virtuosity, that these works grow. They do not seek to be persuasive; they hardly even seek to convince. In Liszt's own words, 'exuberance of heart' gave way to 'bitterness of heart', a bitterness that had various sources: the death of Liszt's children Daniel and Blandine, his inability to marry Carolyne Sayn-Wittgenstein, the disappointment in his friendships with Wagner and Bülow, and the lack of appreciation of his works. 'Infirmary music' was his own term for much of what he then composed. He apparently let Hungarian friends believe that he wrote the *Csárdás macabre* to irk his powerful adversary, the Viennese critic Eduard Hanslick.

This piano piece, unpublished until the 1950s, is one in the series of *danses macabres* and Mephistophelean waltzes, of elegies and threnodies, memorials and troubled inspirations which afflicted Liszt in his last fifteen years. The macabre element is no longer picturesquely theatrical, as in *Totentanz*; neither is it the motive that triggers revolutionary pathos, as in 'Funérailles'. 'Is it permissible to write something like that, or to listen to it?' asked Liszt's pupil August Göllerich when he saw *Csárdás*. His question sounds like an echo of what Liszt himself had written thirty years earlier about Chopin's *Polonaise-Fantaisie*; it shows how greatly Liszt had changed.

What Wagner's musical friendship amounted to at this time is revealed in a comment on Liszt's late works. Wagner considered them the 'picture of a world in decline', with 'decadent Paris', which he so much hated, as its centre. The remark, though meant contemptuously, contains a grain of truth. Most of Liszt's late piano pieces are indeed documents of two declines, that of tonality and that of human personality in old age.

Liszt was probably the first composer to experience the dissolution of tonality in his work, and to free himself from its domination. In his late piano music he avoids traditional cadences. He hardly ever modulates; instead, he puts keys or harmonies side by side, gliding from one to another chromatically, modally or by means of the gypsy scale. The assurance with which this happens caused Busoni to remark that 'the harmony of a revolutionary lies in the steady hand of a sovereign'. When impressions of tonality in the customary sense are conveyed, their effect is one of wistful or ironic reminiscences of the past, or of excursions into a sphere of childlike feeling (as in the *Christmas Tree* suite dedicated to Liszt's granddaughter Daniela). Frequently, as in *Aux cyprès de la Villa d'Este I*, *Unstern* or *Schlaflos, Frage und Antwort*, a dissonant and obsessive first section is answered by a consonant section – usually in a church mode – which could be taken as a gesture of humility, as an appeasement hardly approaching consolation, a desire to be protected by the shelter of a convention that has become an enigma and no longer offers safety or hope.

The Classic-Romantic forms drew their meaning from the functional harmony of major and minor; once their tonal foundation was shattered, they became meaningless. Instead of symmetry, development and recapitulation, Liszt now used the simple confrontation of extreme contrasts or the coexistence of two keys: F major and D major in *Csárdás macabre*, F minor and B major in *Unstern*. Other pieces are not afraid to present the arbitrary or fragmentary, to become torpid, to fade away, to forget where they started when they stop. In this they reflect the symptoms of ageing. We must be careful to distinguish between a shrinkage of elements of the personality in old age, and a decline of creative power (of which Liszt was rather unjustly accused). No composer stayed younger to the very end in his urge and ability to create something new. 'Accidental form', which brought an element of insecurity to many of his earlier works, now comes into its own. It finds suitable material: the dread of senility, as well as displaced harmony – displaced largely by the use of the gypsy scale (originally Indian) and its derivatives. The old man himself is displaced; not even Hungary wants to listen to his music, while he strays between Weimar, Pest and Rome.

What is new in Liszt's late piano pieces is presented without mitigation, spotlit by radical simplicity. The melody dispenses with traditional ideas of *cantabile*. Lonely unison effects are explored. Tone colour remains an important source of the music's impact, but now it is predominantly the dark and the glaring, the ashen and the ethereal that move or unsettle us. The rhythm is obsessive, harassing, oppressive, or it tries to dissolve into the air. Even the smallest piece has breadth; there are hardly any miniatures of the order of Schumann's *Papillons* or *Kinderszenen*, or Schoenberg's Op. 19.

It seems as if the shrinking of the ageing personality has left room for the imper-
sonal, for an archaic force. Liszt's former lavishness, at the time artistically legitimate,
has disappeared. There is an unexpected link with late Schubert. In his virtuoso
days, Liszt overwhelmed the public, even that of Vienna, with his transcriptions of
Schubert's songs; but in them he often treated Schubert badly, transposing him to
the level of his own rhetorical exuberance. As an old composer, Liszt approaches
the original Schubert at his most depressive. Songs like 'Der Doppelgänger', 'Der
Leiermann' or 'Die Stadt' lead in a direct line to pieces like *Unstern* and *Mosonyi*.
They have in common the union of brevity and monumentality, the declamatory
and the pithy, monotony and refinement.

To me, many of Liszt's late pieces seem to anticipate a discovery that took place
in the visual arts at the turn of the century: that of the 'primitive' or 'barbaric', as
seen for example in Gauguin's Tahiti, in masks from Africa and Oceania or in early
Romanesque sculpture. (Goethe, the paragon of civilised man, spoke in 1805 of an
'irresistible propensity for the absurd which causes the hereditary savagery of gri-
mace-loving primitives to resurface in the most respectable world, contrary to all
culture'.) But there are distinctions: where the Fauves drew their inspiration from
'primitive' tribal art, or Picasso from Pyrenean wood sculpture, Liszt drew his gri-
macing visions from himself. There were, to be sure, additional contributions from
sources as disparate as the gypsies, the younger Russian composers and Gregorian
chant; but the most important impulse came from the musical situation of the time,
from the dissolution of tonality and the forms depending on it. The title of one of
his last pieces indicates that Liszt was aware of what he was doing; in the *Bagatelle
without Tonality* even passing attachments to a key are avoided. Almost independent
of Wagner's *Tristan* chromaticism, and more consistently than any of his contemporaries, Liszt ushers in the music of the twentieth century.

What should interest us most in these pieces, however, is not what they anticipate or prepare the ground for, but what they are. They hardly need excuses – not
even for being experiments; that word can be much more fittingly applied to
early works like *Malediction* or the piano piece *Harmonies poétiques et religieuses*.
The unity of Liszt's late style, and the diversity within that unity, can be compre-
hended only by listening to a whole set of these pieces, one after another – and in
performances that do not impose on them a concept of paralysing slowness and pal-
lor. Liszt's entire range of pianistic refinement, acquired over long years of experience,

has a part to play even in the most awkward sounds this music makes. An enormous stock of nuances should be felt to be available in the background, even when they seem to remain unused.

Two of Liszt's late pieces are exceptions, in that they soon gained a place in the standard repertory. If they are not among the most typical (and that is why they were accepted), they are certainly among the most beautiful. The first *Valse oubliée*, a concise piece characterised by a supremely elegant and slightly diabolical air of seduction, helps to explain why Liszt attracted the favours of the fair sex up to the very end. The waltz anticipates Skriabin by decades, just as *Les jeux d'eau à la Villa d'Este*, 'the model for all musical fountains that have flowed ever since' (Busoni), gives a foretaste of impressionism. Unlike these later fountains, their earlier model is also, and above all, religious music. Most of the other pieces in the third volume of *Années de pèlerinage* are likewise religious in character in contrast to those of the earlier *Années*, which depict nature or evoke works of literature and art. In *Aux cyprès de la Villa d'Este I* the melancholy and menace emanating from the huge shapes of cypresses gives way to Christian consolation in unhackneyed chromaticism. (After 1864, Liszt used to live in an apartment at the Villa d'Este when he stayed in Rome.)

Sunt lacrymae rerum is another threnody, but one with a Hungarian flavour. The words of the title, taken from Book I of Virgil's *Aeneid*, refer to the fall of Troy; Liszt, however, used them as an allusion to the failure of the Hungarian revolution of 1848–49. But there is another, more personal allusion. In 1872, the year the piece was written, Liszt visited Bayreuth for the first time. There he accused Wagner and Cosima of having ruined the life of his outstanding pupil, Hans von Bülow, whose marriage to Liszt's daughter had broken up because of Wagner. Not surprisingly, *Sunt lacrymae rerum* is dedicated to Bülow; it contains some of the blackest sounds ever produced in the bass register of a concert grand.

(1980)

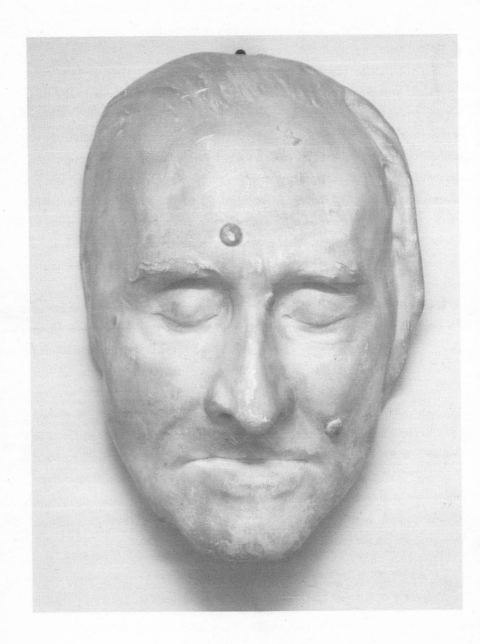

A cast of Liszt's death mask.

Photograph © John Batten, London. (Collection Alfred Brendel)

Liszt's Piano Playing

'LISZT: OR THE school of running – after women.'[97] This spiteful quip of Nietzsche's compresses popular prejudices into a single phrase. As so often with derogatory remarks, the essential point is ignored while the trivial is highlighted. The physical and profane aspects of Liszt's nature are concentrated on, to the exclusion of everything else. One senses the envy behind the calumny: envy of a good-looking man attractive to women, envy of a pianist endowed with a degree of technical facility and bravura that put his colleagues to shame. Two things, 'lusting after women' and Czerny's *School of Velocity* – a thoroughly arid collection of studies – are brought together in an association that might be witty if it were at all relevant to Liszt. It is a moot point whether in his relations with women Liszt was the pursuer rather than the pursued. To identify Liszt the virtuoso with the *School of Velocity*, however, is downright slander.

Robert Schumann, in a letter to Clara, said of Liszt: 'He is quite extraordinary. He played from the Novelettes, the Fantasy, the Sonata, moving me deeply. Many things were different from the way I had imagined them, but this was playing of genius, with a tenderness and boldness of emotion which I doubt if even he can summon up every day'. He went on: 'If you had been here this morning, I wager tears would have sprung to your eyes'. And Clara wrote to Schumann: 'When I heard Liszt for the first time in Vienna, I just couldn't control myself, I sobbed freely with emotion'. It is a testimony of Schumann's admiration for Liszt that he dedicated to him one of his most beautiful works, the Fantasy, Op. 17. Liszt reciprocated with his greatest creation, the B minor Sonata.

The relationship between Liszt and Brahms is sometimes misinterpreted. It is true that they had no great love for each other, but there is evidence of their mutual esteem. The story that Brahms dozed off during his visit to Weimar while Liszt was playing the B minor Sonata is unauthenticated, and not rendered any the more likely by the fact that Liszt bade Brahms a cordial farewell, presenting him with a silver cigarette case.[98] Later on, the two met several times in Leipzig. Brahms sent Liszt his

---

97 *Translator's note*: In an aphorism entitled *Meine Unmöglichkeiten* ('My Impossibles'), Nietzsche refers to 'Liszt: oder die Schule der Geläufigkeit – nach Weibern'. This is based on a pun on the words geläufig ('fluent') – as in Czerny's *Schule der Geläufigkeit* ('School of Velocity') – and *läufig* 'ruttish').

98 Paula Rehberg and Gerhard Nestler: *Franz Liszt*, Artemis, 1961, pp. 607–8.

B flat major Concerto as soon as it had appeared in print, and Liszt acknowledged its receipt in a letter of reserved appreciation; nevertheless, he called it a masterpiece. When he listened to it in his class at Weimar in 1885 he praised it as 'one of Brahms's very best works'. (The diaries of Liszt's Austrian pupil August Göllerich show that between the years 1884 and 1886 works by Brahms were played for Liszt on several occasions in Weimar, Rome or Budapest. Liszt amused his class by inventing a nickname for one of the Paganini Variations: 'a rustle of cockchafers'.)

Even Eduard Hanslick, the feared Vienna critic and unrelenting opponent of the music of Liszt and Wagner, never ceased to respect Liszt as a man and as the outstanding pianist of his time. He held so high an opinion of Liszt that, before publishing his treatise *Vom musikalisch Schönen* ('The Beautiful in Music'), he invited him to write a preface for it – which Liszt, however, declined to do.

Liszt seems to have said little about technique to his pupils. It was taken for granted that anyone playing to him at Weimar would have the requisite mechanical abilities. When this proved not to be the case, Liszt would have one of his rare outbursts of rage – or else his 'Cerberus', Bülow, would feel obliged to bring his sarcasm into action: to a lady attempting to play Liszt's *Mazeppa* he once remarked, 'The only qualification you have for playing this piece is your horsiness.'[99]

Liszt's teaching concentrated on interpretation. There certainly do not seem to have been many pianists who measured up to his ideal of technique; what he demanded was 'a technique created by the spirit, not derived from the mechanism of the piano'. 'All these', he explained ironically, pointing at his pupils when an old lady came to listen to one of his classes, 'are "pianists". At any rate, they all "play the piano"!' He had himself, however, mastered as a youth the whole range of studies and exercises so thoroughly that he could still play them as an old man. In later years he often complained that thumping and pounding was now the order of the day – a view shared by Clara Schumann, who, however, held Liszt responsible for this. Although there were many among his pupils who assiduously copied his hair style, there were few, apparently, who inherited any trace of his *cantabile* treatment of the keyboard. 'Everybody else', wrote Amy Fay about the grace of Liszt's piano

---

99 *Translator's note*: This quip, which alludes to the famous ride of Mazeppa, cannot be roundly translated. *Rossnatur* means 'a horse's nature', but also 'brute strength and patience'.

playing, 'sounds heavy beside him!' This American woman, who has given us an exceptionally lively description of Liszt, relates that she once asked him whether Sophie Menter, a rising star to whom Liszt had given strong support, was his pupil. 'He said no, he could not take the credit of her artistic success to himself.' Liszt did not consider himself a piano teacher.

In pictures and photographs showing Liszt at the piano we see him sitting relatively high and so far away from the instrument that his arms are almost straight. In moments of great elation he is said to have leant backwards. It is reported that he did not favour a strongly bent elbow position.

From the evidence of his works it is clear that the finger technique in general use up to that time was inadequate to his purposes. Nor can the new Deppe method of 'free fall' have satisfied him, since an unchecked arm drop onto the keys usually coarsens the sound. Only a balanced combination of muscle tone and relaxation is of value to the player.

Caricatures used to show Liszt in theatrical poses, with flailing arms and a fierce or ecstatic look in his eyes. In reality, at least in his later years, he did not care for exaggerated arm movements or for throwing his hands up in the air. ('Don't make an omelette!' he told a girl who would not keep her hands still.) This new restraint may explain the curious remark by Stradal, who studied with the master after 1880, that Liszt's entire technique, besides the finger technique, was a wrist technique. But what the great virtuoso Arthur Friedheim tells us is surely more to the point: that Liszt was to the end without equal in the production of powerful sound and towering dynamic climaxes. Such things are not done with the little finger.

(1976)

Turning the Piano into an Orchestra

LISZT'S TRANSCRIPTIONS AND PARAPHRASES

AMONG LISZT'S WORKS, there is a surprisingly large number of transcriptions – surprising to us of this century because we prefer to encounter a composer's works in their original form. Why did Liszt spend so much time and effort recomposing other people's music? (Did you read 'decomposing'? – Let us not prejudge the issue!)

Progress had been made in piano building. The range of colour and dynamics obtainable on a concert grand increased continually, along with the instrument's mechanical strength. The pianist discovered the piano anew – as the instrument capable of any transformation – and he discovered himself as the person capable of working those transformations. He could transform his piano into an organ, an oboe, an orchestra; himself into a conductor, a Lieder singer, a prima donna, into a chorus or speaking chorus (as in Liszt's *Pensées des Morts*), into a storyteller, gypsy, priest, dervish or painter, into birds or the waves of the sea, even into the elements themselves. Alone, the protean player rules over the music, dependent on no one for help, and beholden to no one. In this spirit, Liszt played sections of Beethoven's 'Pastoral' Symphony during an orchestral concert; we can be sure that his performance surpassed the prevailing standard of orchestral playing. In addition, he would vie with the great singers, bringing new music to the attention of the public at the same time. Thus, in an age before music was widely disseminated by the radio and recordings, Schubert, Wagner or Verdi reached a wide audience. Their music was impressed on a public held in thrall by the hypnotic or mesmeric power of the virtuoso.

Transcribing can become an addiction. Many virtuosi of the last century succumbed to it, including some who, unlike Liszt and Busoni, lacked the credentials of being composers in their own right. Every edition of older music, with the exception of those by editors like Bischoff and Kullak, was virtually a transcription. Bülow 'corrected' Beethoven. Adolf Ruthardt, with no qualifications as composer, virtuoso or musical thinker, turned every masterpiece he touched into an Augean stable. Nor were contemporary pieces safe from 'embellishments', even those that could scarcely be said to have suffered from any lack of pianistic strength: Liszt's *Second Legend of St Francis* was inflated by his disrespectful pupil Stavenhagen in such a manner that the original looks by comparison like a simplified version for beginners. Of Liszt himself it was said that in his young days his rendering of other composers' music was best when he was sight-reading, since at that stage he was not yet able to add anything. And Busoni, during his late Berlin years, reportedly arranged passages from *The Merry Widow* in tenths while practising.

Are transcriptions, then, vindictive acts against helpless composers, springing from the transcriber's sense of his own inferiority? Hardly in the case of Liszt. Perhaps his pleasure in transcribing and paraphrasing can be partially explained by the fact that his orchestral works are of lesser stature than his best piano music. Not only was his grasp of larger forms insecure, but the actual scoring proved suitable mainly for the depiction of the crass, as in *Totentanz*. It was greatly surpassed by the subtlety and variety of his 'orchestration' on the piano. Chopin, though no transcriber at all, comes to my mind as a parallel case: with all his admiration for the great singers of his time, with all his ability to draw forth the loveliest cantilenas from the piano, he seemed incapable of putting together a really singable song.

Liszt's transcriptions can be classified as follows:

1) The literal transcriptions, where Liszt makes organ or orchestral works playable on the piano. Here belong his Bach transcriptions, and the piano reductions of the Beethoven symphonies, the Weber overtures, the *Symphonie Fantastique* and the overture to Wagner's *Tannhäuser*. (Anyone playing these pieces today will do well to refer back to the originals. He should not hesitate to rearrange the arrangement if this reflects the original better.)

2) The operatic paraphrases, which are fantasies based on a single number or scene, or on several numbers, forming a cross-section of the opera (*Norma, La Juive, Don Giovanni*).

3) The song transcriptions, which range from relatively respectful arrangements to ruthless adaptations where cadenzas are interpolated, strophic repeats given a new illumination and recapitulations climactically enhanced.

4) At least some of the Hungarian Rhapsodies, in which material taken from 'urban' folk music is paraphrased in a style that is derived from the mercurial performing habits of the gypsies, and from the sound of their instruments.

Liszt's transcriptions still form a unique exercise in 'orchestral' playing for the modern pianist. While in many other piano works the player has to uncover latent orchestral colours, here we have precise originals by which the results may be measured.

In endeavouring to produce orchestral colours on the piano, our concern must not only be with the timbre of each individual instrument, but also with the *manner* in which it is played – with certain peculiarities that arise from the construction of the instrument and that are reflected in the technique required by it. Another consideration is the number of players employed in a certain context. An orchestral *tutti* will have to be treated differently from a passage for strings alone; a *forte* for strings will need more volume than one for woodwind. For orchestral playing it is necessary to have a first-rate grand, voiced not too softly, in a room that is acoustically not too dry. The instrument should have metallic reserves at *fortissimo* level; its *sordino* pedal, however, should be free of metallic noises, and be capable of veiling the sound without making it thin and acid.

How does one reproduce the timbre of other instruments on the piano? Perhaps the following hints will be useful.

Characteristic of the string sound is a wide, easily variable dynamic range, a legato vibrating in the pedal, a tender onset of the notes, the moulding of single notes with the aid of accompanying figures or simply by the power of suggestion. (If you believe that swelling on a note is not feasible for the pianist, you should have heard Edwin Fischer in the concert hall, playing the first entry in the Adagio of Beethoven's *Emperor* Concerto!) Bass entries may be anticipated. Cellos and double basses need time in which to unfold their sound. Pizzicato chords may be lightly broken; they are plucked away from the keys. Muted string passages of course require soft pedalling.

In his 'string playing', the pianist ought to be familiar with the various kinds of bowing, in his 'wind playing' with the techniques of breathing. For the woodwind, there should be a distinct onset of the notes. The woodwind's clear articulation of each single note is best served by the avoidance, or at least a very careful application, of the pedal. The dynamic range should remain narrow.

The sound of the oboe I achieve with rounded, hooked-under and, as it were, bony fingers, in *poco legato*. The vibrato of the oboe requires some pedal, which, however, should not blur the progress from note to note. The pointed staccato of the oboe is pushed lightly into the keys. Dynamic range: *p* to *mp*.[100]

The clarinet has the widest dynamic range – *pp* to *poco f*. Its sound is 'straight': *sempre poco tenuto* and *quasi senza pedale*. The normal sound of the B flat or A clarinets is a noble *mezzoforte* of dark, slightly veiled timbre, calling for the sordino pedal (and flexible wrists). The C and E flat clarinets, on the other hand, are unlyrical, shrill, grotesque; I play them with firm, 'hard' fingers.

The flute stays in *piano*; its dynamics are hardly apparent. Its timbre remains round, mild, somewhat colourless and veiled (I use the *sordino*, as long as it does not produce a thin or sharp sound). Whenever possible, I play every note with the help of a separate arm movement. The staccato should not be too well defined. Low notes on the flute should sound pale.

The cor anglais, whose characteristic *Tristan* sound is echoed in Liszt's *La lugubre gondola*, should be treated like a contralto voice with a very clear onset. The bassoon, on the other hand, remains usually without vibrato; it is rarely a *cantabile* instrument, and needs the *sordino*, but not the sustaining pedal. The touch is finger-staccato, the dynamic range *mp* to *mf*. Similar treatment is needed to achieve the grating sound of the bass clarinet and the double bassoon (dynamics: *mf*).

The noble, full, somewhat veiled 'Romantic' sound of the horn demands a loose arm and a flexible wrist. Although its dynamics extend from *pp* to *f*, the *sordino* pedal should always be used. In legato, every note is put down separately and connected with its neighbours by pedal alone. The staccato is never pointed. In chords played by several horns, the upper voice must recede slightly in favour of the lower ones.

A stiffening of the physical apparatus is required to do justice to the blaring, braying sound of the trumpet, the brilliance of which needs the aid of pedal. Dynamics: *poco f* to *fff*.

Trombones should be handled like horns, but without the *sordino* pedal. They produce the most opulent sound, and in piano writing usually appear as octaves. Brass chorales should be executed *portato*, with air between the chords.

Do not forget that the harp is a plucked instrument! The pianist should play harp notes with round, tensed fingers – *sempre poco staccato* – within the sustained pedal. In rapid, sharply ripped-off arpeggios, the finger-play is assisted by movements of the

---

100 With Heinz Holliger's oboe playing in one's head, dynamics can be extended to *poco f*.

wrist. Harp figuration has a smooth outline; its dynamic curves are of geometrical precision. The rhythmic and dynamic spacing of the notes needs the utmost control. Harp arpeggios are the opposite of careless, chancy arpeggio playing. (Liszt's piano music is full of them, as for example in the recapitulation of the *Bénédiction.*) The dynamics of the harp range from *pp* to *mf*; several harps together can be stronger.

With the organ, a strict distinction must be made between the tone colour and strength of the manuals. Within each manual every part remains at the same level of volume. Declamation, therefore, is not produced by dynamics, but by articulation and the careful use of agogics (subtle inflections of rhythm). Arpeggios are excluded. Organ sound and church acoustics belong together, and the pianist has to reproduce that special resonance. This, along with pedal points and other long-sustained notes, creates fascinating pedalling problems, and here, above all else, lies the attraction of organ transcriptions. I try to manage with the right pedal alone, without using the Steinway middle pedal. In Romantic organ music, the steady rise and fall of tone produced by the swell box will have to be imitated.

Organ transcriptions provide excellent training in colour control, in preparation for 'orchestral' playing.

My list of musical instruments would be gravely incomplete without the human voice. In its freedom of declamation it leaves the orchestra far behind. It is distinguished by warmth and directness. Its articulation is given shadings of vowels and consonants, like sculpture in high relief. Its dynamics extend from whispering and humming to shouting. The voice is capable of every kind of expression. Vibrato, in all its degrees, characterises singing; the arm of the pianist should sail on that vibrato like a ship on the water – a few centimetres above the keys. With the pedal assuring an unbroken legato, piano composers have often used the same finger for particularly 'singable' passages: the fifth in Schubert's G flat major Impromptu, the thumb in the third movement of Schumann's Fantasy, in his F sharp major Romanze or in the second subject of Liszt's *Funérailles.* The sound produced in this way is more relaxed, more 'eloquent' than the *cantabile* of an actual finger-legato.

Singing means exhalation. But the moments of inhalation, too, can be musically significant, as will be felt by any player of song or opera transcriptions who is breathing with the vocal line. A sudden, gasping breath can make a strong dramatic effect – although not if it takes the form of an audible wheeze on the part of the pianist. Most of the time, however, a singer wishing to establish a coherent, large-scale view of the music will take breath as discreetly as possible: the musical ideal of the 'big breath', as we know, goes far beyond the physical limitations of breathing.

Piano literature is pervaded by the musical attitude of singing. Instruments like the organ and the harpsichord discouraged 'singableness'. The further the sound of the Hammerklavier departed from that of the harpsichord, the more accessible it became to cantilenas. Turning the piano into a vehicle of singing is not, to be sure, entirely Liszt's doing. But who else was able to make the *vox humana* vibrate so sensuously on the piano?

(1976)

Fidelity to Liszt's Letter?

THE TRUST ONE can put in a composer's manuscript is a relative matter. The interpreter has to find out not only how the composer's notation is to be understood, but also how appropriate it is to each of his works. Not all masters have developed the same certainty and practical clarity of notation. With a composer like Beethoven, who notates the essential, expression marks and structural logic are often closely interrelated. It is a similar case with Brahms, who in this respect too had learned from Beethoven. Utmost precision is found in Bartók; subtleness bordering on hypersensitivity in Reger and Berg; sparseness, mobilizing the player's adaptive faculties, in Busoni. *Cantabile* composers like Mozart and Schubert present the pianist with the task of translating vocal accents into their pianistic approximations. Schubert, moreover, shows himself to be a young composer lacking the experience that is gained from frequent performances.

Schumann too wrote his most outstanding piano works as a young man. His notation is a very personal mixture of pedantry and inexactness. He is pedantic in his insistence on minute variants by which, more often than not, he merely taxes the memory of the player without adding anything noticeably new to his recapitulations. He is inexact in his *ritardandi*, which at times are not succeeded by an *a tempo*. Two of his markings have often evoked smiles, one being *Durchwegs leise zu halten* ('To be kept soft throughout') over a movement – the third of the Fantasy, Op. 17 – which contains two fulminant dynamic climaxes, the other being *So schnell wie möglich* ('As fast as possible') in the G minor Sonata, which is followed in the coda by *Noch schneller* ('Still faster'). The first example is sheer nonsense. The second makes sense when the emphasis is shifted to 'As fast as *possible*', i.e., musically possible. The end of this movement will then become 'possible' at an even faster speed than the beginning.

The greatest riddle in musical notation is perhaps presented by Chopin. How can such sovereign mastery of the craft of composition go hand in hand with the clumsiness and irresolution shown in some of his manuscripts? I confess that I am not at all convinced by some of Chopin's markings. The liberty with which performers and editors have taken possession of Chopin's texts seems, to a degree, understandable.

And what about Liszt? One can divide his works into two groups. The first comprises those compositions that are fully worked out, and where the text deserves to be followed precisely. (Here belongs the B minor Sonata, the *Legends* and the Variations on *Weinen, Klagen, Sorgen, Zagen.*) The second group makes the intervention of the player possible or desirable.

This group is much larger. Liszt's manner of composing shows all the advantages and disadvantages of working at white heat. Almost always he produces fabulous, highly original beginnings – the tremendous rhetorical gestures in 'Vallée d'Obermann', the Dante Sonata, the *Malédiction*; the ecstasy, at first intangible, then materializing, a mirage become reality, in *Sposalizio* or the Petrarch Sonnet No. 123; the stagnant grief of *Pensées des Morts*; or the great expectations of the *Sursum corda*.

In Liszt's large-scale works, with the possible exception of the B minor Sonata, it is only very rarely that the expectations raised by the beginning are fulfilled. Disenchantment usually sets in during the last third of the piece. Instead of a structural development, which indeed could scarcely be worked out in the white heat of improvisation, Liszt offers a characteristic variant, or a series of repeats orchestrated ever more sumptuously or of ever-increasing excitement. *Mazeppa* rides four times, faster every time, to a contracting rhythm; *Sposalizio*, *Cantique d'amour* and the Dante Sonata are among the pieces where Liszt has indulged his whim of saying everything in triplicate. Sometimes one gains the impression that Liszt has lost interest in the shape of the whole: the A major Concerto and the Norma Fantasy in their printed editions even include suggested cuts *ad libitum!* Here, a composer born long before the development of aleatory methods reveals with disarming frankness his lack of confidence in pre-established and structured large-scale forms.

Another factor which might suggest the notion of 'coincidental form' in connection with Liszt is the number of *ossia* variants found in his piano music. Liszt's proposals for cuts are not promoted by any desire to tighten the argument; the works mentioned above are in any case of modest dimensions when compared with other Romantic piano concertos or with the sonatas of Schubert and Brahms. Just consider for a moment how odd authorised cuts would look in a movement by Schubert or Mahler, and you will realise how small a role the actual length of a piece plays in this matter. (Mendelssohn's conducting of the finale of Schubert's Great C major Symphony in a shortened version and the pianist Harold Bauer's disfiguring cuts in his edition of the B flat major Sonata are based on misconceptions which are no longer prevalent.) Certainly, if one takes Bach, Mozart or Beethoven as the standard, one can speak of 'coincidental form' also in connection with Schubert and Mahler

– a form that at times baffles the listener not only as to how, but also why a piece proceeds in the way it does. But this kind of coincidental form needs wide spaces in which to demonstrate that the usual order of things is here going to be called in question – or rather, from the standpoint of orderliness, to be deformed – and still we have not the slightest doubt about the validity of such a procedure. By comparison, Liszt's works – always excepting the B minor Sonata – seem to be built on doubts, perhaps in the hope that under the hands of a player of genius the suggestion of a new order will arise.

This reluctance to take a definite stand springs to some extent from the nature of the Romantic interpreter and improviser: he must convince the audience at the moment of performance that his, and no other, is the right way. (As a virtuoso, Liszt must have possessed this persuasive quality to the ultimate degree.) But the reverse side of the coin is Liszt's uncertainty in the composition of large-scale works. The grand view of the whole, which Beethoven held so securely, is often lost to him. It is only in the late works that this failing turns into a virtue: there, where there are no longer any apotheoses, where only emptiness, the dread of *senilità*, fixes its bold, bleak stare on us, the form gains from being open on all sides. Transitions occur here, after the example of late Schubert, in the shortest way, chromatically rising or falling, reduced to unison progressions. Endings dwindle over many lines, to trickle away in agony. Coincidental form has found its music.

Among the works of Liszt that invite or demand the intervention of the player are, first, the pieces in which there is a superfluity of notes. Most of these are from his virtuoso period. (Compare the third, more playable version of the *Transcendental Studies* with the overblown second.) Incidentally, there is also a superfluity of notes – not intrinsically so, but for playing purposes – in the B flat major Concerto of Brahms. It contains a number of double-stop passages, the part-writing of which is notated without regard for what is pianistically possible or even necessary. A pianist failing to adapt these passages puts himself at risk: he yields to a compulsion to deliver distinctly every printed note without enquiring into the meaning of the passage; he may impair that meaning if he is then forced, say in the notorious double thirds of the finale, to play at slower speed and in a cumbersome *mezzoforte* what should be fleet, scurrying and *pianissimo*; he underestimates the readiness of a gifted and cultivated ear to restore automatically certain inessential notes that have been sacrificed to the higher purpose – such an ear will not even be aware that those notes are missing, as long as the player does not make things unduly easy for himself.

Secondly, there are works which in places give the impression of a sketch, such as the extremely peculiar *Pensées des Morts* and a number of late pieces where, at the very least, the interpretative intentions of Liszt have to be divined, and where many a metronome mark deserves close scrutiny.

In the third place, there are those works which have induced individual players to tailor them to their technique. D'Albert and Busoni performed their own versions of the First Mephisto Waltz. However, it is a moot point whether the Mephisto Waltz or *La Campanella* are really in need of Busoni's slimming treatment. Liszt himself invented numerous new variants for many passages.

Finally, mention must be made of the *ad libitum* cadenzas, like the one in the Second Hungarian Rhapsody. (D'Albert, Rachmaninov and Cortot have furnished splendid interpolations.)

In Liszt's works, as in those of other composers, there are wrong notes and accidentals that cling tenaciously to the music. On their recording of the A major Concerto, the two Liszt pupils Sauer and Weingartner left uncorrected the wrong pizzicato bass E of the original print, which the Collected Edition has amended; the note must of course be G, as it leads to the A flat of the next piano bass (letter H of the score).

Liszt had a mania for harp-like sounds. While it would be better to avoid certain arpeggios, particularly when they occur in *forte cantabile* passages, it would be a grave mistake to condemn all breaking of chords. Busoni's slender, sculptured sound, Toscanini's tendency to 'detonate' accents and Stravinsky's brittle clarity have left their mark on us, making us suspicious of soft contours. The abolition of the arpeggio ran parallel to the abolition of the portamento in singing and string playing. The result has been an impoverishment of music's means of expression. The breaking of chords is not necessarily a makeshift device for small hands, just as the slurring of sung notes is not necessarily a sign of bad taste. As a vehicle for the attainment of *cantabile* playing and a spatial, plastic sound quality, the arpeggio as well as the discreet, preparatory anticipation of the bass (and, more rarely, the pronounced anticipation of the melodic line) must have been indispensable to an age which, to a much higher degree than our own, strove towards the ideal of a beautiful, singing piano tone. Used automatically and excessively, however, these expressive devices lose their charm and defeat their own purpose, as can be observed from some of Paderewski's records. Indiscriminate and tasteless use may well have been the main cause of the oblivion into which arpeggios and portamenti have fallen. Their rediscovery should be the concern of our more gifted pianists, singers and string players.

Liszt's pedal marks are, like all pedaling instructions, intended merely as suggestions – they have to be adapted to individual instruments and concert halls. Moreover, allowance must be made for the subtleties of minute pedal vibrations which cannot be notated. It is dangerous to ignore them: the three-dimensional character of Liszt's sound-imagination should not be flattened out. Even the long pedals in the exposition of the Dante Sonata or in the bass-octave passage of 'Funérailles' prove their expressive power in certain acoustic conditions. Anyone substituting dry staccato gymnastics for the awesome, gradually increasing dynamic suction demanded here, misunderstands and falsifies Liszt.

Liszt's notation may often be incomplete. Any additions or modifications made by the player, however, must be undertaken in the spirit in which a modern pianist fills in the piano concertos of Mozart: that is, in the style of the composer. To modernise Liszt makes little sense. It is enough to present him on his own terms.

(1976)

BUSONI

~∾~

A Peculiar Serenity

FOR MOST PEOPLE ambiguity holds little attraction. They mistrust the contradictions they find in those who have learned to keep a balance between the opposing forces of their personality. What they look out for is hardly something which will disturb them by enlarging their view of life, but something which will reassure them by simplifying it. Of many possible ideals, they demand that only one be established as absolute and disapprove of an attitude which concedes a certain degree of truth to each of those ideals in the belief that 'every error is a masked truth' – an attitude which, instead of reaching out to barren extremes, strives towards a consciously controlled synthesis.

Busoni's all-embracing spirit – 'a kind of musical Leonardo', as Wilhelm Kempff boldly called him – has few rivals in the history of music. He was a world-famous, phenomenal pianist, a conductor of new orchestral works, a composer of highly significant music for the stage and concert hall, the importance of which has not yet been appreciated; he was a theorist of genius, a highly cultured man of letters, a devotee of theatre as a sublimation of life and of life as an extension of theatre; he was a world citizen, a child of his strife-torn age and the prophet of a music of the future that was to be freed from the shackles of the 'law-givers'.

As a boy, Busoni effortlessly acquired pianistic skill. As a travelling prodigy, he was hailed enthusiastically by none other than Hanslick, the 'law-giver' *par excellence*. As a virtuoso of almost thirty, he made his first investigation of the works of Liszt, which brought about a striking transformation. After a creative pause, Busoni had finally gained an artistic profile of his own; the easy routine which had kept his entire earlier production on the tracks of eclecticism had now been banished. The first works to show to the full his individual style as a composer are some of the Elegies of 1908, expressly designated 'Six new piano pieces'.

The master of the keyboard had long since left behind the 'pianistic Darwinism' of his contemporaries and, as the opposite spiritual pole to d'Albert, had taken the leading place in the Liszt succession. Without having been a personal pupil of Liszt, it was Busoni who was foremost in cultivating Liszt's spiritual heritage – by going beyond it. Through him, piano technique underwent its apparently ultimate differentiation. Lucid awareness cleared away the ruggedly demoniac and the accidental. It is significant that Bach and Liszt were the two nerve centres of Busoni's enormous repertory: the basis and the apex of pianism. The contemplative inwardness of the one was as congenial to him as the theatrical and mysterious tone-magic of the other.

Busoni's allegiance to such dissimilar gods has often been misunderstood. Those unable to grasp the polarities of his nature have tended to brand him a Jack-of-all-trades trying to hide his lack of inner consistency behind a facade of fabricated originality. And indeed, on investigation of his talents, inclinations and pronouncements, the observer is faced with an image that is equivocal.

On the one hand, Busoni's Latin sense of form made him hate the chaotic. His idea of a 'Young Classicism' aimed to incorporate experimental features in 'firm, rounded forms', which, however, should be motivated each time by musical necessity and never simply yield to the pressure of traditional models. On the other hand, there was in him an overwhelming yearning for untrammelled, soaring music, leaving behind formal conventions, as manifested by the fantasies that precede Baroque fugues and by certain free introductions and bridge passages. The consequence of this attitude is made apparent in the following statement from his *Entwurf einer neuen Ästhetik der Tonkunst* ('Outline of a new aesthetic of music'):

> In the present-day musical practice the rest and the pause are the elements which reveal most clearly the origins of music. Great performers, improvisers, know well how to use these expressive tools on a larger scale. The spellbinding silence between two movements becomes, in this context, music itself. It leaves more room for mystery than the actual sound, which, by its higher degree of definition, permits less elasticity.

On the one side, there was Busoni's passionate struggle with the problems of counterpoint, his untiring speculative quest which in 1911 produced the first polytonal fugue exposition and in the *Rondo Arlecchinesco* of 1916 led him to the use of a twelve-note theme; on the other, there was his statement that 'improvisation would come closest to the essential nature of art if only it were within man's power to master inspiration extempore'.

While Busoni demanded that creation should start from the non-existent, should search for the unknown, the never yet experienced, should forget all received ideas and look solely towards the future, at the same time he fostered the cultivation and utilisation of the past, dreaming of a future art that would be aristocratic and reserved, reactionary in the noblest sense. Thus his fondness for the technique of transcription – of which more shall be said later – must also be seen as a characteristic attempt to combine the conservation of historical values with the powerful urge to innovate.

With Busoni, an exceptionally strong identification with the instrument was carried to the point of self-contradiction in such notions as 'abstract sound', the 'dematerialisation' of music, the emancipation of musical instruments from their conventional applications, the concept of a 'de-individualisation' of musical timbre.

In the same breath, he spoke of systems of philosophy and religion as artistic manifestations which would carry conviction according to the skill of their propagators, and, in a fit of religious fervour, called music 'the heavenly child whose feet touch not this earth'.

Again, there was the Faustian side of his intellect, which made him familiar with the melancholy of loneliness. As its counterbalance we find serene confidence, rarefied irony and ready surrender to grace, the mysterious, ethereal virtue, rarest attribute of spirits.

How a character of such individuality was able to avoid those compulsive exertions of the will that often bring ruin to problematic natures will forever remain a mystery. The love of Mozart that took hold of Busoni in his late maturity is a signpost on the road of his inner development. 'In the most tragic situation, he is ready with a joke – in the most hilarious, he is capable of a learned frown' (*Mozart Aphorisms*, 1906). Paul Bekker in his funeral oration commented on the 'peculiar serenity' of Busoni the man, which raised him above others. In Busoni's best works, there is a fusion of the Classicist and the Romantic, the constructor and the improviser, the virtuoso and the transcendentalist of sound, the aesthete and the mystic, the magician and the comedian.

Since Liszt, pianistic progress has been made along many lines. We owe some new nuances to the Impressionists, the modern Russians and Bartók. But it was Busoni alone who realised the full implications of the instrument's technical possibilities over their whole range, beyond the achievements of specialists.

The most individual feature of Busoni's pianistic art was his treatment of the pedal:

> The effects of the pedal remain unexplored because its use is still fettered by a narrow-minded and unreasonable harmonic theory; people treat the pedal in much the same way as they might try to force air and water into geometric shapes ... The pedal has a bad reputation. Meaningless infringements of the rules bear the blame for this. Now let us try some meaning*ful* infringements...

In conjunction with a highly refined non-legato technique this new treatment of the pedal produced tone colours and areas of sound of the most delicate transparency. It was particularly those passages in his piano works which to the uninformed seem technically overloaded that, according to Gisella Selden-Goth, became under Busoni's hands 'a disembodied, floating sound mixture, gliding and whirling past in iridescent shades'.

To Busoni, technical difficulties are merely coincidental. All that matters is the musical meaning of a difficult passage. Until one understands that meaning, one should not touch the keys. The pianist has one implacable enemy: the piano, which continually tempts him to forget the musical meaning of a passage in mastering its mechanical difficulties. Technique can never reach a point where problems cease to exist, precisely because the real problems are not technical, but musical. Liszt's notion of 'technique as the helpmate of the idea' finds a strong exponent in Busoni.

He never tired of protesting against the prejudice that saw in Liszt no more than the conceited acrobat and breaker of hearts. At present, the compositions of Busoni are suffering a similar fate to those of Liszt: they are written in an ink that, as it were, begins to glow only when the right eye falls upon it. But while the creations of Liszt are no longer known,[101] those of Busoni have yet to become known. I would recommend a thorough study of the *Fantasia Contrappuntistica*, that monumental fusion of thesis and antithesis, of counterpoint and fantasy, Bach and Busoni, that confrontation of an infinitely subtle range of keyboard colours with a Baroque-style independence from tone colour. The student of this work may find himself transported into a novel sphere of instrumental art.

---

101   Since 1954, the situation has changed in many countries, as I have indicated earlier in the book.

Busoni's piano playing signifies the victory of reflection over bravura. After Liszt had triumphantly brought the instrument out from its narrow isolation, Busoni continued the process to the point where its challenge seemed to have been overcome. However, impulses are never abolished; they are merely filtered and refined. In his own words: 'Have thunderstorms ceased to exist because Franklin invented the lightning conductor?' For Busoni, too, knew the favour of the hour. In a letter to his wife he describes the happy occasion: 'when the instrument responds perfectly, when the best ideas come during the actual performance and, what is more, sound right straightaway...'

One cannot imagine an art of interpretation farther removed from mindless routine. On the subject of routine, flourishing not least at the conservatories (whose main purpose, according to Busoni, is to provide a livelihood for the teachers), Busoni had much to say from his own experience:

> Routine means the acquiring of a little experience and a few tricks of the trade, and the unvarying application of them to any given context. Accordingly, the number of related contexts must be remarkably high. To my mind, however, music is so constituted that every context is a new context and should be treated as an 'exception'. The solution of a problem, once found, cannot be reapplied to a different context. Our art is a theatre of surprise and invention, and of the seemingly unprepared. The spirit of music arises from the depths of our humanity and is returned to the high regions whence it has descended upon mankind.

Busoni has demonstrated the decisive importance of subjectivity in interpretation, with all that entails; it is not, however, a subjectivity dictated by blind instinct, but one controlled by a sovereign intelligence. As Liszt put it, the work is for the interpreter the tragic and stirring *mise en scène* of his own emotions. A musical transcription, therefore, would be the result of the compromise between what the composer had to say and what the interpreter felt about it. Anyone doubting the propriety of such an artistic exercise should remind himself that the only point at issue is the persuasive power of the arranger. The age of virtuoso worship has been succeeded by one of ancestor veneration for the composer. But let us not forget that above the distinction between composer and performer there is the primal element of music itself to which both are subjected, that elemental power beyond human concerns from which the composer draws his inspiration and to which the true interpreter returns the creations of music. 'The interpretation of music springs from those sublime heights from which the art of music itself has descended. When music is in danger of becoming earthbound, the interpreter has to raise it up and guide it back to its original elevated state'.

A Utopian thought, certainly. But in Utopia art has both its source and its destination.

(1954)

Arlecchino and *Doktor Faust*

A LADY OF THE Busoni circle once asked me what it was about Busoni that so attracted us younger musicians – after all, none of us had been under the spell of his personality or had had direct experience of the magic of his piano playing. None of us had encountered his supreme personal charm, the powerful, even paralyzing presence of Busoni the man. Let me attempt to answer this question.

First, there was that quality that lifted Busoni out from the ruck of his contemporaries, the same quality that had distinguished Liszt fifty years before: the universality of his mind which transcended the confines of his pianistic renown. There was the breadth of his interests and learning; the impact he made on the people he met, enhanced as it was by his splendid appearance; his literary education and activity, besides his ability to correspond in four languages; the witty draughtsmanship of the caricaturist; the aura, at once awe-inspiring and ludicrously fantastic, which, we are told, surrounded him. To all these qualities must be added his achievements as a musician: the composer whose late-style works are to be counted among the most significant of his age; the virtuoso pianist who became a model to the succeeding generation in Europe, paralleled only by d'Albert, who in many other respects was his direct opposite; the conductor who gave first performances of new compositions; the teacher who in Weimar revived the great days of Liszt and in Berlin counted Wladimir Vogel and Kurt Weill among his composition students; and lastly the champion of modern music, in whose collection of essayistic and poeticizing fragments entitled *Entwurf einer neuen Ästhetik der Tonkunst* ('Outline of a New Aesthetic of Music') are foreshadowed not only dodecaphonic and microtone systems, but even electronic music – and that in the year 1906! Such, then, was Busoni's universality.

In the second place I should like to mention a characteristic pertaining to Busoni the pianist, something perhaps unique to him and to Liszt, namely the combination of the great musician and artist with the great bravura player whose strength and precision overcame all difficulties. It is, incidentally, not quite true that we have never heard Busoni play. At least, his recording of the Thirteenth Hungarian Rhapsody by Liszt proves that the admiration of Schnabel, Fischer, Kempff or Steuermann was justified.

My third point seems to me the most important: occupying ourselves with the late compositions of Busoni gives us pleasure. Fischer-Dieskau sings Doktor Faust and the Goethe songs; Hans Werner Henze champions the operas *Turandot* and *Arlecchino*; some pianists, endowed with the requisite large hands, attempt Busoni's Sonatinas and Elegies, the *Fantasia Contrappuntistica*, the Toccata and the organ transcriptions. However, there is a reserve peculiar to his best works which cuts them off from loud acclaim. To quote his biographer, E. J. Dent: 'He was Latin enough to avoid by nature the sentimentality of the second-rate Germans, and at the same time too German to fall into sentimentality of an Italian type.'

His German-Italian heritage is manifest in the titles of his two most important stage works, *Doktor Faust* and *Arlecchino*. In other respects too, these works tell us a great deal about Busoni. They show both the speculative and the playful elements in his nature. But they also represent the two possibilities in which Busoni, equally critical of Wagner and of the *Verismo*, saw the future of opera. These are the concepts of 'supernatural subject matter' (*übernatürlicher Stoff*) and 'downright playfulness' (*absolutes Spiel*). His view that 'opera should create an illusory world which reflects life in either a magic mirror or a distorting mirror' is clearly borne out not only by the *commedia dell'arte*, but also by the puppet play (*Doktor Faust*, Gozzi's *Turandot*) and the fantastic world of E. T. A. Hoffmann (*Die Brautwahl*).

Hoffmannesque traits are also to be found in Busoni's private life: it is reported that in the years before his death in 1924 he sought out the company of the deformed; yet at the same time he was striving for lucidity and lightness (Busoni's nature was activated by its contradictions). One aspect of this striving was his call for a 'Young Classicism', which had little to do with neoclassicism. As he wrote to Gisella Selden-Goth: 'The tapering-scale [*Verjüngung*] – a technical architectural term – implies, as you know, a slimming, a refinement of lines. Therefore we should speak not of New Classicism (a term I resist, since it sounds like a turning back), but of Young Classicism [*Junge Klassizität*].'[102] Busoni was fond of paradoxical formulations, a characteristic he shared with his contemporary Oscar Wilde. One of his remarks that has come down to us by word of mouth, and which was coined with a certain Late-Romantic virtuoso in mind, runs, 'Poetry in performance is a lack of technique.'

---

102 *Translator's note*: As will be obvious to the reader, the English language cannot reproduce the play on the word *jung* ('young') that Busoni intended here.

Some Busoni disciples may well have taken too literal a view of this and similar strange pronouncements, such as his sharp criticism of early Beethoven in particular, his total disregard of Schubert, his low opinion of Schumann, his opposition to Wagner and Debussy. Against these things, however, should be measured Busoni's boundless admiration for Mozart ('With every riddle he gives you its solution'), his incomparable advocacy of Liszt, his sympathy with César Franck, Saint-Saëns, Alkan, his respect for Strauss, Mahler and Schoenberg (who succeeded him at the Berlin Hochschule), his interest in Stravinsky's *Histoire du Soldat.*

The transient nature of some of his views should not blind us to the value of Busoni's works. In Vienna – a city, according to Busoni, that is suffocated by its *feuilletons* – Busoni the composer has not yet been noticed. At most, he is known as the arranger of Bach who arouses the wrath of the purists, for in these days even masterly arrangements are deemed sacrilegious. Elsewhere, the slowly growing fame of Busoni the composer is based on post-war performances of his operas. *Doktor Faust*, in stage or concert versions, has been given in Berlin, London, Florence and New York. It remains to be seen how many more Busoni anniversaries must go by before one of the quintessential operas of the twentieth century finds its way to Vienna.

(1966)

Afterthoughts on Busoni

THE FIRST OF my essays on Busoni, the idiom of which strikes me today as odd, is permeated by Busoni's own individual use of language. It is full of Busoni quotations (by no means always confined within inverted commas), such as his label 'pianistic Darwinism'. In his essay *Das Klaviergenie* ('The Pianist of Genius') Busoni wrote: 'It is very surprising – at the first sight, anyway – that something which until recently could be done only by one man should now also be done by another; but when there are hordes of "others", it becomes Darwinism.' Another Busonian expression, 'law-givers', denotes those to whom the signs are more important than the music. Commenting on Busoni's *Entwurf einer neuen Ästhetik der Tonkunst* ('Outline of a new aesthetic of music'), Arnold Schoenberg, who said of himself that he was 'certainly no law-giver, hardly even a law-taker', repudiated with splendid acuity the right of the interpreter to encroach upon the creator.[103]

Liszt's observation that 'the work is for the interpreter the tragic and stirring *mise en scene* of his own emotions' shows where Busoni's ideas came from. It also shows up the type of interpreter Schoenberg was alluding to – though this did not prevent him from calling Liszt a great man.

My own ideas about the task of the interpreter have moved away from those of Busoni. In my view, the interpreter should function in three capacities: as curator of a museum, as executor of a will, and as obstetrician. The job of the curator is a 'historical' one; he compares the text of the work with the original sources and familiarises himself with the textual conventions and performing habits of the period. In doing so, he will discover that it is not enough to 'observe the letter' – as he will see if he should look, for example, at the Mozart piano concertos, the solo parts of which have hardly any dynamic markings, but contain fermatas and uncompleted passages that have to be filled in by the player. At this point the curator hands over to the executor, who realises that it is his own breath which revives the breath of the composer, and who is aware that emotions and ears, instruments and concert halls have changed since the composer's day. The executor must not only have the ability to project the music of the past into the present, but also a faculty for reopening the gates of the past, for making what was new in its time seem new once again.

---

103 Cf 'On Playing Schoenberg's Piano Concerto', p. 295–6.

Thus, for instance, he will reinvest the chord of the diminished seventh, which wore increasingly thin in the course of the nineteenth century, with its former ominous, demonic, tonality-denying tension whenever this is required by the music.

If fortune smiles, the 'moral' function of the executor will be complemented by the 'magical' function of the obstetrician. It is he who protects the performance from the cold touch of finality, who leads the music back to its origin: the work, so it seems, is brought to life by the hands of the player. The immediacy of such a feat renders pointless any discussion about the merits and demerits of tradition. From a carefully nurtured foundation springs spontaneity.

Some of Busoni's works have recently profited from the vogue for Victorian or Edwardian curiosities[104] and the rediscovery of the Art Nouveau. But compositions like the monstrously overwritten Piano Concerto obstruct our view of his superlative late piano music. How topical still – and undiscovered – are the first two Sonatinas, the Elegies, and the Toccata of 1921! The erosion of the years has not smoothed over their unyielding surface. No patina of familiarity softens their sharpness. *Doktor Faust*, towering over the musical theatre of its time alongside the works of Berg and Schoenberg, awaits its day.

(1976)

---

104 Cf 'Liszt and the Piano Circus', p. 224.

Superhuman Frailty

BUSONI'S INVOLVEMENT WITH opera was linked to his concept of 'Junge Klassizität'. It was not the turning back to older forms, or the ironic comment on past styles, of neoclassicism that Busoni had in mind; his strangely Utopian notion envisaged a music removed from the constraints of purpose, style, form and functional harmony. What 'Junge Klassizität' shares with Classicism is a mistrust of an emotional intensity that goes overboard, of flamboyant gestures, and of a sensuality or 'sexuality' that in music, though by no means in life, Busoni thought ridiculous and untruthful. Love duets, including that of Verdi's *Otello*, made him furious: there is nothing more appalling, he notes, than a little man and a large lady pouring gushing melodies over one another while holding hands.

Musically, Busoni hoped for an end to 'thematic' or 'motivic' composition, called for the primacy of melody in all voices (linear polyphony) and helped, along with Schoenberg, to emancipate dissonance. To him, dissonance rather than the triad represented 'nature'. With all their differences in musical outlook, Busoni patiently continued to support Schoenberg, whose existence in Berlin rested largely on his backing. Alas, Schoenberg declined to complete *Doktor Faust* after Busoni's death, but accepted the offer to succeed him as composition teacher at the Prussian Academy.

Busoni's ideas reacted against the inflated rhetoric and the sentimental pathos of late Romanticism, Italian *Verismo* and expressionism. (Busoni conceded that there is an expressionist in every composer, but rejected any claims of supremacy of one style over another.) He steered clear of kitsch in a musical period that, even in some of its most gifted exponents, was prone to kitsch in unprecedented measure. To an audience used to overheated and over-stimulated music, Busoni's self-control must have appeared almost glacial. In music, he explains, feeling has to be applied grandly and economically. It should not be overly concerned with detail and wasted on the short span (this is what, according to Busoni, the layman and the mediocre artist conceive feeling to be). Feeling needs to be linked to taste and style. The popular concept of feeling ignores taste: the result is sentimentality and over-projection. To feeling that demonstrates itself in 'spontaneous' gestures, Busoni prefers feeling 'that acts quietly' and most of all, feeling that is concealed.

Busoni's phobia about the trivial and ingratiating extended to the musically stereotyped. The 'typical' horn call, the melting string phrase, the chuckling bassoon,
the instantly memorable tune belonged to a past that he greatly admired. As they
became a matter of routine, one needed to avoid them. It was rather late in his
development that Busoni, after writing his prophetic *Outline of a. New Aesthetic of
Music* (1907), imposed such strictures on himself, an austerity that, to him, opened
up vast areas of freedom. If what Isaiah Berlin termed 'moral charm' is applicable
to musical aims, Busoni's offer proof of it.

Busoni believed that opera is the supreme form of musical expression because
it permits, and demands, the combination of all musical means and forms. Opera,
according to him, should not duplicate what happens on stage but illuminate what
goes on in the mind, or soul, of the acting characters, unseen and unuttered. Not
the thunderstorm but the reaction – or non-reaction – to it is what ought to be composed. In some special cases, the music may impress on the listener what happens
outside his vision – behind the stage, so to speak – and ignore what can be clearly
perceived. Singing texts on stage is a convention that has the effect of 'untruth'.
Therefore, opera has to concentrate on the unbelievable and on what is unlikely to
make sense of itself; the public should always be reminded that it is dealing with
the fictional world of the jocular and/or fantastic that is unlike the seriousness and
truthfulness of life.

The operatic subject Busoni sought – 'half religious' and elevating, yet entertain-
ing – had to involve a quintessential and mysterious figure. After Ahasuerus and
Dante, Leonardo was considered; as Antony Beaumont shows in his splendid book
Busoni the Composer,[105] Busoni was able to identify with Leonardo in a variety of
ways. He was discarded when Gabriele d'Annunzio, to our great good fortune,
failed to provide a libretto. Don Juan – though Busoni saw him differently from da
Ponte – was ruled out on account of Mozart's music, Goethe's *Faust* on account of
Busoni's respect for Goethe's text. (In looking for a 'subject' that would not be complete without music, Busoni saw in *Faust II* a prime example of 'operatic drama'.)
Finally, the medieval *Puppet Play of Doctor Faust* proved decisive: it promised, like
the revered *Magic Flute*, a combination of the educational, the spectacular, the awesome and the amusing.

105 Indiana University Press, 1985.

Busoni was a remarkable writer. His essays, and letters to his wife, testify to origi-nality, erudition and stylistic grace. Busoni's libretto for *Doktor Faust* does not quite reach the level of his prose: it remains under the spell of Goethe's diction. Critics of the text of *Zauberflöte* or *Parsifal* – two scores Busoni greatly admired, and two libretti I find no less mystifying than his own – should have a field day. Busoni's Faust, at the end of his life, concentrates on an ultimate 'mysterious deed': he gives his own life to his dead child in order to live on as an 'eternal will'. By finally step-ping out of the magic circle of beliefs, by leaving religious concepts, good and evil, God and the Devil behind in Nietzschean fashion, Faust becomes free to draw his own magic circle and create his own myth. How Faust is able to extract himself from the obligation to serve the forces of evil remains hard to comprehend. 'One good deed' seems an all too easy way out. Does Faust's lifting himself out of the morass – in the style of the German folk hero Münchhausen – by pulling his own hair, thereby undo his past crimes? In the end, the power of Mephistopheles that had frightened Faust out of his wits appears no less riddled with human frailty than that of the Queen of the Night, and Sarastro.

It is, however, hardly the point of opera to be rational. Some of the mystifying events in Busoni's libretto may, to him, have had their private connotations (it should have amused him that Faust's pact with the Devil is sealed on an Easter Sunday – the day on which Busoni was born). Others, such as the two apparitions of Helen of Troy, Busoni's unattainable ideal of beauty and perfection, are frankly Utopian; the fusion of Utopianism and blasphemy in Helen's appearance on the cross remains the most striking invention in Busoni's plot.

At his death, Busoni had not produced the music for the Helen of Troy episodes, or finished Faust's final monologue. To make performances possible, Philipp Jarnach, the most experienced of Busoni's pupils, was persuaded to complete the work. What he contributed, reluctantly and in uncomfortable haste, delighted the press of the day. To my ears it has always appeared diametrically opposed to Busoni's style, an intrusion of Wagner-cum-Leoncavallo into Busoni's rarefied air.[106]

Luckily, this obstacle to the appreciation of *Doktor Faust* has now been removed, thanks to Antony Beaumont's recent solution. His task was uniquely facilitated by

---

106 Of the composers influenced by Busoni, Varèse might have come closest to doing justice to the final scene. Kurt Weill, taking his cue from parts of the church intermezzo from *Doktor Faust*, created in due course his own refreshingly cynical brand of music theatre.

Busoni's habit of using elements of his previous compositions where it suited him, or, indeed, of anticipating *Doktor Faust* in works like the 'Sonatina seconda' or the 'Berceuse élégiaque' that were to break fresh ground.

It would be unreasonable to expect from Mr Beaumont what Busoni himself did not accomplish. His concoction of Busoniana follows Busoni's own prescriptions with remarkable taste and skill. (Only months before his death, Busoni had outlined a musical design of the final scene in a sketch unknown to Jarnach at the time he made his completion.) Beaumont, unlike Jarnach, gives the full text of Faust's final monologue and has restored some lines that are crucial to the understanding, if that is the right word, of Faust's ultimate wisdom. In Beaumont's score, these lines of Nietzschean renunciation contain one instance of mistranslation. Beaumont's book gives a different, literal and accurate if not singable, text for 'Euch zum Trotze, Euch Allen, die ihr euch gut preist, die wir nennen böse' ('In defiance of you, of you all, who hold yourselves for good, whom we call evil'). Beaumont's score reads: 'Let me spite you, wreak my vengeance on all you good ones who in truth are evil', turning the goodies into baddies, and obscuring the issue that Faust rids himself of good and evil alike.

What is the sum of *Doktor Faust*'s parts? I think that, among operatic mystery plays, Busoni's *Faust* is musically superior to Pfitzner's *Palestrina* and Hindemith's *Mathis der Maler*, and invites comparison with Schoenberg's *Moses und Aron*. I find Busoni's score masterly, intensely personal and admirably true to his aims. It seems uneroded, and incorruptible, by time. The tag of eclecticism that is habitually fastened around Busoni's neck fits neither his melodic invention nor his treatment of harmony; where he makes use of older forms he does so with innovative freedom; and his orchestration is never that of a pianist: it shows the most delicate and precise perception of the noblest tints of colour. My only doubt concerns the end of the penultimate scene where Faust welcomes the last evening of his life with quite untypical bombast – avoidable if the drawn-out *allargando* is ignored.

Scenically, there is plenty for an inventive producer to build upon. (Busoni, in his libretto, intentionally left gaps to be filled in by the producer, and the public.) In David Pountney's highly imaginative presentation at the English National Opera, the expressionist in Busoni was over-projected. Busoni himself would have been surprised, and thoroughly horrified, by some of Pountney's scenic coups, and by the reference to political actuality that was imposed on a timeless human problem.

Pountney gave an amusing twist to the students' celebrating Faust's famulus Wagner as 'Rector Magnificus', and made the emergence of the naked boy from Faust's cloak a resoundingly moving experience. But he also turned Helen, who is supposed to appear in a Classical landscape, into a harlot, omitted the required magic circles altogether, and remained tied to the all too dominating set by Stefanos Lazaridis that fitted neither the church scene, nor the Court of Parma, nor the tavern, evoking New York rather than Wittenberg. Busoni maintained that his libretto was free from philosophical intentions, and that the events of the final tableau sprang out of him in an 'entirely poetic' manner. Pountney, I feel, was guided too strongly by rationalisations, symbols and Jungian concepts. He claims, in the programme, that Busoni's Mephistopheles 'offers nothing truly devilish – only something human' (namely another part of Faust's personality), contradicting himself a little later in the same essay by stating that Mephistopheles grants Faust 'the superhuman and lethal ability to act out his thoughts' unrestrained. It is this superhuman faculty indeed that unleashes Faust's fate. All grumbles apart, Mr Pountney deserved his share of the credit for *Doktor Faust's* public success; not a few of those in the audience who were unaware of Busoni's intentions will have perceived his staging as meaningful and highly effective.

Musically, the ENO coped admirably with Busoni's extraordinary demands. Electronic amplification was used where, before its invention, Busoni seemed to call for it: the sound of the organ enveloped the listener as he had suggested. Antony Beaumont conducted the two performances that I heard. It was good to see somebody who writes so well about Busoni bringing his music so stylishly to life. Of all those involved in making this new version of *Doktor Faust* such a memorable occasion, he must take pride of place. Graham Clark, in every way the ideal exponent of Mephistopheles, mastered the 'impossible' tessitura triumphantly. Thomas Allen's Faust was beautifully sung, though, at times, a little lacking in dynamic, and demonic, force. All gratitude to the ENO for finally presenting *Doktor Faust* on the London stage and making it an impressive event. The attendance, and rapture, at the Coliseum indicated that the time for Busoni may, after all, be coming.

(1986)

Ferruccio Busoni.

Original photographer unknown. Photo reproduction © Geoffrey Goode, London. (Collection Alfred Brendel)

On Playing Schoenberg's Piano Concerto

AFTER HALF A century, Schoenberg's Piano Concerto has found its place in the repertory. It may never become fully domesticated; but why should masterpieces necessarily be popular? It has remained a 'problem piece', but not one that is stifled by its problems. They keep on stirring, but the piece, far from collapsing under the strain of its tensions, proves its resilience. Though it may not count among Schoenberg's indispensable scores, it has, to this player, stayed interesting while most other piano concertos of Schoenberg's time have faded away, or ended up as pleasant entertainment. It has turned out to be a lighter and leaner work, a good deal less 'Brahmsian' than it had seemed to commentators like Virgil Thomson during the early days of its life. This is owing to the remarkable increase in familiarity, on the part of orchestras, conductors, soloists and record producers, if not of a very large public, with the intricacies of Schoenberg's style. Re-recording the work recently with the same orchestra and conductor thirty-six years after my first attempt felt like an act of re-generation – as though I were contributing some continuity and progress to a world which, relapsing into nationalism, fascism and madness, appears to have lost interest in both.

The composition of the Piano Concerto was set in motion by Oscar Levant, who had been Schoenberg's student over a three-year period. The celebrated exponent of Gershwin's piano music, radio entertainer and Hollywood film composer commissioned his former teacher to write a piano piece for him in 1942. Schoenberg instead began work on a piano concerto, for which Levant had no use; and the fee Schoenberg now suggested exceeded by far the amount Levant was prepared to spend. (The requested commission of $1,000 corresponded with the sums Elizabeth Sprague Coolidge had paid for Schoenberg's third and fourth quartets.) Levant, with some difficulty, withdrew from the deal. One could scarcely imagine him playing this particular work anyway. Henry Clay Shriver, a wealthy student of Gerald Strang, one of Schoenberg's teaching assistants, took over payment of the commission after the concerto was finished. The pianist Edward Steuermann, a leading interpreter of the music of Schoenberg's circle since the days of the 'Society for Private Musical Performances' in Vienna, played the concerto first for a private audience in Los Angeles with

Leonard Stein at the second piano, and then, in 1944, with the NBC orchestra under Leopold Stokowski.[107]

Schoenberg's new method of 'composing with twelve tones related only with one another' resulted directly from the evolution of musical harmony. For three centuries, music had been dominated by tonality, a system based on the seven tones of the diatonic scale and the relationship of its pitches, with a central pitch, the 'tonic,' as its pivotal point of reference. In the nineteenth century, tonality was gradually dissolved by the increased reliance on the twelve chromatic semitones. Wagner's *Tristan* became the first large-scale work to be governed by chromatic harmony. And Liszt, in some of his late pieces, abandoned not only the frame of conventional harmony but even the requirement of maintaining one basic key or tonal centre.

By 1908, a few gifted and courageous composers decided to leave all tonal constrictions behind. Until the early 1920s, some of the most captivating music of our century, from Anton von Webern's orchestral miniatures to Schoenberg's *Erwartung* and Alban Berg's *Wozzeck*, was composed in the no-man's-land of 'emancipated dissonance', or 'atonality' – a term Schoenberg disliked. Finally, around 1922, Schoenberg's twelve-tone row supplied a substitute order, in effect a genetic code, from which the structure of a whole piece could unfold. His method followed, with much increased rigor, a procedure Beethoven had applied in a number of his cyclic compositions: to introduce at the outset certain motifs (and sometimes even fixed pitches) that would connect all themes and movements of a work as a common denominator. Already in Beethoven, the pitches and their transpositions are usually more important than, and often independent from, the rhythm of the initial musical material or the characteristic contour of a theme.

For Schoenberg, however, the use of the twelve-tone set was not limited to motifs. From the set, he wrote, 'the formal elements of music – melodies, themes, phrases, motives, figures, and chords,' can all be evolved. The tones in the set can be changed in register by one or more octaves, or uniformly transposed by any interval, or inverted, or reversed, or both inverted and reversed. To Schoenberg's pupil Webern, this variety within constraint represented nothing less than the ultimate achievement of a long musical evolution, a view rarely shared today. As a working hypothesis for a number

---

107 See Walter B. Bailey: 'Oscar Levant and the Program for Schoenberg's Piano Concerto,' *Journal of the Arnold Schoenberg Institute*, Vol. 6, No. 1 (1982), pp. 56–79. Above all, I am deeply indebted to Leonard Stein, who, over many years, has been an invaluable and generous source of enlightenment.

of decades, twelve-tone technique has made musical history, and aided great composers in writing masterpieces. It led to the serialism of the 1950s and '60s which, besides
pitch, included harmony, rhythm, dynamics and instrumental colour.

Already in the initial sketches, the opening of the Piano Concerto was conceived
as an extended twelve-tone melody played by the soloist. The rhythm of this opening, alternating short and long durations, survived almost unchanged. The emphasis
given to certain notes by means of longer rhythmic values had a remarkable effect
on the structure of the work; it influenced both the shape of the twelve-tone set and
the relation between sets in various positions, as well as the texture and the development of motifs.[108]

The melodic outline of the opening remained recognisable even when Schoenberg
modified the pitches of the tone row to fit his requirements. These requirements
postulated – for most of his larger works from Op. 25 on – that the first six tones of
the row should be complemented by the six tones of the inversion, an interval
of a fifth below in such a way that this inversion would not repeat any of the original tones. As a result, the combination of both would complete the twelve tones of
the chromatic scale.

Since his great 'Jakobsleiter' fragment of 1917, which opens with a six-fold succession of six-tone chords, Schoenberg took to calling himself a six-tone, rather than a
twelve-tone, composer. Schoenberg's obsession with numbers was, like Alban Berg's,
almost cabalistic. Ancient tradition from Pythagoras and Saint Augustine to a few
Renaissance theorists and Jewish mystics held six to be the perfect or divine number.
It may have been particularly meaningful to Schoenberg that the number of basic
spatial directions – up, down, forwards, backwards, right, left[109] – adds up to six.
In twelve-tone composition, a row can be made to go backwards or forwards: it can
reverse or invert a sequence of tones in techniques called 'mirrors' and 'retrogrades'.
Procedures that gave six-tone sets a particular prominence and allowed the changing around of notes in small groups may have conferred on them a mysterious aura.

Schoenberg's leanings toward the occult found nourishment in Swedenborg's

---

108   See Paul Johnson: 'Rhythm and Set Choice in Schoenberg's Piano Concerto', *Journal of the Arnold Sch-
       oenberg Institute*, Vol. 11, No. 1 (1988), pp. 38–51.

109   See Alexander L. Ringer, 'Faith and Symbol – On Arnold Schoenberg's Last Musical Utterance', in *Jour-
       nal of the Arnold Schoenberg Institute*, Vol. 6, No. 1 (1982), pp. 80–95, and Johnson, 'Rhythm and Set
       Choice in Schoenberg's Piano Concerto', pp. 38–51.

theosophical ideas and Balzac's Swedenborgian novel *Séraphita*. Emanuel Swedenborg (1688–1772), the Swedish scientist turned mystic, claimed to be visited by angels.
They told him that Mars was inhabited by ventriloquists the size of six-year-old
children who crawled on the ground, whereas the population of Venus consisted of
oversized simpletons indulging in robbery. While it is hard to imagine Schoenberg
being amused by such revelations, there is no doubt that Swedenborg's concept of
angels as human beings who had managed to ascend to God in a process of puri-
fication struck a sympathetic chord. Schoenberg knew Wagner's writings, and was
taken by his notion of 'redemption through love'. In *Séraphita* – the name of an
androgynous creature also called 'Seraphitus', depending on the sex and sensibility
of the fellow humans it encounters – Balzac tried to relate such celestial strivings in
a lyrical prose that fused high Romanticism with the idiom of ecstatic visionaries.

So impressed was Schoenberg with *Séraphita* that shortly before the First World
War he contemplated a composition based on it, whether a symphony, oratorio or
stage work. He explained to Alma Mahler that it would need a special theatre to
stage it, and a choir of at least two thousand singers for the 'ascension scene' alone![110]
(Among contemporary fellow admirers of Swedenborg, and of Balzac in his occult
mood, was William Butler Yeats.)

Though in his way as profoundly religious a person as the Russian Orthodox
Stravinsky, Schoenberg defended superstition as a metaphysical urge running parallel to faith, and relished it himself. The strangest manifestations of this naïve side
of Schoenberg's character may be found in the 'War-Clouds Diary' of 1914–15,[111] in
which Schoenberg examined daily cloud formations on the assumption that 'many
people like myself today, will have tried to interpret the events of war by the sky,
since finally the belief in higher powers and also in God has returned'. To Schoenberg, 'golden glitter', 'victory wind', 'deep blue sky' or 'bloody clouds (at sunset)'
preceded Austro-German victories while storm, rain and 'deep black clouds of eery
impression' anticipated bad turns in the war. From such patriotic feelings the Piano
Concerto is far removed. It echoes, in its emotional layout, Schoenberg's flight from
Nazi Germany, and his life as an émigré in the United States.

---

110   In a letter of 11 November 1913. See Nuria Nono-Schoenberg, *Arnold Schönberg 1874–1951: Lebensgeschichte
      in Begegnungen* (Klagenfurt, Austria: Ritter, 1992), a huge, untidy and endlessly fascinating scrapbook.

111   Paul Pisk, translator, *Journal of the Arnold Schoenberg Institute*, Vol. 9, No. 1 (1986), pp. 53–77.

The opening melody of the Concerto, lasting thirty-nine bars, presents the four modes of the tone row in the following order: original set, inversion of retrograde, retrograde and inversion. (Both inversions appear in transpositions.) The listener need not be aware of this. The unifying impact of musical material often remains indirect, whether in Beethoven or Schoenberg. What the listener ought to notice is the masterly control of the melody's seemingly casual unfolding. Some commentators ascribe a 'tonal layout' to the work as a whole. I find that one can, with some imagination, make out intermittent passages of B-flat major, F-sharp minor and C major resulting from the shape of the original row. The appearance of a kind of C major at the end of the initial melody and at the conclusion of the work briefly recalls Stravinsky's use of harmony, which makes simultaneous use of tonic and dominant. (The first traces of such simultaneity, to be found in Beethoven's 'Eroica' Symphony and 'Les Adieux' Sonata, were deemed objectionable well into the nineteenth century.) But there is, to my ears, nothing like a tonal centre to which the whole piece refers, let alone any hint of functional harmony.

Does this make the employment of 'Classical' forms in a four-movement work precarious? I don't think it does, because Schoenberg leaves out the formal concept most dependent on functional harmony: sonata form.[112] Instead of starting with the sonata form in the traditional manner, the Piano Concerto presents a theme and variations with some interludes. This is followed by a fierce scherzo, an adagio full of grave intensity both Romantic and Expressionist in mood; and a rondo finale ('*giocoso*') which brings various strands of the work together. According to Schoenberg's precise notes, he wanted the orchestra to repeat the initial melody played by the piano, with the piano adding a counter-melody also to be taken up by the orchestra, followed by a second counter-melody of the pianist, before all three are combined.

Schoenberg's conservative tendencies can hardly be ascribed to the loss of nerve of an aging revolutionary; already his early twelve-tone compositions, Opp. 24 to 28, had tried to demonstrate that new techniques and older formal concepts were compatible. Schoenberg saw himself as part of the German musical tradition, a descendant of the great masters of the past. His knowledge of the music of his

---

112 The interpretation of the work as 'a single movement form displaying the characteristics of a multi-movement sonata cycle' (Bailey, 'Oscar Levant and the Program for Schoenberg's Piano Concerto', p. 65) is open to doubt.

predecessors was legendary, and explains at least partially his preeminence among composition teachers. His own innovations must have seemed to him to grow from their legacy: Schoenberg continued where they left off. His task was evolution, not revolution. According to Schoenberg, the only truly revolutionary composer during his lifetime had been Richard Strauss.

From the outset, the four movements of the Piano Concerto were conceived as distinctly different in character and texture. Schoenberg's much discussed 'titles' for the movements – 'Life was so easy' (initially 'pleasant'), 'Suddenly hatred broke out', 'A grave situation was created', 'But life goes on' – far from being later explanations provided for Oscar Levant, served Schoenberg as a guiding idea from the start. In his *Fundamentals of Musical Composition* Schoenberg wrote: 'In composing even the smallest exercises the student should never fail to keep in mind a special character. A poem, a story, a play or a moving picture may provide the stimulus to express definite moods. The pieces which he composes should differ widely.'[113] There can be little doubt that Schoenberg himself proceeded in this manner, unlike Schumann or Debussy, who often invented their titles *post factum*. If he kept some of these 'programmes' to himself this may have been because he hoped that a structurally sound piece would explain itself without literary crutches.

In spite of all the efforts of composers to make psychology and structure mutually dependent, I do not believe that the structure of a work automatically discloses its psychological character to the player. In trying to understand a piece the player ought to start simultaneously with both structure and psychology in mind, with the hope that he will find out where he can make them meet. I am grateful to know Schoenberg's – evidently autobiographical – working titles, and glad that, although they were suppressed by Schoenberg, they eventually became available. 'Life was so easy' seems particularly suggestive: it should lead the player away from overly romanticizing and poeticizing the initial waltz. What the waltz needs instead is a certain lightness and Viennese lilt. If any of the titles seems to require modification it would be that of the scherzo; in it, 'hatred' doesn't break out 'suddenly'. On the contrary, the ground for each of the concerto's basic moods is elaborately prepared towards the end of the preceding movement. In the case of the final rondo, the delicious tomfoolery of the solo cadenza serves as a bridge between the adagio and the

---

113   Edited by Gerald Strang (St Martin's, 1967), p. 95.

finale; from the mountain of grief and pathos built up by the 'difficult situation' of the slow movement, there emerges a fidgety little mouse.

The textures of the movements are governed as well by basic contrast: the first calls for singing *legato*, and lightness; the second for aggressive *staccato*; the third for *legato espressivo*, spreading to heavy chordal intensity; and the last for pointed *staccato grazioso*, leading into a variety of sounds, articulations and tempi. The lightness of the first movement becomes opaque in its later stages; when the opening theme appears for the third time, the first violins are surrounded by so many instruments that the theme is easily obscured. (To Schoenberg, a hierarchy of principal and subordinate voices was always crucial, as can be seen in his textual instructions.) The impressive piano solo in the third movement asserts the position of the pianist as the centre of musical proceedings. Here, six-tone patterns are broken up into groups and chords of three tones. The despair and terror of the gestures in these twelve bars bring to my mind images from Picasso's *Guernica*. The final rondo, marked as 'humorous' in one of the earliest sketches, presents grotesqueries bordering on the macabre, complemented by references to the adagio and waltz, whose melody asserts itself in a densely contrapuntal 'apotheosis' (to quote Rudolf Stephan, who edited the 'authentic text of The Complete Edition'). Finally, a 'Stretto' coda closes the work with a statement of emphatic defiance.

Schoenberg's metronome figure for this 'Stretto' overshoots the limits of the possible even further than Beethoven's notorious marking for the first movement of the 'Hammerklavier' Sonata Op. 106. At $\downarrow$ = 120, no woodwind player in the world could even pretend to manage the fast notes and rhythms of bars 478 to 451. Similarly, Schoenberg's $\downarrow$ = 108 for the scherzo is out of the question: in Steuermann and Scherchen's performance for the Frankfurt Radio in 1955[114] it was played some 20 degrees slower; on the other hand, the 'Stretto' was taken so fast that Schoenberg's 'highest principle for all reproduction of music' became resolutely ignored. This principle, admittedly put to paper already in the 1920s, postulates 'that what the composer has written is made to sound in such a way that every note is really heard, and that all the sounds, whether successive or simultaneous, are in such relationship to each other that no part at any moment obscures another…' I am not sure that Schoenberg's advice can – or should – always be followed. In complex passages, the

---

114   The page turner on this occasion was Michael Gielen.

same amount of 'clarity' for each voice easily leads to confusion. Performers of the Piano Concerto will, at times, also have to choose between clear audibility and sweep.

Certain aspects of this score can become vexing and worrying to those who play it. The indicated duration of twenty-eight minutes is wholly misleading. These days, a good performance will take hardly more than nineteen to twenty-one minutes, and scrupulous observation of the metronome figures, if it were possible, would make it even quicker. There are more than a few miscalculations or mistaken notations – of tempi, of balances and of articulation marks (which frequently seem to demand a much slower pace to become playable, and distinctly audible). The lure of writing pieces which stretch the limits of the performer may go some way towards explaining this. I remember a restaurant in Paris called Gaspard de la Nuit, whose proprietor boasted six fingers on each hand. Lately, some younger players of Schoenberg's Violin Concerto, like Viktoria Mullova or Christian Tetzlaff, seem to have grown such an extra finger.

In the Piano Concerto, however, the problem is not fingers but clarity of vision. How far must the clarity of a larger vision – so impressive in Schoenberg – be verifiable in the way details are presented and the execution of the music is made feasible? There is no doubt that Schoenberg wanted to be precise and explicit to the dot – and that, when it came to the requirements of the performance, he sometimes left the firm ground of practicality. Like Max Reger, whose works Schoenberg's 'Private Society' in Vienna frequently rehearsed and performed, Schoenberg tended to be over-explicit in marking his scores. He himself asked 'whether we hear more than our predecessors did, or are merely willing to leave the performers less freedom than they did'. According to Schoenberg the question may be left unanswered. While he orchestrated works by Bach or Brahms with idiosyncratic opulence, Schoenberg seems to have expected obedience from those who played his own music. In his notes on Busoni's *Outline of a New Aesthetic of Music*, Schoenberg counters Busoni's advocacy of improvisatory freedom:

> The more an interpretation respects the written symbols, or rather, the more it tries to deduce from them the true intention of the author, the higher it must be rated. For the interpreter is not the tutor, let alone the spiritual mentor, of an orphaned work of art, but its keenest servant. His desire is to apprehend every wish that composer utters, to cherish his every thought, scarcely conceived. But this ideal is marred by two imperfections: that of notation, and that of the servant

himself. For, unfortunately, the servant is likely to be an individual bent on exhib-
iting his own personality rather than on inhabiting that of the composer. Thus he
will usually become a parasite on the skin of the composer, when he could have
been an artery in his bloodstream.

This is beautifully said, but, in the face of Schoenberg's notation, sometimes impossible to achieve. The situation is particularly aggravated by the fact that Schoenberg
made less than exact use of his own twelve-tone rows. When I started to play the
Piano Concerto in the 1950s, such lapses were explained away as deliberate exceptions to the rule, proof of the composer's whimsy and liberty. Since then, dozens of
wrong notes have been accepted as mistakes and gradually corrected. Such errors
have been attributed to Schoenberg's eyesight; it seems to have given him trouble
since the days of 'Jakobsleiter'. The declining powers of memory in an ageing person
have also been cited. But the frenzied speed of Schoenberg's composing may offer an
even better clue. The fact that he wrote music of remarkable complexity and contrapuntal mastery in a kind of white heat reveals the emotional furnace from which
his work emerged. In this context, his famous pronouncement, '*Kunst kommt nicht
von Können, sondern von Müssen,*' an untranslatable aphorism to the effect that art
is not a matter of 'can' but of 'must' (i.e., comes not from skill but from necessity),
takes on a new meaning.

Schoenberg was delighted by Balzac's description in *Séraphita* of a male character
whose short neck indicated that his heart was close to his head. It was Schoenberg's
ambition, strange as it may seem to some, to bring the functions of the heart and
the head together as closely as possible. While I am constantly reminded of the emotional urge in Schoenberg's music, there are details of pitch, speed or balance which
make me feel that, at points, the clarity of his head was clouded by the urgency of
his heart. For years, Schoenberg's wrong notes have given me headaches. I visualised
what might seem to be a comparable and particularly disturbing situation: that dozens of erroneous pitches would be found in a work by Bach or Mozart, and that, in
order to make up for the negligence of the master, later performers would have to
put them right. But the harmonic situations of Mozart and Schoenberg are too different to bear comparison. Once removed from functional harmony, the relevance
of the single note within an aural context has changed. I have learned to reconcile
myself with the Concerto's occasional lack of focus, or less than perfect notations,

and to be consoled by the fact that this musical organism is sturdy enough to carry its warts. Followers of great composers may compose more impeccably, and eliminate the rough edges of their idols. But smooth finish is not often found in the style of great works. In them, spots and blurs may be accepted, or even cherished, as imprints of genius. In a work like Schoenberg's Piano Concerto, I shall admire the solutions it offers and put up with the problems it continuously presents.

(1995)

PERFORMANCES, PROGRAMMES, RECORDING

~c~

Wilhelm Furtwängler

WILHELM FURTWÄNGLER WAS the performing musician who, more than any other, provided me with criteria for judging a performance. Not that I knew him personally; my career had just begun when Furtwängler's ended, and partnership with a great conductor of his age would have been no easy matter for a youngster anyway. But I had heard several of his concerts in Vienna, Salzburg and Lucerne, as well as a number of opera performances. These, and the records and tapes which since that time have kept me in touch with his conducting, have remained for me a most important source of reference as to what music-making is about.

The greatness of Furtwängler the conductor is, I think, best appreciated if one disregards Furtwängler the composer, the writer of essays, letters or diaries, the thinker (outside the purely musical sphere), the German patriot, as well as the person 'political' and 'non-political', childish and sophisticated, magnetic and absurdly irritable. Those who believe that the character of a musician has to be as elevating as the best of his music-making need read no further – a lot of great music will elude them. A young intellectual who, in conversation with Alban Berg, complained about Wagner's character was told by Berg: 'For you, as a non-musician, nothing could be easier than to condemn him.' Unlike Wagner, Furtwängler hardly qualifies as a villain. Yet I shall have to dissociate myself from some of his views, above all from his obsession with the overwhelming importance of German soul and spirit – that conviction about being chosen which, according to the eminent Zionist leader Nahum Goldmann, was, ironically, for some time a belief common to both Germans and Jews.[115] Then there is Furtwängler's belief, derived from Goethe, that 'the very great is never new', and

---

115 'Both peoples have been of importance in world history, but they have also felt, and feel, their own importance to an unusual degree. Being excessively aware of their importance, they take pride in it as well.' – Nahum Goldmann, 'Warum der Nazi-Schock nicht enden darf', *Die Zeit*, 2 February 1979.

his clinging to tonal harmony, to the heritage of the Classical and Romantic symphony, to popular intelligibility – even in the case of new compositions – which in
the end blinded him to the achievements of twentieth-century music, and made
him overestimate his own. His definition of a composer as 'one who can write his
own folksong' suggests a dangerous affinity with those who regard music as a con-
trollable political tool.

Furtwängler considered himself primarily a composer, and repeatedly spoke of the
day when he would finally stop conducting in order to do something truly worthwhile. But it was not merely a matter of chance that this wish remained unfulfilled.
There was, of course, the fact that Furtwängler had been successful as a conductor,
whereas he remained relatively unnoticed as a composer; but there must also have
been a critical instinct within him which told him that, notwithstanding his belief
in himself as a composer, conducting was where his powers of persuasion lay. All we
need to know about his compositions is that they helped him to look at the works
he conducted from a composer's point of view.

To those of us who do not seek access to music via the detour of literature,
philosophy or ideology, Furtwängler remains indispensable. If Furtwängler had
not existed, we would have had to invent him. He was the conductor under
whose guidance a piece of music emerged as something complete, alive in all its
layers, every detail justified by its breathing relevance to the whole. The prejudice among some English-speaking critics that Furtwängler, carried away by the
musical moment, sacrificed unity and cohesion, is more untrue of him than of
anybody else. No conductor was, in his greatest performances, freer yet less eccentric. No other musician in my experience conveyed so strongly the feeling that
the fate of a piece (and of its performance) was sealed with its first bar, and that
its destiny would be fulfilled by the last. Spontaneously varied as Furtwängler's
performances sometimes were, they always seemed to grow from the seed of their
beginning: they sounded 'natural', if one grants that the artist proceeds in a manner analogous to nature.

In an age such as ours which is fascinated by language and linguistics it is easy
to forget that organised thinking is possible without the help of words. On his own
purely musical grounds, Furtwängler the conductor strikes me as a 'thinker' second
to none; as a writer on music, on the other hand, I find him less satisfying. 'I cannot',
as he says himself, 'get involved with a work in order to demonstrate it reasonably

with love – and at the same time talk about it'. Yet there are a few instances where his words do reflect his musical task.

> It is necessary that both the detail and the whole have gone through the performer's emotions. There are some who can feel a single phrase; only a few who can grasp the complete line of an extended melody; and nearly none who can do justice to the total context of that veritable whole which every masterpiece represents. There is, however, a way of dealing with compositions – overly practical and therefore universally adopted these days – which does not even attempt emotional involvement. It presents the bare facts without their meaning.

Another clue to the character of his conducting is contained in a letter to his childhood mentor and lifelong friend Ludwig Curtius. He writes: 'The work of art should be a mirror not only of one's nerves, of the acuteness of one's observation, the consequence and sincerity of one's conclusions, or of the refinement of one's senses, but of the whole man.'

Lean, bent slightly backwards, and with an elongated neck, Furtwängler in front of an orchestra gave the impression of overlooking vast spaces. His beat had very little in common with that of present-day conductors. In stretches of *pianissimo* it could be minute and extremely precise; elsewhere, outstretched arms undulated downwards in total physical relaxation, so that the orchestra had to guess where the beat should be. The sounds thus produced could be of an elemental intensity that I have not experienced since. The image of 'Jupiter tonans' was what came to me then: Furtwängler's thunder was always preceded by lightning-shaped movements, which made the orchestra play considerably after the beat (if there was a beat), and induced double-basses and cellos to prepare the ground for the sonorities by discreetly anticipating their entry. Arthur Nikisch, according to Furtwängler, was the only conductor who presented a thoroughly unforced appearance; Furtwängler regarded himself, in this respect, as Nikisch's pupil, and believed that any contraction of muscle on the part of the conductor would show up in the sound of the orchestra as if reproduced on a photographic plate.

Furtwängler's technique, though seemingly unfocused and impractical, was in fact well considered. Not only did it help to anticipate the quality of sonorities and the delay of an important beat: it also foreshadowed changes of atmosphere or the gradual modification of tempo. And this leads us to Furtwängler's particular strength: he was the great connector, the grand master of transition. What makes Furtwängler's transitions so memorable? They are moulded with the greatest care, yet one cannot isolate them. They are not patchwork, inserted to link two ideas of a different nature. They grow out of something and lead into something. They are areas of transformation. If we observe them minutely, we notice that, at first almost imperceptibly, they start to affect the tempo, usually a great deal earlier than is the case with other conductors, until their impact finally makes itself felt. Even where I disagree with the amplitude of Furtwängler's tempo modifications – as in the first movement of Beethoven's Fourth Symphony – I do not know what to admire more: the urgency of his feeling or the acuteness of his control.

Tempo modifications are merciless indicators of musical weakness. With Furt-wängler, as often with Casals, Cortot or Callas, they give evidence of supreme rhythmical strength. It would, however, be misleading to look at rhythm, or any other musical element, by itself. If rhythm is to be more than an abstract scheme or a crude obsession it must be influenced by articulation, character and colour. It must be affected by the performer's reactions to harmonic events and – a particular rarity these days – by that feeling for *cantabile* which permeates music in the wid-est possible sense.

Furtwängler made one aware of the interdependence of these and other musical factors. What is called 'structure' emerged as a sum of all the parts. Consequently Furtwängler's performances were often less idiosyncratic than those of his fellow con-ductors, and more varied. Listen to his recording of Beethoven's *Leonore* Overture No. 3 with the Vienna Philharmonic Orchestra, with its astonishing variety of col-our and atmosphere, tempo and dynamics, character and meaning. Yet the music is never burdened by 'expression' from outside. Energies within the piece are released; the essence of the entire opera comes to life without the need for words. Ecstasy and strategy are perfectly matched, combining to produce the big line.

Furtwängler's big line is not a kind of long-sightedness, presenting the larger contours while the details of characterisation are lost. It is one of Furtwängler's dis-tinguishing features that, at least within the repertory he excelled in, each musical character is conveyed with a superior clarity of vision, and with the mastery of the superior professional. Even where the music seems to be left alone, where apparently 'nothing happens' during several bars of the softest playing, as in the cello tune of Schubert's Unfinished Symphony, conviction alone would not deliver such stillness. It had to be conducted and rehearsed.

It had, incidentally, to be recorded as well. There is a widespread belief that Furtwängler's genius was only present in live performances – a belief kindled by the maestro himself, who disliked recording sessions. The glorious Unfinished Symphony with the Vienna Philharmonic, a performance as perfect as any I know, is only one of a number of studio recordings that refutes this opinion. On nearly all counts it seems to me more satisfying than the live recordings I have heard. Equally outstanding are Schubert's Great C major Symphony (Berlin) and Beethoven's *Leonore* No. 3 (Vienna) which, judged as a whole, stand up to any recorded live performance. And the studio recording of *Tristan* seemed to have pleased even Furtwängler himself, who, for once, admitted that a record can have musical merits. I wish Furtwängler could have known how much his performances still mean to many of us today.

At the beginning of these notes I wrote of my debt to Furtwängler for providing me with criteria by which to judge a performance. Looking back over my remarks, I find I must add some afterthoughts.

I have mentioned the variety of musical factors and their interdependence. Let me add an example. Furtwängler's *pianissimo*, extremely remote, yet without a meaningless moment, was more than a degree of dynamic quietness; it was a matter of colour, and Furtwängler's colour – even at its most sensuous or nervously refined – was always a matter of emotion. Thus *pianissimo* and *misterioso* were often identical.

I have hinted at the decisive importance of the very opening of a piece, its dominating impact over what is to follow the way in which it reveals a particular musical vista, causing one to enter a stage set for an inevitable dramatic action. I have yet to declare my admiration for some of Furtwängler's codas. In the concluding sections of the first movement of Mozart's G minor Symphony or of Beethoven's Ninth Symphony, he managed to make us feel that the life of a piece had been lived through, and that the coda expressed the tragic summation.

I have also referred to his ability to characterise, and to change the chemistry of character and atmosphere during transitions. One of my early piano teachers told me, with a smile, that performers can either play beautiful themes or beautiful transitions, but rarely both. Furtwängler made nonsense of that theory. He seems to me the exact opposite of Charlie Chaplin in one of his early films. Chaplin carefully takes an alarm clock apart under the eyes of its owner; finally, when every single component lies spread out on the counter, he sweeps the lot into the owner's hat.

(1979)

Edwin Fischer

REMEMBERING MY TEACHER

EDWIN FISCHER WAS, on the concert platform, a short, leonine, resilient figure, whose every fibre seemed to vibrate with elemental musical power. Wildness and gentleness were never far from each other in his piano playing, and demonic outbursts would magically give way to inner peace. It was as little trouble to him (as Alfred Polgar once said of an actor) to lose himself as to find himself. His playing of slow movements was full of an unself-consciousness beside which the music-making of others, famous names included, seemed academic or insincere. With Fischer, one was in more immediate contact with the music: there was no curtain before his soul when he communicated with the audience. One other musician, Furtwängler, conveyed to the same degree this sensation of music not being played, but rather happening by itself. His death was a grievous blow to Fischer.

Just as Furtwängler liked to play the piano in his very personal manner, so Fischer loved to conduct. Here, too, his achievement was at times breathtaking. His way of directing the concertos of Bach, Mozart and Beethoven from the keyboard remains inimitable. Anyone in doubt should listen to his recording of the second movement of Bach's C major Concerto for Three Pianos: perfect unity reigns from the first note to the last.

However, Fischer should be remembered not only as a solo pianist and conductor, but also as a chamber musician, Lied partner and teacher. Fischer's ensemble with Mainardi and Kulenkampff – whose place was later taken by Schneiderhan – reached the heights of trio playing, and as a partner of Elisabeth Schwarzkopf the master achieved the ideal fusion of simplicity and refinement. As an inspiring teacher he led two generations of young pianists 'away from the piano, and to themselves', and provided them with proper standards for their future careers. As an editor he helped to restore the *Urtext* of Classical masterpieces, and as a writer he formulated such memorable precepts as 'Put life into the music without doing violence to it'. Can there be a simpler formula for the task of the interpreter?

Fischer admired Alfred Cortot, as many-sided a musician as Fischer himself.

The two masters were poles apart in their repertory; one could say that they complemented one another. Fischer was in his element in the Classic-Romantic realm of 'German' music, with Bach, Mozart, Beethoven, Schubert and Brahms. Cortot was particularly happy with Chopin, with some of Liszt's works, with César Franck and French piano music. In Schumann, their spheres met. At home, as he once told me, Fischer liked to play Chopin, whereas Cortot is reported to have had a sneaking affection for Brahms.

Fischer was anything but a perfect pianist in the academic sense. Nervousness and physical illness sometimes cast a shadow over his playing. But in the avoidance of false sentiment he was unrivalled. Moreover, as the initiated will know, it would be presumptuous to underrate a technique that made possible performances of such fabulous richness of expression. The principal carrier of this expressiveness was his marvellously full, floating tone, which retained its roundness even at climactic, explosive moments, and remained singing and sustained in the most unbelievable *pianissimo.* (In conversation, Fischer once compared piano tone to the sound of the vowels. He told me that in present-day musical practice the *a* and *o* are neglected in favour of the *e* and *i.* The glaring and shrill triumphs over the lofty and sonorous, technique over the sense of wonder. Are not *ah!* and *oh!* the sounds of wonder?) By bringing the middle parts to life, Fischer gave his chord-playing an inward radiance, and his *cantabile* fulfilled Beethoven's wish: 'From the heart – may it go to the heart.'

As a teacher, Fischer was electrifying by his mere presence. The playing of timid youths and placid girls would suddenly spring to life when he grasped them by the shoulder. A few conducting gestures, an encouraging word, could have the effect of lifting the pupil above himself. When Fischer outlined the structure of a whole movement, the gifted ones among the participants felt they were looking into the very heart of music. He sometimes helped us more by an anecdote or a comparison than would have been possible by 'factual' instruction. He preferred demonstration to explanation: again and again he would sit down himself at the piano. Those were the greatest, the unforgettable impressions retained by his students. In the days before his prolonged illness, his vitality knew no bounds. He was happy to be surrounded by young people who trusted in him, and his playing for us was at its most beautiful. On such occasions, we experienced what he told us in these words: 'One day, the piano has all the colours of the orchestra; another day, it brings forth sounds that come from other worlds.'

(1960)

Edwin Fischer.

Photograph © Georges Maiteny, London. (Collection Alfred Brendel)

Afterthoughts on Edwin Fischer

WHAT IS PIANO playing of genius? Playing which is at once correct and bold. Its correctness tells us: that is how it has to be. Its boldness presents us with a surprising and overwhelming realisation: what we had thought impossible becomes true.

Correctness can be attained by the expert. But boldness presupposes the gift of projection, which draws the audience into the orbit of one's personality. The personal, 'impossible' element in Edwin Fischer was twofold: his playing sprang from a childlike nature, yet, if the signs were favourable, it also possessed all the wisdom of the experienced master. The childlike characteristics were his sincerity and spontaneity, his ready sense of wonder, constantly rediscovered, his joy in playing, clowning, daring – with what breathless gusto he sometimes romped through a Mozart Allegro! The master in Fischer was proclaimed by his gift for emotional differentiation, by the beauty of his tone and its extreme refinements, by his vision as well as by his grasp of the grand design. Child and master formed a perfect union in Fischer's happiest achievements; there was nothing to pull them apart.

Piano playing is a strict discipline. Practice – the task of clarifying, purifying, fortifying and restoring musical continuity – can turn against the player. Control can 'sit' on one's playing like a coat of mail, like a corset or like a well-tailored suit. On lucky occasions, it is just there, as if in league with chance. I have never come across a control of line and nuance more exciting than that achieved by Fischer in his performances of the slow movement of Bach's F minor Concerto, in the long paragraphs of the A minor Fantasia, or in some pieces from *The Well-Tempered Clavier*. (These examples should suffice to call to order the detractors of Fischer's technique!) Yet this excitement does not obstruct the listener – it liberates him. There is something untamed even about Fischer's most decorous playing. 'In the work of art,' says Novalis, the German Romanticist, 'chaos must shimmer through the veil of order.' (*Im Kunstwerk muss das Chaos durch den Flor der Ordnung schimmern.*) Fischer's order does not betray the pressure of reason; it represents creation in a state of innocence. So, does control appear in the guise of improvisation, as with the great Cortot? I would rather say that Fischer completes a circle: setting out from improvisation, he takes the route of a finely regulated awareness which eventually leads him back to improvisation.

There are pianists whose playing is so predictable that if they fell into a faint it would create a welcome diversion. Fischer could spring a surprise at every note; he could also alarm you with his nerves, or make your hair stand on end with his childish fancies (as in his peculiar cadenzas!). There are pianists who hang on the music like parasites, and there are the platform hyenas who devour masterpieces like carrion. Fischer was a giver; he let out his breath and recommended his pupils to practise exhaling every morning. (Inhaling, he said, was easy.) This 'musical exhalation' was made possible by a singularly relaxed technique. Though it also gave rise to some inaccuracies, these in the end mattered little; the gain was overwhelming.

'You're trying too hard!' he would say to highly strung and self-aware students. But Fischer's influence was not necessarily a relaxing one. He was apt to make the phlegmatic deliberately nervous in order to coax from them a spark of temperament. And he liked to put the pressure on when it was a question of establishing the grand design: he encouraged us not to take things apart and show their components, but to put them together, place them in perspective, and see the detail in the context of the whole.

How can I convey the impact of Fischer's playing to someone who never heard him 'live'?

During the 1950s, an orchestral player once came up to me after rehearsal. He said he used to play in Edwin Fischer's chamber orchestra, and in his imagination was still doing so. He recalled particularly how fresh the Bach concertos used to sound in each performance. Even now, twenty-five years later, he still had goose pimples whenever he thought of a certain passage. 'Look at this', he said, rolling up his sleeve.

Fischer, particularly after the last war, was afraid of the microphone. The recording he made of Brahms's F minor Sonata, for example, gives only one glimpse – at the entry of the D flat major 'patriotic' theme in the last movement – of his real conception of that work. Fortunately, there are among his records some which come fairly close to the reality of his playing. A few even set a standard of unmannered perfection which transcends the bounds of fashion. Best among his earlier records, in my opinion, are a number of wonderful Bach interpretations, as well as the Schubert Impromptus and the Mozart Concertos K.466 (D minor) and K.491 (C minor); among his later ones Bach's C major Concerto for Three Pianos (with Ronald Smith and Denis Matthews) and Beethoven's *Emperor* Concerto under Furtwängler. The recording of Bach's C major Concerto was not done with his usual partners (who were former pupils); all the more admirable, then, is the unanimity of style, impressive proof of Fischer's power of communication. A disc of Schubert Lieder with Elisabeth Schwarzkopf, and the wonderful recording of Brahms's G major Violin Sonata with Gioconda de Vito bear eloquent testimony to his mellow late style.

(1976)

Remembering Katja Andy

I OWE MY ACQUAINTANCE with Katja Andy to the pianist Edwin Fischer, a great artist almost unknown in the United States. In 1958, during his last masterclass in Switzerland, a small mouse-like person sat in the back row as a listener. Over a number of days Fischer would beg her to play for us until she finally sat down at the concert grand and performed, unforgettably, Mozart's A minor Rondo. There, the most unclouded musical and personal friendship of my life began. The following memoir is based on Katja's own recollections.

Katja was born in 1907 as Käte Aschaffenburg in the German town of Mönchengladbach. The whole family was musical; her father, a fabric manufacturer, being a decent pianist, and both parents having studied with pupils of Clara Schumann. While Rudolf, her older brother by four years, had his piano lessons, Katja sat on top of the piano, and afterwards tried to find the keys of what she had just heard. Years later, the siblings played the same Bach Invention simultaneously on two pianos in different keys when the parents happened to be cross with them. Katja's father, in her own account the funniest man she ever knew, regularly travelled to Berlin to hear the concerts of the Philharmonic. One day, when he stood at the artist's entrance without a ticket, he noticed that the great Ferruccio Busoni went in, passing his hand over his hair and saying 'Busoni!' to the concierge. Short, roundish Otto Aschaffenburg followed suit, stroked his bald head and said, 'Aschaffenburg!'

For many years, the Aschaffenburgs housed instrumentalists and singers who appeared with the municipal orchestra. The violinists Huberman, Busch and Szigeti turned up, the latter showing Katja at the piano that the first eight bars of a Bach Invention already contained the complete material of the piece. There were the pianists d'Albert and Gieseking – who apparently memorised a Bach Partita overnight and played it without practice the next evening in concert, having changed his programme. Carl Friedberg, Clara Schumann's most prominent pupil to whom Katja played as a child, recommended her to Lonny Epstein, one of his own well-known disciples.

When Katja was nine, Edwin Fischer started to be a most cherished guest. Fischer, according to Katja, hated to practise, but when it ever happened Katja was allowed to listen. At sixteen, Katja went to study with him in Berlin. While Fischer was on tour his students were taken care of by a pupil of the supreme player of Chopin Mazurkas, Ignaz Friedman.

Sometimes, Fischer held his classes at home. No one was sure what was going to happen. 'I would never have called him a pedagogue,' said Katja. Yet he remained to her the incomparable source of delight, full of charisma and temperament, and with wonderfully lively eyes. When one of his classes that had started at four in the afternoon only ended at 2 a.m., the lady with whom Katja stayed as a lodger mobilised the police.

Katja was also welcome in Schnabel's classes. Schnabel had a sense for fun, took his students to the movies or to restaurants, and played waltzes for his guests on Sunday afternoons. His son was desperately keen for Katja to marry him, but she declined.

The third pianist leaving a decisive impression was Eugen d'Albert, who had stunned Liszt when he was eighteen. Unfortunately, as Katja said, there are no recordings that would do justice to his overwhelming playing.

Some of the music-making at the time was rather casual. But Fischer and Schnabel were striving for textual accuracy, and Toscanini – as Katja inimitably put it – did everything the composer demanded, whether you liked it or not.

Among conductors, Katja particularly admired Bruno Walter, who offered her a concert date in 1933. She had already played in duet with Agi Jambor, and with Fischer's chamber orchestra, participating in performances of all Bach Concertos while being Fischer's favourite partner in Mozart's Double Concerto. With sixty appearances booked for 1933–34 Katja's career was about to take off in a grand way. At this moment, Hitler came to power. Her last concert took place with the Leipzig Gewandhaus Orchestra in March 1933. In April, she left Berlin, and soon after, Germany. Her departure had been triggered by an official letter that told her she could, by way of exception, continue concertising but was forbidden to teach 'non-Aryan' students. 'In this country,' Katja said, 'I couldn't live any longer.' And so her ordeal began.

Without any funds she travelled to Paris where she couldn't get a work permit. Each week, she had to register with the police, surviving mainly on Fischer's clandestine contributions. As concerts or teaching were out of the question, she coached singers and played for dance studios and gymnastic establishments. In 1937, without a valid passport and under the threat of being put into a camp, she boarded a slow night train to Germany. Only there could she try to obtain the document that would enable her to enter the US.

In her compartment, there was just one fellow traveller. At the border controls, a customs inspector asked the man to open one of his two suitcases. It proved to contain nothing but worms because the man was on a fishing trip. 'Close that thing!'

shouted the official, who then disappeared, only to be back a while later. 'Now it's my turn,' thought Katja. But the official was interested only in the man's second suitcase. Calmly, the man got it down – once more, nothing but worms. Infuriated, the customs inspector rushed out, and was gone.

Having managed to arrive in Berlin, Katja waited for a month to obtain a passport. In her words: 'My dressmaker was a very pretty blonde girl whose male companion was Jewish. In order to protect him she went out with Nazis like Göring who provided some necessary signatures. And that's how she got me the passport.' The dressmaker lived in a studio in which during a police raid her friend was found hiding in a cupboard. The accounts differ as to whether it was he who was shot after Katja's departure, or the dressmaker herself.

With the help of an affidavit she could now enter the States where, at that time, no work permit was required. However, chances for a concert career were slim. Many musicians had emigrated to New York where a relief fund had been established. The worst drawback was that women had a much tougher time to make their mark in concert life than they have today. Both Piatigorsky and Feuermann, who had been principal cellists under Furtwängler, would have liked Katja to be their piano partner, but the agents didn't want to hear about it. Though Feuermann was married to her cousin Eva, touring with an unwedded lady was deemed immoral. Already in 1932 Katja had appeared in Berlin with Feuermann who, at her parents' house with her brother Rudolf, had played Boccia in the garden. In Berlin, Katja frequently enjoyed sitting next to Feuermann in his newest car as his driving assistant, shouting 'red!' or 'green!' – Feuermann was colour-blind.

With the dancer Lotte Goslar, Katja toured for a year throughout the US before settling down in Detroit. There were hardly any pianists there, and the main one had begged her to stay – there was nobody he could talk to. A psychoanalyst couple, survivors of Freud's circle, took her under their wings. Richard and Editha Sterba, the authors of a book on *Beethoven and his Nephew*, were amiable people who, at weekends, went on horseback rides unless Richard had hired musicians he could join playing quartets. Up until his old age, he travelled to New York for violin lessons with Adolf Busch, and considered Freud a saint.

Ten years later, Katja accepted a teaching post in Chicago that placed her under the obligation of including nuns in starched headdress. Katja derived some pleasure from making them play pieces that required crossing their hands. At that time, as she described it, her spine collapsed. After threefold disc surgery she was back on her feet; but concerts were out of the question. Evelyne Crochet arranged for her to be invited to teach at Boston Conservatory and, thereafter, Katja joined the New England Conservatory, where she concluded the active part of her life as a highly esteemed teacher, and the recipient of an honorary degree.

Nearly blind, scarcely mobile and equipped with hearing aids, Katja spent her last thirty-six years in New York, a musician of the rarest kind, revered by friends and former students, and cherished as a character in whom warm-heartedness and matter-of-factness struck a beautiful balance. Katja was also blessed with humour – a main force in carrying her through her difficult life. Her quips didn't waste words. Of the great, wall-eyed violinist Huberman, Katja said: 'When he asked someone a question in the artists' room, everybody answered.'

I love to remember you on this note. Goodbye, dear Katja.

(2015)

Katja Andy and Edwin Fischer, Lucerne, 1966

Coping with Pianos

'THERE ARE NO bad pianos, only bad pianists.' An impressive statement, one that looks round for applause. A statement that will at once ring true to the layman and make him feel initiated as well as amused. A statement addressed perhaps to some revered virtuoso who did not refuse to play at a private party – Busoni would have left the house right away – and who, in spite of the detestable instrument, managed to hold his audience spellbound.

It is a statement to confound any pianist. Admittedly, many a piano will sound less awful under the hands of an expert than under those of an amateur; but does that make it a good piano? To 'carry the day' on a badly regulated, unequally registered, faultily voiced, dull or noisy instrument implies as often as not that one has violated the music for which one is responsible, that control and refinement have been pushed aside, that the 'personal approach' has been greatly exaggerated and a dubious sort of mystique has taken over, far removed from the effect the piece should legitimately produce.

How often does the player find a piano he can rely on, a piano which will do justice to the exactness of his vision? Is it to be wondered at that many of his performances remain compromises? After all, he should not have to struggle with the instrument, or impose his will tyrannically upon it, any more than the instrument should turn into a fetish, an object of idolisation that dominates him. On the contrary, the player should make friends with the piano and assure himself of its services – especially when Pianism with a capital P is to be transcended. He should give the instrument its due by showing how capable it is of transforming itself.

A piano is not a mass-produced article. Every instrument, even from the same renowned maker, presents the pianist with a new experience. What shapes his reaction is not only the 'individuality' of a particular instrument, but also the materials used in it and the processes of manufacture: in other words, the difference in quality between one instrument and another. Enviously he watches the cellist dragging his own cello around; his only consolation is that the adjustment problems of organists and harpsichordists exceed his own. What energy is sometimes needed to 'listen to' a particular piano, and what pertinacity to make it amenable to a certain piece of music! The pianist will find that the instrument readily responds to some pieces, but balks at others. He may, unexpectedly, be reminded of the piano he used in his youth, or on which he studied a certain piece: intention and execution suddenly coalesce once more; something of the joy and concentration of his early strivings comes back to him; old, crumpled fingerings regain their pristine smoothness – it is a homecoming into the lower reaches of memory.

Once in a while a piano will surprise the player by demonstrating to him the nature of the instrument on which a composer conceived a particular work: a piano with a singing tone, a tender treble, gentle bass, and a harp-like, whispering soft pedal will bring Liszt's *Bénédiction* to life, and the lower middle range of a Bösendorfer will remove Schubert's accompaniment figures to their proper distance. A Pleyel upright amid velvet draperies, cushions, carpets and plush furnishings might perhaps reveal the sense of Chopin's pedal markings. Pianos and rooms are generally interdependent: anyone who has ever travelled with a piano knows that the same Steinway or Bösendorfer not only sounds different in different halls, but also seems to react differently in its mechanism. Indeed, the resistance of the key, over and above the measurable mechanical aspect, is a psychological factor. The characteristics of a concert hall – its greater or lesser resonance, brightness, clarity, and spaciousness of sound – are reflected in the player's technical approach and have an influence on his sense of well-being. There are halls that coarsen or deaden the sound; others absorb one's pedalling like blotting paper or, conversely, require constant non-*legato* playing. Thus (to return to Chopin's pedal signs) there can be no universally valid pedalling instructions – these exist only in the imagination of some piano teachers. Excepted, of course, are pedal markings which determine the colour of entire sections, indicate pedal points, or ask for some kind of pedalling which is not self-evident; most of Beethoven's infrequent pedal markings belong in these categories.

Much will depend on the previous concert: are the new hall and instrument reassuringly similar, or will the pianist have to readjust himself? If the latter, his aural and technical reorientation before the concert will have the additional aim of ridding his memory as far as possible of all recently acquired habits of listening and playing. However, the pianist's attempts to adapt himself to instrument and hall are beset by a multitude of difficulties.

In the first place, the full hall during the concert sometimes sounds completely different from the empty one during the rehearsal. The halls of the Vienna Musikverein, for instance, famous for their acoustics, overflow in a welter of sound when empty. (The only time that Viennese orchestral musicians can hear one another at all clearly is during the performance.)

Moreover, the sound reaching the public in the auditorium only rarely corresponds to that heard on the platform. In extreme cases, the player may know perfectly well what is happening on stage, but not at all what is coming across. He must then try to translate his musical intentions into a presumed sound which he himself can control only indirectly. This acoustic equivalent of reading the tea-leaves can at times lead even the most experienced pianist astray. Unless he has sat in the hall himself as a member of the audience and knows exactly what the sound is like from there, the player will have to rely on the advice of musical friends. At recording sessions, the sound of test tapes through the speakers in the playback room will tell him whether and in what proportions he will have to split his musical personality.

Another problem is that, on the rare occasions when he has the luxury of choice, the pianist cannot often compare the available pianos side by side in the hall. He has to go to the storage room of the hall or hiring firm, or encounter each instrument in a different location. The divergent acoustics can widely mislead him in his choice.

Lastly, there is no denying the fact that we pianists do not always 'function like clockwork'. I am referring not only to the changing lubrication level of our physical apparatus, which at times enables us to throw off with the grace of an acrobat what at other times weighs upon us like a ton of bricks; I am referring also to the quality of our hearing, which may vary under the influence of tiredness or freshness, anxiety or repose.

There are some pianists fatalistic enough to assail the platform blissfully unaware. However, they are rare birds. In spite of all the obstacles, the experience gained at the rehearsal will be useful at the performance, even though, as might happen, the pianist may well have to revise his impressions yet again. At any rate, he has overhauled the instrument with the help of the tuner. He has positioned the piano correctly, not too close to the edge of the platform, the keyboard near the centre of the hall. He has removed the music stand, tried and rejected three piano stools (the fourth, at last, did not creak or wobble), arranged the lighting so that no shadow falling on the keys should disturb his concentration, and located an old upright on which to warm up briefly before facing the audience. He has also, with luck, almost at the back of his mind, recalled the whole programme he is to play. Now he may sleep through the afternoon.

Reactions to a piano are a personal matter; they are not always sharply defined, and are subject to continual change. The pianist has to take into account whether he is going to accompany songs or brave the orchestra in the First Bartók Concerto; whether he is to perform before an audience of fifty or five thousand; whether he is to play Schubert or Stravinsky, Beethoven's 'Waldstein' Sonata or Beethoven's Op. 110. Can one, nevertheless, lay down some general guidelines for the evaluation of an instrument, which could be of assistance to most pianists in most situations? Let me do so by submitting the following propositions:

1) The piano should be dynamically even in all its registers and at all levels of volume. This evenness can only be achieved by careful regulation of the action, together with the technique of voicing, which I shall come back to later. Eccentric pianists who are accustomed to an overly loud bass or a piercing treble should bring in their own piano. The upper middle range (the 'second stave') where so many of the *cantabile* melodies are located must not be duller than the lower half. Unfortunately this is often the case on present-day instruments unlike, say, on pre-war Bechsteins which, in this register, showed a particular radiance. I see no justification for an unevenness of registers – the balancing out of the musically required sound should remain entirely in the hands of the player.

2) The tone of the piano should be bright and radiant, but have no cutting edge. The rounder, duller, blunter the tone, the less chance one has to colour it, to mix timbres, to detach one layer of sound from another. Faced with the choice between a concert grand with an inherently beautiful but invariable tone, and a less noble but more colourful instrument, the pianist will usually prefer the more colourful one.

3) The volume of the piano should range from a whisper to a roar. This again depends on a carefully regulated action, which does not require the player to possess superhuman strength, and yet is responsive to his control of the most tender *sotto voce*. Furthermore, resounding splendour must be attainable even in passages and trills within the upper middle range without unduly tiring the hand.

4) The sustaining pedal must dampen precisely. Even when lowered quite slowly

on to the strings, all dampers must remain completely noiseless. The much feared grinding and soughing of the dampers at the point of contact will, as likely as not, be blamed on the pianist as a technical shortcoming. Without properly shaped and regulated dampers made of good felt, refined, atmospheric pedalling is simply impossible. The lever of the pedal should not have too great a degree of play.

5) The tone of the soft pedal; i.e., the depressed left pedal, should not be thin and acid, but should retain sufficient lyrical roundness and plasticity of sound variation.

6) The pitch of the piano should be able to survive a concert without major dislocation. (If a concert grand goes out of tune, the fault often lies not with the instrument, but with the inadequate skill of the tuner.) Where I expect some disagreement is over the question of the soft pedal. There are pianists who prefer a shallow, nasal *con sordino* tone, decidedly removed from the normal gamut of sound. This 'grotesque' tone can, by virtue of its sharper definition, be of advantage in over-resonant halls. However, it may be so intolerant of nuances that the result is a single, unvaried tone colour. I find this too much of a restriction. Distinct whispering, important as it may be, is after all only a very small part of the musical function of the soft pedal. I recommend three test passages:

   a) The A flat major second subject of Schubert's Impromptu Op. 142, No. 1. (Its many repeated *pianissimo* notes, surrounded by a halo of pedal, should retain their singing delicacy without an accumulation of ugly metallic noises and unpredictable 'snarl-ups'.)

   b) The high treble trill towards the end of Beethoven's Sonata Op. 111. (Many modern grands turn its atmospheric vibration into an *étude*-like succession of prickly single notes that pierce the ear like tin-tacks.)

   c) The first lines of Liszt's *Bénédiction de Dieu dans la Solitude*. (Liszt asks for *mezzoforte* cantilenas in the middle range! The soft pedal sounds should allow plenty of room for dynamic gradations – a reproduction, as it were, of the full volume on a reduced scale. It is wrong to believe that the *sordino* permits only gentle playing. This assumption had already been contradicted in the *una corda* sections of Beethoven's 'Hammerklavier' Sonata.)

The position of the hammers during the depression of the left pedal is regulated by an easily adjustable screw at the right edge of the keyboard. A nasal-sounding *sordino* can sometimes be corrected by reducing the distance by which the left pedal shifts the action to the right. As a rule, the left string should still be touched by the hammer, but only just. In this position, it is possible to do soft pedal voicing 'between the strings'; i.e., between the grooves visible on the top of the hammer.

What does the term *voicing* mean? It refers to the equalisation of volume and quality of sound with the help of needles which prick or otherwise touch the hammer felt. For the treatment of notes that are too soft, chemicals are available which harden the hammer. Fortunately, in recent years there has been a marked improvement in such chemicals; they can now be applied selectively with tiny brushes without doing damage to the felt, drying within a few minutes. Before this is done, however, the crown of the hammer should be examined: it may be that it does not strike all three strings evenly. In that case the hammer-top has to be filed until it is perfectly horizontal.

Skilful voicing is rare. The difficulties begin with the prerequisites: the ear must be trained to perceive the finest gradations of dynamics and timbre; moreover, only a perfectly even *legato* touch in *piano* and *forte* will reliably show up the deficient notes. Both fall within the province of the professional pianist and cannot in all fairness be expected from most tuners. Only a collaboration between an experienced pianist and tuner can therefore achieve the proper voicing of the instrument, a view readily endorsed by the most expert piano technicians while doubted by the less capable ones. The ignorance of some tuners in matters of voicing, even in major cities, is sometimes staggering. Time and again I have met concert tuners who had never realised that one needs to check, with the help of wedges, each of the strings individually, that one must listen for evenness separately with and without the left pedal, and that one can use the voicing prong independently in both positions of the action! How to prick the hammer head without doing harm to the basic quality of the tone is another mystery to some. The most frequent deficiencies, even of new pianos leaving the factory, are the noisiness of the middle dampers and the neglect of the soft pedal sound. It is obvious that only a small minority of technicians is trained to set up the soft pedal properly.

It needs to be added that the resident piano technician is not the only one responsible for the quality and condition of the instrument. Frequently, concert organisers and halls are at fault in not giving the technician enough time and opportunity to keep it in shape. Alas, there are halls that do not even provide a separate, undisturbed storage room for pianos. No concert hall of repute should tolerate such a grievous state of affairs.

Two remarks are frequently made by piano technicians: 'Voicing is a matter of taste', and 'There's never an end to the job of voicing'. But if one restricts oneself to the general aim of dynamic evenness; i.e., the adjustment of over-prominent notes or groups of notes to the overall level of sound, then voicing becomes not so much a question of taste as one of skill. Where there is skill, and also sufficient time and patience, one can certainly bring to completion the voicing of a well-regulated piano. It is only when the tuner disturbs the core of the tone or overshoots the mark, instead of carefully doing what needs to be done in progressive stages, that he will 'never come to the end of it'. For if he is careless he will be forced, as his work proceeds, to take the notes that have become too soft as a new point of reference, adapting neighbouring notes to their level. Dullness of tone is the likely result.

Piano tuners and technicians should be given every possible encouragement in their profession. Their status and standard of living needs to be improved in many countries; they should be supported by scholarships during their long training period. Today, we have an incomparably larger number of passable pianists than of piano technicians. The few good concert tuners are usually overworked, and after doing their jobs in concert halls, recording studios and radio stations have no time left in which to impart their skill. Some of them anxiously guard their secrets. If only one could make some piano players understand that they would be of greater service to music as piano technicians! The training of the tuner should, in any case, put more emphasis on the artistic education of the ear. And tuners should – in my Utopian view – be better pianists. On the other hand, all pianists should be expert voicers – if only in self-defence. A course on the regulating and voicing of pianos should be obligatory for all piano students at music schools. (An examination in organ building for organ students has already been introduced at some musical institutes.)

Much of the uncertainty and indifference of tuners has its roots in the ignorance of pianists, who are unable to perceive clearly and put into words what worries them about an instrument. Many pianists do not even realise how much they are entitled to expect from a concert grand. It almost seems as if the piano firms turn that ignorance to their advantage and sometimes release from their factories instruments with the most amazing congenital defects or teething troubles. Looked at from this angle, the statement 'There are no bad pianos, only bad pianists' reads like the motto of a piano dealer trying to divert attention from the impending decline in the art of piano building. I have played on brand-new concert grands whose dynamic range in the upper middle register would have been just adequate for accompanying an elderly singer in *Die Winterreise*. I have played on others where whole bundles of notes failed to react to forceful repetition: they just did not work. Many pianos are like unmade beds; a tuner, apart from his actual tuning, will rarely have the initiative to prepare a piano thoroughly for a concert. He will say to himself, 'When the pianist tries it, he will soon tell me what he wants done'. This means that the pianist has to expend precious time on mechanical matters. It also means that, considering the shortness of time available and the sorry state in which so many pianos are found, it will be possible to undertake only part of the necessary work. The remaining defects of the instrument will then press upon the pianist during the performance, and he will have to make a conscious effort to ward them off.

In the age of the gramophone record, concerts on inadequate pianos make less sense than ever. The player should be given the opportunity of competing with his own recordings. But does he have a chance at all, when the instrument used at the recording sessions is more carefully chosen and kept in better order than is usual for concerts? When the tuner is always in attendance, ready to deal with every crackle, every change in pitch, every loud key? Surely, when there is the possibility to repeat and improve things in the studio, to overcome the fluttering of one's heart, to banish the blind spots of concentration, to commune with oneself in perfect peace, to be undistracted by the coughing fits of the audience – surely all this results in an end product which comes nearer to the player's ideal? And is it not true that the art of the sound engineer, beguiling the ear with the best of all possible piano sounds, makes the listener independent of the acoustic disadvantages of his seat in the concert hall?

Happily for live music-making, the reality is less rosy. In coping with pianos, modern recording technique appears to run into one problem after another. Why was it so easy to make good piano recordings in the 1930s? When listening to the records of Cortot, Fischer or Schnabel, I feel as if I were sitting in a good seat in a good hall; the timbre of each great pianist is there, the piano sounds homogeneous in all registers, dynamic climaxes and hushed tones come over with equal conviction.

And that impression cannot be shaken by technical explanations designed to prove to me that the limitations of early recording techniques did not permit a faithful musical reproduction.

To me, it seems more likely that with the over-refinements of modern techniques one is apt to miss the wood for the trees. Thus, certain discs nowadays need very special speakers, which, in turn, have to be placed in the right sort of room for the sound to acquire its proper physical consistency – for otherwise the treble and bass of the piano may split apart as if coming from different instruments or different distances. While the engineers of the old 78-rpm days may still in all innocence have heard the music as a horizontal succession of sounds, their present-day colleagues, with their imposing musical and technical qualifications, have difficulty in breaking away from the habit of vertical listening, the close scrutinizing of knife-edge synchronisation of sounds, which the modern practice of tape editing has inculcated in them as second nature.

And what about the artist's self-communings in splendid, peaceful isolation? Is he really impervious to the malice of the instrument, the touchiness of the equipment, the host of possible noises? Does not every visit to the playback room cut off his physical contact with the piano? Does a concert pianist actually want to soliloquise? – surely only when the composer seems to wish him to do so, as in some of Beethoven's slow movements, where the music withdraws into an inner world. And even here the player's approach is conditioned by his intention to let himself be overheard; even a whispered utterance, an aside, must remain intelligible to the audience. This illusion of the listener being admitted to the player's confidence becomes a moving experience in the concert hall. The individual listener is picked out: the player favours him with his inmost secrets. This shrinking of the distance between audience and platform is an achievement which should never be taken for granted; the player has to work for it. In front of the loudspeakers, the listener's privilege turns into stale reality; he is alone with his gramophone in any case, and he can, if he is so inclined, overhear the 'secret' at double the volume: it will lie before him, huge and penetrating, within arm's reach. The recorded performance does not depend for its success upon the listener's concentrated attention. It has already happened and now rolls along without any contribution from him, until he turns off the machine. In the concert hall, each motionless listener is part of the performance. The concentration of the player charges the electric tension in the auditorium and returns to him magnified; thus the audience makes its contribution, helping the pianist to cope with his instrument. At home, in front of his stereo equipment, the ideal listener will strive to attain a similar state of concentration, drawing on his experience of past concerts – just as the pianist did when he played in the recording studio for an imaginary audience.

(1974)

A Lifetime of Recording

LOOKING BACK AT the sixty years of my pianistic life, the quantity of my recordings seems to me one of its most unusual features. Let me try to explain how this multitude came about.

If one assumes a successful career to be linked to having been a child prodigy, to early triumphs and transcendental pianistic control, my development has to be called atypical. My family was neither musically active nor aesthetically inclined, neither from Eastern Europe nor, as far as I know, Jewish, neither intellectually ambitious, nor adventurous. Before my fifteenth year, I had not witnessed a symphonic concert, a piano recital or the performance of an opera. Only the radio provided occasional glimpses of distant musical bliss.

Apart from attending a few short masterclasses, I had no piano tuition after my sixteenth year. For good measure, I also composed, painted and wrote. Ludovika von Kaan, my piano teacher in Graz, told me to put on a public recital, arranged for me to meet the great pianist Edwin Fischer, and bade me a genial farewell. In the following years I participated in three of Fischer's Lucerne summer classes and also played for Edward Steuermann in Salzburg. My first recital at the age of seventeen in Graz went down well; it sported an unusual programme of my own design ('The Fugue in Piano Literature') and, for the time being, pacified my mother who was a professional pessimist.

In the 1950s, smaller American record companies flocked to post-war Vienna where they could record cheaply. My first recording happened when I was twenty. I had received a telegram around Christmas asking whether I would be prepared to record Prokofiev's Fifth Piano Concerto in January. Neither myself nor, I believe, the Vienna Volksoper orchestra had played a note of Prokofiev before but we bravely staggered through the piece in two sessions. Soon after, an elderly gentleman turned up who owned another American record label. Mr F. Charles Adler had conducted for Artur Schnabel somewhere in the American provinces which resulted in a newspaper clipping headed by the jocular words 'Schnabel and Adler' ('beak and eagle' in German). He asked me to record Busoni's *Fantasia Contrappuntistica*, a work that I had scribbled down on a lengthy list of repertoire suggestions. Already in my teens, Busoni had fascinated me as a figure whose reach, for me as an artist, far exceeded piano-playing.

My recording of Liszt's *Christmas Tree Suite*, meanwhile, started my involvement with Liszt's late piano music that was still virtually unknown at that time.

The next personality eager to scout Viennese talent was George H. Mendelssohn, who seemed to have modelled himself on the movie star Anton Walbrook. Being the president of Vox/Turnabout, he kept me busy recording over the next ten years. Under his auspices I spent many an hour in the halls of Vienna's Konzerthaus and Musikverein where most of the recordings took place. One of my first programmes was all Russian: Stravinsky's *Petrushka*, Balakirev's *Islamey* and Mussorgsky's *Pictures at an Exhibition*. While studying *Petrushka* I invented a new method of covering my fingertips with Band-Aids to stop the fingernails from disintegrating.

There were also at least seven Liszt recordings as well as some Mozart concertos before I confronted all of Beethoven's piano works, spread over five years. (The Vox label was the first to exploit commercially the idea of issuing boxes containing whole series of works by the same composer.) Of Beethoven's piano music, I left out only very few pieces like his early Nine Variations on a March by Dressler. I had started with the smaller variation works, which, even if of lesser importance, contribute substantially to the understanding of Beethoven's range. By chance, the recording of the thirty-two sonatas came to a close on my thirty-second birthday, although not with the late sonatas which I had already done at the end of the '50s. Next to Beethoven, I tried my hand at Schubert's Impromptus, *Moments musicaux*, the three *Klavierstücke* and the *Wanderer Fantasie*, a work that, along with Liszt's B minor Sonata, remained a staple of my repertoire. Further I should mention Arnold Schoenberg's Piano Concerto Op. 42, recorded in Baden-Baden with Michael Gielen, who also conducted my third, and best, version of the work, while the second with Rafael Kubelík for DG was recorded in Munich. I can hardly describe how difficult a performance of this concerto had initially been and how much simpler it appears today.

In many of my Viennese recordings my producer was a double-bass player who followed the bass line with avid concentration. He was assisted by just one sound engineer who operated the tape recorder but couldn't read music. During the editing, I waved my arms at him like a conductor in order to show him when to edit. At that time, the tapes were still spliced with the help of scissors. I benefited greatly from these recordings – both in terms of technical know-how and in gaining my first overview of the vast panorama of Beethoven's output for the piano which allows for lightness, playfulness, gracefulness, comedy and wit no less than for drama and tragedy, intellectuality and emotional power – the brevity of the Bagatelles next to the giant organism of the *Hammerklavier* Sonata. Towards the end of my association with Vox, I recorded for the first time Beethoven's *Diabelli Variations*, a great favourite of mine. Like some of the sonatas, I played it first for the microphones before presenting it in concerts over the next forty years.

In the late '60s, I had a brief encounter with Vanguard that led to my first Schumann recording (*Symphonic Etudes* and Fantasy), and to a Schubert disc including the Sonatas in C minor and C major. When, a few years earlier, I had played the C minor Sonata in a Vienna recital, the great Schubert scholar Otto Erich Deutsch was among the listeners, and he had never heard the work performed before. I also recorded a programme of Chopin Polonaises and Liszt Rhapsodies. In order to enter the particular spirit of these works and meet their pianistic demands I treated myself to a sabbatical of several months. Although I never considered myself a genuine Chopin player, it intrigued me to come to grips with his Polonaises, works that, with the exception of the notorious one in A flat, rarely cropped up in concerts.

After a Beethoven recital in London towards the end of the '60s, a number of large record labels suddenly woke up. I opted for Philips (later Decca), a company that took me under its wing for the rest of my career. Besides all the studio work, there was now the chance to publish live recordings as well, some of which still warm my heart. Among my studio recordings I should point out the second and third series of the complete Beethoven sonatas and three cycles of his piano concertos. In addition to two sets of Schubert's later piano works (1822–28) there are also live recordings of five of his sonatas. With the Academy of St Martin in the Fields and Sir Neville Marriner I recorded all of Mozart's Piano Concertos, later followed by six of them with the Scottish Chamber Orchestra and Sir Charles Mackerras and complemented by most of Mozart's sonatas and piano pieces. There was also a selection of Liszt's late music and the second and third recordings of his B minor Sonata. (Take the third.)

Two versions of the Brahms Concertos – the second with Abbado in Berlin – were succeeded by a live performance of the D minor with Sir Colin Davis in Munich, to me the most satisfying. I played some more Schumann and, to my particular delight, a dozen of Haydn's sonatas.

Among chamber music discs there is a lovely Schumann record with Heinz Holliger and Beethoven's piano-cello works with my son Adrian. A Mozart CD with the Alban Berg Quartet was issued by EMI. Finally, there were recordings of *Winterreise* and *Schwanengesang* with both Fischer-Dieskau and Matthias Goerne. One more

Winterreise with Fischer-Dieskau is preserved on DVD from a live performance for the Sender Freies Berlin (1979); here, the great singer is in fine voice.

What makes the career of a soloist continuously successful? Next to talent, skill and a good constitution, I should mention the esteem of orchestras and conductors, and the weight of a good recording contract. There is also the work of devoted agents, the voices of well-disposed critics and, of course, the presence of a sizeable public.

In considering what maintained the success of my career well into old age, the role of publicity and the media seems to me the least pertinent. Even after I had acquired some repute as a Philips artist, this company's publicity expenditure remained comparatively modest. What, then, explains the fact that I could record my core repertoire more than once, and in some cases even three or fourfold? Leaving the appreciation and curiosity of public and press aside, I submit the following:

I turned up at all sessions in time, and well prepared.

To record the programme of an LP, I needed on average two days. Once, when the recordings had finished a day early, we taped, at my suggestion, a Bach record within a single day. Only at an advanced age, and on account of the longer duration of CD programmes, did I rely on more recording time.

Since my young days in Vienna I was in the habit of routinely writing notes while listening to playback and making suggestions of where to edit. In spite of taking liberties in the playing of detail, my performances followed a concept which always made it possible to join takes at certain editing points (which shouldn't suggest, by the way, that there was an inordinate amount of editing; nor do I believe that, at least in my later recordings, the listener can detect whether a piece is edited or played in one go). In addition, I had the good fortune of collaborating with outstanding producers (Volker Straus, Martha de Francisco) and sound engineers.

Throughout my life I have cancelled very few concert or recording dates.

The development of recording technology led from mono to stereo to digital, from LPs and cassettes to the compact disc. New technologies called for new recordings.

And finally: I did not stall as a musician and pianist. This is crucial. My recordings are not carbon copies of past achievements. An old lady who had listened to many of my concerts used to tell me each time, 'But you played this quite differently today!' This was surely an exaggeration – I don't quite see myself as Woody Allen's 'Zelig'. But there was enough novelty to keep listeners curious.

What did it mean to me to make all these records? And what does such a flood of records mean to others?

Some performers feel the unquenchable thirst to get things right, to broaden and deepen their acquaintance with masterpieces, to accommodate contradictions under one roof, to become simultaneously simpler and more imaginative, freer and more accurate. From the growing store of experience arises the chance to reach the essential. My sequence of recordings kept me aware of my development.

There are musicians like the late Sergiu Celibidache who despised recording. There are those who, when having to repeat a passage, seem unable to regain the same tempo, and others who play a piece a number of times, each time quite differently, to decide only afterwards which takes should be used or combined. There are performers who relish manipulating each single note, and their opposites for whom editing is a cardinal sin: only pieces played in one single take are ethically sound.

I did not belong to any of these. As long as I found a beautiful, conscientiously prepared piano in a hall with good acoustics I embarked on recordings with keen anticipation, all the more so since technology has made it possible to use computers for editing on location. This gives the player the chance to react to playback immediately, and enhances the collaboration between producer and artist.

There are two groups of producers. The first has the ambition to assist the artist and realise his conception as faithfully as possible. The second, while attempting to be helpful, considers the end product as the producer's creative achievement – a stance confirmed by musicians who are not sure what they want. (Let me relate to you two cases where the engineering turned out to be a disappointment: in the final mix of the Brahms D minor Concerto with Abbado, the piano lacks presence – it sounds as if it were placed within the orchestra, and not in front of it; and the concluding record of my second Schubert series from 1988 featuring the B flat Sonata and the *Wanderer Fantasie* is, to me, devalued by the inferior quality of its piano sound.) In Martha de Francisco I found a brilliant and sympathetic producer belonging to the first group I describe; with her, piano sound, definition, resonance and other components of editing could be jointly determined.

Having been presented with a tape recorder as a youngster, I had the chance to inform myself about my playing 'from the outside', namely from the distance that is created by playback. This improved my ability to listen to myself while playing. Later, I collected radio broadcasts of my concerts. Since, in my Vox years, I frequently supervised the editing of my recordings myself, I felt hardly less familiar with the procedures of so-called studio recordings than with the conditions of a concert hall. For five decades, I could therefore stay abreast of myself, listen critically and refine my ears. As a further bonus, there were the live recordings, usually drawn from radio tapes, that complemented the picture of my studio projects. These included large and ambitious works like the *Hammerklavier* Sonata (twice), the *Diabelli Variations* (also twice), Liszt's 'Vallée d'Obermann' and Busoni's Toccata.

The trouble is that such recordings need to be looked for. And here a main problem reveals itself: who, besides manic collectors and rabid fans, would pile up all those discs, and attentively listen to them? Most will be familiar with three or four records, and form an opinion. Some years ago I saw a comparative review of Schubert's great A major Sonata that embraced a number of pianists. Of my own three recordings of the work, the critic only knew the first from more than thirty years ago. That seemed to him sufficient to pronounce a verdict.

It gives me pleasure to see that so many of my recordings are still available. But here, a small question mark seems appropriate, when I consider those recordings that I would have preferred to see deleted or that have been issued without my knowledge, or even against my will. (Such things have happened.) At times, old recordings resurface, newly packaged and recommended. Recently, my series of the five Beethoven concertos from the '70s with Bernard Haitink has appeared for the first time on CD. Haitink is a justly admired and venerated conductor, but his conducting thirty-five years ago was different from today's, as was my playing and my way of dealing with conductors. Also, more accurate scores and editions of these works have meanwhile appeared which I was able to use in the ensuing performances with James Levine and the Chicago Symphony Orchestra, and Sir Simon Rattle with the Vienna Philharmonic. Apart from some instances of absorbing simplicity, the later performances seem to me more sensitive, lively, and colourful. In both cases, the collaboration with the conductors in setting up the concertos was more intense.

My advice would be to look up the date of a recording or of its initial release. Where the necessary information on the record sleeve or in the booklet is missing, think twice before acquiring it. Lately, my earliest recording of Beethoven's thirty-two sonatas was made available through obscure companies. Piano students who get these recordings at rock-bottom prices may now live in the illusion that they know me.

I have to confess that even I cannot claim to have a complete musical recall of all my recordings. It had been my intention to listen to some of them again in connection with this article; unfortunately, sudden hearing problems have prevented me from doing so. Even so, relying on my memory, I have tried to point out some of those discs in which I recognised myself more readily. To be sure, my choice is bound to remain incomplete. Thus it dawned on me only recently that I had forgotten about my Philips version of Beethoven's *Eroica* Variations Op. 35.

The six CDs within the 'Great Pianists' series (now out of print, but available to buy as downloads) as well as the more extensive sequence called 'Artist's Choice' should provide some orientation.

To the 'Great Pianists' CDs, the last piece from Schumann's *Fantasiestücke* ('Ende vom Lied') has been added against my wishes and the transfer of the sonority of Liszt's *Sposalizio* has misfired while, in 'Artist's Choice', I had hoped for a live performance of Liszt's A major Concerto with the Berlin Philharmonic that, alas, did not become available.

In general, I would plead for my later recordings, although there are exceptions, such as the finale of Schubert's Sonata D.959 that I still prefer in my first Philips recording from Salzburg; similarly, my heart beats for the live recordings of five of Schubert's sonatas, no matter that the engineering may not always have been of the highest order. The TV (and DVD) versions of the last three Schubert sonatas recorded at London's Middle Temple suffered from the hurdles and mishaps of TV technology on location, the large windows unprotected by curtains, and the limited time frame of just three days.

Even more precarious were the thirteen instalments of Schubert's piano works (1822–28) in Bremen. In the '70s, certain technical devices as well as editing opportunities were still in their infancy. And the summer heat was extreme. It puzzles me how, under such circumstances, the *Wanderer Fantasie* could have turned our decently.

Among my favourite recordings I count some of Haydn's lovely sonatas (that of the hilarious one in C major, Hob XVI:50, preferably in a live performance from the Salzburg Festival, 1981), Mozart's A minor Rondo, K.511 (in the second Philips version from 1999), Schubert's Impromptus (mostly from the 1988 Philips set), and

Liszt's 'Vallée d'Obermann' (live from Amsterdam 1981), a performance that fully engages in the piece's magnificent rhetoric.

Last but certainly not least, my gratitude goes to the public. Without meaning to belittle the resolute support of concert promoters or the impact of a benevolent press in the slightest, I am certain that my pianistic life would have taken a different course without the readiness of the public to continue listening to me both in the concert hall and through the loudspeakers. Nothing could have made me happier than the awareness that I did not owe my reputation to a giant publicity drum but to the appeal of my playing.

(2015)

A Case for Live Recordings

MY SUBJECT IS a stepchild – live recording. Standing between the two officially canonised sources of musical experience, concert performance and studio recording, the recorded concert has had less than its due.

There has been a good deal of discussion about the differences and similarities between concerts and studio recordings. I should like to offer my own catalogue of distinctions (bearing in mind that a concert hall may turn into a studio if recording sessions take place in it):

In a concert one plays just once, in the studio several times if necessary. In a concert you must convince the audience at once; in the studio it is the accumulated result that counts.

In a concert the performance is only experienced once; in the studio it can be reproduced. In a concert the performer must get to the end of the piece without a chance to make corrections. In the studio he can make corrections, learn while he records and get rid of nerves.

The player before the public must do four things at the same time: he must imagine the performance, play it, project it, and listen to it. In the studio he has the opportunity to hear it again after playing, and to react accordingly.

In a concert it is the broad sweep that counts. The studio demands control over a mosaic; while it offers the performer the possibility of gradually loosening up, there is also the danger of diminishing freshness. And there is the painful business of choosing between takes.

When playing before the public, details must be projected to the furthest ends of the auditorium, just as the whispers of an actor must be heard throughout the theatre. In front of the microphone one tries, on the contrary, to get away from exaggerations and aims for an interpretation that will bear frequent hearing.

In the concert hall the concentration of the audience brings about a mutual influence between the performer and his listeners. In the studio nobody has to be conquered – but there is nobody to disturb you. The player sits as though in a tomb.

A fit of coughing or the chirping of the alarm on a watch may break the spell of the most delicate moment of the concert. The studio offers silence.

Weaknesses in a concert performance tend to result from spontaneity, from a break in concentration or from nervous pressure. In the studio they may have their roots in excessive critical awareness.

The ability to convince the public in the concert hall is quite independent of absolute perfection. The studio is ruled by the aesthetics of compulsive cleanliness.

All these are observations from the player's point of view. Concert-goers and listeners to records may like to add that a concert involves physical presence, while the 'pure music' of the record avoids it (a bonus for those who suffer from agoraphobia or feel uncomfortable in crowds); moreover, the sound reaches the listener unmanipulated and as directly as the acoustics of the concert hall permit. The sound of the recording, on the other hand, is decided by the technical staff, the musical effect depending on such factors as editing, balance, reverberation and the qualities of the reproducing equipment. Lastly, not only must the player perform an entire work in a concert, but the audience must sit still and listen until it is finished. (Such respect for the concentration of both musicians and audience is one of the tacit agreements of a cultured public.) But when you listen to a record you can turn the music off, savour it in instalments or try bits here and there; you can move, talk, eat and groan – in a word, you feel at home.

Despite the funeral orations Glenn Gould delivered on concert halls, they continue to be the setting for the most vivid music-making. I do not wish to be dogmatic and will admit that there are concerts without a breath of life, and records of electrifying vigour. All the same, it follows from the way they come about that concerts are more likely to be characterised by spontaneity, tension and risk, studio recordings rather by reflection and superior method. To quote Robert Musil's *The Man without Qualities*, with its 'Generalsekretariat für Genauigkeit und Seele' (Administration of Accuracy and Soul), I may say that in the studio accuracy is more readily manageable than 'soul'.

Studio recordings have enormously increased the acuteness of detailed listening, including that of the musician listening to himself. In conjunction with the influence of modern *Urtext* editions and the demands of contemporary music, the gramophone record has profoundly upset listening habits. Its effects on the player, however, may not only be purifying but also sterilizing; it may be petrifying as well as concentrating and distilling. The interpreter who aims at accuracy risks less panache, lesser tempi, less self-effacement. The gramophone record today sets standards of perfection, mechanical not musical, which the concert hall seldom confirms. It induces some artists to play in a concert as though for a record, in the fear that the audience is listening as though to a record.

But a concert has a different message and a different way of delivering it. Now that we listeners to records and studio troglodytes have learned so much from studio recordings, it seems time to turn back and learn from concerts once again.

For the sake of objectivity, let us consider the recordings of the 1930s, such as those of Cortot, Fischer or Schnabel. One may not have been aware then of certain imprecisions, in the way modern wrong-note fiends are. Where the leading of voices, the grading of dynamics, the control of character and atmosphere, timbre and rhythm are handled with the mastery of Cortot at his best, it appears to me that a few missed notes are not only irrelevant but almost add to the excitement of the impact.

In the 1930s people seem to have played in the studio almost as in a concert. But was this really so? Even then, players must have been worried about providing lasting evidence on a record, unless they could summon up the unbelievable nonchalance of a Richard Strauss. Apart from that, the limited duration of the 78-rpm disc was basically at variance with the nature of playing longer pieces as a whole. But then, as Emil Gilels told me about his own early recordings, a side may have had to be repeated thirty times if the producer so commanded, and the players had no opportunity to hear the results themselves, since a wax matrix was destroyed by one playing.

Above all, there was no audience. Why, if I may believe my own experience as a listener, does an impressive concert tend to leave stronger traces than a record? Because the listener, no less than the player, has had a physical experience, not only hearing the performance but breathing in it, contributing to it by his presence and sharing his enthusiasm with many others. The listener encounters the composer together with the performer and the rest of the audience in one place and at one time.

In the studio the player is alone with his own self-criticism and with the Argus ears of the producer. Even if he possesses the important gift of playing there with all the tension of the concert platform, and however vividly he might imagine the presence of the public, it is still imaginary. There is no direct exchange. He will, of course, try to remain as close as possible to his concert performances, using takes of a complete piece as a basis. But whoever subscribes to the belief that tape editing is a deception and that only complete takes should be used, deceives himself; he or she would renounce the advantages of the studio and still fall short of the enchantment of the concert, for it is not just the tension of the single uninterrupted performance that counts. (No one listening to my records could tell which movements remained unedited and which were put together from a number of takes.)

Here the live recording serves as a bridge. What is it able to convey? For me, there is above all the attractive feature that the uniqueness of a concert has been thwarted. The concert took place on a certain day: the public was present, as we can sense in the background, and we can imagine being present ourselves – a fancy much less ridiculous than wishing to imagine ourselves in the bare studio.

What you hear and enjoy is an indiscretion, something that was only intended for those present and cannot be exactly reproduced. It is not the technical level of reproduction I am referring to: the fact that live recordings cannot always achieve the quality of the best studio products hardly worries me. It is the participation of the public, the aura of physical presence, the contribution of which cannot be altogether assessed on a live record; and yet, in some happy instances, these leave their mark in the heightened intensity of a performance, in the increase in the player's vision, courage and absorption.

Why have live records been so rare until now, except for those of famous artists of the past enjoyed by connoisseurs and collectors? First, because a concert becomes more difficult when it is recorded. The sight of microphones on the podium does not fill the artist with glee. Incidentally, one must make a clear distinction between radio recordings and live productions for commercial gramophone records. The former are more easily bearable since they will only be broadcast once or twice, while the latter are bound to terrify the player, being aimed at an international body of critical contemporaries, and future generations. Live productions are therefore only worthwhile in special cases, one of which I shall mention later. On the whole, live records should come about by chance; they should use radio or private recordings that give the artist pleasure. (Of course it is outrageous that, in some countries, they are still sold without the artist's agreement.)

Here we come to the second difficulty about live records: the prejudice against their alleged technical, and even musical, inferiority. Losses in digital quality and realistic balance, accidental noises, inaccuracies in the playing or fatigue in the instruments are mentioned as deficiencies that cannot be tolerated. True enough, there is no call to make a commercial record of a performance that has caught the interpreter off colour, the public during a flu epidemic, or a fleet of fire-engines passing by. Apart from that, the latest developments in recording technique will sometimes make an expert in electroacoustics happier than a musician. There are chance recordings that bring a piece of music to life and studio performances that destroy it. Those who consider spotless perfection and undisturbed technical neatness the prerequisite of a moving musical experience no longer know how to listen to music.

In pleading for live recordings here, I do not by any means wish to turn my back on the studio. I have spent innumerable interesting and some happy hours in it, owe it much essential experience, and shall continue to acknowledge my records, though with certain reservations. But in future I should like to place more frequent live recordings next to them.

My first live record was devoted to the longest masterpiece of the older piano literature, Beethoven's *Diabelli Variations*. Since then I have been waiting for a suitable performance of the 'Hammerklavier' Sonata Op. 106, and recently found one in a London concert given in April 1983.[116] Why am I drawn, of all things, to the biggest and most dangerous works? Because they best provide evidence of a mastery that is not available to some 'studio artists' and because it is works of that scope which stand to gain most in boldness, absorption and vision. The objection that no player can function uniformly well for an hour or so, however justified in itself, misses the point of a concert performance. Compared with the evened-out results of the studio, it may show greater dedication and that unexpected success that differs from a premeditated result as a poem differs from a timetable.

Although I would not normally wish to make a planned live recording, an exception came about in Chicago in June 1983. On this occasion the effort of performing the cycle of the Beethoven piano concertos was added to the risks of a live recording.

Performances of cycles make the stature of a composer more clearly recognisable. They are especially appropriate to great composers like Beethoven, who constantly have something new to convey. The unmistakable character of each movement, when played in close succession with the rest of the cycle, shows its profile even more distinctly to performers and listeners alike.

The Chicago Symphony Orchestra, James Levine and I are old acquaintances. My contact with that splendid orchestra goes back to 1970 and has continued with welcome regularity. The Ravinia Festival of 1977 gave us the opportunity to play all the Beethoven concertos under James Levine. On the first evening the temperature

---

116   Another one, from 1996, has been included in my latest complete set of Beethoven Sonatas from Philips.

was around 100°F and the humidity 95 percent, which disturbed the orchestra not a whit: concentration and control of the playing remained virtually unaffected. The cycle was repeated two years later. Finally, in June 1983, two series of Beethoven's concertos were recorded digitally in Chicago's Orchestra Hall.

The undertaking had a double goal: we intended to examine and to realise a concept of these works in several stages. The rehearsals were used to go, among other things, into the difference between *sforzando* and *forte piano*. Levine and I found ourselves in friendly agreement about what Beethoven's scores communicate, while the musicians of the orchestra never tired of re-examining pieces they had long ago mastered.

At the same time we hoped to document that tension and directness which manifests itself more readily before the public, a kind of spontaneity within pre-set boundaries which would rather discover than reproduce.

The confidence of all concerned in one another was the safety factor that made the risk of this live recording for once a calculable one, but it would have been extremely unwise, not to say foolhardy, if only for technical reasons, to have relied on the tight-rope-walk of a single series of performances. The availability of two cycles gave us the possibility to combine some benefits of concert and studio: the freshness of the moment with the advantages of having a choice. I am not giving away any secrets if I say that live productions nearly always work in this way, seeking a synthesis or a compromise between both worlds.

All the same, despite every precaution, the audience could still have spoilt the lot. Over the years I can remember concerts with screaming babies (Japan), a barking dog (New York), a mewing cat (Istanbul), somebody falling down in a faint, a maniac clapping in the most impossible places and a power cut plunging us all into darkness. (In Chicago itself I once had to stop during a recital, a few bars into the hushed beginning of Liszt's *Sposalizio*, and tell the audience: 'I can hear you, but you can't hear me'.) None of these things occurred; on this occasion the exceptional stillness and concentration of the Chicago public filled me with gratitude. It was almost possible to forget how dangerously one lives when one records live.

(1984)

On Recitals and Programmes

'LE CONCERT, C'EST moi.' When Liszt wrote to the Princess Belgiojoso that, in this pronouncement, he was affecting the style of Louis XIV, he had just launched a new type of public concert: the solo recital.[117] To be precise, the announcement in London used the plural 'Recitals on the Pianoforte', starting on 9 June 1840 – recitations of pieces of music, testimonies, one would guess, to both Liszt's declamatory playing and the Romantic closeness of music and poetry. Hitherto, soloists had contributed to a programme that employed a variety of participants, including an orchestra. Joint recitals, rather rare these days, were still fairly frequent at the beginning of our century when Busoni shared a concert platform with Ysaÿe or Melba.

Between each 'recitation' Liszt went to converse with people in his audience, a habit we have fortunately shed. (Another discontinued habit of old days, and a rather endearing one, was to modulate, *arpeggiando*, from one piece to the next; Wilhelm Backhaus still improvised discreetly in this manner.) While Liszt's newly created recitals may have lasted a couple of hours, some of Anton Rubinstein's mammoth programmes of the 1890s cannot possibly have taken less than three. Today we have settled on concerts of roughly eighty minutes' playing time, forty in each half. Of course, there may be the odd exception of a longer one, or a different balancing-out of the two halves, should an oversized work such as Beethoven's *Diabelli Variations* demand it.

How ought these eighty minutes to be filled? Of two standard programme schemes that come to mind, the old-fashioned one treated a programme like a menu: starter (or soup) and main course, followed by various salads and puddings, and topped by omelette flambée. Artur Schnabel, in *Music and the Line of Most Resistance*,[118] wrote extensively about, and against, such musical meals. According to him, 'the first condition of a good menu is that all dishes should be prepared by the same chef or several chefs of equal merit; that all should be prepared with first-class raw materials, and that the gourmet should concentrate with the same seriousness on all of them!' The usual concert menu is far removed from these requirements. In my

---

117 See Alan Walker: *Franz Liszt, The Virtuoso Years* (Faber & Faber, 1983), p. 356.

118 Princeton University Press, 1942.

younger and more wicked days I invented, for an encyclopaedia, a list of compositions which included a work entitled 'Suite gastronomique'; during its last movement
an omelette is supposed to be set alight on the performer's head. The bald virtuoso
to whom it is dedicated has so far declined to give it a try.

The other standard programme scheme proceeds in a roughly historical order. Yet
the reverse, or an apt historical mixture, is equally justified. I would accept no hard
and fast rule in programme-making except one: that works in the same key should
not follow one another. A varied succession of keys is required to stimulate the listener's attention. If the whole recital does not have a true key scheme, its sequence
of pieces should at least be checked for suitability. I maintain, as Artur Schnabel
did, that it is a mistake to connect in performance Mozart's C minor Fantasy K.475
with the C minor Sonata K.457. The fact that they were published in one volume
proves nothing. Each of these works is an autonomous masterpiece; together, they
cancel each other out.

A whole evening in one basic key is even more tedious. I once heard Beethoven's
Sonata Op. 106 played after Schubert's D.960, both in B flat. It proved to be a miscal-
culation on every possible level. Even the succession of major and minor on the same
tonic tends to be, in larger works, precarious. A combination as tempting as that of
Beethoven's Diabelli Variations and his last sonata, Op. 111, should therefore be ruled
out. But there is yet another reason: for both works, the only position within a programme that seems to me permissible is at the end. The *Diabelli Variations* present a
complete universe, while Op. 111 leads irreversibly into silence. Encores here, for that
matter, are out of the question. I remember once seeing an advertisement for a recital
that started with Op. 111 and continued with the Liszt Sonata. I cannot recall how the
programme went on after the interval, and prefer not to recall the pianist.

The idea that recitals have to end brilliantly or mightily belongs to the past. If I ask
myself how they should *begin*, my first advice would be to avoid pieces which may
break the player's neck. To sit down and throw oneself into Schumann's Toccata may
prove too much for even the most dextrous and cold-blooded of virtuosos. On the
other hand, it would never have occurred to me to start a Beethoven cycle with Op. 28,
as Schnabel apparently did. For this most relaxed of sonata beginnings I prefer to
have settled down and thoroughly acquainted myself with the instrument. If I caution the player against immediately daring the devil I do not want to imply that I

encourage the 'warming-up piece'. This notion suggests to me that the player has not seen fit to try out the piano or that the initial piece need not be taken quite seriously. Right away, the player ought to be fully involved and challenge the audience to share his or her concentration. Instead of playing down to an audience, the player should make the audience 'listen up'.

Good programmes are based on sufficient contrast. But they usually also reveal connections. Obvious connections are demonstrated when specimens of certain forms like the sonata, or of freer concepts like the fantasy, are assembled. In such programmes the diversity of possible solutions within a concept should become apparent. My own debut recital ambitiously offered a choice of works from Bach to the present day, all containing fugues. Busoni, in 1909, toyed with the idea of two entire dance programmes, the outlines of which are given in a letter to Egon Petri.[119] As for a full recital of variations, here prudence is required. I have tried out, and discarded, a programme of Beethoven's Opp. 34, 35 and 120 sets. The only successful variation programme I could possibly think of is that of Mozart's Duport Variations, Brahms's D minor variations from his String Sextet Op. 18 (in his own transcription for Clara Schumann), Liszt's *Weinen, Klagen, Sorgen, Zagen* and, once again, Beethoven's *Diabelli Variations* – works in which the diversity of the short span is absorbed in a comprehensive psychological whole. Each of these sets is markedly different in its basic character – graceful, heroic, suffering, humourous – as well as in the technical treatment of its common formal idea.

Connections and contrasts of another sort were laid out in a programme that tried to make a case for late Liszt. It started with a selection of eight of his late pieces, interrupted in the middle by Schoenberg's Six Little Pieces Op. 19 or, alternatively, Bartók's *Naenies.* Half an evening of late Liszt should, I imagined, prove not only possible but highly rewarding. The juxtaposition with short twentieth-century works would underline Liszt's modernity. After this group of pieces, united in their opposition to Classicism and functional harmony, the second part of the recital was given over to examples of neoclassicism or Neo-Baroque: Busoni's Toccata and Brahms's Handel Variations. Busoni, having absorbed influences of Liszt and Brahms, could be seen to have united both worlds in the central Fantasia of his Toccata.

Depending on the performer's ability to switch from one style to the next, a

---

119   See Antony Beaumont: *Ferruccio Busoni, Selected Letters* (Faber & Faber, 1987), pp. 96–7.

programme of extreme contrasts can be hugely satisfying. On paper, the idea of putting three of Liszt's Hungarian Rhapsodies between Fantasies by Bach and the *Diabelli Variations* may seem perverse. In reality, the profane complements the sublime. Not only do Liszt's pieces hold their own surprisingly well; they also reveal, in their quasi-improvised introductions, Liszt's familiarity with Bach's improvisatory fantasies, and link Liszt's virtuosity with that of Beethoven. After all, the *Diabelli Variations* display, besides other things, a considerable amount of bravura.

It is amazing to what degree works (and composers) can be shown, by the context in which they appear, in a new light. If, in a programme of well-matched Haydn and Beethoven sonatas, Haydn's are played first and last, they are given a new status and might be listened to with different ears. When Beethoven's 'Appassionata' is presented – after works such as Haydn's G minor Sonata, Brahms's Ballades Op. 10, Weber's Sonata in A flat and Mendelssohn's *Variations sérieuses* – as the evening's conclusion, it almost sounds like a different piece, and certainly feels different under my fingers. This programme has a double effect: it upgrades not only a number of undervalued or lesser known masterpieces but also the 'Appassionata' itself. Not that I have ever been one of those who have become wary of this great work's 'heroic' attitude, resentful of its popularity or doubtful about its place among Beethoven's special achievements. But hearing it in close connection with Weber, Mendelssohn and Brahms, composers who beside, or after, Beethoven had to find a voice of their own, may produce the sensation of watching all the pieces of a puzzle come together, and grasping what completeness is about. (Note: Weber's strangely neglected Sonata, the one basically graceful and radiant work in this generally dark programme, is placed in the middle.)

Among the programmes that I particularly enjoy playing are those that feature one composer only. When Clara Schumann heard Anton Rubinstein perform four Beethoven sonatas in one evening she deemed it inartistic. 'Doesn't *one* Beethoven sonata need one's entire soul? How, then, could one play four sonatas in a row with one's entire soul?'[120] On top of this, Rubinstein added a fifth as an encore. Unimaginable what Mendelssohn or Robert would have said. Bülow's feat of playing Beethoven's last five sonatas en suite would have given Clara a heart attack. Admittedly, in taking on such an exhausting programme Bülow overstated his case. But,

---

120 Clara Schumann's *Diaries*, 18 February 1893.

in his time, certain late works by Beethoven were still the property of a few – and every generation seems to have its endurance tests. (At present, Messiaen's *Vingt regards* and Stockhausen's *Klavierstücke* might qualify.)

If the right composers and works are chosen, one-composer programmes should be far from monotonous. To me there is a parallel with the major exhibition of a painter. Does he gain in stature when his pictures fill several rooms, or will this reduce the pleasure that we derived from seeing a few of his works interspersed between those of other artists? Here is my personal choice of keyboard composers whom I would volunteer to listen to on their own: Bach, Scarlatti, Haydn, Mozart, Beethoven, Schubert, Schumann, Chopin, Liszt and Schoenberg. Others would probably add Brahms, Debussy, Bartók and Messiaen; or Alkan, Ravel, Skriabin and Rachmaninov. I should advise against Carl Czerny, though – and I know what I am talking about; in the 1950s I had to sit through an all-Czerny recital which was delivered with missionary zeal by a friend of mine.

The range of what a great composer can express seems mysteriously incompatible with his limitations as a visible, and tangible, human being. I cannot imagine anything more thrilling than to explore that range. In works suited to fill a whole series of concerts, such wealth and breadth become gloriously evident – always provided that the performances rise to the occasion. At the same time, the individual character of each work is etched more clearly. Concerts in a cycle differ from single ones. In a cycle, the majority of the audience remains the same. There is a feeling of sharing, a cumulative effect, the experience of a spiritual journey jointly undertaken with the performer. With the end of the cycle, a goal has been reached.

While Schubert cycles are a relatively recent venture, and the first Mozart concerto cycle I know of was launched by Ernst von Dohnányi as late as 1941, all of Beethoven's sonatas had already been performed in the 1860s by Sir Charles Hallé, in 1873 by Liszt's pupil Marie Jaëll, and in the 1890s by Eugen d'Albert and Edouard Risler. Busoni's six Liszt recitals in Berlin in 1911 accomplished something that none of Liszt's own students had ever dared attempt. The first great pianist to survey the 'history of piano music' in seven recitals was Anton Rubinstein (1885–86). In the Beethoven programme of his series he surpassed himself, and even Bülow, by playing, in one go, Opp. 27, No. 2; 31, No. 2; 53, 57, 101, 109 and 111. Since the last war, Beethoven's sonatas have sometimes been done chronologically, a practice I find rather pedantic. Those who are interested in the evolution of Beethoven's style and range can pursue it with the help of records. In the concert hall, well-balanced contrast and a variety of style in each recital seem to me preferable. I would opt for a careful placement of the minor-key sonatas (a minority of nine), and for the distribution of the five late sonatas on different evenings.[121]

Recital programmes may have to accommodate various necessities. What did I play when I visited a certain city the last time? What would I like to add to my repertory? Which works have been agreed on for future recording? Which twentieth-century works do I include? Is the recital part of a programmatic series, needing to be adjusted accordingly? Do I want to comply? Of such pressures and queries, a good programme should reveal nothing. Even if it subscribes to a guiding idea, a programme is a balancing act. The balancing is done mainly by instinct, helped by experience. More often than not, programmes explain, or justify, themselves only in retrospect. A basic disposition – whether to play it safe or to administer a dose of disquieting surprise to the public – will leave its imprint on the whole enterprise.

In terms of repertory, two extreme positions are embodied by the player of hits and the player of oddities. The hit player, persuading himself that the best is also the best loved, caters for the biggest public attendance. The player of unfamiliar music, on the contrary, resents popularity as debasing or shies away from competition in the established field. Programmes of rarely performed works can be highly sophisticated and illuminating, or wonderfully dotty, as that of a violin solo arrangement (if I may, for a moment, switch my attention from pianists to string players) of Wagner's *Siegfried* dedicated to Cosima Wagner and performed at Wahnfried. The three final sections of this event, arguably one of the most indispensable one-man shows and one-composer programmes ever to hit the eardrum, were named: 'Siegfried on Top of Brünnhilde's Rock', 'Siegfried Awakens Brünnhilde' and, presumably in double stops, 'Siegfried and Brünnhilde'.

A close contender might be the piano recital given in Vienna in 1926 by a certain Wilhelm Bund. It started with a lecture in which Bund criticised the Viennese critics – all mentioned by name in the printed programme – and ended with a composition by Bund described as follows: 'Longing to die in voluptuousness – rearing and sinking back, shimmy-foxtrot as song of destiny, orgiastic dance (disrupted),

---

121   In my last Beethoven cycles I have kept the trilogies of sonatas (Opp. 2, 10, 31) as well as the consecutive works Opp. 26–7 and 109–11 together, and found this particularly satisfying.

exclamations of desire, desperate struggle, apoplexy.' I wonder whether Mr. Bund survived the concert.

While such programmes are collectors' items, there are those that betray a collector's obsessive mind. We have the collector of fast notes, chords and octaves, of which as many as possible are supposed to be delivered per second and square inch; and the player of miniatures (*Lozelachs*, to use a Viennese pre-war term) who, abhorring larger structures, deals exclusively with musical bric-à-brac. Of these, Paul de Conne, a pupil of Anton Rubinstein and specialist in arranging tricky passages for fragile hands, piled up in one recital twenty-three pieces by seventeen composers, if I may trust my informant.

I would not want to bully anybody into anything. But I feel it ought to be a matter of personal pride for younger performers to play a fair share of the new repertory, and for older ones whose resilience may betray signs of erosion at least to listen to new works, and live in their aura. Among all the programmes I could name, those promoting important new music get my highest marks. Of course, as we live in an imperfect world, the attention and credit such concerts earn is often scanty. Few all-round performers will be able to muster the heroic dedication and specialised skills that are required to cope with a recent work like Ligeti's admirable Etudes. Yet this is precisely one of the tasks that a gifted young player should try to work at. To someone like myself who, as a performer, is absorbed by playing the old but enjoys listening to what is new with passionate curiosity, there is some consolation: the old does not simply have to be well lit and expertly preserved, like Titians in a museum. It continuously needs to be brought to life, and to relate to our own time. If handled rightly, the result should be far removed from musical consumerism and mental sloth. Ideally, the performer should champion the neglected and the new along with established masterworks, and by no means exclude famous pieces just because they are famous. In his programmes, Maurizio Pollini has admirably stayed this course.

The piano literature, even if we only consider its finest works, is too extensive to be mastered by one single player. An intelligent and far-sighted choice of repertory is therefore paramount. Which are the works that one can plead for with conviction, that one hopes to grow into, that one would want to spend a lifetime with? Which is the music players can discover, or audiences ought to notice? Recitalists are rhetoricians; they have something publicly to convey. In classical rhetorics the main propositions are to instruct, to move and to amuse. The performer should not dodge the obligation to be edifying. His sense of quality has to inform the audience. In his programming, he should not give in to commercial demands. The more uncompromisingly a performer follows his own convictions, the better for his self-esteem and, in the long run, the esteem in which he is held by others.

'Le concert, c'est moi'? The programme is the player's visiting-card. But make no mistake – an intelligent, ingenious programme does not guarantee convincing performances. It still needs to be projected, generating a spiritual link between composers and listeners but also turning into an intense physical experience, an event unique and unrepeatable, tied to the day and hour, the sound of the hall and instrument, the sudden burst of sweat in a spasm of anxiety and the bravely stifled coughing fit. All being well, the executant's grasp of his programme and his audience will be surpassed by the grip of an unseen hand that keeps its hold over player and listeners alike for the duration of a few timeless moments.

(1990)

Hearing

HEARING IS JOY and agony. Chronically strained, a musician's ears will be able to relax only in complete silence. (His inner hearing may pursue him even in his dreams.) To the hotel staff, he complains about the moaning of the elevator, the humming of the air conditioner or the vibrating of the generator in the courtyard. What the musician perceives can torment, and even traumatise him. The piercing outer voices in the balance of a colleague's playing, the now obligatory eruptions of extreme noise in theatre and film, the neighbours' electronically amplified celebrations, the horror of an increasingly louder world mired in violence and vulgarity, the principle purpose of which seems to be to damage our ears.

But what we hear can also delight us, if not lift us into a veritable state of bliss: the experience of musical cohesion, the equilibrium, energy and delicacy of a fine performance, the timbre of a cherished voice, the singing of birds, the encounter with a composition that opens new vistas, the purity of a chord in part-song.

Hearing has its own memory. It registers the dog whose sudden barking startled me as a child. The folk songs my nanny used to sing. The Dadaism of a cabaret song from Berlin: 'I tear out one of my eyelashes and stab you dead with it,' innocently sung by my mother. Hitler conjuring up the almighty. The crowing voice of little Goebbels. Alarm sirens, the roar of aircraft, the blast of bombs. Ljuba Welitsch being Salome. The sonorities of Edwin Fischer's piano playing. Maria Casares as Lady Macbeth in Avignon. Ralph Kirkpatrick's two Scarlatti recitals. Gré Brouwenstijn as Leonore in Fidelio. The epiphany of Ligeti's *Aventures et Nouvelles aventures*. The magic application of noise in Peter Brook's 'A Midsummer Night's Dream'. All sorts of laughter.

As a pianist I find it difficult to separate hearing and feeling (here to be understood as the sense of touch). Whenever I hear music there is for me, even when not personally involved, a three-dimensionality that distinguishes shapely performances from flat ones. The art historian Bernard Berenson has introduced 'tactile values' as a criterion in painting. Music as well, if I am allowed to believe my ears, is something palpable, and its sensuous manifestation is no less impressive than its compositorial shape and structure. But sensuality of sound needs to be linked to the other feeling, that of emotion. Without this connection, it would remain no more than a surface phenomenon.

Only the connection of notes generates music. But even a single tone can be significant. Depending on how short or long, dry or resonant, vehemently or tenderly it is played, we can already perceive it as characteristic. The expressive power of the single note is easily overlooked. Maybe it is here that an understanding of interpretation should start – unless you prefer to succumb to the Moog Synthesizer.

Music is spatial. Among the senses, it is hearing that is developed earliest in the mother's womb. In music as well, pulse is decisive. Music is surrounded by space that allows the sound to blossom, or suffocates it, but that can also expand into the open and infinite, liberating or threatening.

The musician wants to hear the silence. She is there before and after the sound, tacitly breathing in the rests, at times, as in Schubert's Sonata in B flat, the source of the beginning, elsewhere, as in Beethoven's last three Sonatas, the designation to be reached: as the withdrawal into an inner world, the throwing off of all chains, the ultimate merging with silence.

The musician on stage is a hearing conglomerate. He has to listen to himself, perceive what he plays, and react to it. At the same time, he has to anticipate his playing and overlook the complete piece. Simultaneously, he plays for the listeners in the tenth or twenty-third row, and listens, as it were, with their ears. He will also register disturbing noises – open coughing, compulsive clearing of throats, the whistling of a hearing aid, a mobile telephone – and decide whether and how to interfere. Finally, he asks himself whether the audience had lent him their multiple ear.

I hear myself. The public hears me. Do I hear the composer?

(2015)

On Some Performance Habits

WE ALL KNOW that a musical composition isn't present in the way a picture, a sculpture or a novel is present – it needs to be performed and listened to. In this, it resembles a work for the theatre, a play, a drama. My teacher Edwin Fischer coined an admirable formula for the task of the performer: Give life to the work without violating it. Now this should not suggest that the work on the page is still dead and needs the genius of the performer to rise from limbo. A leading musician of our day declared that 'the score is not the piece of music. A piece exists only when the score is turned into sound.' No, the life of a work is already to a large extent, if latently, encapsuled in the score. In the performance, this latent life should become manifest.

Let me give you an outline of some basic aspects of performance. Some of these aspects appear here like a head with two faces looking in opposite directions – which does not necessarily preclude mediating positions in between.

I shall start with the fact that a piece of music doesn't just consist of form and structure but also of character, atmosphere, 'psychology', 'expression' (as Rousseau called it) or 'the affections' (as C. P. E. Bach would have said). This is not an either/or situation but rather a constellation of non-identical twins. In a not fully analogous way, there is, in music, the allotment of intellect and feeling.

Secondly, one can illuminate a work from the outside or bring it to life from the inside. The first directs a spotlight on the work pointing out certain features, the second opens it up from within in several directions at once.

Thirdly, one can restrict oneself to playing 'only what is written', or rather aim to permanently deliver surprises. Here, we have two extremes. There have been prominent exponents of both.

Fourthly, the performer proceeds either historicising or modernising – to state extreme positions once more. We all have come across performers who, with greatly divergent results, have reached back into period performance practice. That, on the other hand, one's experience of contemporary music should influence the perception of past styles was the position of Schoenberg, Steuermann, Adorno, and even Bartók, as exemplified by his edition of Scarlatti sonatas.

The performer's starting point should never be the rigid and unduly simplifying dogmatism of certain textbooks written to pronounce the personal slant of their authors, and tied to a particular place and time. Let us rather be inspired by the variety and multiplicity of the masterpieces themselves, by the fact that each masterpiece, by my definition, adds something novel to musical experience, that each theme, each coherent musical idea is divergent from any other. Not just the similarities (which are more easily detected) but the features that are distinctive and unique deserve our attention.

The same applies to the technical side of performance: a few recipes and established habits will never be sufficient. In each single case we have to look for the precisely adequate technical solution. The pleasure of searching and learning never ends.

Of course, obsessive ideas are not the prerogative of our trade. May I remind you, in the field of medicine, of Linus Pauling's Vitamin C craze, of gulping up gallons of water, of the coercion towards knee surgery, or of the infinite benefits of hard beds. These days, performances sometimes sound as if a few keys of articulation should be able to unlock every eighteenth-century door. Here is a small list:

The habit of playing *diminuendo* in two-note groups, or repeated notes, or at ends of phrases, or over whole phrases;

stereotyped accentuation of so-called heavy beats;

the view that repeats invariably have to be played;

general rests as interruptions of the musical flow;

getting louder when the music goes up and softer when it goes down;

the short tearing-off or biting-off of end notes;

the vibrato-less start of a sustained note with later vibrating;

the automatic pointing-out of the outer voices in piano playing;

alla breve as an indication of double speed; and

the separation of the final chord by inserting a hiatus.

To deal with all these ideas a whole series of lectures would be necessary. Today, I want to start with the cherished habit of invariably playing or singing *diminuendo* on two-note groups, on short or longer phrases, repeated notes or endings, and take some time to pursue this phenomenon as it nowadays seems to be taken for granted in many quarters.

There is a story that tells about an inquisitive person visiting a historicising performer and musicologist in order to get some competent information about certain 'authentic' performance practices. After the delights of a carefully prepared dinner the visitor mentions the widely accepted habit of playing two-note groups by pointing out the first note more or less obtrusively while the second one is short and soft, sometimes bordering on the inaudible. Instead of the expected reference to Baroque treatises the expert pronounced: 'Well, somebody must have played and recorded it this way, and others heard and imitated it.' Immediately, one feels the urge to hurry to the expert's defence. Alas, the story is not fabricated. I witnessed it myself.

There are melodic, harmonic and psychological reasons that can speak against the *diminuendo* treatment of two-note groups – not to forget rhythm. I have heard the Andante theme of the slow movement of the Ninth Symphony played like this:

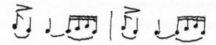

This *espressivo* theme does indeed include appoggiaturas. But they are connected to syncopations which, to my mind, embody the core of the *cantabile* of this theme, giving it ardent warmth, carrying on the singing line, as *cantabile* syncopation always should do.

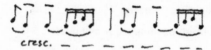

Please note that Beethoven, at each recurrence of this theme, started the crescendo marking underneath the first syncopated tone! Whoever dealt with Beethoven's autographs should know that he generally marks the beginning of a crescendo with great precision.

I have heard performances in which the incessant pointing-out of two-note groups seems to convey the message that the piece had been composed predominantly for that purpose. In an interpretation of the Allegretto from Beethoven's Seventh Symphony, conductor and orchestra never got tired of playing

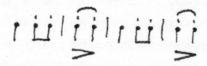

The forthcoming change of harmony alone should indicate that the two end-crotchets need the same weight throughout.

Besides psychological reasons there is also the musical structure that often enough contradicts *diminuendo* endings. What precedes endings of sections is usually, and particularly in Beethoven, a musical intensification, a telescoping or foreshortening of the musical material. A dynamic drop would suggest the picture of an increasingly taut balloon suddenly bereft of air. The impression is particularly painful when the vigour of an altogether powerful piece evaporates at its very end. With period performers, truly energetic endings have become rather a rarity.

There has been a time when Mozart had to be graceful and Beethoven heroic. It was Schumann's word of Mozart's 'floating Greek gracefulness' that seemed to articulate the distinguishing feature of Mozart's music for many. Even Busoni didn't grant Mozart a demonic side. I truly love Mozart's gracefulness – where the music is truly graceful. During the last decades some performers tried, and succeeded, to be as anti-graceful as possible. With *diminuendo* formulas like

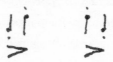

gracefulness returned through the back door. In a piece like the first movement of Mozart's C minor Concerto gracefulness has no place.

One deplorable habit is the cutting-off of end notes. Christian Morgenstern talked, in a grotesque poem, about a fence with spaces to peek through. Short-breathed fragmentation is detrimental to singing. That a long line necessarily thwarts musical declamation is simply not correct.

Here is a fitting pronouncement from Leopold Mozart's Violin School:

> A singer who would separate each little figure, breathe in, and stress this or that little note would cause irrepressible laughter. The human voice connects one note with the next in the most unforced way … And who doesn't know that vocal music should always be what every instrumentalist has to keep in view – because one needs, in all pieces, to come as close to being as natural as possible. One should therefore, where the singableness of a piece does not call for separations, aim to leave the bow on the violin in order to connect one bowing properly with the next. (V, 14)

The neat separation of longer phrases has often enough been counteracted by the great composers themselves. Notably in Beethoven we frequently discover phrases the last note or chord of which already coincide with the start of a new one.

The idea that a phrase invariably has to have the shape of an arch leading to a soft conclusion is another simplification; in my younger years I adhered to it myself. There are phrases that have to begin with a clear onset – though not all of them as has been claimed in the Baroque – and those that lead to the last note as its goal. There are also phrases which have to carry on into the next one.

Diminuendos are particularly disturbing where musical contrasts have to remain contrasts. In a recording of an orchestral rehearsal by a noted post-war conductor you can hear him insisting, with his high tenor voice, on so-called terrace dynamics. Contrary to such rigour, there are musicians today who feel the compulsion to round out everything and insist on mediating between sections that must stand apart.

There are also those phrases that increase dynamically right up to the end. In the second movement of Beethoven's Op. 109 such crescendi are clearly indicated. Beethoven's *subito piano* would lose its meaning if the tension of the crescendo is not sustained to the last. In its recordings of the early '30s , the Busch Quartet has demonstrated beautifully how such sudden switches, as for instance in the first movement of Beethoven's Quartet Op. 132, should be executed.

'Firm rules' merit to be called into question. We are told by some that in the performance of pre-nineteenth-century music, sustained long notes should gradually decrease, while others swell them out in the middle, and yet others advocate a soft onset with belated vibrato. Why should we yield to one concept above another when there has been such a variety of instruments, including the human voice? An organ, an oboe, a harpsichord produce long notes quite differently, not to speak of singers or string players with their manifold possibilities of modifying sound and dynamics.

'Music before 1800 speaks, music after 1800 paints.' When I read this pronouncement I immediately want to ask: And where does that leave singing? As a pianist, I feel particularly keen to come to its defence. The piano can sing, even if not everyone seems to be aware of it. Bach, in his preface to his Two-Part Inventions and Three-Part Sinfonies, explicitly calls them pieces for the instruction of *cantabile* playing. Some period performers have done away with *cantabile* to the best of their abilities. In my own musical understanding, however, singing remains, at least before the twentieth century, at the heart of music. (There is another view of music that claims that all music is dance. What a treat to hear a *Miserere* or *Agnus Dei* skip along.)

There is variety in beginnings and endings, in *staccato* and *legato*, trills and arpeggios. Talking about trills, there are players who execute each trill as if ringing the same doorbell. Trills can be played faster or slower, consistent or varying in their speeds, with or without onset or suffix, brilliantly or pensively, sensuously or mechanically. Trills and other ornaments should fit into their emotional environment. They are frequently not what Ernst Gombrich thought they were in his book on *The Sense of Order*, namely something attached to the melodic line on the surface, but rather, particularly with Beethoven, an agent of expression integrated into the music – if not the end of a process of structural foreshortening. Trills can be intensely expressive! At the outset of Beethoven's so-called 'Appassionata', they immediately denote a high degree of inner tension. Within the Adagio of Op. 111, on the other hand, trills twice appear as the outcome of rhythmic foreshortening, first at the focal point of mystical experience, transporting us into E flat major, and ultimately as an utmost manifestation of rhythmical density, elevated high up in the air. In these arguably most beautiful and moving of all trills, even the last remnants of the ornamental have vanished. These trills are at once structurally motivated and deeply emotional.

Once more, the guiding concept for our dealings with ornaments and embellishments should be variety. While C. P. E. Bach still considered the addition of embellishments to be a crucial part of the art of performance, the same could hardly be said of Haydn. And Mozart's first great masterpiece, his Piano Concerto K 271, is written out to the last detail. But some of his later autographs which are not finished for the engraver frequently include passages that need fill-ins, as well as themes that may be embellished at their returns. Beethoven decisively spoke out against additions to his scores. His notation is more literal and modern than that of Salieri's pupil Schubert, and even of Chopin. Where Mozart's works need additions and elaborations the master himself is our only trustworthy model. J. N. Hummel spent a couple of years in Mozart's house as a child; however, his elaborations of some of Mozart's slow movements are not an echo of Mozart but an excrescence. In his chamber music arrangements of Mozart Concertos, Hummel ruthlessly interfered with the structure of the works, and administered cuts. No less distant from Mozart's style are Ph. K. Hoffmann's adornments.

Performance practices can sometimes change, as it were, overnight. If you travel across southern Germany looking at architecture you will notice how rapidly Neoclassicism succeeded late Baroque and Rococo around 1790. It seems, however, more probable that, for a while, different possibilities will coexist next to one another. In his Piano School (Klavierschule) of 1822 Hummel, the leading piano virtuoso of his day, sanctioned the start of trills with the main note and requested a suffix for every true trill! In a recent edition of Beethoven's Piano Sonatas, the editor explains that Beethoven wrote suffixes down only where he really wanted them. A glance at the fugue of the 'Hammerklavier' Sonata tells us a different story. In its exposition the suffixes are written out in the theme but later on only sporadically, and then usually where the notation of accidentals is necessary. Of the six trills right before the final chords only the third and sixth have received suffixes because they required accidentals. It goes without saying that suffixes need to be played in all six.

Staccato can indicate many different ways of separating notes. In each individual case, the length, the kind of touch or bowing have to be determined. The use of pedal is not necessarily excluded: short notes, played into the pedal, sound different from long ones. Schubert writes repeatedly '*sempre ligato*' over passages that contain *staccato* notes (Impromptu D 935/1), and where he obviously means continuous *cantabile* – one more example for the fact that the most beautiful declamatory singing line is often not produced by finger *legato*. Continuous finger *legato* doesn't speak. Listen to Schubert's Impromptu in G flat. Here it is mainly the fifth finger that produces the suggestion of singing, of course with the help of the wonderful accompanying voices and the aura of the pedal. In Schumann's F sharp Romance the *cantabile* is produced by the thumbs.

Distinct declamation is, of course, also a matter of tempo and rhythm. In Wagner's musical dramas, one should be able to understand the words. This will not only depend on the diction of the singers but on the choice of tempi as well. The fugue of Beethoven's Op. 106 should, to a discerning listener, still remain intelligible as a piece of music. It is, by the way, considerably harder to play if the tempo is slightly more moderate yet firm. Beethoven's own indication of $\downarrow$ = 144 results in ten minutes of a turbulence which soon becomes tiring to listen to. Sustaining a fast pulse in eighth notes will prevent the player from getting caught in a torrent, and enable the listener to take in the main changes of harmony. That the piece should play the player is a neat ideal – which, however, should not result in a loss of control.

Fermatas lead out of strictness. I do not believe that they always require the double length of the rhythm's duration, or that they ought to be 'counted' at all.

Sometimes a small halt will do, as in the finale of Beethoven's Eroica Symphony or in his Eroica Variations Op. 35. In Liszt, fermatas may even shorten a bar. The fermatas in the Adagio of Schubert's C minor Sonata on the other hand, call, to my feeling, for an approximately threefold prolongation of the chord. The duration of fermatas will depend on their emotional significance. If fermatas are an interruption of the musical flow, the tension of the music must still carry on. That general rests should be prolonged even without fermatas as a matter of course I consider to be nonsense. Such rests must not be holes punched into the sound but places where the music holds its breath or gets a chance to breathe in. The music stops abruptly before presenting something surprisingly new or it may give the onset of the continuation a little break. The tension has to remain tangible. One floats through the air before touching the ground over there, or one dives and surfaces on the other side. Much depends on how the conductor or pianist handles such rests visually.

Let me add a word about piano sound and balance. The best model for the player's sound is the balance of an excellent orchestra under an experienced conductor. The first violins must not be understaffed, cellos and double-basses should not sound as if being positioned in front of the stage, woodwinds and brass must not get unduly prominent, and the timpani not perforate the ear. What we sometimes hear, particularly from younger players, is a pointing-out of the outer voices, and especially of the bass line due to a rigidly adjusted little finger. The idea that, in older music, the upper voice and the bass (as the fundament of harmony) are of primary importance may be intellectually unassailable. In practice, though, the player should underline the bass only when it has something special to say. Octaves in the left hand merit particular care – in *forte* playing, they may easily drown out the rest.

Once in a while we find ourselves, during a performance, in the innermost core of a secret. In Furtwängler's great recording of the 'Unfinished Symphony' with the Vienna Philharmonic, the cello section plays the second theme on one dynamic level in ravishing *pp*, without what is called declamation, controlled yet unselfconscious, removed from the constraints of time and breathing. No declamation could produce such mesmerising stillness within singing. The performer has disappeared behind the music.

(2015)

Music Life in Flux

HOW DID THE musical repertoire, and musical perception, change during my lifetime? Here are a few observations.

Most importantly, 'Modern Music' needed after World War Two to be resuscitated, if not altogether discovered. When I lived in Vienna in the '50s and '60s the city was musically dominated by Neoclassicism and Neo-Baroque. Stravinsky had switched to an eclectic line, and Hindemith as well as the Swiss patron of contemporary composers, Paul Sacher, appeared as guest conductors. For some time, this prevented the appreciation of Schoenberg and his school. The early post-war years of the Salzburg Festival similarly remained, with composers like Carl Orff and Frank Martin, in moderate territory. With the Vienna Symphony and the young conductor Michael Gielen I went to Warsaw in 1966 where the first international festival of contemporary music behind the Iron Curtain had invited us to perform Schoenberg's Piano Concerto. Urged by the public we had to repeat the last movement. Nadia Boulanger, the teacher of a number of Polish composers, sat sulking on the balcony; her idol Stravinsky hadn't yet discovered the Second Viennese School. Subsequently, I introduced Schoenberg's Op. 42 on three continents. The readiness and ability of orchestras to do justice to this piece have meanwhile improved to a staggering degree.

A principle catalyst of contemporary music was, of course, Pierre Boulez. His founding of the ensemble 'Domaine Musicale' in 1954, his work at IRCAM in Paris as well as his activity as chief conductor of the BBC Orchestra in London and the New York Philharmonic gave the modern repertory purpose and direction. It had been Sir William Glock who had called Boulez to London. A pupil of Schnabel, Glock wielded his wide and beneficial influence as Controller of Music of the BBC's Third Programme and as organiser of the Promenade Concerts. Under his guidance, English music life shed its insularity, and the radiance of both institutions turned London into a musical metropolis of international importance.

Later on in Salzburg, personalities like Hans Landesmann, Gerard Mortier, Peter Ruzicka and Markus Hinterhäuser vigorously promoted new music, giving it lustre as well as gravity.

By mounting a complete performance of Mahler's symphonies and song cycles in 1960, Vienna had attempted to follow the footsteps of the legendary 1920 Mahler

Festival in Amsterdam, albeit without the presence of a conductor of Willem Mengelberg's stature. As it happened, Mahler's symphonies soon started to be programmed internationally with an emphasis that lent this music special importance. While Beethoven symphonies had hitherto served as the touchstone of orchestral playing, it appeared now that, thanks to the ambition of many younger conductors, Mahler had taken his place. Meanwhile, decades after the great old Beethoven exponents had passed away, Beethoven's orchestral music has returned to its central position, whether *molto con brio* or *con somma espressione*.

Parallel to the approval of Mahler's musical spaciousness, Schubert's piano sonatas caught the attention of pianists and the public. Old prejudices gradually evaporated. What before had seemed sprawling and aimless could now be accepted as an asset and necessity. The assumption that Schubert, who had not been a virtuoso player himself, did not create an innovative pianistic style was refuted once and for all. In a few countries like Russia, however, a wider appreciation of Schubert is still pending.

Another composer who benefited from this expansion of musical tolerance was Bruckner. So far, his symphonies had been mainly the privilege of German-speaking countries tied to an orchestral sound that was specifically middle-European. It seemed hardly foreseeable that after the exit of Furtwängler, Jochum, Klemperer, Knappertsbusch, Celibidache or Günter Wand this music would be blessed with a new, international lease of life. Bruckner is now promoted worldwide by orchestras and younger conductors. And who would have imagined that protagonists of new music like Boulez, Gielen, and Zender would warm to these amazing works? It was a lovely surprise that they can be played without imagining the Vienna woods and the incense of Catholic mysticism.

Changes also occurred in the reception of Liszt and the presentation of Chopin. The distorted picture fuelled by Ernest Newman's malicious 'The Man Liszt' was thankfully set right; what now became visible is the figure of a singularly magnanimous personality, a 'genius of expression' (Schumann), a human being that not only played the piano incomparably, smoked cigars, consumed cognac, prayed, and gave ladies a good time, but also supported his colleagues in the noblest way, coached pianists without remuneration and neglected the promotion of his own compositions in favour of helping others, notably Wagner. Gratifyingly, the appreciation of the finest of his own works, including the late ones, has considerably risen.

While to be called a 'Liszt player' fifty years ago amounted to a put-down, the

Chopin specialist, much esteemed over several generations, has ceased to exist. In the past, such specialisation was deemed to be justified, and not for nothing. Did Chopin's music not absorb the player like no other? Independent as it was from the discipline of ensemble playing, Chopin's own style of performance must have been highly idiosyncratic, little wonder as he was unique among the greatest piano composers in hardly writing ensemble or vocal music. True, young Schumann or Liszt didn't do it either; however, they already liked to treat the piano orchestrally. After the death of the last of great Chopin players, Alfred Cortot, such awareness of Chopin's single-mindedness got lost. By now, Chopin has been swallowed up by the musical mainstream.

A special, and significant chapter constituted the practice of 'Old Music'. The virtuosity achieved by now in the playing of historic instruments and the jettisoning of some nineteenth-century habits generated unfamiliar results. While only decades ago the performance of Gesualdo's Madrigals strained technical possibilities to the limit, their bewildering chromaticism is beautifully rendered by present-day singers. Here, British choirs provided the yardstick. It was thanks to the use of original instruments and the application of 'authentic' practices that a master like Monteverdi truly came to light. The desire to return to the musical outlook of Baroque and Renaissance, however, led to very different conclusions. Dogmatic insistence on a few, exaggeratedly presented rules of performance as well as the seduction of overly brisk tempos tended, at times, to obstruct an awareness of the expressive range that masterpieces exhibit.

On the other hand, the gain was overwhelming, and particularly so in the playing and singing of Handel. To me, the fact that so many of his works were now expertly resurrected was a gift of special magnificence. For all too long, Handel had only been granted scant attention next to Bach, and his operas were considered dramatically unfit for contemporary ears and minds. What melodic power, what generosity of musical breadth but also what a genius of characterisation can be discerned in this composer whom Beethoven admired above all! The one-dimensional Handel of yesterday has been replaced by a figure whose dramatic compass reaches all the way from the tragedy of *Hercules* to the comedy of *Xerxes*. The emergence of a cornucopia of singers who excel in the mastering of coloratura while simultaneously igniting a musical fire was a precondition for the new Handel boom. Among the obstetricians of his art we should also include some practitioners of the current vogue of 'Directors' Theatre' (*Regietheater*), whose manner of staging I have frequently disagreed with but which, in Handel's operas, seized a fitting field of activity. It is an achievement of present-day musical theatre that our successors of primadonnas and castratos have acquired the skill of moving their bodies with the greatest adroitness, a faculty that should not come amiss in the staging of Purcell and Rameau.

In terms of keyboard music the situation is somewhat different. Thanks to two of Ralph Kirkpatrick's recitals I had the good fortune to hear, I clearly prefer Domenico Scarlatti's sonatas played on the harpsichord. On the other hand, I never saw the point of restricting Bach to this instrument, his own keyboard music being so hugely diverse. Also, his propensity for adapting pieces from, and for, different instruments should be known well enough. After decades that kept Bach players off the modern piano – unless the name happened to be Glenn Gould – it is reassuring to see that the composer of *The Well-Tempered Clavier* and the Goldberg Variations has, once more, found a home on our concert grands.

Our picture of Haydn, as well, is in the process of disposing of its nineteenth-century varnish. The always-welcome friend of the house who has nothing new to tell (Schumann), the man who was still mainly seen as a stepping stone for Mozart and Beethoven by Hanslick or Adorno, is giving way to the figure of an explorer and adventurer, a grandmaster of surprise, a creator of his own musical universe who introduced the comical into absolute music. For his string quartets alone he should deserve to be called one of the supreme masters. The performance of all six of his Quartets Op. 76 in one evening by the Tokyo Quartet counts among the pinnacles of my listening life.

This leads me to the mushrooming of cyclical performances. Cycles of all of Beethoven's Piano Sonatas, in the past rather an exception, have become everyday events. The distribution of series of works by one composer that had been promoted in boxes by some record companies served as a contributing factor. The task to cope with thirty-two markedly different works has proved, for players and listeners, to have a pull of its own, signifying a joint effort, a journey at the end of which an inner destination is reached. Beethoven's 33 Variations on a Waltz by Diabelli are a cycle of a different kind. Compressed into the duration of slightly less than an hour, this towering work has only belatedly been accepted and celebrated as a concert piece. It is encouraging that the public of our day is willing to summon the concentration to listen to it.

Another beneficiary from this inclination towards completeness was Schubert with his piano works. The compositions of the last seven years, 1822–28, in particular have turned into a beloved feature of the repertoire.

Among the most outstanding achievements of cyclical presentation must count the performance of the entire Bach Cantatas. In roughly a hundred concerts, grouped according to themes, and in chronological order, more than 200 works were played in Milan's churches to great acclaim by leading international ensembles. At the same time, the series offered a survey of the diversity of current Bach interpretation.

A protuberance of such serial endeavours is the so-called marathon. There have been attempts of feeding the listener all Beethoven's Symphonies and Piano Sonatas in one go, played or conducted by one single musician. (In the case of the conductor, three different orchestras were used.) In spite of canapés served during the intervals they have so far remained rarities. Let us hope for their complete extinction.

(2010)

Audacious Chamber Music I

SCHUBERT'S STRING QUARTET IN G MAJOR

WHAT ARE THE origins of the string quartet? We owe the genre, as we know it today, to an easily undervalued composer – Joseph Haydn. Indeed, one can say without exaggeration that the string quartet, one of the most precious musical forms, was his creation. There had already been divertimenti, cassations and serenades, and during the eighteenth century instrumental music gradually surpassed vocal music in esteem. But only thanks to Haydn did the form and style of the string quartet become established since 1750. The private character of music-making, the soloistic rendering of the instruments and the abandonment of continuo playing now enabled a discourse of four individual players.

Haydn's fifty-year-long involvement with the string quartet opened up a new musical world. The fact that the creator of a genre emerged as its pre-eminent figure reminds us of Schubert, who remained the supreme exponent of the Lied, the art song, that he himself had initiated.

Beethoven's Op. 18, his first quartet series that was much admired by Schubert, demonstrated the exceptional case of a young composer who immediately succeeds the master at a comparable level. While Beethoven had gradually found his way towards the quartet via sonatas and trios, Schubert wrote quartets for domestic use right away but also enlisted quartet writing to express orchestral ideas. Perhaps because of his connection with the orchestra of the Imperial Boarding School in Vienna, his compositions show a proclivity toward orchestral writing that would also include the later piano works, most strikingly the Wanderer Fantasy. Within the quartets, the orchestra is hinted at through passages played in unison, double stops, and tremolo. Preceding his late quartets were other superlative chamber music works like the Octet, the two Piano Trios and the Quartettsatz from 1822, while the great String Quintet was written at the end of his life.

Beethoven's and Schubert's quartets face each other well nigh independently. Both look far into the future. It seems to me that only the twentieth century would build on their audacity, with the quartets of Mendelssohn, Schumann and Brahms remaining in a kind of parenthesis.

In contrast to Beethoven the architect, I have called Schubert a sleepwalker. Let me explain this. In Beethoven's forms we never lose out orientation. His music, in a series of foreshortenings and intensification processes, always propels forward. There is a sentence by Goethe which admirably summarises his personal impression of Beethoven: 'More concentrated, energetic, and affectionate I have never seen an artist.' These qualities give a clue to Beethoven's music as well. Next to Beethoven's concentration, Schubert appears as a musician who lets himself be transported, just a hair's breadth from the abyss, not so much mastering life as being at its mercy. His somnambulist style of working is borne out by the fact that, in a life of less than thirty-two years, he was able to produce nearly a thousand works. Which is not to say that he composed uncritically. Nevertheless, in regard to Schubert, I feel closer to the Kantian view that the creator of a product of genius doesn't know himself how his ideas are generated, and that to generate them at will is beyond his powers.

Schubert may be the most immediately moving among composers. But be forewarned about the bias that, in Schubert, everything is a matter of feeling or, as people used to put it, of the heart. There is such a thing as an autonomous musical intelligence. But there was also, simultaneously, the ability of consciously planning novel forms, as in the Wanderer Fantasy and the four-hand Fantasy in F minor.

The composition of Schubert's three great quartets in A minor, D minor and G major had obviously been stimulated by the return of the violinist Ignaz Schuppanzigh after years of living abroad. Before the burning down of the Palais Rasumofsky, Schuppanzigh and his string quartet, which was sponsored by Rasumofsky, had been the leading interpreters of Beethoven. Whereas Schubert's early quartets were written for amateurs, and not infrequently played by Schubert's own family, Schuppanzigh, with his professional players and his own series of subscription concerts, offered the possibility of placing demands on the musicians that went above the domestic level. Schubert was a subscriber to this concert series. The A minor Quartet, the first one of the late string quartets, is dedicated to Schuppanzigh, who premiered it in 1823. For the subsequent D minor Quartet 'The Death and the Maiden', he had no use.

In 1850, the Viennese Hellmesberger Quartet performed Schubert's Quartet in G Major. A year later, it finally appeared in print.

Movements of a macabre character – veritable dances of death – are a Schubert hallmark. We find them in the D minor Quartet as well as in two of the piano sonatas.

In the G major Quartet the finale is eerie in a somewhat different way. The movement is actually in a major key but constantly attacked by the minor – for instance by a piercingly accented minor note in the initial theme.

Has there ever been another composer who had such an unmediated relationship to major and minor? More often than not, minor seems to represent here the world's reality, while major suggests a yearned-for happiness or even a sweet and comfort-bringing death. Already the very beginning of the G major Quartet confronts us with the juxtaposition of major and minor. This conflict remains one of the most glaring features of the piece. In the recapitulation we experience the opposite: first minor, then major (I 278–88). The energy of the movement's start is now attenuated – the theme sounds as if it had aged. Walter Frisch called this change one of the most radical in all music. At the movement's end the battle is just barely won by G major.

We can see Schubert as lyricist, epic poet, and dramatist – the latter being far more persuasive in his instrumental music than in opera or Singspiel. I would now like to add the expressionist: In the slow movement of the G major Quartet (II 43–60), as in the Andantino of the great A major Sonata, conscience becomes shattered. The outcry of the notes G and B recalls the beginning of the work. Both of these notes remain unchanged even if the harmonies do in fact change.

Another feature of the G major Quartet is the use of a wide variety of note repetitions and tremolos. They are a token of inner unrest that can lead to delirium. Dieter Schnebel even talks about 'the secret material of the entire work'. It would appear as if Schubert wanted to demonstrate the wealth of things that can be done with repeated notes. Tremolos, for example, have the capacity of electrifying and galvanising chords, as in the double theme of the first movement. Tone repetitions of a thematic and motivic kind are to be heard in the third and fourth movement. Here every single note counts.

With its tremolos, the G major Quartet links up with the Quartettsatz of 1822.

The first movement is marked *Allegro molto moderato*. The *moderato* refers to the tempo and not to the temperament – in this movement extreme intellectual and emotional tensions counterbalance each other. It starts with a strongly contrasting double theme: first major-minor, then a premonition of Bruckner. Later, a third, dancing theme is added which leads to a whole series of varied repetitions. Carl Dahlhaus speaks of a sonata form approaching a cycle of variations.

At the beginning of the development, tremolos of the cello move in harmonic no man's land (I 168–80). In the descent of this bassline we can notice the whole-tone scale providing its principal notes, a striking novelty in Schubert's time. Within the recapitulation, contrary to Schubert's custom, hardly anything is repeated verbatim. Even performance markings are varied and legato and staccato modified when themes and their variations are re-introduced.

The basic character of the second movement (*Andante poco mosso*) is lyrical. The cello has wonderful things to tell. On the other hand, the various episodes of this rondo fill us, as we already know, with dread. Out of the hopelessness of its conclusion, the last four bars lead unexpectedly to a kind of redemption. It affects us like a miracle – providing that the first violin is capable of making it happen.

What follows is a spectral scherzo in A minor with the most loving and tender lullaby as its trio.

The dancing finale, *Allegro assai*, is of a grotesque and sinister gaiety. It contains a melody in C sharp minor that appears in pianississimo like a phantom (IV 320–39). Beethoven as well has composed passages where he surprises the listener by fiat, as it were. In his Fourth Piano Concerto there are no less than three such episodes in the first movement: brief, unique glimpses into another sphere.

Before the finale's conclusion, there is a startling intensification over almost twenty bars that carries us from piano to triple forte, an intensification that is constantly widening as treble and bass move away from one another in contrary motion.

Only belatedly has the greatness of the G major Quartet been recognised. Even Joseph Joachim, the supreme violinist, said as late as 1860 that, although he loved individual sections, he found the work 'immoderate and without feeling for beauty in its contrasts'. Since the twentieth century, at the very latest, Beethoven's and Schubert's quartets have been listened to with different ears. Seeming boundlessness set new boundaries.

There is a memorable phrase from Friedrich Krummacher, a string quartet initiate, that encompasses Schubert's late chamber music: Perfection in antithesis.

(2015)

Audacious Chamber Music II

BEETHOVEN COMPOSED HIS late string quartets within a period of two-and-a-half years. Roughly during the same timespan Schubert, whose 'unbelievably great originality next to a crushing presence like Beethoven' so deeply impressed Arnold Schoenberg, wrote his last three quartets. Independently of one another if not in contradiction, works of the highest quality emerged, the significance of which only became apparent in the twentieth century. Reportedly, it was Schubert's last musical wish to hear a performance of Beethoven's Quartet in C sharp minor, Op. 131. It seems to have been granted to him five days before he died.

In the introduction to an older edition of Beethoven's late quartets we read:

> This music is so completely dissociated from all that is material, so thoroughly the expression of a spirit governing beyond all earthly matters that it well nigh reaches the borders of music itself; [it is] music that could perhaps only have been written by some- one who, like Beethoven, ceased to be 'of this world'... alone with himself and God.

Let us discount such projections and try to summarise Beethoven's late style more concretely. To start with, there is an expansion and synthesis of musical resources. Contrasting elements collide and merge: naïvety and complexity, intricacy and apparent artlessness, abruptness and lyricism, the sublime and the profane, solemnity and comedy, musical past as much as musical present and future. There is the dancing of children and peasants. There is instrumental singing in the Cavatina of Op. 130 as well as in the Arioso dolente of the Sonata Op. 110 and the Arietta of Op. 111. We find canon, chorale and recitatif. We find church modes and, in many of the late works, fugues and fugatos. The polyphony of Beethoven's part-writing does not shy away from clashes of dissonance and false relations. At the same time, we notice, and do so particularly in Op. 130, Beethoven's striving for immediacy.

The advent of Beethoven's late style in his Piano-Cello Sonatas Op. 102 strikes us notwithstanding all premonitions in the Fantasy Sonatas Op. 27, in the F minor Quartet, or the song cycle 'An die ferne Geliebte', with an almost shocking force. Large-scale works – Ninth and *Missa solemnis*, the last five piano sonatas and the

Diabelli Variations – then precede the final quartets. But there were also the Six Bagatelles Op. 126; Beethoven himself called them a 'Ciklus' which reminds us of the cyclical arrangement of six movements in Op. 130. Only the final Quartet Op. 135 pursues the classical sonata pattern once more.

In the late quartets, the motive G sharp/A/F/E and its variants create evident connections. Schubert had composed his *Wanderer* Fantasy in 1822, the four sections of which are joined by one single short motif, while Berlioz's *Symphonie Fantastique* with its *idée fixe* was composed only a few years later. Similarly, in his 'Grosse Fuge' Beethoven linked its several sections with the help of one principal theme and its modifications. The staggering boldness of this work has hardly ever been surpassed; for a century, it was held in disfavour. Schindler called it the relic of a manner of mathematical composition that belonged to the past, and the great violinist Joseph Joachim had no use for it in his cycles of Beethoven quartets. It needed twentieth-century ears and minds to bring about an understanding of this work. For Stravinsky, it was 'the most perfect miracle of music'.

Beethoven had added the words '*tantôt libre, tantôt recherché*' to the title of the first print. According to Joseph Kerman, a leading expert on Beethoven's quartets, it should better read '*plutôt libre que recherché*' owing to the fact that the work is by no means a continuous fugue. The actual fugues within the piece are in B flat and A flat; they persist in *fortissimo*, and demand unusual stamina from players and listeners alike. The work begins with an highly unusual introduction called 'Overtura' that presents, in the way of an index, the four manifestations of the principal theme, each a fifth apart and different in character. Ahead of the end, there is again a similar survey of the characters but now in the basic tonality B flat. The B flat double fugue following the Overtura introduces a new idea in *fortissimo*, with the principal theme of the whole work serving as a syncopated counterpoint. The striking interval of this new theme, the tenth, had been featured by Beethoven before in another major B flat work, the 'Hammerklavier' Sonata Op. 106. There, the subject of the fugue starts with leaps of a tenth while, at the beginning of the first movement, the tenth is supplemented by the twelfth. But already in his first piano trio Op. 1 leaps of the tenth distinguish one of Beethoven's wittiest movements.

Whereas his dynamic markings in the 'Grosse Fuge' are largely confined to spells of *fortissimo* and *pianissimo* they are elsewhere remarkably detailed. One can only marvel at the sophisticated precision the stone-deaf Beethoven was able to muster in imagining the execution of these works. In his fugues, though, the addition of a few markings will prevent, or at least mitigate, monotony over large areas. For the extended *ff* sections, the question will also arise about the character they are supposed to relate. Is it a desperate exertion conveyed with cruel obstinacy, or rather a display of warmth, luminosity and, where the music calls for it, gracefulness and wit? Should the piece produce angry noises or sounds of ecstasy? For the ending as well, there is a choice between frenzied self-immolation and hymnic relief.

The correlation of movements in this quartet has remained a puzzle. Should one see the whole work (and Beethoven's late quartets in general) as being under the spell of romantic aesthetics? At the time, Friedrich Schlegel, the German romantic writer, presented fifteen lectures to the Viennese in which he explained his ideas dominated by imagination, whim and irony.

It is possible to envisage the fugue from the point of view of the first movement, or look back at the preceding movements from the fugue. One can see the fugue as a monumental and oversized event that has merited a separate place or rather as something that was missing in the other movements of Op. 130, and finally provided. One can interpret the new supplementary finale as an attempt to undo the tensions of the quartet in a jocular way. It may however be that Beethoven who lived in constant need of, and anxiety about, money produced the piece willingly because he had been promised an additional sum of fifteen ducats. In a number of letters, it is clearly affirmed that Beethoven was pleased with the result.

When he wrote it down in 1826 he was in severe emotional distress. His nephew Karl, to whom he was desperately attached, attempted suicide, and his own health was shattered. The new finale proves once again that composers are able to write music that is light and cheerful when in dire straits, or even facing death. A work comparable in key and character is the finale of Schubert's sonata in B flat, which along with his *Shepherd on the Rock* can serve as a further example of the fact that the person of an artist and his art should not be taken as an equation.

Beethoven insisted on producing a four-hand piano version of 'Grosse Fuge' himself. Unfortunately he didn't bother to take into account its playability and left crossings of the inner voices unarranged.

To deal with a late Beethoven quartet invariably amounts to a voyage of discovery – in spite of George Bernard Shaw who famously declared that the late quartets were simple, unpretentious and thoroughly accessible. He also wrote about Schubert's

Great C major Symphony that it was one of the most provocatively brainless compositions ever penned on paper. Rossini would have been able to do it better in half the space. While the other four quartets convey a remarkably strong feeling of coherence, Op. 130 is more loosely knit. It recalls Beethoven's 'Sonata quasi una fantasia' Op. 27, No. 1 where the succession of the movement is surprising, and almost dreamlike.

The first movement is an Allegro with a lyrical Adagio introduction fragments of which return later. I have sometimes heard it played all too slowly and with exaggerated expression. Next is a Presto that is short, bold and burlesque. The third movement, the first of two slow movements of this quartet, keeps the players in a precarious balance between lyricism and comedy. Its beginning bears the indications 'Poco scherzoso' but also 'Andante con moto, ma non troppo'. Obviously, Beethoven deemed it important to encircle the character precisely.

After this movement's key of D flat major the far removed one of G major sounds abrupt and unusual. This 'a la tedesca, Allegro assai' movement belongs to a family of pieces that refine the rural character without losing it. It leads to the core of the work, the Cavatina (Adagio molto espressivo) the prevailing colour of which is *sotto voce*. Here, the first violin, intermittently partnered by the second, has the chance of telling itself a secret. According to Beethoven it was the Cavatina among all his compositions that moved him most. We can sense that in those uncanny bars marked '*beklemmt*' (stifled) which interrupt the cantilena and suspend time the music is, as it were, barely suppressing tears.

For the end, the performers are allowed to choose between the light-minded finale and the elemental event of 'Grosse Fuge' – the 'very great fugue', as Stravinsky called it. What an odd constellation to be confronted with such a choice! For anyone who seeks to establish every single note that Beethoven wrote as being 'organic', here is a good opportunity to think again.

(2015)

Children's Orchestra

A TEN-YEAR-OLD DRAWS ALL gazes upon himself. Small and handsome, he sits at the first desk of the cello section right next to the conductor and hardly looks at the music, obviously mesmerised by Sir Simon Rattle who instils into him and the others Mahler's First Symphony. The orchestra, consisting exclusively of children from nine to thirteen, comes from Venezuela. Brilliantly prepared, as well as inspired to the last detail by the evening's conductor, it gave one of the most affecting performances I have witnessed in Salzburg in half a century. I had listened to other more adult ensembles of this Venezuelan enterprise in which the superabundance of players who were allowed to participate did not always result in the most gratifying sound. It was the youngest generation of 'El Sistema', the officially sanctioned scheme of musical education, that made an indelible mark.

The 'National Children's Orchestra of Venezuela' seems to operate without any freelance substitutes or senior players. But these youngsters did not play like beginners or amateurs. A combination of freshness, concentration and devotion lent the performance an air of professionalism. The TV recording of the Austrian Radio made it possible to verify this; it constantly showed players from all orchestral departments. I found it profoundly moving to be able to witness their faces and bodies.

The folkloristic elements, comprising *Wunderhorn* and *shtetl*, of the Symphony's themes clearly appealed to these young players. During dance-rhythms, their bodies started to sway; but they also proved capable of executing proper tempo modifications. Rattle's skill in dealing with children is well known from his work in Berlin. The orchestra followed him enraptured. What he communicates is not merely the large overview but also the particular within the whole. Differently to some of his colleagues, Rattle does not simply beat time: he conducts character, colour and atmosphere to an extent few have been able to convey since Carlos Kleiber.

At the end, the players joined in the ovation. Rattle hugged the little cellist and lifted him up – something that corresponded precisely with what we all felt.

Music education is, in many countries, sadly neglected. What 'El Sistema' has achieved in Venezuela since 1975 is now widely seen as a model and emulated in various places. But the benefit of mobilising children to make music together did also have a remarkable social impact, particularly in a country where large parts of the population live in extreme poverty. Children now join forces in doing something that lifts them above the daily round and prevents them from succumbing to juvenile delinquency, violence and drugs. Has the power of music ever generated such comprehensive social benefit? Dr Abreu, the founder of 'El Sistema', has stressed that he aims to bring about better human beings, not just better musicians. How does one get to be a better person? Possibly, by becoming aware of each other, listening to each other and, in doing so, finding a higher purpose.

José Antonio Abreu, the mentor and veritable soul of 'El Sistema' has been one of the few who, with the help of tenacity and luck, were able to realise a dream. Economist as well as musician, he also served in elevated political positions as that of a minister of culture. Thanks to the government of President Chávez he was readily assisted on the highest level. These days in Venezuela, there seem to be more than 280 music schools and about 1000 instrumental and vocal groups. An altruistic concept was aligned with political ambition. The cultural politics of Venezuela have something to offer that the world admires.

My own development was that of a sceptical individualist who, from early on, saw it necessary to find out things for himself. As a child, I had witnessed fascists, Nazis, Ustashi, SA and SS, the babble of blood and soil, and the chaos of the last years of war. Consequently, I became suspicious of all crowds, found 'community' painful and nationalism abhorrent. To my best ability I have avoided groups, clans and organised institutions whether religious or dogmatic. From my sceptical corner, I look at the Venezuelan miracle with amazement. The concert crowd is the only one I have made my peace with as long as it refrains from coughing. May I dare to hope that in the wake of their triumphs the young Latin-American musicians shall not get consumed by musical and political chauvinism, and that their early professionalism will lead to an adulthood that gives individuality its due.

(2013)

Farewell to the Concert Stage

LOOKING BACK, I ask myself: What is it that makes it possible for a performer to face such a life?

There is, firstly, the triad of talent, constitution and luck. But there is much that needs to be added: self-confidence and self-criticism, ambition and patience, perseverance without fanaticism, good memory, good nerves (we shall need them not only on stage but also while glancing at some reviews), vision – namely the imagining of how one's talent, repertoire and personality can be provoked to unfold, the gift of concentration, pleasure derived from work, the readiness, ability and relish of transmitting something to the public (and be it musical soliloquy), a sense of humour, an inkling of the absurdity and paradoxy of the situation as well as a healthy dose of scepticism that ought to prevent us from taking ourselves too seriously.

All the more seriously, however, we need to take the composer's intentions even if, and when, the music happens to be funny. In a masterclass, the violinist Sándor Végh jokingly called humour a kind of superior seriousness ('Superernst'), while the great German writer Jean Paul defined it as 'the sublime in reverse'.

We need lightness as well as gravitas. We need an appetite for transformation – openness towards a multitude of musical characters.

The composer wants to be loved. Arnold Schoenberg urged the performer to be 'his most ardent servant'.

The performer, as well, hopes for some love. My gratitude goes to all the love I have received.

Great composers have made my life possible, and meaningful. More than I can express, I feel in their debt. It should be our token of gratitude to try to do justice to their works, not obstruct them. From the masterpiece performers can derive, to a large degree, what they have to do. To receive this message is demanding enough, and, where it succeeds, deeply gratifying.

I have never played concerts out of compulsion. It seemed a matter of choice to perform, but also to stop in good time. Thank you for having listened to me, and goodbye.

(2008)

From 'Analysis' to 'Zubiaurre'

A REVIEW OF *THE NEW GROVE DICTIONARY OF
MUSIC AND MUSICIANS*, 1981

I F THERE ARE people who are frightened by encyclopaedias I am not one of them. When I was thirteen I read, from cover to cover, Hermann Abert's German *Musiklexikon* of 1927. It has remained the basis of my modest musical erudition. The size of the book, some 500 pages (considerably less than the letter *A* in the *New Grove*), seems to me ideally suitable for an introduction to musical names and matters. I marked the text with pencils in four colours, and returned many times to the pages of photographic reproductions, each of them either devoting the whole space to one 'major composer', or containing nine smaller, neatly arranged portraits of lesser musical mortals, like performers, musicologists and those unfortunate composers who were not considered fit to exemplify greatness. Of 'living composers' thus illustrated there were no fewer than seventy-two, without counting Strauss and Pfitzner, who each had a page to himself. On the other hand, a figure like Liszt was not deemed worthy of a large picture, a blow that was hardly mitigated by three smaller photographs scattered in different departments. Incidentally, Abert's dictionary is not listed among his writings in the *New Grove*.

I went on savouring dictionaries up to my early thirties, with the Vienna telephone directory thrown in for fun – and a funny book it was at that time, still presenting full names, professions and addresses, sometimes in glorious accidental combinations. The most entertaining music dictionary in my possession remains Julius Schuberth's *Musikalisches Handbuch* of about 1860. It informed me that Johann Christian Bach 'only wrote music in order to be able to lead a frivolous and dissolute life'; that François Hünten composed while catching flies in his studio, preferably during the autumn; that Gottfried Piefke made a respected name for himself by transcribing Liszt's tone poems for his military band; and that Anton Rubinstein was, 'at this moment', the greatest living composer. It also listed 'Pubertät' (puberty), offering a German translation of the word without further comment.

Until well into the 1930s, musical dictionaries appeared to be a one-man enterprise. They reflected the taste, and satisfied the ambition, of one learned personality, even if he was, like Abert, assisted by four other writers.

Sir George Grove, on the other hand, was not a professional musicologist or music historian. He was a great Victorian amateur whose interests included biblical history and geography. From the outset, his dictionary was a collective venture. Originally planned in two volumes, the first edition of 1879–89 appeared in four. It has continued to grow beyond recognition: the twenty volumes of the *New Grove* remind me, in the musical field, of that story by J. L. Borges in which the whole universe is confined to one vast library.

Its army of contributors would fill Trafalgar Square, yet I conceive the editor, Stanley Sadie, less as a field marshal than as a supervisor, coordinator, computer engineer and talent scout. It is almost endearing that in spite, or because, of all those thousands of specialists a name as important as that of Francesco d'Andrade, the most celebrated Don Giovanni who ever lived, could get lost. I also looked in vain for Lamar Crowson, one of the finest chamber music pianists of his day, while, on the credit side, my collection of bizarre names was enriched by the Spanish composer Zubiaurre y Unionbarrenechea.

Those who feel that I should rather practise the piano than count the heads of musicians may rest assured: I shall not read through the 18,000 pages of the *New Grove*. Besides honouring it as the most recent and the most extensive musical reference library, I shall greatly value it as a tool for self-investigation. Where does my own knowledge falter? What has happened to my musical mind since, as an adolescent, I had hazy visions of what I would try to achieve, up to my present age of fifty?

While my curiosity and eagerness to learn have hardly diminished, I do find myself a great deal more critical, and sceptical, in the face of such a magnificent mountain of information, and such a diverse conglomeration of style and opinion. There are, within the experience of my piano playing, areas which profit from a high degree of awareness while others have to remain in the dark. Similarly, it has now become a matter of choice and of priorities where I should inform myself, and where stay ignorant.

An area where my curiosity continues to be insatiable is that of the creative process. How does the mind of a composer function? To work through the forty-page survey on 'Analysis' in the *New Grove* was amply rewarding. As I shall remain one of the few performing musicians to do so, I hasten to express to its author, Ian D. Bent, my admiration and gratitude. Misconceptions about analysis abound: it is assumed that it means taking a piece of music apart instead of showing why it is coherent; it is often regarded as being the starting-point for an understanding of a work, instead of the gradual outcome of growing familiarity with it; and it is thought of as being an exclusively intellectual task, whereas good analysis depends on emotions and senses no less than on reason. By describing several approaches towards analysis, Mr. Bent made me realise even more clearly how relative their merits are. Masterpieces are powerhouses of energy. They open perspectives of inexhaustible complexity. My sympathies, therefore, are not with those who claim to have defined their essence once and for all. I do not believe, for instance, that the nature of music can be explained as the 'music of nature', derived entirely from the overtone system, the triad and its consequences. But I remain convinced that more than a few features of a masterpiece can be made evident without undue complication, provided that, besides the engineering, one grants the composer some elbow-room for tinkering or fooling around. In my own way, I shall continue to pursue the luxury of trying to discover why masterpieces are superior to the compositions I produced in my teens.

The inclusion of a large piece on analysis indicates how musical dictionaries have changed. Abert had skipped the term altogether, while the old *Grove* merely referred to 'Analytical Notes', the habit of furnishing concert programmes with introductory essays, in England established largely by Grove himself. I looked up 'Structure' but found it mentioned only in the context of 'Form', with which, for many writers, it is not identical. I am still waiting for the day when 'humour', 'wit' and 'irony' will be discussed as topics of musical importance: it should be a red-letter day in the appreciation of Haydn.

There is some progress in the appreciation of Schoenberg. While H. J. Moser, in 1935, spoke about this intensely emotional composer's work as a 'blind alley', 'basically related more to mathematics than to music', and Abert thought it would 'never qualify for the kind of German music which is based on a national culture', the *New Grove* rightly tells us that 'perhaps no other composer of the time has so much to offer'.

The notion of a German culture which would lead the world to recovery has disappeared. So, it seems, have Victorian ethics: it is good to have a Schubert article by Maurice J. E. Brown, replacing Grove's own, although I shall miss Grove's priceless statement, 'Schubert was neither selfish, sensual, nor immoral.' Since Brown's death in 1975, it has been documented that what the *New Grove* reproduces as Schubert's death mask is in fact a life mask – and what a sensuously powerful, un-Biedermeierish face it reveals! (Not all the articles, even on living musicians, are up to date: James Levine had not appeared at Salzburg, Abbado had not conducted his wonderful *Carmen* at Edinburgh and Seymour Shifrin, the American composer, still alive in the *New Grove*, has been dead for two years.)

There is marked progress on Furtwängler. In his splendid piece, David Cairns makes up for much of the scorn which has been poured upon the great conductor in England. I noticed, elsewhere, a change of attitude in some of the writing on performers, pointing towards a style which alarmingly resembles everyday criticism. To assess a distinguished singer by noting that her remarkable voice is 'not always perfectly controlled' seems, to a fellow performer, irrelevant and, in the context of a dictionary, out of place. It was said about Grove himself that, as a critic, he 'would rather love than condemn any day in the week, and was little concerned with niceties of technique in performance'. Three cheers for Sir George!

The glory of the *New Grove* is its long and detailed articles on important personalities or subjects. Expecting to be enlightened on a subject in which my knowledge most frequently falters, I looked up 'Piano playing'.[122] The essay I found is as brief (barely three pages, after a twenty-seven-page survey of pianoforte construction) as it is amusing. The first sentence is a collector's item: 'On a practical level piano playing is concerned primarily with matters of touch, fingering, phrasing and interpretation.' (Once the player has arrived at interpretation he may be so bored that he may want to try something impractical.) Later, it is suggested that 'one can now confidently expect regard for the text from any pianist of stature'. I cannot but admire such a measure of confidence. I do, however, assure Mr. Sadie and his team of my regard for the text of the *New Grove*. This is a library, a source of stimulation, a sparring partner, a mirror to live with. Offering the sublime and the hilarious, it reflects the (musical) world not as it could or should be, but as it is.

(1981)

---

122 The article on piano playing has been replaced in later editions.

CONVERSATIONS

◦∿◦

Talking to Brendel

WITH JEREMY SIEPMANN

JEREMY SIEPMANN This may seem an odd sort of question to be asking you, but I know enough about performers to know that the answer is by no means a foregone conclusion: do you enjoy performing?

ALFRED BRENDEL Yes. Yes, I do. I've enjoyed it particularly during the last few years, when I've had the impression that much of what I do comes across. Of course, one very rarely knows if the right things come across; I collect tapes of my concert performances to check what I've done, but the sound captured by the microphone may be quite different from the sound in the twenty-third row.

SIEPMANN Not to mention the *meaning* of the sound, which may vary in as many degrees as there are seats in the twenty-third row. Does it disturb you that musical communication can't be more precise?

BRENDEL Yes. A lot of it disturbs me. Even the appreciation of the audience disturbs me sometimes, because it appreciates good things and bad nearly alike. Although one is extremely dependent on an audience's appreciation, because one has to convey a message, one must try, if it is possible, to remain completely independent of other people's judgments.

SIEPMANN You say that an audience may appreciate something which is 'bad', yet what is bad to one listener may be good to another equally qualified to form a judgement. Do you think that there *is* a distinct right and wrong, a distinct good and bad, in musical performance? Or does it in the end, beyond a certain level of professional attainment, boil down to personal preference, resulting from a particular psychological or spiritual bent?

BRENDEL To a certain extent it does, yes; but maybe not entirely. If one takes as a basis of judgement a very high professional level, and a real knowledge of the music involved – knowledge born from talent, from experience, and informed by psychological insight into what happens in a piece of music – then one gets nearer, I think, to judgments which are not so opposed.

SIEPMANN You've said that performers exist to be a link between the composer and the audience. That's true, of course, but is it as simple as that?

BRENDEL No. I must say that I myself am far more interested in the relation to the composer than in the relation towards the public. What fascinates me is to make sense of a piece of music while it sounds. That I convey something to the public is partly a necessary evil, but it's also a wonderful challenge. I say it's an evil because it may give the performer feelings of power which oughtn't to come into it. He may so enjoy having a hold over his audience that he forgets what he's for as a musician. Musical values and a performer's grip on his audience aren't always quite the same thing!

SIEPMANN Is it a performer's job to 'teach' his audience? I remember hearing a distinguished performer who'd been asked if he would bring out each appearance of the subject in a fugue. He said, in effect, 'Not when I'm playing it for myself. I know it's there. I can see it; I can hear it; I can even feel it. But in a concert I would.' To what extent do you think this double standard is justified?

BRENDEL There are two points. First of all, the performer has to clarify a piece, to make it as clearly accessible as possible. Listening should always be made easy, whether it's to late Beethoven quartets or Mozart sonatas. There should be a blend of the performer's feeling and the music which doesn't give the impression that there's any great strain involved. The second point is that the moment an audience feels that a performer wants to teach them, his case is lost. If you teach an audience, they mustn't ever notice it.

SIEPMANN Do you think musical analysis is of any value to the performer as a performer?

BRENDEL I think every performer should have a sound background as a composer, and know enough about traditional harmony and counterpoint so that it won't give him much trouble to write a cadenza which is without obvious faults of voice-leading [part-writing] and so on. As for analysis, there are many ways of analysing music, some more helpful to performers than others. But it's interesting to note that composers have rarely spoken at all about musical analysis. They've avoided the subject to an extent which seems to me very revealing. One finds, on the other hand, a lot of comment about atmosphere, about character, about poetic ideas – even in the most unlikely places. Performers who nourish poetic ideas are excused by the composers themselves. Analysis should never be taken for the key to the sort of insight which enables a great performance. If we know that there is an extremely important harmonic progression – if, for instance, we analyse a piece in Schenker's way – and we do not feel, while we are playing it, the exact amount of tension, the way atmosphere changes at this point, the balance of all the elements involved, then our knowledge will not help us at all. It was Schoenberg who said, in a letter, that formal analysis is often overrated because it shows *how* something is done, not *what* is done. This, from one of the supreme analysts, is something valuable, I think.

SIEPMANN Do you think live and recorded performances encourage, or perhaps even require, different approaches to listening? The very nature of a recording, after all, is unnatural (even, arguably, unmusical) in that in life a performance is never repeated time and again without change. Does this require us to adjust our attitudes?

BRENDEL There are, certainly, basic differences; but after fifty or sixty records I'm still not able to cite them all! When I made my first records I decided that a recorded performance was something quite different, in that one doesn't see the performer and that, for the performer, there is no audience. What counted was the result (the edited tape), not the risk. But the more I progressed in recording experience, the more I tried to play as though in a concert, imagining that an audience was there, listening to me. I came to this after listening to tapes from my own concerts and comparing them with some of my records. Many more concerts, I think, should be recorded and issued on disc, with all their imperfections and coughing and so on. As far as piano recordings are concerned, the over-refinement of our tools nowadays seems sometimes to be a disadvantage.

SIEPMANN Do you consciously alter the details of a performance for a recording?

BRENDEL I do not – unless when I listen to the playback I find that something sounds out of proportion and wouldn't have the same impact as when one could see me, or feel my bodily presence in a hall.

SIEPMANN Do you feel, as I would gather you do, that there is a musical function in the gestures a performer makes? That he can, or even should, use his physical presence to support or draw attention to certain moments in the music?

BRENDEL Yes, I do. When I saw myself on television for the first time, I became aware that I'd developed all kinds of gestures and grimaces which completely contradicted what I did, and what, musically, I wanted to do. I then had a mirror made, a big standing mirror, which I put beside the piano, not really making me visible all the time, but always there; unconsciously, one noticed things. It helped me to co-ordinate what I wanted to suggest with my movements with what really came out. There are many examples of pieces where this is necessary. Things like the end of Liszt's B minor Sonata, where before the three *pianississimo* B major chords there is a crescendo on one chord which one has to convey bodily, with a gesture. It's the only possibility.

SIEPMANN You've made an enormous number of records over the years. What is your relationship to all these progeny?

BRENDEL Records are a kind of offspring of which one can't, unfortunately, say that one has to nurse them until they grow up and then forget them as soon as possible and let them lead their own lives. They lead their own lives at once, and are scarcely ever grown up! There's always something infantile about a record, at least as far as the artist is concerned. Records are interesting to learn from but not always to enjoy.

SIEPMANN What do you think has been the effect on general musical life of the advent of the gramophone and the radio, and the easy accessibility of music which it has brought? Certainly it seems to have greatly diminished the amount of amateur music-making.

BRENDEL Yes, which I think is a great pity. On the other hand, it has enabled so many more people and classes to participate in the enjoyment of music. It's now much less the privilege of, financially speaking, the upper classes.

SIEPMANN I've read that you're interested in writing about music.

BRENDEL Yes.

SIEPMANN As you've seen, one of the questions I've written down is 'Is music a subject to be written about?' Presumably your answer is yes, in certain circumstances and by certain people.

BRENDEL Yes. Yes. I think one should sometimes try to do the impossible!

SIEPMANN What can, or should, writing about music achieve, and, if you like, what must it not try to achieve?

BRENDEL First of all, I think it must not be arrogant. That may seem very irrelevant, but I think it's very important. If one decides to talk about something as elusive as music, something which is so difficult to grasp in words without talking nonsense all the time and being imprecise to an enormous degree, and personal to a degree which is no use to anyone, then one has to be modest about it. I haven't read many books on music which were worth reading once the purely historical and biographical material ended and the analysis, the attempt to illuminate something about music, began.

SIEPMANN Your own extra-musical interests are wide-ranging. Do you think that a knowledge of other arts, such as painting, architecture, literature, etc., and acquaintance with other spiritual-cum-intellectual pursuits such as philosophy, can affect a musician *as a musician?* And would you recommend the study of them to those not naturally drawn to them?

BRENDEL One can only answer questions like these for oneself. For me, it definitely has. It's all part of my aesthetic food, really. I wouldn't feel properly fed without it, but I wouldn't necessarily recommend it to others. After all, there are enormously talented musicians who are completely unvisual, even colour-blind. What I *would* recommend, to all musicians, is to see what is happening around them, to face reality and not to take any of the many, many ways of escape which people so often do; I doubt if there have ever been so many problems of such actuality, in the whole history of mankind, as there are today. If people would face the reality, then one could do something about it. But it would change their lives. Our lives.

SIEPMANN Do you see dangers in the concept of 'music as refuge'?

BRENDEL It can be a refuge, certainly. Music can be so many things. It can lift one into a sphere which is remote from time, and from reality. That is one of music's marvellous possibilities. But it's not the only one.

SIEPMANN I've read that among your many interests is the study of Baroque architecture, but I think I'm right in saying that you rarely, if ever, include Baroque music in your programmes. Do you ever play music which was written for the harpsichord?

BRENDEL Virtually never.[123]

SIEPMANN Why?

BRENDEL It's a very personal question, really. One of the reasons, certainly, is the use of the instrument – though I don't object to someone who manages to play

123 My outlook has since changed.

Bach convincingly on the piano. Unlike Scarlatti, which I cannot bear to hear
on the piano.

SIEPMANN No matter who plays it?

BRENDEL No matter who plays it. In comparison with an excellent performance
on the harpsichord, this music makes no sense to me at all on the piano. But
there is some of the old English music – the Fantasia by Gibbons in *Parthenia*,
for example – which I think is better suited to the piano than to many of the
old instruments, because it is so madrigal-like. It is music of singing voices, of
sustained sound.

SIEPMANN What are your feelings about what I call 'reconstructionist' performances,
in which musicians aim to recapture precisely the style and sound of music as
it was in the days of the composer? Do you think it's possible, with all our subsequent musical experience, to recapture that? We can perhaps reconstruct the
sound, but can we recapture the experience? And is it worth trying?

BRENDEL It certainly seems to be worth trying. Because even if it doesn't recapture the experience as a whole, the sound has a strong bearing on the quality of
the experience. The timbre of some of the instruments involved, and the way
of treating the music which these instruments suggest, may have very great significance. For instance, take Monteverdi – hearing the actual instruments of his
time, even if we don't know exactly how they were used, makes all the difference
to me. Especially after so many transcriptions by Hindemith and Malipiero and
God knows who I listen with completely new ears. Now with piano music…

SIEPMANN In Mozart concertos, for instance, to what extent do you try to tailor your
playing on a modern concert grand to the ideal of the Mozartian piano sound?

BRENDEL I think of the whole piece, and of all the players involved. As I don't play
with players who use 'old' instruments, it would make little sense for me to try and
adjust my playing to an old instrument. For myself, I find it much more interesting and important to make as much as I can of the present-day piano, to make
the limits wider and wider in every respect. I try to see each work as a problem
by itself – less a historical than a psychological problem, a problem of character.

SIEPMANN In view of the widespread availability of what I shall call 'mainstream'
performances, do you think there is any justification for the attempts of certain
players to shed new light or encourage a new way of listening to the extent that
they deliberately distort, or, if you like, pervert the composer's markings?

BRENDEL It depends on the way in which one wants to shed new light. I think, actually, that the attempt to do it is wrong in the first place. If one sheds new light on music, it should be the *outcome* of an effort, not the input! As is originality. If one sets out to be original, especially as a performer, one is bound to get lost. Indeed, if one sets out with that aim it's likely that one has very little talent in the first place. If one alters a composer's markings in order to be interesting, then one is simply foolish. But it's fascinating to see that quite a lot of people are attracted by this approach and seem even to find it intellectually justified.

SIEPMANN Do you make a point of keeping abreast of contemporary music?

BRENDEL Yes, I do. I haven't enough time to do it as I would like, but I go whenever I can to listen.

SIEPMANN Do you feel, as a performer, any obligation to contemporary composers?

BRENDEL No, I must admit I do not. But I feel that they ought to be encouraged. I don't play them because I would have to specialise completely in a certain field of music in order to do it really well. I would have to confine myself to a rather limited number of works instead of playing an enormous repertory, and I decided otherwise.

SIEPMANN Do you, on the whole, learn quickly?

BRENDEL Yes, although I haven't got a visual memory. My memory isn't phenomenal, but it's quite good on the whole.

SIEPMANN Is your memory extremely retentive, or do you have to keep re-learning?

BRENDEL I have to keep re-learning – which is, I think, a very good thing. It makes for many new encounters and never allows one to feel unduly secure in reproducing some old hat!

SIEPMANN Do you ever feel the necessity to get away from music for a time, to go away from the piano and away from where you hear music?

BRENDEL Each year, for about two weeks, at the beginning of my vacation, I don't touch the instrument. And while I may hear music, I don't plan or expect to. I like to look at architecture and to drive around. And every four or five years I try to take off a period of some months which I devote completely to study, and maybe sometimes to recording as well.

SIEPMANN Do you ever feel a temptation to branch out? To conduct, perhaps?

BRENDEL I'm very interested in conducting, and in the techniques of conducting. I imagine myself conducting, but I would never do it. I am interested in the piano.

I think I would be too shy to attempt to impose something on an orchestra without being completely professional. However well I know a piece, and what the orchestra can do, there would always be a gap between my standard as a pianist and my standard as a conductor.

SIEPMANN You are now a very successful concert performer. Should success grant you the freedom to order your professional life precisely as you see fit, what changes, if any, would you be tempted to make?

BRENDEL I don't know. So far I don't feel at all exploited. I play a lot, though not as much as some other people, but I play because I like it. I have a lot of other interests, of course, for which time will always be too short. But there it is.

(1972)

Bach and the Piano

WITH TERRY SNOW

TERRY SNOW You have avoided playing Bach's works in concerts for a number of years. Why have you changed your mind?

ALFRED BRENDEL The expert use of old instruments is a fairly recent achievement. I spent the post-war years listening, sometimes with a great deal of admiration, to the development and application of this expertise; the question was how convincing such performances would prove in the long run. Another thing was that I had studied with Edwin Fischer, whose Bach playing conveyed, in its own way, such powerful authority that I felt unable to free myself from its grip. The moment had to come when I became secure enough to deal with Bach on my own terms.

SNOW This implies that 'historical' performances did not win you over?

BRENDEL They didn't entirely. I feel that many of Bach's works are less dependent on the instruments of his day than are the works of Monteverdi or Domenico Scarlatti, or Purcell, Rameau or Couperin. And I think that a coexistence of 'historical' and 'modern' Bach performances is possible, and necessary.

SNOW What are the advantages of playing Bach's keyboard works on the piano?

BRENDEL First of all, the sound of pianos suits modern halls. That of old instruments does not. A critic who thinks that Bach performances should be confined to old instruments should also insist that one travel to a Baroque marble hall to listen to them; or stay at home to hear them played on a record. Now, to my mind, Bach should remain part of the living concert repertory. Thanks to critical opinion his music has nearly vanished from piano recitals, and pianists are about to lose the skill of 'polyphonic playing', once held in high esteem, a loss that makes itself felt not only in Bach, and not only in dense contrapuntal structures.

Bach's keyboard music is full of latent possibilities. It is sometimes difficult to decide for which of his keyboard instruments a piece was written. The A minor Fantasy and Fugue, for instance, has many features of an organ work. There are, on the other hand, among his keyboard compositions typical ensemble pieces, orchestral works, concertos or arias which found their way onto the keyboard at the expense of more varied instrumental or vocal timbre, declamation and dynamics. They seem like a two-dimensional reduction of something three-dimensional.

How did these works get there? Because one keyboard player can master a whole work alone without having to compromise with partners. The modern piano, thanks to its greater sensitivity to colour and dynamics, can sometimes restore this third dimension.

SNOW Should the absence of interpretation markings on the autographs be remedied today by adhering to the conventions of Baroque playing – with regard to the use of rubato, for example, or the choice of tempi and dynamics?

BRENDEL On the piano, certain modifications of rhythm and tempo are obsolete. There is a link between rubato and dynamics. Where the instrument does not permit phrasing and declamation to be moulded in dynamic terms, more rubato playing will be necessary to make the music breathe, particularly in *cantabile* music. There are, however, cases where the importance of a strict pulse will overrule all other considerations, as in the *perpetuum mobile* motion of the final movement of the Italian Concerto.

SNOW Are there any characteristics of the harpsichord sound which you would consider reproducing, as, for example, the contrast of 'big' and 'small' registers?

BRENDEL I do not hesitate to underline dynamic contrast with octave doublings where it seems musically necessary. Generally, however, I am more interested in suggesting those qualities of the music which stay dormant on Bach's instrument. And there is a special group of pieces of a prophetic kind, such as the remarkable A minor Fantasy, or 'Prelude' (Bach-Gesellschaft XXXVI/138, BWV922), which seems to have been written for an instrument of the future in any case. As a harpsichord piece this Fantasy seems to me unsuccessful; as a piano piece it turns out to be quite marvellous, communicating surprises from bar to bar, never giving away to the listener where it will go.

SNOW To look out for surprises in the music and fully employ the development in keyboard interpretation up to the present day – doesn't this inevitably lead to 'Romanticizing' Bach's music?

BRENDEL Not necessarily. Does any music convey the spirit of improvisation more immediately than Bach's Fantasies? Is not the execution of the *arpeggiando* chords in the Chromatic Fantasy left to the imaginative gifts of the player? I remember the days when the backlash against the excesses of 'Romantic' performance resulted in unemotional and drily mechanical abstraction. Nowadays we hear Couperin on the harpsichord played in a way that amazingly resembles the 'Romanticism'

of Paderewski's records: no chord without an arpeggio and the left hand constantly anticipating the right.

SNOW As for the use of modern dynamics…

BRENDEL Forkel's edition of the Chromatic Fantasy and Fugue, published towards
the beginning of the nineteenth century and allegedly based on a tradition of performance handed down by Wilhelm Friedemann Bach, already contains many
tempo changes and dynamic markings, including that huge, hideous crescendo
over the last lines of the Fantasy which has been reproduced in so many subsequent editions. I think that some 'historical' performances, and the development
of twentieth-century music, have led us to a new structural understanding of
Bach's works, contrary to interpretations which indulged in values of colour and
atmosphere for their own sake.

SNOW Can you give an example?

BRENDEL Since Busoni, the *arpeggiando* chords of the Chromatic Fantasy have
often been played in a new, subdued and mysterious manner which to me is
structurally unjustified.

SNOW How important are transcriptions (such as those by Busoni) in translating
Bach to modern instruments? Do transcriptions help to convey or impede the
'real voice' of Bach?

BRENDEL I don't know about the 'real voice', but some of Busoni's versions of Bach's
organ chorale preludes do convey Bach gloriously, provided that one restores a few
details according to the original text. Others at least give the pianist an opportunity to conjure up the sound and volume of an organ, plus the reverberation of
a church. And, though it seems that the piano is a nearer relation of the harpsichord than of the organ, it lends itself much more readily to imitating the organ.

SNOW Should the greater sonority and resonance of modern instruments place
some constraints on ornamentation for modern players?

BRENDEL It should, sometimes. And there is also the question whether the unadorned line may strike us as more impressive. Not that we should ignore those
ornaments which are authentic. But we may use our own judgement and discretion about whether to add unwritten ones.

SNOW Instead of slavishly reproducing practices of the past, should the Bach pianist
examine former conventions of performance as to their validity to present-day
ears and musical minds?

BRENDEL Certainly, and he should ask himself whether they are tied to the musical
structure, and contribute to the basic character of a piece. No 'rules' of performance should be automatically applied. Does a string player really have to swell
out each *tenuto* note as much as the bow permits? Should he turn every two-note
group into a vehemently accented sigh? Even if it had been a passing habit to
emphasise certain rhetorical elements, we may find them of minor significance
today. Rhetorical elements have always been an important part of a good performance. If they are over-projected, and given undue prominence, they sound – to
my ears – hysterical. Music, instead of speaking, shrieks and moans.

SNOW Does it make any sense to say, as Nikolaus Harnoncourt did, that music
before the French Revolution was primarily rhetorical and declamatory, after the
Revolution emotional and atmospheric? Do we really have to choose between
declamation and the big line, or between logic and atmosphere?

BRENDEL I do not see these elements as alternatives. They are interdependent and
balanced out in a masterpiece. The performer, on old or modern instruments,
should try to reveal this balance.

(1976)

In the years following this interview, amazing things have happened. There are now
period orchestras – reaching in their repertoire even beyond the Age of Enlightenment – whose precision and refinement match that of splendid conventional ones.
Effortlessly, they can play in tune. Convincing balances have been found. The brass
does not invariably attack you in full blast, and the timpanist is not encouraged to
perforate his instrument or your eardrums, at least by some conductors. Styles of
historicising performance have diversified, ranging from the near-objective to the
wildly idiosyncratic. The competence in dealing with period instruments is now
staggering – so staggering that leaving the concert hall I sometimes ask myself: Had
there ever been a moderate tempo? Even conventional orchestras have now taken
on some period routine: an avoidance of vibrato, the stressing of two-note groups,
the clipping of end notes. (See 'On some performance habits', p 350.)

At the same time, the pianists have rediscovered Bach. Mainly thanks to András
Schiff, his piano music has reestablished itself in modern concert halls, to the delight

of listeners and executants alike. A coexistence of 'historical' and 'modern' performances is now taken for granted.

(2015)

On Schnabel and Interpretation

WITH KONRAD WOLFF

KONRAD WOLFF IN the preface which you wrote for the new editions – in German and in English – of my book about Schnabel's interpretative ideas on piano music,[124] you say at the end that what you feel about these ideas is 'admiration' on the one hand, 'opposition' on the other. I want to ask you about the substance of your opposition, for two principal reasons (apart from sheer curiosity).

First, you have become the first pianist since Schnabel – two generations apart – who again enjoys full authority in the field of interpretation of Mozart, Beethoven and Schubert. (Your other repertory was hardly shared by Schnabel.) Secondly, in the opinion of many, and also in mine, your approach has much in common with Schnabel's, both in details of phrasing, tempo and dynamics, and in your basic attitude, and this against a different approach by nearly everybody else. Yet, when you played the G major Sonata of Schubert the other night, you told me afterwards that you did everything contrary to Schnabel's rules, or words to that effect. He would not have been aware of a disagreement except in details.

There is one basic point where I see a very different approach between you and Schnabel, but I am sure we shall get to it.

1 Metre, Rhythm and Tempo

ALFRED BRENDEL What I remarked about the G major Sonata was mainly referring to its beginning. I remember one of the examples in your book which suggests that the G major chords, as they are something like the spine of the beginning, should be played with a certain amount of weight whenever they come. I don't agree, because I think that if one plays the last chord with weight instead of 'taking it away', the roundness of the phrase is gone. This brings me to some metric articulations by Schnabel – his idea that in a phrase there are one heavy bar, two

---

124 *The Teaching of Artur Schnabel, A Guide to Interpretation* (Faber & Faber, 1972).

light bars and then one heavy bar at the end, or at least a light bar in the third bar and a heavy bar at the end. If one were to apply this to this beginning, I think it would be contrary to what I see in it.

I see in this beginning a whole phrase, and by phrase I mean something like a curve, a bridge which starts down here and then goes up into the air and leads down again.[125] So what interests me about phrases is often much less the count-ing of the bar-lines and the functions of bars, but the whole shape. In another example from your book which is supposed to illuminate the heavy-light-light-heavy scheme, the C minor episode in the finale of the G major Sonata, Schubert's own accents tell the player to do the exact opposite:

Only the minuet theme, for once, adheres to Schnabel's pattern. I think what Sch-nabel does with his metric articulation is to overestimate bar-lines. Very often for me the art of phrasing consists of forgetting about bars, ignoring bars and seeing large units. If I think, for example, of Schubert's B flat Sonata, then I think that the whole point of playing the beginning is *not* to disclose where a light or where a heavy accent may be, not to disclose where there is an upbeat (is it just the first upbeat or does it lead to the next bar-line?); to play as if this theme would have to continue something which had been going on for some time already. The music really has begun already and one sits down and continues something. One does not emphasise the upbeat – one leaves the mystery of how the theme is organised undisclosed! By leaving it undisclosed it becomes more mysterious, in my opinion.

WOLFF That is beautifully said, but I don't think you have the slightest disagree-ment with Schnabel – especially with this beginning. I believe I mention in my

---

125 I have, in the meantime, left this image behind. There are plenty of phrases which do not conform to it. Schubert's dynamic indication in this theme points to the fact that many phrases, instead of petering out, increase their tension immediately before their end.

book that he thought of it as a 6/4 bar that starts one beat before the first note.[126]
Schnabel is the one who said, 'If I were rich enough I would have all my music
printed without bar-lines'.[127] I don't think it is the bar-*line* that he emphasises.
Rather it is two things, really. One is that he wanted to know how far he was to
play before there was a breath (the length of the breath – including harmonic
rhythm); the other is that he said that a phrase begins and then goes *from* there,
or else it ends and goes *to* there. He also said that in every phrase either the beginning or the end is the more important.

BRENDEL   Well, there are two things I should like to say. I'm sure that Schnabel
did not have such a simple mind that he had simple rules. Everything I know
about him suggests that he often contradicted himself and had new ideas about
the same things – he even wanted, to a certain degree, to amaze his pupils and
confuse them, thus showing them in how many ways the same music may be
understood and how the person may change who performs it. But I find several
references in the book, and I hear, sometimes, certain things – not so much in
his own playing, but in the playing of some of his pupils – which tell me that he
must have taught a bit of this bar-line business.

WOLFF   All our music is filled with the numerals V or III, where he dictated to us –
or wrote himself – that the metrical period in question was five or three bars long.

BRENDEL   And yet within his periods he loves to emphasise bars: 'light bars' or
'heavy bars'. Now, for instance, there is an example at the beginning of Beethov-
en's Op. 2, No. 3 where he wants the first four bars to be heavy, light, light, heavy,
which to me is absurd.

Why should the dominant be light and the tonic at the beginning and the end
be heavy? If anything, for me, it is the opposite. If we look at the piano writing
of this opening we find one tenth in the left hand, in the third bar. This tenth for

126   p. 71.

127   p. 99.

me indicates the high point of the whole phrase. Then it relaxes, because with all the energy of this beginning it still has a certain graceful quality about it. I think that what Schnabel attempts to do here sounds a little bit forced.

The other thing is that when I listen to his playing, and the playing of some of his pupils, I find an organisation of the playing which refers to what you said about thinking about how long the breath should be and where a new breath should start. I'm not sure that I agree with this kind of musical thinking at all. I feel that inasmuch as the pianist should sing inside himself, and on his instrument, he should not accept the physical limitations of a singer. I would go further and say that the singer himself should not accept his own limitations. When the singer has to breathe, he should do it in a way that is as unobtrusive as possible. There's a lot of music – for example the vocal music of Beethoven – which does not take into account the breathing of the singer at all. The singer has to be, like a very good instrumentalist, able to bridge all those gaps where breath is necessary. There is such a thing as 'accented breathing'. It should only occur where the drama of the music requires it, not as a matter of course.

Also, for me, Schnabel's playing sometimes likens music too much to language, with full stops, commas and all. Music is not as simply organised as that. Even when it has a very eloquent quality – a speaking quality, a telling quality – it does not have sentences or commas or the organisation of words into rhythms in a way that would make it easily comparable to language. Obviously, Schnabel himself knew better, according to your book. 'Where something new begins, something old is continuing all the same. This is the first clue to the idea of phrasing. The last note of one phrase is frequently the first note of the next ...' I totally agree. Very often there are several things going on at the same time. You may have a *melodic* ending and *melodic* beginning, but there may also be a *harmonic* ending and a *harmonic* beginning which is so important that a breath, a musical comma, would take away the necessary continuity. For example, at the end of Beethoven's C minor Concerto, in the coda, you have the presto theme.

WOLFF Somewhat Rossini-like?

BRENDEL Yes, and there is something like a downbeat at the end, a *forte* downbeat of the orchestra which I have sometimes found corrected in the orchestral parts into *mezzo forte*, because somebody saw in it only the end of a phrase. In actuality the new phrase starts there as well. There is a switch of phrasing. This is the *forte* platform for all the downbeats which happen later. I have very rarely heard it played energetically enough to project the meaning of the whole end. So I feel that *Punkt und Komma* in musical interpretation is an undue simplification of musical matters. I shall always remember a performance by a very well-known trio of the second movement of Beethoven's 'Archduke' Trio. There was a horrible little stop after each four bars.

WOLFF   I love this phrase, because Beethoven leads to a *forte* in the fourth bar but not in the eighth.

BRENDEL   Yes, indeed. Even after eight bars such a stop would be horrible. Such slight separations of phrases are sometimes taught. They disfigure the rhythmic context. For me, it is much more interesting to connect phrases than to separate them, as a principle. That is something I have probably acquired from my teacher, Edwin Fischer, who did not speak about this in such terms but would demonstrate it all the time.

WOLFF   I have been sort of forced into the role of the Boswell or Eckermann of Schnabel (a role in which I don't feel adequate, especially not now after forty-five years), and I don't know what he would have said about it. As for me, I agree with all you have just said. Only I think that in the music before Beethoven, and especially in Mozart's music, there is still a great deal of *rhetoric* tradition stemming from the time when instrumental music was really a surrogate for vocal music. The speaking, the recitative-like quality, like the sighing motives of Mozart's music and some other music of the time, is much greater, and I see one of the principal innovations of Beethoven as being that he created an abstract rhythm that was not to be filled with words.

BRENDEL   I want to repeat that a lot of my musical thinking is vocal. And I find, especially in Mozart's piano concertos, many operatic traits which make me treat the piano part in as vocal and declamatory a manner as I can. Yet the operatic singing of Mozart has also changed quite a bit in the last thirty years. I think this is probably the greatest change in musical performance which has happened during our lifetime. If I listen to Beecham's *Zauberflöte* nowadays (recorded in the 1930s) it's a very strange experience. The style of the singers could hardly be tolerated today.

WOLFF   I agree – there has been a gradual change.

BRENDEL   And yet I would expect that even a singer could create the big line, could connect whatever he had to sing. 'Connection' is not even the right word. What I mean is that one thing leads into another. This is an area where I sometimes disagree with Schnabel's playing – the area of rhythm and tempo. What I am sometimes missing is the rhythmic continuity. He is very much concerned with clarifying harmonic progressions, and with giving the impression of declamation – even in passage-work.

WOLFF Also with melodic rise.

BRENDEL And with, of course, the melodic organisation, but often unconcerned with purely rhythmical matters – the importance of an even, rhythmical flow.

WOLFF This is exactly what I had hoped you would get to because this is the point, mentioned earlier, where I do see a difference in approach. To illustrate, I want to tell you that Schnabel once admitted in a lesson that, as a game, he sometimes would have, especially in slow movements, a metronome going when he practised and he would try to play as rubato as possible against the metronome so that he would come together on every strong beat – but be entirely unfettered between beats. I don't think you would do that.

BRENDEL I would possibly do it in slow movements which have a speaking quality and where one of the main features of the music is not a regular rhythmic pattern which has to be maintained. I do not think that where there is a regular accompaniment it always has to be as strict as in a Stravinsky piece. But let me get back to one of the examples in your book. You talk about the harmonic articulation in the Brahms D minor Concerto, in the coda (Più animato) of the last movement.[128] Of course, I also know Schnabel's record, and I think that the rhythmic articulation he suggests and plays there is harmful because the overriding importance is the regularity and energy of each little beat. It is one of the most disturbing aspects of some of his performances that the rhythmic priorities are sometimes not accepted, or recognised. For instance, towards the end of the C minor Concerto by Mozart, wherever there are broken chords, Schnabel lumps them together harmonically in portions and separates them from each other. Similarly, wherever there are broken octaves, he will not play them evenly but plays them like grace notes before the main note. These things happen so often that one gets the impression of mannerisms, of bad habits. It is something, I have the feeling, which he failed to control.

---

128 pp. 90 ff.

WOLFF Sometimes he probably did, but in the finale of the Beethoven C major
Concerto it was his way of showing how Beethoven foreshortens the phrases. Of
course it was not out of control. It had a musical purpose. It may have been the
wrong means...

BRENDEL Let me put it differently. The musical purpose is too thickly underlined.
Musical ideas cannot be presented as fixed ideas. Schnabel's treatment of rhythm
too often gives me the feeling ... well, that he thought a continuous rhythmic
pulse was boring. There is a matter of principle in his playing where principle
should not come in.

WOLFF He had a great fear, which came out in his teaching, in his criticism of his
students, of being what one usually calls 'notey' – that one would hear too many
single notes. He always quoted a negative review that he had had many years earlier,
where a critic wrote, 'His semiquavers sounded like peas counted by a prisoner'.
Apparently that was what he wanted to avoid under all circumstances. Do you
have some of that same fear – of playing one note after the other in fast music?

BRENDEL Well, first of all I wouldn't listen too attentively to critics. I try to make
out what the music requires. There may be a situation where evenness of rhythm
is essential. I think this is more often the case than Schnabel's playing would
disclose. But does evenness of rhythm exclude expressive playing? Wasn't it Schnabel who, when asked, 'Do you play with feeling or in time?' responded: 'Why
shouldn't I feel in time?' But let me go on to another matter. The central area of
my disagreement with Schnabel is not the treatment of rhythm, it is the treatment of tempo.

WOLFF Yes. It is probably a generation difference too.

BRENDEL I ask myself whether this is the case. If I compare performances of
other great players of Schnabel's generation, like Cortot and Fischer, then I
find that fast movements and fast pieces are often played faster than some people would dare to play them today, whereas the treatment of slow tempi varies.
For instance, Cortot never played extremely slowly in his whole life. Not that I
missed it, but he got away without playing a real Largo. Fischer tended to play
slow movements fluently, particularly Andantes, and told his pupils that there
is a marked difference between Andante and a really slow movement. On the
other hand he could expand the tempo of a Largo, as the one in Beethoven's
First Concerto, to wonderful effect. With Schnabel I get the impression (and

he says so in the book) that he wants extremes of tempo. He suggests it to be a virtue to play a slow movement slower than anybody would expect. He also suggests that it is an interesting way to amaze the listener to start a fast movement faster than the listener thinks one can manage, and I have the feeling that he is really doing that in some of his own performances. Here I do disagree. I think that playing music as slow or as fast as possible makes music into something bordering on sport.

Dealing with tempo, as with dynamics, as with colours, as with every means of musical expression, there should be as much variety as possible at the command of the player. There is an enormous variety in all music, and the player has to look for it. Preconceived ideas will limit his or her possibilities. To concentrate on extremes of tempo means to neglect the wide area of tempi in between.

WOLFF May I say that you simplify his approach to tempo a little bit? For instance, in certain symphonic first movements, he tried to have the tempo slow enough to have the music develop with a certain majestic quiet. The examples that come to my mind are not from piano music but chamber music. In two B flat trios, the 'Archduke' and the Schubert B flat, he usually criticised everyone for being too fast in the first movements. There again he was not quite alone in his generation.

BRENDEL And yet if I think of the recordings I have heard, of most of the Beethoven sonatas, the general impression remains of extreme tempi. Of course, I ask myself whether he always played like that, whether that was his intention, or whether a certain amount of nerves made him play too fast and, in slow movements, extremely slow.

WOLFF You must remember that records in those days were only about four minutes long, and therefore the tempo of slow movements was occasionally slightly modified for recordings. For instance, I don't recall the slow movement of the Beethoven Fourth Concerto played as fast by him as on his record. It had to fit on two sides.

BRENDEL This is a great pity, because it is an Andante con moto and I think it should be played flowing!

I remember being told that Schoenberg was listening to a performance of Schnabel playing the Beethoven C minor Concerto on the radio. There was the first chord of the slow movement, then the second one never came, and Schoenberg said, 'I can't count any longer!'

2 Sound

BRENDEL I never heard Schnabel in the concert hall. I only have second-hand experience from the records.

WOLFF I heard him often in his house and in the concert hall. In my opinion, the pirated records are the best reproduction of his real sound.

BRENDEL I must say that from the records I do admire his sound very much. It is one of the reasons why Schnabel is a constant source of inspiration to me. And yet when I read through your chapter about regulating sound I have to disagree with certain ideas. For example, does the piano tone remain the same throughout the entire range of the instrument? I ask this because on the pianos of Beethoven's and Mozart's time this was certainly not the case. The interesting thing is that the bass sound and the treble sound and the sound of the middle range sometimes differed nearly as much as the voices of a string quartet would differ. There was enough variety to exclude the statement that the basic characteristic of the piano was the evenness of the sound, an evenness which inspired composers to take this into account as a basic quality of the instrument. Of a first-class modern piano I would expect that in dynamics and quality the sound should remain similar throughout the registers. It is then up to the pianist to produce the necessary variety of balance and timbre. And I think that not only the listener should imagine sounds of other instruments coming from the piano; the pianist has to imagine them and produce them in the first place.

WOLFF Well, if I didn't say that in the book, it is a bad omission, because certainly Schnabel wanted that.

BRENDEL Unlike the harpsichord or the organ, the piano sound can be moulded in many ways. 'In the great majority of compositions for the piano I think the composer wanted his music to sound like piano music and nothing else.' This is a quotation from the book, and as far as I am concerned the contrary is probably true. I would think, if I looked at the latent possibilities in most piano works, that piano pieces are rather reductions. They are usually reductions of musical ideas which belong to the orchestra, to chamber music, to the voice – whatever you name. A reduction so that one player, without having to compromise with others, can master them – at a price. I think the price should be as low as possible. The present-day piano lowers the price more than older instruments could – with a few exceptions.

It is interesting that in your book there is little talk of Liszt. Schnabel in his last decades did not play him in public, I think.

WOLFF I never heard him play Liszt, but when he was young he played the Mephisto Waltz and the Sonata – and I think the Second Concerto.

BRENDEL He seems to have enjoyed teaching Liszt, as you have written. Liszt, of course, makes the pianist aware of all the possibilities of the piano. If I have a principle it is in agreement with this one – that the piano, in itself, is not enough. That it is an instrument not with a strong character of its own, like the human voice or a string instrument, but rather like a character actor – it wants to play roles. It can turn into nearly everything you can think of. So much for principles.

WOLFF You said today's piano lends itself more to most piano music – with certain exceptions. What are the exceptions?

BRENDEL There would be pieces like certain Haydn sonatas which need a particular bite and clarity. They sound more idiomatic on the early Hammerklavier, which has still retained part of the harpsichord sound. There is music like Scarlatti which is very close to the hard edges of the guitar (after all, he lived in Spain for some time). It needs very clear contours, Mediterranean clarity. Returning to the word 'timbre' which I used a little earlier, I have written down a quotation from your book which says: 'Obviously, with the exception of the soft pedal, the piano has no means of altering its timbre.'[129] That again is something I cannot easily agree with.

WOLFF This you can blame on me. Schnabel is not responsible for that statement. Of course this is meant as a *physicist's*, not as a *musician's* statement.

BRENDEL I would think that the touch, the dynamics, the balance, the right pedal can also alter the timbre to a great extent, even to the extent of clearly suggesting certain instruments or certain combinations of players.

WOLFF I once read in a Hindemith book that it makes no difference on the piano whether it is touched with the tip of an umbrella or with the finger of Arthur Rubinstein. It is an argument that is very hard to refute in a convincing way, although we all don't believe it. It is true in a way and untrue in another – and that

---

129 p. 157.

is what I was talking about. When you strike the key with the tip of an umbrella the only difference in timbre will be if you put your left foot down or not.

BRENDEL Let's examine this. I think what is important is the *connection* between sounds. If you make single sounds it can possibly be argued that one sound is like the other, no matter what strikes the key. (Though, on second thoughts, even this is not correct. You can strike the same note softer or louder, faster or slower, gently or violently, with or without the pedals; this already gives it a certain amount of character.) But when it comes to the connection of sounds the matter looks entirely different. It needs fingers, it needs feelings, it needs a musical temperament and brain to produce what makes music worth listening to. Then all the elements like harmonics, the pedalling, the articulation come in to alter the sound, to alter the meaning even of single notes because they live within a certain context. Of course, if you like the piano played like an automaton – there was a period in the 1920s when composers tried to achieve exactly this; i.e., Hindemith in the Suite (Op. 26) – then the pianist can produce this too. But there's little piano music to which this treatment does justice. And the pianola can do better.

WOLFF How do you react to Schnabel's rules for the ratio of loudness within chords?[130]

BRENDEL I think that the ratio of loudness of chords depends very much on the character of the music. For example, at the beginning of the 'Waldstein' Sonata you have four-voiced chords. If you play them in the manner recommended in the book (the soprano and bass leading and the middle voices slightly in the background) you will get a great deal of clarity but a totally wrong atmosphere. The atmosphere of this beginning is *pianissimo misterioso*...

WOLFF In the book there are several categories, if I may contradict you, and you have to find the right category: the category where they are all in the same register, as is the case in this beginning. The category of the soprano and the bass being stronger than the inner voices would not obtain but, instead, the category is where they all belong 'to one family'.

BRENDEL Yes, but even with chords in the same position it is imperative to see which colour is required, which atmosphere, which distance (I mean that space-like quality which music can convey). In the case of the 'Waldstein', it is not

---

130 pp. 159 ff.

daylight but dawn, I would say, not bright energy but mystery – even within the strict rhythmic pulse – and for me that tips the balance in favour of the inner voices. I play the inner voices slightly stronger than the outer voices. That makes the chord sound softer. This is an important matter. If the outer voices are played louder than the inner voices it does not sound *pianissimo*, no matter how soft you try to play them. The inner voices, in certain positions, give the *dolce* character, the warmth. Within a chord of four voices the interval of the third is the lyrical voice, the fifth is the horn – the mysterious voice – so if you have the normal position of a chord from C to C it would mean that the player who is interested in this poetical approach would favour, rather often, the middle voices and not, for instance, the bass line. I personally feel, after listening to pianists like Cortot, Fischer and Kempff (who in his best playing is a supreme master of sound and of balance), that to bring out the bass line is usually unnecessary. It is the basis of the harmony, of course, and it should be controlled perfectly, but it only needs to be pointed out where it denotes energy or where the bass has a special melodic or motivic or atmospheric importance. Otherwise, in music with functional harmony every musical listener will hear the bass more or less automatically, even if it is played very softly.

WOLFF Yes, that is the difference between you and Schnabel which I have also sometimes noticed when you play.

BRENDEL Yes? Sometimes my bass line is perhaps too soft?

WOLFF It sometimes seems that way to me.

BRENDEL Yes?

WOLFF I can't recall a recent occurrence where it seemed so to me, but several years ago there were moments.

BRENDEL There were, yes. I realised that myself and hope I have corrected it. I still think that to favour melody and bass as the two most important components of musical writing is, in practice, not always very successful.

WOLFF My father was an old-fashioned music lover, especially an opera lover. I remember him saying that he didn't like to listen to Schnabel because he heard the left hand too much. Of course, that was the generation of the 1870s.

BRENDEL Well, it depends on many things. If the piano piece presents the sound of a soloist with an accompaniment, then the melodic voice has to come out very prominently – more prominently than nearly anybody dares to do it today. For

me, Cortot is an example of a player who could bring the melody to the fore-
ground with a whole orchestra in the background without losing the different
timbres and voices. And without ever forcing the sound. I should also like to
mention balance rules for the playing of octaves, of which Schnabel says that they
are usually duplications of the main voice. From the standpoint of part-writing
this may be very true, but as a principle of giving more value to the main voice
during the performance, I would not always agree. Again, when I think of the
orchestra, when you duplicate something in a score, the duplication may be in
a stronger timbre and may, by its strength and by its intrusion into the purity of
part-writing, give special significance to the octave. I would not accept the principle that in an octave there is necessarily one leading voice and an accompanying
one. There are octaves where both notes have to be exactly equally loud, sound-
ing, so to speak, like one instrument. There are octaves where the inner voice,
even in melodic passages, comes in like a duplication with a horn. For instance,
let's take the Schubert G major Sonata, about which we talked earlier – the beginning of the first movement. I do not play the upper voice louder than the octave.
I favour the sixth in the right hand and make the high voice accompany, gently,
and that gives warmth and body to the sound, whereas if I were to bring out the
soprano it would, to me, sound too direct.

WOLFF But Schnabel thought, I believe, as he usually did in such cases, of the third
on top, like a soprano and alto singing in duet, and that's why he took the B in
the left hand – the B below middle C.

BRENDEL But then, what is the role of the thumb in this theme? There is a continuity of colour in the line of the thumb, and nearly all of it is a doubling of
the soprano. It should sound particularly relaxed, and it lies so well in the hand.
Why interrupt this continuity?

To my ears, the sound of thirds and sixths should often be on the dark side.
That means that the lower voice in Schubert and Brahms has to be at least as
prominent and expressive as the main voice – particularly in minor keys. If I listen to the slow movement of Schubert's B flat Sonata, at least the thought that
the inner voice is the most meaningful is valuable to me, even if it is not louder
than the soprano. Maybe it comes just a split second after the soprano and thus
draws imperceptibly a little attention to itself.

WOLFF I hear and enjoy these things when you do them. The other day you did something extraordinary and beautiful. In the B flat Impromptu (Schubert Op. 142, D.935, No. 3), just before the end, is a *sforzato* that I am always afraid of. You played it so that it was a *sforzato* but it had no violence, no harshness – you gave it the right dose.

BRENDEL I changed the balance. That, for me, is often the solution and there is no secret about it. Other people have done it before. If I look at the accents of the A minor Sonata (D.784), in the second movement, they are not positive accents which stand out dynamically; they ask for a change of colour in favour of inner voices, which gives the impression of pointing to a particular meaning or conveying something which is more private than anything before.

WOLFF To end, let me ask you this: is there any one point or points, in general, where you think that Schnabel's doctrines, in the way I have tried to explain them, are still valid and important?

BRENDEL Your question tells me that I must have given the impression of being entirely critical. I apologise! The subject of our conversation was to find out where Schnabel's approach, as you put it forward, differs from mine. I often feel close to Schnabel: when he speaks about general matters I usually share his opinion. When he goes into certain details of performance, such as rhythm and tempo, I sometimes have to disagree. I would say that the majority of things in the book are totally natural to me. I estimate that I would accept about two-thirds of your book with joy, and leave one-third open to discussion. And with all my queries, it remains the most stimulating and thought-provoking professional book that I have read in many years – to be precise, since Schnabel's own *Music and the Line of Most Resistance*.

(1979)

Looking through this interview ten years later, I feel that I should add a few instances of my dissent, if only for the sake of argument. Musicians who prefer to remain unaware of what they are doing may look at such scrutinizing as a useless contest in cleverness. This, I think, would not be quite fair. Konrad Wolff's, and Schnabel's, focus was on the discussion of musical matters, not on the promotion of personal glory and superiority. So is mine.

In the opening of Schubert's B flat Sonata, Schnabel 'wanted to avoid any point of gravity prior to the second downbeat' (p. 71). But is the second downbeat a point of gravity?

'Beethoven's rare pedalling instructions are without exception essential to the musical structure' (certainly not all of them) 'and do not leave any liberty to the performer.' Schnabel believed that, in these passages (Op. 31, No. 2, I, recitatives; C minor Concerto, Largo; 'Waldstein', finale; G major Concerto, I; Bagatelle Op. 126, No. 3), the 'bass note must be audible until the next bass note is played'. I cannot see why the C minor Largo should qualify. And how about Op. 126, No. 2, and Op. 106, II? 'If the pianist chooses the appropriate tone proportion and tone colour there will be no disturbing confusion in sound' (p. 84). Listening to Schnabel's record of the 'Waldstein', I have to voice my doubts. Under no circumstances should Beethoven's pedal markings be ignored. But these were the early days of pedal notation. In Beethoven's pedals the idea, whether structural, declamatory or atmospheric, should be conveyed, not the letter. There are ways of doing this without sacrificing transparency.

Talking about Mozart (pp. 102 ff.), Schnabel maintained that there should be no addition to the text. 'The pianist must play the exact number of notes the composer has written'. I would say that the pianist must give this impression (which is not quite the same!) unless there are patches that demand, or permit, elaboration.

On embellishment, 'the most important factor is the preservation of its decorative character'. There are embellishments which are decorative, and others which become part of the melodic line or have structural implications. 'Schnabel himself always played embellishing notes, and more *leggiero* than the principal ones'. I am afraid he did not. In his recordings they often draw all the attention towards themselves. And his highly personal, very fast trills often sound uneven by emphasizing the lower note. (Liszt had a name for it: 'Kartoffeln abladen' – unloading potatoes.) Should trills not be varied, in speed, colour and dynamics, to fit into their musical surroundings? There are plenty of different trills, if one listens to Edwin Fischer or Kempff, and a good many of them have preserved the nature of an extended appoggiatura, meaning that the higher note must not be neglected.

Schnabel avoided 'playing measured trills and turns exactly coinciding with the figurations of the left hand'. An idiosyncratic statement, to me unacceptable as a rule. Schnabel claims that 'a left-hand staccato does not exist in Mozart'. In Mozart's notation it does, though only when motivic ideas of the right hand are played by the bass. Accompaniments are sometimes slurred, but mostly unmarked; then they should be adjusted to the context. When in piano concertos the orchestra plays the same theme with staccato accompaniment, the soloist will usually comply, as in K.414, III.

'The brilliant figurations in Mozart's concertos ... have to be played legato. This rule is practically without exception, since they are modelled on vocal coloratura and not on violinistic articulation' (p. 108). Why should they be modelled on vocal coloratura alone? And why should vocal coloratura not include articulation which a woodwind player or violin player would make? The nineteenth century considered legato playing to be standard practice (see Czerny's *School of Piano Playing*, Op. 500, and the old Mozart complete edition). Paul Badura-Skoda, on the contrary, is convinced that Mozart's passages have to be played non-legato unless they are slurred. I cannot accept either prescription. For me, the model instruments for Mozart's passages are the woodwinds. (In Beethoven's early E flat Concerto this kind of articulation is written out in detail.)

'Quick notes, following a dot, in so-called dotted rhythm should neither be played as part of a triplet, nor double dotted'. They can, and often have to, be varied according to character and rhythmic surroundings.

Schnabel, during a crescendo, 'would not admit any drop in loudness between beats, not even in the event of two-note phrasings' (p. 112). Why not? I see the completely even crescendo rather as the exception, the crescendo that incorporates smaller declamatory dynamics as the rule.

'*Ritardandos* should only be made where they are marked'. In another essay[131] I have reproduced a list of unmarked opportunities for *ritardando*, or *ritenuto*, given by Czerny in his *School of Piano Playing*, Op. 500.

If, in contrapuntal music, 'two equally important parts are to be brought out with equal clarity, they should not be played equally loudly'. Agreed. But 'in a two-part setting the lower of the two parts must always be softer than the upper' (p. 160). No, it must not. Either way is possible.

The performer should be 'shedding a surprising new light on the composer's deepest meaning' (p. 169). I am worried about the stress on 'surprising' and 'new'. Is it not difficult and absorbing enough to look for 'meaning', and to distil its essence?

---

131 '*Werktreue* – An Afterthought', p. 39.

To surprise oneself, or let oneself be surprised, by musical discoveries is legitimate and satisfying as long as such discoveries illuminate the purpose of the piece. The intention to surprise one's audience, however, breeds eccentricity. Wanting to be different, the player easily exaggerates what is right or contradicts what is necessary.

I never met Schnabel, and I do not belong to the legion of his enthralled pupils. Yet he remains one of the great musicians I relate to, both in admiration and in criticism. I should like to close these pages by quoting some of Schnabel's (and Konrad Wolff's) statements I am only too glad to share.

Schnabel 'always encouraged students to find out as much as possible about the structure, harmonies, motivic technique, etc., used in each score. But there is no basis for interpretation in most of this ... To *begin* the study of a new work by analysing its form, in school term paper fashion, is more harmful than helpful ... True analysis is but a clarification and intensification of musical sensitivity, an additional push in the right direction as established by musical instinct' (pp. 18–19). Like Schnabel, I feel that few analytic insights have a direct bearing on performance, and that analysis should be the outcome of an intimate familiarity with the piece rather than an input of established concepts. At the same time, 'every music student should be obliged to write music, whether or not he is gifted for it or attracted by it. Such an obligation is, unfortunately, not even recommended nowadays, although it was a matter of course in former times' (Schnabel, *Music and the Line of Most Resistance*). 'He easily associated this or that section of a composition with pride or humility, outdoors or indoors, morning or evening, privacy or officialdom, cold or heat, remoteness or directness, agitation or sobriety, etc.' (p. 127). To be able to put into words matters of musical character, colour and atmosphere implies some kind of a literary effort. We need not only to understand what words mean and to feel what they suggest, but also to stretch the scope of our vocabulary. As Schnabel's (or Wolff's) examples show, the perception of contrasts is our starting-point. But let us not forget that they need not be mutually exclusive; there are, indeed, areas of overlapping, of musical twilight, as in several of Haydn's themes. And many characters are complex rather than clear-cut.

'It is a mistake to imagine that all notes should be played with equal intensity or even be clearly audible. In order to clarify the *music* it is often necessary to make certain *notes* obscure' (p. 157). Complete and permanent clarity of execution is a manner of playing which, instead of serving the music, is content with itself. It happens to be the beau ideal of most record producers.

'The performer's inner ear hears everything twice: each little bit is mentally anticipated as well as checked out by later control.' If all goes well, these two perceptions
are blended into one or, as Schnabel phrased it: 'The conception materialises and
the materialisation re-dissolves into conception.' An event as mysterious as parallel
lines meeting in the infinite. If all went well, Schnabel made them meet.

(1989)

Afterthoughts on Life and Art

WITH MARTIN MEYER

MARTIN MEYER You are an exceptionally successful musician. But if you looked back on your career, what aspects of your life as an artist would you change?

ALFRED BRENDEL I cannot complain. Things have gone well enough for me. Therefore, instead of altering the details of my destiny, I'd rather like to invent a series of scenarios which would have steered my life in a different direction.

MEYER Knowing your black humour, I'd hardly expect them to be particularly cosy. Could you give some examples?

BRENDEL Firstly: musical parents. No wars, no memories of Nazis and fascists, no Hitler or Goebbels on the wireless, no soldiers, party members and bombs. Piano tuition from a nephew of Rachmaninov in America. Composition lessons from Schoenberg in Los Angeles. Film music for Woody Allen.

MEYER That certainly sounds promising, and I'm pleased about the rapprochement with Rachmaninov. But I could imagine something more provocative.

BRENDEL All right, then: artistic parents – my father a sculptor and taxidermist, my mother a dancer and diseuse. Myself one of the first to supply *objets trouvés* for Joseph Cornell, for whom I worked as an assistant. It was actually I who created all those Cornell boxes that feature birds or ballerinas. In addition – I wrote scripts for Buñuel and designed the Graz Dada Memorial, at the unveiling of which the mayor, true to his pledge, managed always to say the opposite of what he had just said.

MEYER To play the opposite would presumably have been in homage to Rachmaninov ... But seriously: I have never been utterly enamoured by your enthusiasm for Dada, with or without monument. Masks, rhetoric and the cabaret stage do not suit the seriousness of a concert pianist.

BRENDEL When I play Beethoven, I am not a Dadaist. Yet even the most serious of musicians cannot exist without some sort of connection with masks, stage and rhetoric. Which leads me to my third scenario: actor parents. My father the most down-to-earth Hamlet of his generation, my mother a tragedienne whose screams as Messalina terrified the public. Numerous appearances as a child at the Burgtheater, before I transferred my allegiance to Vienna's underground stages. In the

Viennese premiere of *Waiting for Godot*, I played both Estragon and Vladimir on alternate nights, then Vitrac's 'Victor' with triumphant success. I also appeared in Antonioni films alongside Monica Vitti, who nearly became my third wife.

MEYER That would have made me jealous, at least at that time. But back to reality. What new projects do you have as a pianist?

BRENDEL To do what I already do, but better. Play more Mozart sonatas. Perform with the nicest conductors and the best orchestras. Take into account the constitution of a 75-year-old. Look at architecture, visit museums and exhibitions – in other words, have more spare time. See old films. Re-read great literature. Write poems. Give lectures. Try to look happy and grateful despite the wretched state of the world.

MEYER That is a great deal, but with a good balance, it seems to me, between contemplation and the *vita activa*. The 75-year-old appears, if I may say so, remarkably sprightly. Do you feel the need to think about a possible 'late style' of interpretation?

BRENDEL A good question. Even when I was young, I had the distinct impression that the so-called late style was a compromise with arthritis. For arthritis read articular degeneration, myositis and neuritis, and other conditions that come with advanced age. A musician who maintains his natural vitality after seventy is a rarity.

MEYER Could you name any?

BRENDEL Arthur Rubinstein was one such. Astonishing examples among conductors include Claudio Abbado and the octogenarian Charles Mackerras. Bruno Walter, by the way, said that one's music-making was more fluent in old age because, with a greater overview, one needed less time. Which in his case was certainly not true. I remember a late performance of Schubert's *Unfinished* in Vienna in which, after a wonderful first movement, he made the wind players blow their lungs out in the second. It sounded like a solemn, endlessly extended valediction.

MEYER But there were, and still are, a great number of musicians who wish to forget old age in favour of a late-flowering youthfulness – even rather introverted figures such as Rudolf Serkin or Horowitz.

BRENDEL I note with interest that you call Horowitz introverted. There are, it's true, examples of ageing artists wishing to be more youthful than the young. The aged Casals, who as a cellist was no hotspur, conducted performances in Marlboro of Beethoven's Eighth and Mendelssohn's Fourth that were downright frantic. The ideal late style would be a blend of wisdom and freshness. When aged virtuosi, however, find it necessary to prove themselves by still thundering out Chopin's A flat Polonaise, I am embarrassed.

MEYER Would you yourself find it difficult to say farewell to an active life as soloist? Or to put it more bluntly – are you preparing for the time when you might possibly play no more?

BRENDEL There are people who are ill-prepared in everything. 'Let's wait till we fall sick and then decide how to react.' That is not my style. There will never be a lack of surprises in life – things that cannot be predicted. My poems, for example, were one such surprise. But there are other things that should be anticipated, and prepared for, to prevent them from occurring or to reduce the shock.

MEYER I have to say that sounds to me more than a little abstract.

BRENDEL Of course there will be a time when I stop playing – either through necessity or because I wish to. That won't be easy. For although one's musical insights develop and become more precise in detail, although one senses essence more readily, one's physical strength and mobility will at some point diminish – just like one's ability to concentrate for long periods. It is easier for conductors, because the orchestra will go on playing.

MEYER Thomas Mann imagined late in his life that the body was still able to perform relatively efficiently, whereas one's mental vigour dried up. Proust, on the other hand, feared that his diminishing physical powers would no longer be sufficient for him to put his ideas and thoughts onto paper. Which would be worse?

BRENDEL Probably the horror imagined by Thomas Mann, especially when I think about what I might do when my career as a concert pianist comes to a close: give lectures and occasional masterclasses and write – provided that my eyes, ears and mind can still function. What at any rate I look forward to is having more time to do what I wish: travel, look at art, hear new music, sit on the edge of my chair in theatres, and fill gaps in my knowledge of movies.

MEYER Any surprises?

BRENDEL When my first volume of poems appeared, a friend wrote to me saying that he expected me now to design a church in Hampstead.

MEYER The praise of an atheist architect would certainly have delighted the good Lord. But returning to our theme: would you really find it interesting to give masterclasses? Teaching seems not till now to have been a high priority.

BRENDEL In the last thirty years my preference has been to teach only a few individual pupils. But the idea might nonetheless interest me again. For in a good masterclass all those present should feel it is not they but the music, the work in question, that is at the centre of things. The performance should spring from the composition, revealing its uniqueness, which cannot be plumbed through general rules or formulae.

MEYER I see and hear legions of gifted but grey pianists, crouched over the piano, boring us with their fidelity to the original score.

BRENDEL I sense in you a predilection for eccentric giants of the keyboard. Which of the two is worse: fidelity to the work or fidelity to the player's huge ego? Let's leave fidelity out of this, shall we? It is from the works themselves that pianists – male and female – should derive their inspiration, and blossom. Of course, one must teach young players to be independent. On the other hand, one should demonstrate to them exactly how a performance, down to the very last note, needs to be worked out. That can only be conveyed with the aid of one's own imagination and one's own experience: as an example, but not as the one and only truth.

MEYER Could you give a few more specific tips for the younger generation of pianists?

BRENDEL What I mean is this – there are problems that cannot be solved through imagination or rules. The pianist must experiment with the instrument, listen carefully, and then hold on to the moment when suddenly a passage sounds convincing. Aha! This note must be stressed and not the next. But even perceptions of this nature are not sufficient unless they are combined with the utmost accuracy – how great must the nuance be and how does it affect the phrase?

MEYER Can you cite examples from particular pieces of music?

BRENDEL The examples that come to mind are not from music but from films. Jean-Claude Carrière tells of Jacques Tati's concern with sounds in his film *Mon Oncle*. It was a question of finding the right sound for a glass as it shattered on the kitchen floor. Tati got hold of a variety of glasses which he then 'with the utmost seriousness dropped one after the other onto a variety of surfaces'. And Chaplin was said to have spent many hours rehearsing in great detail the dialogues with the flower-girl in *City Lights*, although the words in a silent film would remain inaudible. A fine model: prepare something in great detail and then hide the final result as much as possible!

MEYER What advice – from an artistic and human perspective – would you give today's young musicians?

BRENDEL Young pianists should acquaint themselves with music of all kinds – not just piano music. They should study composition and, as far as possible, compose. They should, if they wish to be virtuosi, not be virtuosi of the stupid kind, but should subordinate their virtuosity to the music as a means to an end – nothing more, nothing less. They should regard their talent as a promise that can be realised in the long term through patience, energy and a good mixture of enthusiasm and scepticism. They should, instead of applying stereotypes, always be prepared to learn – every new piece, every new bar is a new challenge.

MEYER That seems to me to be the work of a lifetime.

BRENDEL Exactly, that should hopefully continue through their life. They should however learn not just from other instrumentalists but also from singers, conductors and actors. Music is so many things: poetry, storytelling, but also grand theatre. And finally, they should live, love, suffer respectably and be happy. Which is, of course, asking too much...

MEYER Music drawn from life, or better – from other energies in life. Which reminds me that you yourself acted as a child. Your father ran a cinema, when you were a schoolboy. What importance do theatre and cinema have for you today?

BRENDEL Both remain, at their best, something magical. Good actors are my brothers and sisters, great actors are my models. After all, the musician must play roles, characterise, transform himself according to the composer's will. What the musician puts into the music, the actor on stage achieves with his face, his voice, his body.

MEYER Could one adapt Nietzsche's words: he should draw the shape of the music from the spirit of tragedy?

BRENDEL It doesn't have to be interpreted so narrowly. Comedy too should have its say. But a part of music is certainly drama, which mirrors human actions and reactions. In the spoken theatre there is also music, stage-music, and good music too. I remember Maurice Jarre's music for the Théâtre National Populaire. And the great Harrison Birtwistle was for many years composer-in-residence at the National Theatre in London. Theatre music seems, as a rule, better than film music. Film music, or soundtracks, to use a present-day term, are mostly ghastly.

MEYER That seems to me somewhat harsh and perhaps starts from the wrong assumption that film music should stand on its own, whereas it should work in conjunction with the image. That is how both Hitchcock and Fellini could, through clever cooperation with their composers, underpin their films with masterly sound.

BRENDEL I wish I could agree with you. The only masterly thing I find about these composers is the routine, if that is not a contradiction in terms. What they supply, with few exceptions, is pretentious entertainment music, or else sentimental rubbish. Worst of all are film scores with artistic pretensions, especially when they are pastiche. I'm thinking above all of films in which music has a central role, such as Jane Campion's *The Piano* or Kieślowski's *Trois Couleurs: Bleu*; sitting in the cinema, I'm surrounded by people with tears in their eyes who fail to note that the most extreme boundaries of taste have been 'understepped'. There's a word for it.

MEYER You mean kitsch?

BRENDEL I mean kitsch. But I will for a change mention an example of splendid film music: that of *City Lights*, composed by a musical amateur, namely Chaplin himself. It was probably improvised at the piano, but it is exactly what the film needs. Films, of course, can be especially wonderful when there is no music at all – as with Tarkowski (only those inspired noises) or with the last films of Buñuel (who was rather deaf), except when someone sings.

MEYER Film – compared with musical composition and written-down theatre – is a medium *sui generis*: free and open, created from the ideas and images of the director, who is his own interpreter.

BRENDEL Correct. In the theatre, as on the concert platform, the performance must show a responsibility towards the play and the text – which today happens all too rarely. Something latent should be brought alive. Films, if they are not re-makes, are indeed creations. There is, of course, or there used to be, the occasional film with an outstanding script, in which every word fits: *All About Eve*, for example, or René Clément's *Jeux interdits*. Mostly, however, a film seems to be created in a state of flux and – as a combination of order and chance – to end, if not culminate, on the cutting table. In my own life, this process resembles the genesis of my poems.

MEYER Since you mention your poems, quite a few of their images and metaphors, and even the rhythm, seem to be inspired by the visual richness of film.

BRENDEL I hope you are right. But there is something else, something important: the courage of films to be grotesque. Chaplin, who in some circles is despised today, is still for me, in his earlier films, cinema's universal genius. As a seasoned collector of kitsch, I should like to say that the final scene of *City Lights* has nothing to do with kitsch; it is, on the contrary, great and tragic theatre. Whenever Chaplin plays with the picture postcards of kitsch, he changes lies into truth.

MEYER I confess that I don't quite follow you. I also fear that we intellectuals often read a little too much into Chaplin's intentions. I do, on the other hand, get excited about another filmmaker who you especially admire: Luis Buñuel.

BRENDEL Buñuel is for me unique. The word 'surreal' describes him better than anyone else. Buñuel's best films are higher, concentrated reality. This combination of clarity and calm with the subversive world of dream makes the dream real, and reality anarchic. *Viridiana* and *Le Fantôme de la Liberté* are liberating films, if not exactly a lesson on how to lead a good and sensible life.

MEYER Isn't such a subversion like 'playing jokes on horror' as Goethe formulated it critically? I am, after all, familiar with your affection for, so to speak, a higher intellectual anarchy.

BRENDEL Well, as far as I can see, Goethe's susceptibility to comedy of all types was rather limited. I, on the other hand, especially in my youth, found that something very considerable was happening in the new drama and music on this ridge between the grotesque and the macabre – as exemplified in music by Ligeti's *Aventures et Nouvelles aventures*, and in the theatre, of course, by Ionesco and Beckett.

MEYER In other words, a radical demystifying plus comic effect, or else, human frailty with a gentle hint of possible redemption. And while on the subject of comedy – do you like laughing? Or do you rather laugh at the thought of a conceivable laugh?

BRENDEL I am not that complicated. I like laughing but don't laugh as much as I used to. The secularist in me delights in attacking the absolute, anyone who takes himself wholly seriously, anyone who puffs himself up. The enlightenment spirit in me also delights in blasphemy. That is beautiful, healthy subversion. Faced with the havoc caused by religion throughout history, and the havoc it continues to cause most liberally today, there can hardly be sufficient subversion. A wonderful film that belongs to this genre is René Clément's *Jeux interdits* of 1952. Here, on the same theme, is a poem:

Just look at these angels
clad in their celestial armour
that make short work of anyone

who doesn't instantly
sink to his knees drivelling
a butchery of apocalyptic completeness
a mangled blend of body and soul
irretrievably deadly to those of us who cannot boast a guardian devil
an entity hard to overestimate these days
whose ability to set up house
in New Jerusalem's hideouts and ruins
will doubtless
save us from the worst

MEYER I see that the devils here have assumed a downright rescuing function – I hope, however, that they don't lose their propensity to intervene subversively. In this connection, I put you this question: is Alfred Brendel a Dionysian or Apollonian type?

BRENDEL There is a key way of looking at alternatives that perhaps comes from Austria: not 'either-or' but 'either-and-or'. That seems to me, in politics as well, to be sometimes the only sensible approach, a combination of change and conservation. In relation to art, Nietzsche's dichotomy reminds me of the opposing positions of C. P. E. Bach on the one hand, and Busoni or Diderot on the other. According to one of them, only he who is himself moved is able to move his audience. The other two assert the exact opposite: he who wishes to move his audience must not himself be moved, or else he will lose control over his means. Both, in my view, are necessary. Intoxication will not create a work of art, without the assistance of control and reflection. Chaos is then allowed – to quote a thought of Novalis – 'to shimmer through the veil of order'.

MEYER Which composers, which musical styles are, generally speaking, favoured by the Apollonian age, in contradistinction to the Dionysian elan of youth?

BRENDEL I cannot answer that in general terms. It presumably depends on what one became involved in when younger. My friend Isaiah Berlin, who for a long time admired Italian opera more than any other music and travelled regularly to the Rossini Festival in Pesaro, turned in his final years to the chamber music of Beethoven and Schubert. Having been delighted by 'naïve' music, he was now caught up by the 'sentimental'.

MEYER And what about yourself? Have you set aside any provision for the future?

BRENDEL Apart from new music, I take more and more pleasure in Haydn and
Handel. I still have many of Haydn's symphonies and string quartets left to enjoy
in my old age. Haydn – that master of the surprise, the half naïve, half rococo
discoverer of new forms and rules who, at the same time, delights in humorously
contravening them. And then Handel, the 'plein air' composer with the most
open of horizons, the inexhaustible and generous melodist, balancing out the
contrapuntal density and obsession of Bach.

MEYER Both Handel and Haydn were, so to speak, well-disposed towards this
world, and never ventured too far into metaphysics, either of the theological or
pantheistic variety.

BRENDEL Yes, although both are wonderfully capable of gravitas, they are, despite
all their diversity, bright and positive composers by nature and no angels of death.
Perhaps there is not so great a desire in old age for the abysses of melancholy, for
the most ineluctable levels of complexity or for superhuman perfection. It does
not disturb me much, by the way, that Handel borrowed considerably from other
composers. Not one of them was a Handel. Even when adapting the music of
others, he creates his personal and powerful style.

MEYER When I listen to your performances, one naturally wonders whether you
intend to keep writing about music.

BRENDEL I rather have it in mind to lecture on the various possibilities – both positive and dubious – of interpretation, much of which cannot be written down; it
has to be demonstrated.

MEYER The poet in you, however, continues to be active and productive. How do
you view the significance of your activity as a poet?

BRENDEL Not as a hobby! Those poets who do nothing but write poetry inevitably
have the following view: here is someone who plays the piano and writes poetry for
fun. Or: even in his poems he plays with his little finger extended. One extended
little finger too many. No, no. Writing has been second nature to me for a long
time. But my poems have from the very beginning been written by an alter ego.

MEYER What does that actually mean? Can you really look over your own shoulder, as it were?

BRENDEL I read and listen to my poems and criticise them as though they were
by another poet, and although they affect me in a strangely intimate way, they

also lead me away from myself into the unknown. Without this black ghost of distance, I would not find the reflection worthy of attention. The black ghost, however, is not only black, it also has its curious and comic sides. An authority on contemporary poetry called my collected poems a 'negative (cheerful) cosmology'. When I recently mentioned one of my favourite books, Italo Calvino's *Cosmicomics*, to Seamus Heaney, he replied that my poems were, after all, 'cosmicomics' as well. Though not all of them are comic. Or cosmic.

MEYER Since you've been writing poetry, you have recited them in public. I remember an evening in Lucerne when you, together with the pianist Pierre-Laurent Aimard, presented a highly enjoyable blend of readings and music. What, for yourself, is the difference between performing poetry and performing music?

BRENDEL To begin with – the fact that I recite my own things and not those of other poets. Which is why I make fewer mistakes than when I give concerts. And there's almost never any coughing. During my first visit to Dortmund, however, the audience let me down badly: no one laughed and an unbelievably ugly woman looked at me with disdain. I like reading my poems because they should be heard. After all, I hear them as I write them down.

MEYER Do you permit others to recite your poems? Should they?

BRENDEL Of course. Only – when they are read or recited by others, something easily goes wrong, even when the reader is a Jutta Lampe or an Isabelle Huppert. A most notable exception was Harold Pinter who once recited six of my poems – he got it absolutely right, in his own way. At a ceremony in Vienna, however, two students from the Max Reinhardt Seminar demolished everything with their old-fashioned and high-flown declamation.

MEYER Some venues have a magic about them, others are unremarkable and dull. Do you react sensitively?

BRENDEL Sometimes. A particularly enjoyable reading took place in Frankfurt's Städel. The museum was being rebuilt, which meant that I was miraculously allowed to choose pictures which were then hung around me in an empty gallery. Behind me was a painting with mice, with a hardly visible monster lurking in the background. Another unforgettable venue was a small baroque church in Amsterdam that had been secretly installed in the attic of a house on one of the canals. Having been introduced by Margriet de Moor, I sat in front of the high altar and recited my not especially God-fearing poems.

MEYER You mentioned Pierre-Laurent Aimard, a pianist who specialises in contemporary music. How did you come together?

BRENDEL My wife invited him out of the blue to take part in a charity event for
London's Almeida Theatre. He attended, and already knew some of my poems.
After an initial improvisation, we began to give our joint recitals which, thanks
to Pierre-Laurent's versatility, also are staged with skill. Pieces by György Kurtag
– which are sometimes small theatrical scenes – and by György Ligeti are played,
either according with my poems or contradicting them. The way Pierre-Laurent
can conjure up a Ligeti Etude with a funny expression on his face is rather inspired.

MEYER A propos new music: is it actually becoming a constant quest for novelty –
in that 'progressive' sense of the avant-garde – or is it experimenting with models
in the style of what Gottfried Benn called 'Unaufhörlichkeit' – 'open-endedness'?

BRENDEL A fundamental characteristic of any masterpiece – and not just in contemporary music – is innovation: breaking new ground, inventing new combinations,
developing something in a new direction. Backward steps are sometimes permitted provided they are not retrograde steps. For me, there are endless ways in
which music can progress – which is not the same as progress! In this respect I
am, exceptionally, an optimist.

MEYER A question now on the public's reception of music. Do you think that today's
audiences respond to concerts, given by you and others, in a more informed and
enlightened way than in the past? Or has there been a decline in knowledge and
competence, due to a different attitude to education?

BRENDEL Probably both. Any increase in the number of musical amateurs or connoisseurs is offset by the threat of electronically amplified music. The ear, the first
of the sensory organs to develop in the womb, is today exposed to a level of noise
pollution, is coarsened and brutalised in a way that attacks one's whole being.
Noise pollution is to the mind what cigarette smoke is to the lungs.

MEYER Could you give more concrete examples? The way you put it sounds too
generally critical.

BRENDEL Willingly. I'm thinking of the many young people who systematically
ruin their own hearing and sometimes the hearing of their fellow human beings
– as you are well aware! I'm thinking of the influence of television which gives
an audience the erroneous view that it's listening to the sound from the platform through a loudspeaker placed in one direction – while coughing, clearing

the throat and sneezing does not echo back. So – on the credit side we have an auditorium full of people who, if one is lucky, listen attentively to Beethoven's *Diabelli Variations*, which they would hardly have done a few decades ago. And on the debit side we may be forced to interrupt a concert and tell the audience: either you cough or I play – otherwise the coughing would simply continue. The audience, by the way, after such announcements, is usually utterly silent for the rest of the evening, which proves conclusively that it is not necessary to cough.

MEYER To return once more to possible sources of inspiration: in what ways are you inspired by other art forms such as literature and the visual arts?

BRENDEL From early on I have kept in touch with all the arts. I therefore find it difficult to say in which ways the musician in me has gained from all that. At any rate, it was more a complement than a blending of elements.

MEYER No synaesthetic intoxication, like a Gesamtkunstwerk?

BRENDEL I learned early enough to keep all the arts separate. There are of course connections with music in the figurative sense, like words and concepts which, from the visual arts and literature, are applied to music. But at the same time music remains autonomous, even in Arthur Honegger's *Pacific 231*, an orchestral work in which the composer used the journey of a specific railway engine from one station to another as a pretext for writing new music.

MEYER Music, therefore, remains more or less absolute and self-contained, while the rest of life profits from the other arts?

BRENDEL Music is the most natural thing in my life. Music: that's me, as it were, and I have never been very interested in thinking about myself. If I dig deep into my memory, it is not necessarily musical impressions that come first to mind, but things 'from without', such as my first encounter with Chaplin films, the first performance of *Waiting for Godot* in Vienna in Erich Neuberg's production, or my first visit to the Romanesque churches of Tuscania, my first encounter with Alexander Calder's mobiles in a Munich gallery during the early '50s, or the chance discovery of Tinguely's kinetic sculptures in a whitewashed garage in Rome – to name but a few. Who knows whether Tinguely's wriggling and rattling machines, delightfully without point or purpose, are not reflected in my performances of Haydn's sonatas or the *Diabelli Variations*?

MEYER If that were the case, then we should cry out: 'Tinguely, be thanked!' Does a performer, by the way, have to be an intellectual?

BRENDEL I never think of myself as an intellectual, that is to say as someone who
is guided primarily by his intellect. I am a musician and a writer who also thinks.
There are instinctive musicians of great stature, but one must not conclude that
they alone can move us. That is nonsense. It is through the combination of chaos
and order, feeling and reflection that the heat of chaos should be reduced through
order to warmth – which in turn warms the coolness of order. Whether that
happens consciously or subconsciously is hardly important, as long as the result
is right. One result of such a combination is *Gefühlsdeutlicheit* – distinctness of
feeling, a word coined by Robert Schumann.

MEYER Congratulations on this third Brendelian law of thermo-dynamics. I think
it can be applied to many outright intellectual musicians, even to Glenn Gould
who, though in his interviews he gave only an artificial impression of spontaneity by reformulating certain questions which he then put into his interviewer's
mouth, could as a pianist play spontaneously and with warmth.

BRENDEL No comment.

MEYER Our conversation is drawing to a close, which is why I now ask you this
question: How does an awareness of the finiteness of life relate to the supposed
timelessness of music?

BRENDEL Art and life was never for me an equation but rather a calculation that
does not work out. Not that music has nothing to do with life. The connections
with human character, emotions, conflicts, reactions should after all be obvious.
Great music is concerned with a world which embraces human experience, but
it also has the ability to reach out beyond human experience into the fateful, the
fantastic, the demonic, the seraphic, reach out to timelessness and silence. Music
can immerse itself in the tragic and the fatal, but can also, in humorous superiority, rise above human matters.

MEYER That sounds to me almost mystical, spiritual. Are you a secret mystic?

BRENDEL You'd better ask the devil. It's feasible that my performances may sometimes release – for the audience too – such kinds of energies. In which case, one
could say: 'The music plays itself.' I'll give you a more concrete example. Not
long ago I heard a performance of Bruckner's Seventh Symphony which made
the work come originally and convincingly alive. The music in this performance
was to my ears far removed from Bruckner's personality as we know it from eye-
witness accounts. No one would have had an idea from this performance that

Bruckner was naïve, gauche and humble. It would be equally wrong to connect this arch-Catholic walking the Vienna woods with this highly sophisticated and grandiose music. Attempts to explain a composer as comprehensibly as possible through biography are often misleading – and not only in the case of musicians. That is precisely what the film historian David Thomson tries to do with celebrities of the screen in his highly praised *Biographical Dictionary of Film* – with partially absurd results.

MEYER What is your attitude towards recordings, both generally and with reference to your own?

BRENDEL I'm grateful for the fact that there are recordings by great masters which still, after years of familiarity, set standards – so fresh and brilliant have they remained. With my own recordings there is a different, personal yardstick. I've had the opportunity of making a great number of studio recordings. That increases the chance of there being a few that represent me at my best – the best concerts are, after all, rarely recorded. A selection appeared on six CDs in the 'Great Pianists' series, which deliberately omitted both Beethoven and Mozart piano concertos, as well as Schubert's sonatas. Live recordings of some Schubert sonatas, the Beethoven concertos with the Vienna Philharmonic and Simon Rattle, as well as a number of Mozart concertos with Charles Mackerras should complete the picture. I'm pleased that a new, larger selection of CDs, likewise chosen by me, is now beginning to appear, which will eventually include a number of unpublished live recordings by which I set great store.

MEYER What music should be heard in heaven – if there is such a thing – and what music should not?

BRENDEL There is something child-like about the idea of heaven and hell. Isaiah Berlin, in a celebrated essay, applied Schiller's concept of the naïve and the sentimental to music. Verdi was for him a great naïve composer. If one had to hear Verdi incessantly in Paradise, I'd ask for leave and the occasional visit to Purgatory or perhaps even Hell.

MEYER Where the rest of us will take pleasure in welcoming you! One final question. How would you respond to anyone who implied that the modesty you revealed during our conversations in *Me Of All People* was merely a pose?

BRENDEL I am aware that some people do not wish to accept me as I am because they expect an artist always to be narcissistic. My position is as follows: I am surprised by myself but I cannot admire myself. I have certain gifts. That is no achievement. It is only sensible to try and make something of one's talent. It's also a need, because it sucks you in. It's something that helps to fill life. That one has the necessary energy, the necessary enthusiasm, the necessary persistence, the appropriate constitution, is likewise not an achievement. They are qualities one has. That I can communicate with an audience musically and fill halls despite my grimaces is for me not a source of pride but astonishment.

(2015)

Me, Myself and I

ABI: To start with, let's establish how to communicate with each other. First names only?

AB2: What a question! Who uses first names these days besides aristocrats and Americans? Do you feel aristocratic or, perish the thought, do we feel like an item? Come to think of it: Do we love each other?

ABI: I wouldn't go that far. What about hating each other?

AB2: Hardly. Even allowing for all the mistrust, we certainly won't be tearing each other into little shreds. Although I would have liked to clip you over the ears recently when you didn't start that trill with the grace note...

ABI: Pedant! Anyway, that's no longer a matter of discussion. These days, I trill in silence. But let's get to the point. As we both, until recently, have been pianists, I've always wanted to ask you what's going on – all right, *was* going on – when you played Op. III. Were you moved at all?

AB2: Most certainly. I'd even go so far as to say that I levitated – though only inside myself.

ABI: In that poem of yours about your colleague Fischkemper you actually made a joke about...

AB2: Come on, *you* wrote that poem!

ABI: It's just as well that I'm there for you. While you are right into the music, I am outside and beyond. Not a bad combination.

AB2: Yes and no. To penetrate to the heart of a work, to lose yourself in it with relish, to actually disappear in it – this is, and remains, one of the loveliest things that can happen to us.

ABI: Okay. I leave it to you without qualms – just as long as I, as a *deus ex machina*, can keep an eye on you as to whether things are functioning, making sure the fingers know what they are doing, that the back isn't tensing up, the rhythm isn't slackening off, the fact that you are creeping into the work isn't just hollowing it out but also putting something in.

AB2: My dear helicopter policeman, couldn't you just hover over me quietly and unobtrusively? Keep control without rattling on? Don't you ever feel the need to make yourself superfluous?

ABI: A nice utopian vision. When music seems 'to play itself' I'm always there, at least with one hand at the wheel. Have you ever heard of something called Romantic Irony?

AB2: A pleasant state to be in – but one that carries the risk of placing yourself above and beyond responsibility. Which brings us back to levitation, not in terms of floating *above* the work, but floating *with* it. After all, we're only performers.

AB1: To recapitulate: You levitate inwardly, I steer things from the outside. Sorry to be such a nuisance to you. Didn't we get on pretty well with each other as a circus act? The Brendel Twins – not identical, of course.

AB2: Allow me a very personal question: Do you ever find yourself on the verge of tears? In Schubert, perhaps?

AB1: Are you serious? Expecting me to do what Diderot and Busoni have warned us against? That is, lose control, control over the ways and means, but also my control over you? Sob as much as you like – but please do it clandestinely. As soon as you go overboard becoming all weepy and whiny, and overstep the bounds of musical decency, I shall start rattling again.

AB2: Incorrigible purist! Your notion of decency is nothing but a straitjacket. For God's sake, can't you give me just a few inches leeway?

AB3: Morning, gents! Been listening to you with some interest. Doncha know that times have changed? These days we've got, on the one hand, the two-note group, on the other the adaptation, the paraphrase, the personal take on things, the commentary that is more pertinent than the work itself. Let's be honest: Without us, the music is just waste paper. Show it to them: Galvanise the composers! The force is with us! Shake off your chains! (Getting progressively worked up) Let off steam! Be a Dadaist!

AB2: (Covers his ears.)

AB1: (Pulls out an eyelash and stabs AB3 to death with it. Then scatters spinach all over him.)

Here is the poem the Brendels were referring to:

> *During his recent recital*
> *I saw my celebrated colleague Fischkemper*
> *levitate above the piano*
> *I could hardly believe my eyes*

but there he hovered
while the piano keys
all by themselves
went on playing the E flat trill from Op. III
thus demonstrating
even to the staunchest skeptic
that a mystical experience
accessible to all
was being enacted

(2010)

Thanking the Critics

FIRST OF ALL I would like to thank you for the honour that brought me here, slightly bemused because I have never been in a room full of critics before. I confess that even now, at a point of my life when I fill the large halls, play with the great orchestras, and continue to turn out recordings, there is a residue of apprehension left from earlier days when I tried to make a name for myself with the help of the press, and sometimes without it. My gratitude goes out to two of the three reviewers in Graz, Austria, who, after my debut recital, predicted a brilliant future, and to William Mann who described one of my first London concerts in *The Times* as 'a recital in a thousand'. But I should also be grateful in hindsight to the *New York Times* which for a number of years had put me down, for showing me that it is possible to gain a following and establish one's reputation in spite of it.

There is a collection of art criticism by Robert Hughes which is called *Nothing If Not Critical*. The title is taken from Shakespeare's *Othello* where the full line reads: 'For I am nothing if not critical.' I hope that not everyone present here will readily identify with Iago who speaks it.

Of course I have no way of knowing how the minds of professional critics are wired as I am not one of them. I remember writing three reviews myself. I wrote a piece about a young violinist in order to describe as fully as possible all the wonderful virtues of her playing. I have commented on the *New Grove*, taking particular delight in its information on 'Piano Playing'. And I delivered a lengthy survey of a German encyclopaedia of present-day performers which was produced predominantly by computers and the viruses inhabiting them. Further, I have occasionally voiced my misgivings about Glenn Gould whose talent was certainly exceptional but whose style of dealing with his profession – which also happens to be mine – I found unacceptable. On the other hand, my admiration for some of my fellow musicians has helped me to become aware of what a great performer can achieve, and to outline the task of the performer as I see it.

That brings me to the critical faculty I am most familiar with, namely self-criticism. The 'culture of complaint', to mention another of Robert Hughes's book titles, should be turned towards oneself. One's own performances, musical goals and perspectives need to be continuously aired, scrutinised and measured with the yardstick of the compositions themselves. In order to pursue this task with patience and grace the performer will have to take his cues from the pieces and not put himself above the composer.

What troubles me about the title of Robert Hughes's brilliant book is the word 'nothing'. If performers aimed to be nothing if not critical they would forfeit their role. Among the many contradictions a performer has to live with is being sceptical *and* loving, questing *and* elated at one and the same time. Never should the bliss of dealing with masterpieces get buried under a pile of self-deprecating rubble – which doesn't mean that the intervention of one's critical abilities is anything less than decisive. Where there is a healthy balance between elation and scepticism the performer is on the right track providing that there is also talent, patience, perseverance, vision, a sound constitution and luck.

When the Romantic poet Novalis said, in an aphorism which I have often quoted, that, in a work of art, chaos shines through the veil of order, I take chaos to be the unchecked emotion and imagination, the raw energy that needs to be tamed, filtered, civilised in order to make art possible. The performer will be an echo of this symbiosis, trying to keep the chaos alive while reining it in according to the shape and character of each individual piece.

In this kind of self-criticism, which can extend to the minutest detail of a performance, we remain on strictly musical grounds. Whereas criticising oneself as a person, a responsible citizen, a law-abiding patriot, a God-fearing Christian or an atheist, is quite another matter. A famous pianist once stated that the ethos of a performance was inextricably linked to each and every bite the performer undertakes to swallow. This, I believe, is nonsense. The human being and the artist often operate on very different levels, if not in different worlds, and no one has yet been able to explain the gap between the almost limitless range and accomplishment of the great artist and his limitations as a private person. The idea that the artist necessarily mirrors the man is a fallacy. And this carries me back to Iago, the master of innuendo and character assassination – not, perhaps, the best model for aesthetic criticism of any kind.

Whatever else I have done on the critical line seems to me linked to self-scrutiny. I have thought and written about matters of my trade in order to clear my own mind, and in order to effectively handle words, which gives me pleasure. I set myself the task of writing clearly enough for others to share my thoughts, and, if not accept my arguments, at least enjoy the writing. I have tried to be critical about the quality of pieces. There, my early experiences in composition have helped me to look at pieces from a composer's point of view and have kept my curiosity alive in trying to understand how the mind of a great composer works. Piano literature being so vast it seems important that young pianists should start considering at a very early stage which pieces they may spend a lifetime with, and which others they might play out of curiosity, or as a luxury. I have been self-critical in playing little contemporary music as my talents lie elsewhere. But I go to concerts of new music whenever I can, listen to performances of the unfamiliar with passionate interest, and take my hat off to artists who have given their services to new music as splendidly as my friend Pierre-Laurent Aimard.

Finally, I'd like to mention an obituary that Goethe and his friend Zelter wrote after the death of Haydn. In it they say that in Haydn's music we find both naïveté and irony, the distinguishing features of genius. I have never considered myself a genius, yet this dichotomy – next to that of chaos and order – has told me something about my own frame of mind. I think it may serve well, not just for geniuses, but as the bond that unites them with civilised critics and performers. In the name of naïveté and irony, I thank you for your esteem.

(2003)

On Humour, Sense and Nonsense

WE SAY SOMEONE has a sense of humour. Which implies that there are others who miss out on it. What seems hilarious to some may be ridiculous to others. While the colour-blind have been informed about their condition, humourless people rarely realise that they are humourless; they even may be inclined to treat comical matters with scorn. There used to be a species of humour that remained within the confines of the cosy. Today the word humour more commonly relates to the comical in the widest sense. For the profoundly serious the affinity of the comical with absurdity and nonsense is an obstacle. Things should make sense, and laughter is something a considerate person ought to wield with caution. Dostoyevsky thought that it greatly depends on how someone laughs. In his novel *The Youth*, he writes:

> If we want to become familiar with a person and his soul we do not examine his silence or his way of speaking, his weeping or even his enthusiasm for the noblest ideas. Rather, we should observe him when he laughs. If he laughs well, then he must be a good person.

But laughter is not invariably tied to the comical. In a movie of the 1930s a man appears whose profession is that of a laughing expert, a ridologist, traveling around with a gramophone and a suitcase full of recorded laughter. Meanwhile, there are academics who subscribe to this alluring occupation. One of them, Scott Weems, relates that on 30 January 1962 three students of a missionary school for girls in Tanzania started laughing. Their laughter was contagious, and soon about half of the students of the campus joined in. Before long, uncontrollable laughter spread within the entire village. When after a month and a half of laughing it hadn't stopped, the school was closed and the students were isolated. However, after reopening the school there was laughter again: one third of the alumni couldn't help laughing. The school was shut down once more. Meanwhile, the laughter had reached some neighbouring towns and villages, spread particularly by those girls who had returned home and infected the adults. Before the end of the year, fourteen schools had to close. More than a thousand people were helpless with laughter. Eighteen months after it started the laughter had finally stopped. The reason for this epidemic seems to have remained in the dark.

As a second example, the members of an American congregation were encouraged by their preacher to laugh as hard as they could, an operation during which some fell on the floor. Laughter, that was the objective, brings you nearer to God – a strange idea, as there is no evidence that God ever laughs. The gods, on the other hand, seem to have enjoyed laughing, albeit sardonically.

Humour shows that the world is absurd, and that absurdity is easier to cope with if we focus on its funny side. A number of thinkers have tried to determine what makes things funny. It was a Scottish philosopher of the Enlightenment who launched the idea of incongruity. In *Humour: A Very Short Introduction*, Noël Carroll has explained this kind of view: something appears to be discordant with something else. This generates a short circuit that surprisingly illuminates the picture. The 'other' that is contradicted is our image of the world as it is, or should be. Our expectations are undermined and led *ab absurdum* whether ideas, rules, principles of logic, norms of morals and decency or notions of taste and the sublime. A precondition of comic amusement is the derailment of sense, whether at the cost of ourselves or others, or at the cost of no one and nothing. It is noteworthy that it was a moral philosopher like Francis Hutcheson who should have brought up the concept of incongruity ('Reflections upon Laughter', 1750) as anyone who looks for the moral in the comical has knocked at the wrong door. Humour is by definition amoral. It reaches well into the anarchic, breaks taboos and makes light of our certainties.

There are a few other perceptions of the comical that are sometimes right: laughter seen as a device for laughing away the horrendous and catastrophic, or the notion of Baudelaire, that sees comic amusement as caused by a feeling of superiority. There are, however, sufficient cases that do not tally with such ideas. A good reason for the comical, quite on the contrary, is our appreciation of the superiority of the humourist. We honour him as we laugh.

According to George Orwell whatever is funny is subversive. Some cartoonists live dangerously. If they deal with the sublime, they are threatened, or even killed.

The words cartoon or caricature do not do justice to the literary cartoon, a genre easily underestimated within the arts. Its supreme examples display a perfect unity of picture and words. The precision of what is said is no less decisive than what we see. For comic effect, the brilliance of presentation is quite essential – the attraction and appropriateness of its style. Jean Paul's sentence 'Shakespeare painted all characters, one excepted, his' delights by its unexpected structure.

I have mentioned nonsense. As a father and citizen but also as a musical performer both my feet are firmly planted in sense. The musical work should be presented, and not its travesty. Only when the music itself is comical should the performer turn into a comedian.

As a writer of poetry, on the other hand, one of my feet is grounded in sense, the other in nonsense. There is, in nonsense, a dialectical connection with sense. Of all the groupings of the last hundred years Dadaism of the Zurich variety was nearest to the comical. In a later definition, Raoul Hausmann said: 'The Dadaist hates silliness and loves nonsense.' In Zurich's Cabaret Voltaire, the catastrophic stupidity of the First World War was confronted by liberating nonsense. The Viennese satirist Karl Kraus fittingly pronounced that 'Chaos is welcome because order has failed'.

Max Ernst wrote a Dada sentence particularly suited for guestbooks: 'According to an ancient, anxiously guarded monastic secret even octogenarians can learn to play the piano without any trouble.'

When Edward Lear discovered Nonsense Poetry, Chesterton greeted him as a new Columbus. But nonsense poetry had been around, in one form or another, since the Middle Ages, and not just in England. The minnesinger Reinmar the Old had cultivated it already, and it is a nice thought that nonsense poetry, or *Lügendichtung*, may have been invented by a practitioner of love songs. In a German text of the fourteenth century, a vinegar jug rides on horseback into a country that was situated behind Monday. A fierce battle between a hedgehog and a flying earthworm is arbitrated by a swimming grindstone. There exists a poetry of the impossible that moves in a world turned upside down. But already antiquity and the Bible have dealt with 'impossibilia', as did Shakespeare.

The sense that nonsense makes is that it leads, unfettered by rational restrictions, into the infinite. One enters, if one is disposed to do so, a religious sphere. Of the Dadaists, it was Hugo Ball who was inclined towards mysticism. What intrigues me more is the intimate connection of nonsense with the comical. Besides Lear's and Carroll's grotesque poetry there is Christian Morgenstern's. 'The Knee' that's lonely moving through the world is the supreme German nonsense poem.

Nonsense within sense, on the other hand, reveals itself when we notice how firmly sense is immured in rationality. A purely rational world that disregards the play of chance would be a sad misunderstanding. The geneticist François Jacob described the driving spirit of the universe – in case you have the urge to imagine one – not as an engineer but a tinkerer. Einstein's pronouncement 'God doesn't throw dice' may well belong to the past.

Sense and nonsense intertwined: that sounds sensible. It is a concept that is sufficiently absurd to be realistic. It may be capable of mirroring the world as it is.

How about humour and the comical in music? Who would deny that Mozart, in some of his operas, pulled out every stop of the comical? But what about music without words and the stage? Can music be comical on its own?

I shall start with the fact that tones are not merely tones, or parts of a tone constellation. A major and a minor triad will, to most listeners, impart different emotional signals. But it all starts with the single note already having an expressive significance depending on how it is played. If the player is visible, the movement of his arm can contribute to making a very short single note appear funny. However, this is only the beginning. With the connection of notes, the simultaneity of voices, with harmony and rhythm we reach beyond mere sound play. Pieces of music have a character of their own, or contain a variety of characters. Even to an unexperienced listener, a funeral march will not appear to be a matter for laughter, or a polka by Johann Strauss a cause for lament.

The big music encyclopaedias of our day do not give humour any space. I had to go back to a German one of 1875 to find a lovely article on this topic. 'For the humorist', the article says, 'there are no fools, only foolishness and a mad world … [This is another formula by Jean Paul.] He will therefore perceive man and the world to be not ridiculous or revolting but pitiable.' What we encounter here is a benign interpretation of humour, an understanding of life generated in the eighteenth century, of a 'world humour that never aims at, or blames, the single individual'. In Schumann's piano pieces we can read the indication '*Mit gutem Humor*', meaning 'in good humour'. For Goethe, who was no humorist, only this variety was worthy of attention. But humour is not always good.

To unambiguously define the meaning of humour, irony and wit seems hardly feasible – too numerous are the differences of a national and linguistic, historic and cultural kind. In being a highly personal matter, humour offers a link to religion. For some of us, music, or at least great music, is exclusively quasi-religious. Jean Paul, the great humorist, called humour the sublime in reverse. The lack of humour in the sublime is made up for by turning it upside down. According to Francis Hutcheson, 'Nothing is so properly applied to the false Grandeur either of Good or of Evil, as ridicule.'

There are ravishing examples of the sublime in reverse in Haydn and Beethoven, whose treatment of Diabelli's Waltz in his 33 Variations is a catalogue of the musically comical but also a satire on its theme, while at the same time the interspersed sublime variations along with the gracefulness of the final minuet supply the enraptured background. Already in his early variation works Beethoven likes to toy not just with the themes but also with the public, and relishes in making a fool of the listener, as in the conclusion of the hilarious set of variations on Salieri's 'La Stessa, La Stessisima'.

It was one of Haydn's supreme achievements to make the so-called absolute music amenable to humour. Many of his finales are distinguished by high spirits that at times cross the borderline of nonsense. When a B major chord repeatedly appears in a C major piece the effect can be that of a playful deviation, a slip or a deliberate insult. Comic music contravenes musical expectations. We find such expectations in Haydn's and Beethoven's time whereas Romanticism shows the unexpected as its norm. As for Berlioz, surprise is everything – how should the comical still be discernible? In Rossini's *Sins of Old Age*, pieces virtually untouched by Romanticism, we find not only funny titles but also genuinely funny music. The train ride that he makes us participate in stops after some 'satanic whistling' at a station. When the train continues its journey there is a horrible derailment. We hear the moaning of the injured before the first victim quickly flies to heaven while the second one goes to hell. There follows a funeral march.

In spite of Schumann's inclination towards romantic irony I do not detect genuinely comical music again until the twentieth century. Ligeti's *Aventures et Nouvelles aventures* and Mauricio Kagel's *Marches to Fail Victory* are striking musical grotesques. In literature, theatre and film as well, important manifestations of modernity have happened in the emotional territory between dread and laughter. Black humour has replaced the good one.

To be sure, not all great music is comical. Kant, by the way, held laughter in higher esteem. Of both music and laughter, he felt, however, that they were overly dependent on nonsense, 'aesthetically impure', removed from the sphere of critical judgement. They stimulated good health without reaching the 'supreme capacity of the soul'.

For me, the most phenomenal blessings I could discover on this planet next to love were music and humour. They imbue life with sense. (And nonsense.)

(2015)

SELECT BIBLIOGRAPHY

Beethoven

Adorno, Theodor W. *Beethoven*. Suhrkamp, Frankfurt, 1993.

Beethoven, Ludwig van. *The 32 Piano Sonatas*. In reprints of the first and early editions. Tecla Editions, London, 1989.

Birnbach, Heinrich. 'Über die verschiedene Form grösserer Instrumentaltonstücke aller Art und deren Bearbeitung'. *Berliner Allgemeine Musikalische Zeitung*, 1827.

Cooper, Martin. *Beethoven – The Last Decade, 1817–1827*. Oxford University Press, London, 1970.

Fischer, Edwin. *Ludwig van Beethovens Klaviersonaten*. Insel Verlag, Wiesbaden, 1956. English edition: *Beethoven's Pianoforte Sonatas*. Translated by Stanley Goodman with the collaboration of Paul Hamburger. Faber & Faber, London, 1959.

Khittl, Christoph. *Nervenkontrapunkt*. Böhlau, Wien-Köln-Weimar, 1991.

Kinderman, William. *Beethoven's Diabelli Variations*. Clarendon Press, Oxford, 1987.

Lenz, Wilhelm von. *Beethoven et ses trois styles*. St Petersburg, 1852; Paris, 1955; new edition: Legouix, Paris, 1909.

Lenz, Wilhelm von. *Beethoven – Eine Kunststudie*. Hoffmann & Campe, Hamburg, 1855–60.

Marx, Adolph Bernhard. *Die Lehre von der musikalischen Komposition*. Leipzig, 1838.

Morgenstern, Christian. Poem 'Die unmögliche Tatsache' from 'Palmström' in *Alle Galgenlieder*. Bruno Cassirer, Berlin, 1932. The end of the poem, in its German text, reads:

> *Und er kommt zu dem Ergebnis:*
> *Nur ein Traum war das Erlebnis,*
> *Weil, so schliesst er messerscharf,*
> *Nicht sein kann, was nicht sein darf.*

Nagel, Wilibald. *Beethoven und seine Klaviersonaten*. 2 vols. Beyer & Söhne, Langensalz, 1923.

Nottebohm, Gustav. *Beethoveniana*. 2 vols. Peters, Leipzig, 1867.

Prod'homme, Jacques-Gabriel. *Les Sonates pour Piano de Beethoven*. Delagrave, Paris, 1936, 1951.

Ratz, Erwin. *Einführung in die musikalische Formenlehre*. Österreichischer Bundesverlag, Vienna, 1951; third edition: Universal Edition, Vienna, 1973.

Réti, Rudolph. *Thematic Patterns in Sonatas of Beethoven.* Faber & Faber, London, 1967.

Riemann, Hugo. *Ludwig van Beethovens sämtliche Klavier-Solosonaten.* Max Hesse, Berlin, 1918–19.

Ries, Ferdinand, and F. G. Wegeler. *Biographische Notizen über Ludwig van Beethoven.* Koblenz, 1838; reprint: Schuster & Loeffler, Berlin, 1906.

Ritzel, Fred. *Die Entwicklung der 'Sonatenform' im musiktheoretischen Schrifttum des 18. und 19. Jahrhunderts.* Breitkopf & Hartel, Wiesbaden, 1968.

Rosen, Charles. *The Classical Style.* Faber & Faber, London. Revised edition, 1976.

Rosenberg, Richard. *Die Klaviersonaten Ludwig van Beethovens.* Urs Graf Verlag, Olten and Lausanne, 1957.

Schenker, Heinrich. *Beethoven – Die letzten Sonaten, Erläuterungs-Ausgaben.* Universal Edition, Vienna.

Schindler, Anton. *Biographie von Ludwig van Beethoven.* Munster, 1840. English edition: *Beethoven as I knew him.* Edited by D. W. MacArdle. Translated by C. S. Jolly. Faber & Faber, London, 1966.

Schmalenbach, Werner. 'Das Museum ist kein Luxus'. *Frankfurter Allgemeine Zeitung,* 3–4 August 1968.

Solomon, Maynard. *Beethoven.* Schirmer Books, New York, 1977.

Tovey, Donald Francis. *A Companion to Beethoven's Pianoforte Sonatas.* The Associated Board of the Royal Schools of Music, London, 1931.

– *Beethoven.* Oxford University Press, London, 1944.

– *Essays in Musical Analysis,* supplementary volume. Oxford University Press, London, 1944.

Uhde, Jürgen. *Beethovens Klaviermusik.* Philipp Reclam, Stuttgart, 1968–74.

Busoni

Beaumont, Antony. *Busoni the Composer.* Indiana University Press, Bloomington, 1985.

Busoni, Ferruccio. *Entwurf einer neuen Asthetik der Tonkunst* [first published 1907] *mit Anmerkungen von Arnold Schoenberg und einem Nachwort H. H. Stuckenschmidt.* Suhrkamp, Frankfurt, 1974. American edition: *Sketch of a New Esthetic of Music.* Translated by T. S. Baker. Schirmer, New York, 1911.

– *Briefe an seine Frau.* Rotapfel Verlag, Erlenbach, 1935. English edition: *Busoni – Letters to his Wife.* Translated by Rosamond Ley. Edward Arnold, London, 1938.

– *Selected Letters.* Translated and edited by Antony Beaumont. Faber & Faber, London, 1987.

– *Wesen und Einheit der Musik.* Max Hesse, Berlin, 1956.

Dent, Edward J. *Ferruccio Busoni – A Biography.* Oxford University Press, London, 1933; reprint: Eulenburg, London, 1974.

Pfitzner, Hans. 'Futuristengefahr' in *Gesammelte Schriften I.* Augsburg, 1926–29.

Selden-Goth, Gisella. *Ferruccio Busoni.* E. P. Tal & Co., Leipzig-Vienna-Zürich, 1922.

Stuckenschmidt, H. H. *Ferruccio Busoni – Zeittafel eines Europäers.* Atlantis Verlag, Zürich, 1967. English version: *Ferruccio Busoni – Chronicle of a European*, Translated by Sandra Morris. Calder & Boyars, London, 1970.

Fischer

Fischer, Edwin. *Musikalische Betrachtungen.* Tschudy Verklag, St Gallen, 1949. English edition: *Reflections on Music.* Williams & Norgate, London, 1951.

– *Von den Aufgaben des Musikers.* Insel Verlag, Wiesbaden, 1960.

Haid, Hugo. *Dank an Edwin Fischer.* F. A. Brockhaus, Wiesbaden, 1962.

Polgar, Alfred. *Ja und Nein – Schriften des Kritikers* (4 vols), Rowohlt, Berlin, 1925 etc.

Furtwängler

Furtwängler, Elisabeth. *Über Wilhelm Furtwängler* F. A. Brockhaus, Wiesbaden, 1979.

Furtwängler, Wilhelm. *Aufzeichnungen 1924 – 1954.* F. A. Brockhaus, Wiesbaden, 1980.

– *Briefe.* F. A. Brockhaus, Wiesbaden, 1954.

– *Gespräche über Musik.* Humboldt Verlag, Wien, 1948.

– *Ton und Wort.* F. A. Brockhaus, Wiesbaden, 1966.

Liszt

Dömling, Wolfgang. *Franz Liszt und seine Zeit.* Laaber Verlag, Laaber, 1985.

Fay, Amy. *Music Study in Germany.* Macmillan, London, 1885.

Friedheim, Arthur. *Life and Liszt.* Taplinger, New York, 1961.

Göllerich, August. *Franz Liszt.* Marquardt & Co., Berlin, 1908.

Gottschalg, A. W. *Franz Liszt in Weimar und seine letzten Lebensjahre.* Arthur Glaue,
    Berlin, 1910.

Jerger, Wilhelm. *Franz Liszts Klavierunterricht von 1884–1996, dargestellt an den
    Tagebuchaufzeichnungen von August Göllerich.* Gustav Bosse, Regensburg, 1975.

Kodály, Zoltán. *Folk Music of Hungary.* Barrie & Jenkins, London, 1971.

Lachmund, Carl. 'Living with Liszt'. From *The Diary.* Ed. Alan Walker. Pendragon Press,
    Stuyvesant, New York, 1995.

Pfeiffer, Theodor, and Jose Vianna da Motta. *Studien bei Hans von Biilow.* Friedrich
    Luckhardt, Berlin, 1894.

Ramann, Lina. *Lisztiana.* Schott, Mainz, 1883.

Searle, Humphrey. *The Music of Liszt.* Williams & Norgate, London, 1954.

Siloti, Alexander. *My Memories of Liszt.* Breitkopf & Härtel, London, 1913.

Stradal, August. *Erinnerungen an Franz Liszt.* Paul Haupt, Berne and Leipzig, 1929.

Walker, Alan. *Franz Liszt.* Alfred A. Knopf, New York, 1990–1996 (3 volumes).

Watson, Derek. *Liszt.* J. M. Dent & Sons, Ltd. London, 1989.

Mozart

Badura-Skoda, Eva and Paul. *Interpreting Mozart on the Keyboard.* Barrie and Rockliff,
    London, 1962.

Braunbehrens, Volkmar. *Mozart in Wien.* Piper, München, 1986.

Busoni, Ferrucio, *Von der Einheit der Musik.* Max Hesses Verlag, Berlin, 1922.

Deutsch, Otto Erich. *Mozart: Die Dokumente seines Lebens.* Barenreiter Verlag, Kassel,
    1961.

Hildesheimer, Wolfgang. *Mozart.* Suhrkamp, Frankfurt, 1977; Farrar, Straus & Giroux,
    New York, 1982; J. M. Dent & Sons, London, 1983.

Leitzmann, Albert. *Mozarts Persönlichkeit.* Urteile der Zeitgenossen. Insel Verlag,
    Wiesbaden, 1914.

Schneider, Otto, and Anton Algatzy. *Mozart Handbuch.* Verlag Brüder Hollinek, Wien,
    1962.

Solomon, Maynard. *Mozart.* HarperCollins, New York, 1995.

Schnabel

Schnabel, Artur. *Music and the Line of Most Resistance.* Da Capo Press, New York, 1969.

– *My Life and Music.* Colin Smythe, Gerrards Cross, London, 1970.

Wolff, Konrad. *The Teaching of Artur Schnabel.* Faber & Faber, London, 1972.

Schoenberg

Bailey, Walter B. 'Oscar Levant and the Program for Schoenberg's Piano Concerto'. In *Journal of the Arnold Schoenberg Institute*, vol. vi, no. 1, June 1982.

Johnson, Paul. 'Rhythm and Set Choice in Schoenberg's Piano Concerto'. In *Journal of the Arnold Schoenberg Institute*, vol. xi, no. 1, June 1988.

Schoenberg, Arnold. *Briefe.* B. Schott's Söhne, Mainz, 1958. English edition: *Letters.* Selected and edited by Erwin Stein. Translated by Eithne Wilkins and Ernst Kaiser, Faber & Faber, London, 1964.

– *Fundamentals of Musical Composition.* Ed. Gerald Strang and Leonard Stein, Faber & Faber, London, 1967.

– *Style and Idea.* Ed. Leonard Stein. Faber & Faber, London, 1975.

Schubert

Badura-Skoda, Paul. 'Fehlende Takte und korrumpierte Stellen in klassischen Meisterwerken.' *Neue Zeitschrift für Musik*, Mainz, November 1958.

Brown, Maurice J. E. *Schubert – A Critical Biography.* Macmillan, London, 1958.

– *Essays on Schubert.* Macmillan, London, 1966.

Cone, Edward T. 'Schubert's Beethoven'. *The Musical Quarterly*, New York, October 1970.

Deutsch, Otto Erich. *Schubert Thematic Catalogue.* J. M. Dent & Sons, London, 1951.

– *Schubert – A Documentary Biography.* Translated by Eric Blom. J. M. Dent & Sons, London, 1947. German edition: *Schubert – Die Dokumente seines Lebens.* VEB Deutscher Verlag für Musik, Leipzig, and Barenreiter Verlag, Kassel, 1964.

Dvořák, Antonín (in cooperation with Henry T. Finck). *Franz Schubert.* In John Clapham, *Antonín Dvořák*, Faber & Faber, London, 1964.

Gülke, Peter. *Franz Schubert und seine Zeit*. Laaber Verlag, Laaber, 1991.

Költzsch, Hans. *Franz Schubert in seinen Klaviersonaten*. Georg Olms/Breitkopf & Härtel, Wiesbaden, 1927, 1976.

Nägeli, Hans Georg. *Vorlesungen über Musik*. Stuttgart and Tubingen, 1826.

Reed, John. *Schubert – The Final Years*. Faber & Faber, London, 1972.

Rosen, Charles. *The Classical Style*. Faber & Faber, London, 1971.

Schnabel, Artur. 'The Piano Sonatas of Franz Schubert.' *The Musical Courier*, New York, 1928. (Mentioned in César Saerchinger, *Artur Schnabel – A Biography*, Cassell & Co., London, 1957.)

Schumann

Boetticher, Wolfgang. Opus 13, (1) *12 Etudes Symphoniques*. (2) *Etudes en forme de Variations*. Henle Verlag, München.

Réti, Rudolph. *The Thematic Process in Music*. Faber & Faber, London, 1961.

Schumann, Robert. *Tagebucher*. Stroemfeld/Roter Stern, Frankfurt, 1971–82.

– *Gesammelte Schriften über Musik und Musiker*. Georg Wigand, Leipzig, 1875.

ACKNOWLEDGEMENTS

'Notes on a Complete Recording of Beethoven's Piano Works', 'Liszt Misunderstood', 'Liszt's Piano Playing', 'Turning the Piano into an Orchestra', 'Fidelity to Liszt's Letter?', 'A Peculiar Serenity', '*Arlecchino* and *Doktor Faust*', 'Edwin Fischer: Remembering My Teacher' and 'Coping with Pianos' were translated from the German by Paul Hamburger. 'A Mozart Player Gives Himself Advice', 'Form and Psychology in Beethoven's Piano Sonatas', 'The Text and Its Guardians', 'Beethoven's New Style', 'Theme and Variations II', 'Liszt's Hungarian Rhapsodies', 'Liszt's Bitterness of Heart' and 'A Case for Live Recordings' were translated by Eugene Hartzell. 'Minor Mozart' was translated by William Kinderman, 'Musical Character(s) in Beethoven's Piano Sonatas' by Mark Evan Bonds, 'Reflections on Life and Art' by Richard Stokes. All the other essays were written in English or translated from the German by myself. In 'Me, Myself and I' I had a welcome helping hand in Michael Morley.

The lecture on 'Form and Psycology in Beethoven's Piano Sonatas' was first given in German at Professor Harald Kaufmann's Institut für musikalische Wertungsforschung in Graz in 1969, and in its English version at the 1970 Darlington Summer School. 'Musical Character(s) in Beethoven's Piano Sonatas' was given at Cologne University in 1998 as 'On Character in Music'. 'Must Classical Music Be Entirely Serious?' was delivered as the Darwin Lecture at Cambridge University in 1984; 'Schubert's Last Sonatas', in an abridged version, as the Edward Boyle Memorial Lecture at the Royal Society of Arts, London, on 30 November 1988. 'Schubert's Piano Sonatas, 1822–28' was given at the Santa Fe Chamber Music Festival in 1973.

In a similar or considerably divergent form, the following articles were previously printed:

'A Mozart Player Gives Himself Advice' in the *New York Review of Books*, 27 June 1985; in *Die Zeit* ('Ermahnungen eines Mozart spielers an sich selbst'), 15 November 1985; as an accompaniment to a Philips boxed set of the Mozart Piano Concertos, 1990.
'Minor Mozart' ('Mozart für die Klavierstunde') in *Frankfurter Allgemeine Zeitung*, 19 October 1991.
'Notes on a Complete Recording of Beethoven's Piano Works' ('Anmerkungen zu einer Gesamtaufnahme der Klavierwerke Beethovens') in *Hi Fi Stereophonie*, Karlsruhe, May 1966.

'Form and Psychology in Beethoven's Piano Sonatas' in *Music and Musicians*, London, June 1971.

'The Text and Its Guardians' as an accompaniment to a Philips boxed set, 1983.

'Musical Character(s) in Beethoven's Piano Sonatas' ('Gehörte Seelen und Landschaften') in *Frankfurter Allgemeine Zeitung*, 26 October 1996; in *Beethoven Forum* vol. 9, University of Nebraska Press, 2001, in the *New York Review of Books*, 2001.

'Beethoven's New Style' as a sleeve note for Philips, 1976.

'Schubert's Piano Sonatas, 1822–28' as an accompaniment to a Philips boxed set containing my recordings of Schubert's later piano works, and, simultaneously, in *Hi Fi Stereophonie*, Karlsruhe, June 1975; it was also used as the basis for a BBC discussion with Stephan Plaistow in 1974.

'Schubert's Last Sonatas' in the *New York Review of Books*, 2 February 1989; in the *Royal Society of Arts Journal*, London, June 1989.

'A Footnote on the Playing of Schubert's Four-Hand Works' as a sleeve note for a set of Erato records of Imogen Cooper and Anne Queffélec, 1978.

'Testing the Grown-Up Player: Schumann's *Kinderszenen*' in *Musica*, September/October 1981.

'Theme and Variations II' as an accompaniment to a Philips recording of Schumann's *Symphonic Etudes* and variation works by Beethoven, 1991.

'Liszt Misunderstood' ('Der missverstandene Liszt') in *Phono*, Vienna, 1961.

'The Noble Liszt' in the *New York Review of Books*, 20 November 1986.

'Liszt's *Années de pèlerinage* I and II' for the programme accompanying a performance at the Royal Festival Hall, London, on 2 February 1986.

'Liszt's B minor Sonata' as a sleeve note for Philips, 1981.

'Liszt's Hungarian Rhapsodies' as a sleeve note for Vanguard, 1968.

'Liszt's Bitterness of Heart' as a sleeve note for Philips, 1980; in *The Musical Times*, London.

'A Peculiar Serenity' ('Busoni, Vollender des Klavierspiels') in *Österreichische Musikzeitschrift*, Vienna, 1954.

'*Arlecchino* and *Doktor Faust*' in *Die Presse*, Vienna, 2–3 April 1966.

'Superhuman Frailty' in the *Times Literary Supplement*, London, 13 June 1986.

'On Playing Schoenberg's Piano Concerto' in the *New York Review of Books*, 16 February 1995.

'Wilhelm Furtwängler' in *Die Zeit*, 13 November 1979; in the *New York Review of Books*, 28 March 1991.

'Remembering My Teacher' ('Edwin Fischer zum Gedenken') in *Österreichische Musikzeitschrift*, Vienna, 1960.

'Coping with Pianos' ('Vom Umgang mit Flügeln') in *Hi Fi Stereophonie*, Karlsruhe, December 1974.

'A Case for Live Recordings' ('In Favour of Live Records') *Hi Fidelity*, May 1984.

'On Recitals and Programmes' ('Das Konzert bin ich') in *Frankfurter Allgemeine Zeitung*, 27 October 1990; ('The Pianist and the Program') in the *New York Review of Books*, 22 November 1990.

'From "Analysis" to "Zubiaurre"' in the *Sunday Times*, London, 22 February 1981.

'*Werktreue* – An Afterthought', 'Liszt and the Piano Circus', 'Liszt's Piano Playing', 'Turning the Piano into an Orchestra', 'Fidelity to Liszt's Letter?', 'Afterthoughts on Busoni' and 'Afterthoughts on Edwin Fischer' were first published in *Musical Thoughts and Afterthoughts*, 1976.

Jeremy Siepmann's interview originally appeared in *Music and Musicians*, London, December 1972; it is reprinted here in a slightly abridged version. The interview with Terry Snow was the accompanying text for a Bach record issued by Philips in 1977. The interview with Konrad Wolff appeared in the *Piano Quarterly* in 1979. Although the form is not that of an essay, I decided to include them because they make a number of points that I considered to fall within the scope of this book.

Of the newly included essays, lectures and interviews, *Katja Andy, Music Life in Flux, Beethoven Grosse Fuge and the Quartet Op. 130*, as well as *Afterthoughts on Life and Art* were published in Neue Zürcher Zeitung, *A Lifetime of Recording* in the Gramophone.

Hearing, Farewell to the Concert Stage, and *Me, Myself and I* ('Selbstgespräch') appeared in AB: 'Nach dem Schlussakkord' (Hanser, 2010).

On Some Performance Habits is a condensed version of the third of my lectures 'Alfred Brendel on Music' (2 DVDs, Unitel).

Schubert's G Major Quartet was delivered at the Wissenschaftskolleg in Berlin 2013.

Children's Orchestra was included in AB: 'Wunderglaube und Misstonleiter' (Hanser, 2014).

On Humour, Sense and Nonsense opened the Lucerne Festival 2015.

My thanks go to all the publishers concerned, as well as to Mr Lawrence Schoenberg, who kindly gave permission to quote from Arnold Schoenberg's notes on Busoni's *Entwurf einer neuen Ästhetik der Tonkunst*.

INDEX